MIMESIS
INTERNATIONAL

LITERATURE

n. 4

C000156153

WORD AND IMAGE
In Literature and the Visual Arts

Edited by Carmen Concilio and Maria Festa

With a Preface by Federico Vercellone

MIMESIS
INTERNATIONAL

Published with the contribution of the University of Turin – Department of Foreign Languages, Literatures and Modern Cultures.

© 2016 – MIMESIS INTERNATIONAL
www.mimesisinternational.com
e-mail: info@mimesisinternational.com

Isbn: 9788869770838
Book series: *Literature* n. 4

© MIM Edizioni Srl
P.I. C.F. 02419370305

TABLE OF CONTENTS

PREFACE

Federico Vercellone
(University of Turin)

Word and image pursue each other within a continuous frame stretching from Plato's devaluation of aesthetic appearance to Guy Debord's "society of the spectacle". It is self-evident that — in principle — there is no reason to ascribe a theoretical primacy to one of the two expressive means over the other. A logic of conflict between the two is rather what has imposed itself and become the rule over the centuries. The relation between East and West is at the origin of this confrontation, which, from the very beginning, has seen a clash between *logoi*, as one might say, using a journalistic lexicon — a persistent clash of civilizations opposing the advocates of iconophilia to the iconoclasts.

This is an ongoing challenge that we have inherited and are faced with even today. As far as we are concerned, by way of updating the debate, we need to decide whether the civilization of the image is a corruption of the civilization of the word, or rather a further step forward which we have to take into account and become responsible for. Choosing the second horn of the dilemma definitely implies adopting a momentous cultural and political stance. It means that the precarious balance between the two *logoi*, recurrently sought, for instance, in the contexts of the Renaissance and the Baroque through emblematics and iconology, is now lost, and that the wished-for correspondence between the imaginary and the real has undergone a profound, pain-ridden alteration. When Thomas Mann, at the very beginning of *Joseph and his Brothers*, invited the reader to look behind the stage of history, he was still convinced that the past could reverberate onto the present thanks to descriptions that revived it in its original freshness.

At that point the world was on the threshold of an announced catastrophe and of a final attempt to conciliate the irreconcilable. From that moment, the two clashing attitudes that have entrapped the western *logos* in an endless diatribe would diverge so violently as to lead us to the contemporary "civilization of the image", a sort of extreme, belated and generalized victory of iconophilia. Images deprived of *logoi* and *logoi* deprived of images seem to constitute our present destiny. The aseptic rhetoric of scientific discourse is accompanied by vast clusters of images which provide an identity to subjects who have a desperate yearning to know who they really are in an estranged world. The catastrophe affecting *ekphrasis* embodies the agony of a whole civilization that had believed in description and in the absolute coherence between the *logos* and the imaginary. The implicit promise was the integrity of the world as a coherent cosmos. The ancient fracture is engaging the present with a violence that was originally unconceivable. The project of modernity — to use Bruno Latour's words —, which had attempted to restore order by ascribing truth to the world of words, while assigning appearance to the world of images, is on the verge of a shattering crisis.

Mending the fracture means crossing the chasm in order to reimagine a habitable world — a world where it is possible to receive the infinite extension of discourse within moments of the collective imaginary in which the flow of time may be temporarily re-invested with the seal of eternity. This would be almost a new Renaissance. Rethinking this nexus through literature takes us back to the core principle of the unity of the arts, whose separation derives — in modern times — from that fatal oblivion of Horace's *ut pictura poesis* which dawned with Winckelmann and continued with Lessing. The present, newly-rediscovered unity of the artistic media leads us well beyond art, towards the reconstruction of a single world and the retrieval of the subject's integrity, which the modern arts system had considered lost. Dividing the arts according to their specific objects, as happened between Batteux and the great systems of German idealism, meant breaking that synesthetic unity which made it possible to have a correct perception of the world, that is to say, a total sensorial perception. This led to an increasing fragmentation of sensorial experience on the basis of a rationalistic subjectivity mirrored by the arts system, in a pattern of mutual reflections. In such a context, the task of art is that of plunging once again into human praxis so as to help its essential unity to come to light. Centuries of rationalism have worked in the opposite direction, shaking off the unity to facilitate the advent of a pragmatic form of reason, exclusively devoted to performativity, and to favour a universe of appearances entrusted to an ineffectual imaginary. The aim of the present volume is to probe this nexus. Its main merit consists in the fact that conducting this kind of research means working hard at bridging the gap between two fronts which are not only related to art but also to human experience, as well as, first and foremost, to art as a human experience.

(*Translated from the Italian by Lucia Folena*)

INTRODUCTION.
WORD AND IMAGE FROM TEXT TO FILM: RICHARDSON'S FIELDING

Paolo Bertinetti
(University of Turin)

Novels, stories, literary texts, both popular and refined, have served as the base, when not as a pretext, for all sorts of film adaptations. The results achieved by directors and film companies have varied greatly: some have been fascinating and others horrible. But the indignation of the literary world, when it considered that the original text had inevitably been degraded to a sort of raw material, has almost always been unjustified; and equally unwarranted, in the eyes of today's more attentive critics, appears the concern about "faithfulness". On the contrary in many cases the strength of an adaptation has been found in the conflict with the work on which it is based. Changes, differences, cuts are always revealing, not only in the different sensibility and interpretations of the world that they manifest, but also because they make evident the diversity with which other codes for the expression and communication of experience function. The new version may repeat or reduce the "vision" of the original text, or it may construct a new meaning. And in many cases it is this last possibility which has yielded the most interesting results, when the director is in conflict with the original text, challenging it, in the dialogue and in the transformation of characters.

Because of the expectations of the audience, though, most films based on classic novels attempt to give the impression of being faithful, literal translations of the text into the language of the film. There must be a good deal of selection when a six hundred pages novel is transposed into a film of approximately two hours: scenes and subplots must be cut, minor characters have to be eliminated, but this necessity does not exclude the possibility of respecting the deep meaning of the original text and of its author's central concern.

Tony Richardson, one of the founders of the British "free cinema" and one of the greatest British film directors of the second half of the twentieth century, directed the film version of Henry Fielding's *Tom Jones* in 1963. Fielding's novel, stylish and entertaining, is full of highly comic episodes and maintains a consistently lively tone thanks to the irony and humour with which Fielding presents characters and events.

Tom is a foundling who towards the end of the novel finds out that he is the nephew of Squire Allworthy, the likeable, impetuous and generous man of property who had adopted him. But Allworthy, believing the lies of Blifil, his hypocrite and seemingly virtuous nephew, turns Tom out of his home. The adventures and misadventures of Tom and Sophia, the woman he loves and who loves him (the best of which are in the middle of the novel, where they form a sort of epic of the road) carry on for a few hundred pages, but Fielding keeps the reader glued to the plot by the invention of spectacular incident, and constantly entertained by a use of irony almost amounting to a regular dialogue between author and reader. At the end of the novel Tom Jones, rash, exuberant, imprudent, but a man of generous heart, is restored to his inheritance and to Sophia, whereas the hypocrisy of Blifil and his allies is unmasked.

Characters and events are told by the voice of an omniscient narrator, whose ironic tone sets the character of the story. Richardson' film version recreates its source by incorporating the voice of a narrator and by using a series of cinematic techniques that "translate" Fielding's verbal fireworks into visual inventions.

As Fielding alludes to the origins of literature, so Richardson recalls the origins of film through a sequence presented as a silent movie. At the beginning of the film, title cards announce the narration and dialogue; and the music intensifies the archaic mood as a harpsichord assumes the function of the piano heard in the cinemas at the beginning of the twentieth century (Richardson decided to use a harpsichord because the action takes place in the eighteenth century, when the piano had not yet been invented).

This sequence masterfully condenses into five minutes of film Fielding's long exposition of the events surrounding Tom's discovery and adoption by Squire Allworthy. The fast pace plunges the spectator into the novel's comic spirit; and the use of another "classic" device, accelerated action, extends the tone of the opening sequence. Such device clearly diverges from the rhythm of Fielding's novel, which pretends to be the rhythm of a tale told by a (highly cultured) gentleman to his quiet listeners. Richardson "betrays" Fielding. And by doing so, he is faithful to the spirit of his novel.

The pace is also quickened for transitions between scenes and the passage is marked with an ornamental device, either a flip frame or a wipe. For example, when Tom is going to make love to Molly, in the novel the narrator says: 'It shall be our custom to leave such scenes where taste, decorum and the censor dictate'.[1] In the film at this point a double vertical wipe closes in from both sides of the screen towards the centre, like a pair of sliding doors. When the camera returns to the lovers, a double wipe appears in reverse, as though the sliding doors where now opening.

On two occasions Tom covers the lens of the camera. The first time occurs after Allworthy's recovery at Paradise Hall: Tom pulls the draperies off the window and throws them over the face of the hypocrite Blifil and then throws one over the camera. Later, while going to Upton with Mrs Waters (one of his lovers), Tom covers the camera with his hat in order to protect his half-undressed friend from the audience's "prying eyes". When Tom receives a new and sophisticated wardrobe from Lady Bellaston (his lover in London, definitely older than him), Richardson uses a spiral-shaped wipe to represent the young man's excitation and delight. Towards the end of the film, when Tom goes to Newgate prison, a wipe consisting of a row of vertical stripes descends like prison bars over the screen.

One of the most successful devices is the iris, which once again alludes to the awareness of silent film. The gradual opening

---

1   Henry Fielding, *The History of Tom Jones: A Foundling* (New York: Collier & Sons, 1917), p. 101.

or closing of the camera eye not only directs attention to an important detail, but comments on the character's possibilities in space: it can be expanded or contracted, freeing or isolating its subject. In silent movies, the camera often irised in on the villain. Richardson's film irises in on Dowling, the lawyer. At Bridget Allworthy's funeral (Bridget was Tom's mother) he gives Blifil the letter which reveals Tom's true parentage. The iris signals the importance of Dowling while indicating his villainous nature.

The display of narrative control that the camera "translates" from the novel's voice is particularly well served by freeze frame. For example, Tom visits Molly and discovers his tutor Square, a hypocrite who dislikes him and favours Blifil, in her bedroom: Richardson ends this episode with a freeze frame, depicting Tom and Molly laughing, and Square standing by in gauche embarrassment. Near the end of the film, when Allworthy takes Jenny Jones, who is believed to be Tom's mother, and then Lawyer Dowling, behind closed doors to uncover the truth about Tom's birth, Richardson does not allow the audience behind these doors. Instead he shows Mrs Miller and Partridge (who was believed to be Tom's father) listening at the keyhole in a series of freeze frames. They can hear what is said inside, but the audience cannot. Like Fielding, Richardson creates an awareness of time, for he will not allow us to learn certain facts until the narrative is ready to spring them on us: the film asks us to be patient while undercutting our expectations.

The film also makes use of stop-motion photography, which fools the eye much as Fielding's prose often plays games with the reader. On this device, for instance, is based the montage sequence of the romantic idyll during which Tom and Sophia fall in love. At one point they appear to make a procession on horseback, each following the other in an apparently impossible sequence, but made possible by the stop-photographic technique. The humour of these moments provides a counterpoint to the potential sentimentality of the scene. By doing so, it remains faithful to Fielding's light mockery: Tom's citadel, proclaims the book,

> was taken by surprise. All those considerations of honour and prudence, which our hero had lately with so much military wisdom placed as

guards over the avenues of his heart, ran away from their posts, and the God of Love marched in triumph.[2]

All these techniques call attention to the presence of the camera (which corresponds to the underlined presence of the narrator in Fielding's novel). Moreover, the irony of the narrator's comments corresponds to the visual demystification offered by the characters in the film: they often turn directly to the camera and engage the audience with a complicitous wink (suffice it to remember two instances: when Tom asks Sophia to give his mistress Molly a job as her maid, and when Lady Bellaston receives Tom's proposal of marriage and her own maid reads it over her shoulder).

The playful relationship established between the characters in the film and the audience represents Richardson's ingenuity in adapting Fielding's novel. The cinematic techniques mentioned above realize in visual terms the effect created by Fielding's brilliant, ironic, and "confidential" prose.

In his adaptation (1978) of Fielding's *Joseph Andrews*, Tony Richardson faced again the formidable task to provide cinematic equivalents to the unique narrative voice of the original. The story is told in the third person and Fielding declares his presence as narrator explicitly from the outset, and throughout the narration there are constant reminders to the reader that she/he is reading a novel.

Joseph Andrews initial impulse and its opening section are parodic in style (the object of its parody being Richardson's novel *Pamela* and, according to Fielding, his hypocritical moral view of virtue rewarded). Joseph, Pamela's brother, is the footman of Lady Booby, the aunt of Squire Booby (who has married his servant Pamela). Lady Booby, in her London house, makes explicit advances to Joseph. But the young man, who is pure and is in love with the beautiful Fanny, rejects them and is thrown out on his ear. Poor Joseph decides to return on foot to his Somerset village, which is the country seat of the Boobys. This is his homecoming, like Ulysses's homecoming after the Trojan War. And like that

---

2   Fielding, *The History of Tom Jones*, p. 128.

of Ulysses, Joseph's return turns out longer, more complicated
and more adventurous than it should have been. After his first
misadventures, Joseph bumps into Parson Adams, the vicar of
his home village, and they set out for Somerset together. Here the
novel changes course. Parody is left on one side and the narrative
proceeds under its own steam, as a bizarre English version of the
adventures of Don Quixote and Sancho Panza. Adams saves a girl
from an assault in a wood, only to discover that she is Fanny. The
three travellers, after encountering every sort of misadventure,
finally reach their village, where they find Pamela married to
Squire Booby. Overcoming the hostility of Lady Booby (backed
up by Pamela), Fanny and Joseph (who turns out to be the son of
a gentleman) are allowed to marry.

In the film there are some changes in the narrative and subtle
shifts of emphasis in character and theme that make the satire of
Richardson's *Joseph Andrews* meaningful to modern audiences.
One major shift is sexual. Fielding distinguishes the love of Joseph
and Fanny from the baser lusts of those around them. Joseph's
rejections of Lady Booby's advances and his adherence to chastity
is both a comic reversal of expected masculine behaviour and a
moral statement of the possibility of the individual controlling his
desire: natural instinct subordinated to rational order.

In the film the values are shifted. The natural instincts of Joseph
and Fanny are still valued above the lust of Lady Booby, her maid
Mrs Sleepslop, and the young beau Didapper (brought by Lady
Booby to Adam's house to seduce Fanny), who are rejected by
the two young lovers. But Joseph's and Fanny's natural instincts
are also valued above strict adherence to moral order when that
order stands between two honest lovers.

The love of Fanny and Joseph is clearly sexual; but at the same
time is clearly innocent. Her lovemaking is shot in soft-focus,
amid tall grasses and blooming flowers. The novel and the film
share the view that their love is pure and innocent, as compared to
the hypocritical affectation and wantonness of the others; but the
film includes explicit sexuality as part of that purity.

Religion and religious hypocrisy is another theme that the film
treats differently from the novel. Richardson adds a long scene

in which Parson Adams, Joseph and Fanny are the victims of a gothic-religious kidnapping and attempted rape (a scene that recalls Polanski's *Rosemary's Baby*) and makes several changes in the character of Parson Adams. In the film Adam's flaws are emphasized and his theological and doctrinal competence is not taken into consideration; on the contrary, the religious bases of his moral values are almost brushed aside.

It is important to note that the film shares the self-conscious narrative technique of the novel, as it calls attention to itself as a work of art. There are several scenes in which Richardson alludes to earlier films and film genres: the parallel with *Rosemary's Baby* in the "gothic" scene, the fight *à la* Errol Flynn between Joseph and the kidnappers, and a series of rescue scenes reminiscent of cliff-hangers serial (like the Western and *Flash Gordon* serials). Richardson even alludes to his own *Tom Jones* for the use of silent film for flashbacks.

Joseph Andrews's adaptation, even more than his *Tom Jones*, allows Richardson to see the present (the Seventies of the 20th century) reflected through the prism of the past. It is not a traditional costume drama film: it is, so to speak, a "historical" film which operates like those great historical novels that find in the past the way to speak of the present distancing it (in the Brechtian sense of the word) from the reader. When speaking of moral choice and moral action while describing the ferociously class-structured world of *Joseph Andrews*, Richardson ultimately speaks of the political evaluations and of the political choices to be taken in the present.

PART ONE

LORD OF THE FLIES: WILLIAM GOLDING'S REALISM AND PETER BROOK'S CINEMATIC "REALITY"

Paola Carmagnani
(University of Turin)

Published in 1954, *Lord of the Flies* was William Golding's first novel; the one that established his reputation and that is still most widely acclaimed as his major work, capturing popular imagination and critical attention. Nominated for the *Palme d'Or* at the 1963 Cannes Film Festival, Peter Brook's *Lord of the Flies* was its first adaptation, and also the cinematic debut of one of Britain's most innovative theatre directors.[1]

Brook's film was based on a deep knowledge of Golding's text and a clear understanding of the specific questions it posed for a cinematic adaptation. Page after page, Golding's imagination 'becomes the reader's reality', writes Stephen King in his *Introduction* to the novel, 'It glows, incandescent and furious.'[2] What can a cinematic adaptation do with a text that is in and of itself so visually powerful? Brook's bet was to show that the vivid images it provoked in the reader's mind were indeed so powerful that they could glow on the screen as 'incandescent and furious' as from the novel's pages. Thus, adamantly refusing to use a screenplay, Brook chose to trust the novel's narrative power and worked directly from Golding's text.[3] As we will see, through an almost obsessive adherence to the letter of the story, the formal

---

1   *Lord of the Flies*, directed by Peter Brook (UK: British Lion; US: Continental Distributing, 1963). Produced by Lewis M. Allen. Photography by Tom Hollyman and Gerald Feil. Music by Raymond Leppard. Cast: James Aubrey (as Ralph), Tom Chapin (as Jack), Hugh Edwards (as Piggy), Tom Ganman (as Simon).

2   Stephen King, 'Introduction', in William Golding, *Lord of the Flies* (London: Faber & Faber, 2014), www.oxfordsd.org, p. 3.

3   See Peter Brook, *The Shifting Point: Forty years of theatrical exploration. 1946–1987* (London: Methuen Drama, 1989), pp. 192–198.

peculiarities of the novel's realism reveal themselves and find a stunning translation in a specific cinematic language.

Peter Brook's impressive filmography is entirely comprised of adaptations from the theatre, the opera, as well as from several narrative texts. Throughout all these experiences, he was concerned with finding an autonomous cinematic language that was capable of capturing each text's meaning and atmosphere. For him, the key element of that language has always been the "reality" of the image, which he considered both the cinematic medium's strength and limitation. Brook wrote that the power of the cinematic image entirely grasps the viewer: 'It is only possible to reflect on what one is seeing before or after the impression is made, never at the same moment. When the image is there in all its power, at the precise moment when it is being received, one can neither think, nor feel, nor imagine anything else.'[4]

This immersive cinematic "reality" finds a worthy challenge in Golding's literary realism. The novel's story, organized within a perfectly mastered structure that gradually takes us from an idyllic setting towards a dark core, is told by an invisible narrator who functions as a camera. Showing more than telling, the narrator leads us through the beach and jungle of an uninhabited tropical island among a group of marooned children, in and out of their different visions and thoughts, to and fro in a sort of alternate editing of simultaneous events. It is indeed a "cinematic narrative", which provokes in its reader a deeply emotional, immersive response, very similar to the viewer's reaction to the "reality" of the actual cinematic medium. As Stephen King recalled:

> I was […] unprepared for what I found between the covers of *Lord of the Flies*: a perfect understanding of the sort of beings I and my friends were at twelve or thirteen […]. To the twelve-year-old boy I was, the idea of roaming an uninhabited tropical island without parental supervision at first seemed liberating, almost heavenly. By the time the boy with the birthmark on his face […] disappeared, my sense of liberation had become tinged with unease. And by the time the badly ill

---

4   Brook, p. 190.

— and perhaps visionary — Simon confronts the severed and fly-blown head of the sow, which has been stuck on a pole, I was in terror. 'The half-shut eyes were dim with the infinite cynicism of adult life,' Golding writes. 'They assured Simon that everything was a bad business.' That line resonated with me then, and continues to resonate all these years later. [...] No teacher needed to tell me that Ralph embodied the values of civilization and that Jack's embrace of savagery and sacrifice represented the ease with which those values could be swept away; it was evident even to a child.[5]

The ground on which Brook's images meet Golding's cinematic writing is partly that of the *cinéma vérité*, where the camera was employed as a means to create a new kind of relationship with reality, revealing it through documentary work that refused any aesthetic gratifications. The work of Jean Rouch, a pioneer of the *cinéma vérité* who used the camera as an essential tool for his ethnological research, seems to resonate throughout Peter Brook's *Lord of the Flies*. Rouch's docufiction, *Les maîtres fous* (1955), chronicled the rites, which involved dancing and mimicry of the colonial power's military ceremonies, performed in a state of trance by some African tribes. As in Rouch's film, in Brook's *Lord of the Flies* the camera works as an "*agent provocateur*", stimulating the children's reactions and attitudes and developing their characters as they are being filmed. 'I believed,' said Brook,

that the reason for translating Golding's very complete masterpiece into another form in the first place was that although the cinema lessens the magic, it introduces evidence. The book is a beautiful fable — so beautiful that it can be refuted as a trick of compelling poetic style. In the film, no one can attribute the looks and gestures to tricks of direction. Of course I had to give the impulse to set a scene in motion, but what the camera records is the result of chords being struck on strings that were already there. The violent gestures, the look of greed and the faces of experience are all real.[6]

---

5   King, p. 2.
6   Brook, p. 197.

With a cast of children who had never acted before, the film was shot on a tropical island off Puerto Rico in rough conditions and with poor technical means. Using several cameras at the same time, leaving them to run even as he was talking to the children and filming sequentially as per the novel, Brook ended up with sixty hours of unbroken screening to be edited. The result was a film where the rough, black and white images, the often-confused camera movements and the improvised performances intentionally display its documentary nature. Consequently, Brook's unadorned work-in-progress somehow reconnects with the sociological experiences of the novel's origins, when Golding was a schoolteacher and he studied the dynamics of children playing. 'Many of (the children's) off-screen relationships,' recalls Peter Brook,

> completely paralleled the story, and one of our main problems was to encourage them to be uninhibited within the shots but disciplined in between them. We had to cake them with mud and let them be savages by day, and restore prep-school discipline by the shower and the scrubbing at night. Even the wise and calm Piggy came to me one day close to tears. 'They're going to drop a stone on you,' the other boys had been telling him. 'That scene on the schedule, Piggy's death. It's for real. They don't need you anymore.' My experience showed me that the only falsification in Golding's fable is the length of time the descent to savagery takes. His action takes about three months. I believe that if the cork of continued adult presence were removed from the bottle, complete catastrophe could occur within a long weekend.[7]

Golding's novel, however, cannot be summed up as a sociological experience, and Brook's adaptation goes far deeper than that, capturing the text's truth within its very literary form. Cleverly handling the potential of its own cinematic "reality", the film indeed manages to bring out the symbolic essence that is embedded in the realistic fabric of Golding's narrative as an organic part of it.

---

7   Brook, p. 198.

Golding's story begins with the arrival of Ralph and Piggy on the island, — 'the boy with fair hair' and 'the fat boy'[8] with spectacles and asthma — explaining through fragments of their dialogue the background of this opening situation (a nuclear war that had caused the evacuation of a group of English schoolboys and a plane crash that has left them on the island without any grown-ups to take care of them). The film instead, summarizes the story's background in a sort of *incipit,* through a series of blurry half-tone still images over which the opening titles roll. An old public school, a long-ago class photograph, scholars bent over their desks and then seen singing in a choir. We hear a bell ring, a somber and distant voice teaching geometry and reciting Latin verses, and then, while the images of the choir are appearing, we hear the melodious, remote sound of children's voices singing the *Kyrie Eleison*'s liturgy — 'Lord, have mercy' — that will become the film's musical leitmotiv.

Opening

---

8   William Golding, *Lord of the Flies* (London: Faber & Faber, 2002), pp. 1–2.

Some stills of a cricket match complete this set of tokens, evoking a distant life regulated by well-established, long-time traditions that are abruptly interrupted by entirely different kinds of images: missiles and nuclear weapons, accompanied by the menacing sound of percussion. For several seconds, the cricket match and the sinister weapons alternate rapidly on the screen, before giving place to a third set of stills: war planes in the London sky, a blackboard announcing the school's evacuation, the boys smiling in their uniforms and holding a photograph of a plane, aircrafts in flight, a stormy sky, a map of the Pacific ocean off the Australian coast and then, accelerating the images and the soundtrack's rhythm, the plane crash. A gong sounds, and then a final still image of dark palm trees blowing in the wind ends this opening whose purpose is to crystallize the novel's main theme: the presence of evil within the deceivingly reassuring heart of civilization. Throughout the entire written narrative, we are systematically reminded that the violence and chaos gradually developing among the children are simultaneously raging within the adult world; a civilization in ruins fighting its terrible war outside the island. This civilization is identified by the novel with a western world that is, more specifically, English. Thus, the boys bring with them to the uninhabited island the weight of their colonial pride; the implicit and explicit references to R. M. Ballantyne's *Coral Island* (1858) function here as a symbolic subtext, setting Golding's dark adventure against the colonial ideology embodied in traditional adventure stories. Brook insists on this cultural aspect, firmly establishing in the film's opening the story's English roots, and also highlighting a class issue that was not so explicitly present in the novel. The still images of the school clearly situate the boys within a social elite. In particular, Jack's character is strongly determined as a result of his belonging to that context. Leader of the choir, endowed with an instinctive commanding attitude, Jack declares at the beginning of the novel: 'We'll have rules! Lots of rules! Then when anyone breaks 'em —' (32); 'After all, we're not savages. We're English; and the English are best at everything' (42). Brook's version retains these lines and the boy who plays Jack speaks with a marked upper-class accent ironically connoting his further development into the brutal, face-painted leader of the 'savages'.[9] The effect produced by the film's opening deeply modifies the emphasis the novel puts on the deceivingly bright and innocent adventure that the island seemed to offer at the beginning of the story. In the first chapter of Golding's narrative we see Ralph overcome by 'the delight of a realized ambition'[10] with no grown-ups and an island full of enchantments: 'the green shadows from the palms and the forest sliding over his skin' (5), and a lagoon that looks 'like an incredible pool' (7) with warm water that he plunges into it with delight. Here, on the contrary, we are immediately confronted with the grim backdrop of the story, whose uncanny effect is enhanced by the blurry still images which convey an irretrievable past into the flowing present tense of cinematic language: a lost world of school boys in uniforms, angelic choirs and cricket matches, where everyone could still pretend to be innocent. The viewer is therefore emotionally prepared for the dark story he is about to watch, as the buzz of some invisible flies significantly accompany Ralph and Piggy's arrival on the beach.

The use of long shots and slow pans translates onto the screen the novel's vivid descriptions of a perennial and indifferent nature. Human figures often appear as small and irrelevant details that develop into narrative characters as the camera gradually draws closer.

> Within the diamond haze of the beach something dark was fumbling along. Ralph saw it first, and watched till the intentness of his gaze

---

9   Tom Chapin, the boy who played Jack, was dubbed over by another actor because he had lived in the United States for some time and didn't possess the proper upper-class British accent. See Matthew Dessem, '#43: Lord of the Flies', in *Lord of the Flies* (New York: The Criterion Collection, 2013), www.criterion.com. On the film's class issue see also Geoffrey Macnab, '*Lord of the Flies*: Trouble in Paradise', in *Lord of the Flies*: 'The reason Jack so despises Piggy is not just appearance but also the fact that he is not of the right caste. Yes, Piggy is fat, wears spectacles, and looks like Billy Bunter, but the real problem is that he's from Camberley. He's suburban, lower-middle-class — an outsider among all these blue-blooded chorists.' (Ibid.).

10   Golding, p. 2.

drew all eyes that way. […] The creature was a party of boys, marching approximately in step in two parallel lines and dressed in strangely eccentric clothing. […] Each boy wore a square black cap with a silver badge in it. Their bodies, from throat to ankle, were hidden by black cloaks which bore a long silver cross on the left breast and each neck was finished off with a hambone frill.[11]

An aerial shot shows the gentle curve of the white beach, with a dark, indistinct mass advancing from the far left singing the *Kyrie Eleison* as a sinister military march. Carefully translating the novel's point of view, the image of the advancing group is preceded by a shot of Ralph, clinging to the trunk of a bent palm while gazing intently towards the beach with the sun in his eyes. The camera follows the dark mass as it approaches and gradually appears as a group of boys, carefully reproducing every detail of their choir cloaks from the novel. As it has been remarked by Geoffrey Macnab, the contrast between the natural whiteness of the tropical beach and the long dark cloaks, belonging to an incongruous faraway world of schools and rules, adds a striking 'strain of surrealism'.[12]

The arrival of the choir

11   Golding, p. 15.
12   Geoffrey Macnab, '*Lord of the Flies*: Trouble in Paradise'.

The choir is guided by a taller figure, dressed in the same way; he will later present himself as Jack Merridew and he will become Ralph's competitor for the role of chief. Nevertheless, it is Ralph who will be elected, and he will generously leave to Jack the command of the hunters. However, the rivalry between the two boys and the contrast of Ralph's democratic rule to Jack's violent and totalitarian tribe will develop into one of the main narrative threads. By showing Ralph and Jack symbolically separated by the trunk of the palm tree, which obliquely cuts the frame, Brook immediately sets the stage for their rivalry. Then, a close-up of Jack shot from below lends him a powerful and fierce aspect, offering a first glimpse of a character that will be further developed throughout the following sequences narrating the first expedition through the island.

Tom Chapin (Jack)

The three boys walked briskly on the sand. The tide was low and there was a strip of weed-strewn beach that was almost as firm as a road. A kind of glamour was spread over them and the scene and they were conscious of the glamour and made happy by it. They turned to each other, laughing excitedly, talking, not listening. The air was bright.[13]

On the screen we see Jack, Ralph and Simon, three of the four main characters of the story, walking away on the beach and then climbing up a mountain in a sunny landscape, happily eating fruit from the trees and laughing as they push a great rock down the hill — 'Like a bomb!' they scream in the novel (25). When they arrive at the top of the mountain, they pause to look out at the island and sea. 'This belongs to us,' says Ralph in the novel (26), expressing the great expectations of a boy in a traditional adventure story who is to be tragically deceived by the subsequent developments. Here, we see the three of them looking out in silence, the camera closing in on Jack's face, then on Simon's, and finally moving behind the nape of Ralph's neck, offering a semi-subjective shot of the wide ocean at their feet. Three boys like any others, their faces like blank pages onto which the destiny of each has yet to be written.

As in the novel, their descent from the mountain opens the way for the development of Jack's and Simon's characters, confronting each of them with their own deep nature.

They found a piglet caught in a curtain of creepers, throwing itself at the elastic traces in all the madness of extreme terror. Its voice was thin, needle-sharp and insistent. The three boys rushed forward and Jack drew his knife again with a flourish. He raised his arm in the air. There came a pause, a hiatus, [...] and the blade continued to flash at the end of a bony arm. The pause was only long enough for them to understand what an enormity the downward stroke would be.[14]

After a first close-up of the three boys looking down from a rock at the piglet, the film shows a prolonged image of Jack's suspended gesture, intently gazing downwards while pointing

---

13   Golding, p. 22.
14   Golding, p. 28.

a knife at the animal's neck. Here, as consistently throughout the entire film, the camera directs the viewer away from the overwhelming adventure and towards something at a deeper emotional level, to which the young actors' stiff awkwardness contributes.

'Why didn't you —?' asks Ralph in the novel after the piglet has run away. 'I was going to,' answers Jack, 'I was choosing a place. Next time —!'. 'He snatched his knife out of the sheath,' says the narrator, 'and slammed it into a tree trunk. Next time there would be no mercy. He looked round fiercely, daring them to contradict.' (29). In the film, Jack's violent frustration is elaborated on in contrast with the first presentation of Simon's character, making reference to a preceding passage of the novel:

> They scrambled down a rock slope, dropped among flowers and made their way under the trees. Here they paused and examined the bushes around them curiously. Simon spoke first. 'Like candles. Candle bushes. Candle buds.' The bushes were dark evergreen and aromatic and the many buds were waxen green and folded up against the light. Jack slashed at one with his knife and the scent spilled over them. 'Candle buds.' […] 'Green candles,' said Jack contemptuously, 'we can't eat them. Come on.' (28)

After the piglet's flight, we see the boys scrambling down a slope and Simon approaching some Birds of Paradise bushes. The contrast between Jack's frustration and Simon's instinctive closeness to the world of Nature is conveyed through two back-to-back images. The first is of Jack, in profile with the knife caressing his nose, and then Simon, also in profile, caressing and smelling the plant.

Tom Chapin (Jack)

Tom Ganman (Simon)

The focus of the narrative is thus transferred from Jack towards Simon. Jack abruptly cuts off one of the plant's leaves with his knife and it descends very close to Simon's face, almost touching it. Simon slowly turns towards the camera and the sequence ends with his close-up, looking at us with a quizzical expression, while we once again hear the ominous buzz of invisible flies.

This ability to crystallize the different aspects of the novel into images and sounds appears particularly striking in the sequences adapting the very core of Golding's story: Simon's confrontation with the Lord of the Flies and his subsequent death, narrated in the eighth and ninth chapters. The film shows Simon climbing up the mountain, where a parachutist's dead body — 'If only they (the grown-ups) could send us something grown-up… a sign or something'[15] — has been seen and identified by the children as 'the beast'. While Ralph and Piggy had previously tried to rationalise the spreading fear, and Jack had catalyzed the hunters' violent urges on an imaginary and terrifying antagonist, Simon says that, maybe, the beast is 'only us' (96). He must now go to the top of the mountain and confront it, embarking on a path of initiation towards the awareness of mankind's hidden evil: 'What else is there to do?' he asks, both in the novel[16] and in the film, offering another quizzical look into the camera.

In the meantime, following the novel's structure, Jack and his hunters are in the forest, on the pig's trail. The film shows them running, accompanied by the sound of percussion that grows faster and louder while Jack pulls out his knife and strikes a pig hidden by vegetation. We hear the pig squealing and a fast panning shot shows the hunters in a motionless half circle, their faces painted and spears raised in a suspended attack. Here, the immersive and intrusive reality of the cinematic image is manifestly played down by concealing the novel's brutal details of the sow's slaughtering and offering instead one of those sequences where the violence of the story is deliberately stylized and contained.

Returning to Simon, we see him half concealed by the vegetation and wearing a stunning white shirt.

---

15   Golding, p. 102.
16   Golding, p. 141.

Tom Ganman (Simon)

He is standing near the same bushes we had seen at the end of the exploration sequence and is witnessing the pig's killing, his head bowed while we still hear its desperate squeals. The pig is dead, and the camera shows us Jack's hands crafting Golding's famous stick sharpened at both ends. While the stick is rammed into the ground, the sound of percussion resumes and the camera focuses on the motionless, painted face of one of the hunters while we hear Jack's voice, 'This head is for the Beast. It's a gift.'[17]

---

17   Golding, p. 151.

A hunter

The Lord of the Flies

It is a quick close-up, that will be followed later on by a second one, even quicker, in which the head appears covered with flies. Between these two close-ups, there is another image of the Lord of the Flies, shown in an almost theatrical setting: a long medium frontal shot of the lush forest with the head in the foreground merging with the vegetation, as in a sort of allegorical painting. In the background, we first see the hunters marching with the skewered pig's carcass and singing *Kyrie Eleison*. Then Simon appears. At first he's a small, faraway figure emerging from the dense-forest background. Then, as he pauses in the midst of the vegetation, he creates a diagonal axis with the pig's head, revealing its almost-hidden presence. Relegated to a supporting role, the Lord of the Flies is indeed the least impressive aspect of these stylized sequences, as if the realness of its images couldn't convey its symbolic appeal without having to resort to other elements (human figures or lush vegetation). On its own, the image of the Lord of the Flies cannot linger too long on the screen, otherwise it risks becoming simply a 'pig's head on a stick',[18] as Simon discovers later on.

In the film, moreover, the Lord of the Flies does not speak. Thus, Simon's famous dialogue with it explicitly becomes an interior discourse, with the boy silently sitting in front of the pig's head and a series of shots and reverse-shots gradually closing in on Simon's intent gaze and the pig's grinning face. 'Fancy thinking the Beast was something you could hunt and kill!' said the Lord of the Flies in the novel, 'You knew, didn't you? I'm part of you? Close, close, close! I'm the reason why it's no go? Why things are what they are?' (158). By renouncing Belzebub's suggestive voice, everything in the film is delegated to the visual power of the camera, alternately moving 'close, close, close' towards Simon's face and the pig's head. Here, the Lord of the Flies obtains at last a prolonged close-up, gradually giving way to the immense detail of its mouth, covered with buzzing flies, until Simon (together with the viewer) actually seems to fall into it: 'Simon found he was looking into a vast mouth. There was

---

18   Golding, p. 158.

blackness within, a blackness that spread. [...] Simon was inside
the mouth. He fell down and lost consciousness'.[19]
    The following sequence proceeds to narrate the final part of
Simon's symbolic path, higher up the mountain to see the 'beast'.
Through Simon's eyes it appears now very different from the grim
puppet that had previously terrified Ralph, Jack and Roger: contorted
on one side, motionless, it has become nothing more than a 'poor
body' on which the camera lingers for a few, long seconds, silently
translating on the screen Simon's pity for that 'harmless and horrible'
(162) symbol of 'mankind's essential illness' (96). Simon's epiphany
is now complete and, from this moment, he takes on the role of a
saint, a Christ-like figure (about which much has been written) who
gives up his life for mankind's salvation: 'The news must reach the
others as soon as possible.'[20] In the film, Simon's last step towards
his martyrdom begins with an impressive close-up set against an
immense and cloudy sky. We see him as an imposing figure shot
slightly from below as he slowly recedes from the dead body into the
background of the sky, as if being swallowed up by it.

Tom Ganman (Simon)

---

19   Golding, p. 159.
20   Golding, p. 162.

As in the novel, Simon's movement towards the 'beast' is preceded by images of the boys cooking the pig on the beach, led by Jack who has by now clearly overcome Ralph's rule. In these sequences Brook offers the most striking example of his documentary style, and the camera captures the spontaneous cries and haphazard movements of the practically naked and crudely painted children who have been set free to play.

Boys on the beach before Simon's murder

Among the almost comical, improvised realism of these images, Brook introduces a different, disquieting kind of vision: a carefully staged shot of Ralph's dark profile that has become an iconic image for Golding's story. Presiding from high upon a rock overlooking the chaos beneath him, Jack, whose face and body are heavily painted in white lines symbolically evoking the Union Jack, is wearing a kind of savage crown made from the leaf he had previously cut off near Simon's face.

Tom Chapin (Jack)

After the sequences of Simon and the 'beast', we are brought back to the boys on the beach who are now plunged into the darkness of the night, illuminated only by their torches as they chaotically move along the shore. The confused yelling is interrupted by another close-up of Jack's profile. With a ferocious look, he distinctly articulates the opening lines of the hunters' war chant, 'Kill the beast!', which is immediately followed by the other boys' voices, 'Kill the beast! Cut his throat! Spill his blood!'. The wild war chant is but another variation of the same *Kyrie Eleison* that we first heard in the film's opening and then again as the marching song of Jack's choirboys. While some of the cameras continue to follow the children's chaotic movements, one remains fixed, filming the faces and bodies that occasionally pause in front of it, eerily addressing us with their shouts and sneers.

The following sequences alternate the images of the boys with those of Simon, explicitly connecting them through the war chant and the screaming, which we continue to hear as we watch Simon

staggering towards the beach. Simon's and the viewer's auditory
perceptions are joined together and the sounds coming from
the beach, which are at first diminished by the distance, grow
increasingly louder as he approaches. Returning to the boys, we
observe a close-up of a painted figure illuminated by torchlight
pointing towards the forest. 'Look!' the painted boy shouts, and
every other sound and movement suddenly stops, dramatically
suspending the narrative flow, 'The beast!' During an unnaturally
protracted, eerie silence, we see Simon coming through the forest
and then, shifting to his point of view, the group of boys at a close
distance on the beach. For a brief moment they remain in silence,
motionless. Then they attack him, drawing us into their chaotic
movement of ecstatic violence.

In the novel, the boys' violence was stylized in a symbolic
war dance performed in two concentric circles, hypnotically
turning and beating 'like a steady pulse', as 'the throb and stamp
of a single organism' (168). The film renounced the stylistic
virtuosities of Golding's description and, if we compare these
sequences to those of the pig's slaughtering, we notice how
differently Boook's cinematic translation functions here, taking
the documentary realism to its very climax. The novel, moreover,
narrates the entire scene by focusing on the children's perception
of Simon as 'a thing' that 'was crawling out of the forest', 'the
beast' that 'was stumbling in the middle of them, […] on his
knees in the centre, its arms folded over its face' (168). Within
the actual reality of the cinematic medium however, the viewer is
forced to see Simon's terrified face and his hands raised to protect
himself.

In Golding's narrative, Simon remains the 'beast' even after
the violence has been consumed, maintaining that appellative
beyond the children's perception in order to convey the enormity
of what has been done and their confused understanding of it:

> Then the clouds opened and let down the rain like a waterfall. The
> water bounded from the mountain-top, tore leaves and branches from
> the trees, poured like a cold shower over the struggling heap on the
> sand. Presently the heap broke up and figures staggered away. Only the

beast lay still, a few yards from the sea. Even in the rain they could see how small a beast it was; and already its blood was staining the sand.[21]

The film does not show us Simon bleeding on the beach but rather keeps its focus on the children's savage violence up until the end when we see them running towards the sea yelling and wielding their spears. While the camera frames the white sea foam, once again we hear Jack's voice screaming the opening words of the war chant, 'Kill! Kill!'. Another voice immediately joins in, disquietingly more childish, repeating the same words and extending the responsibility to every single child on the island, even the very little ones.

Having reached its climax, the violence gives way to the only moment of catharsis offered by Golding's dark story.

> The tide swelled in over the rain-pitted sand and smoothed everything with a layer of silver. Now it touched the first of the stains that seeped from the broken body [...]. The water rose further and dressed Simon's coarse hair with brightness. The line of his cheek silvered and the turn of his shoulder became sculptured marble. [...] The body lifted a fraction of an inch from the sand and a bubble of air escaped from the mouth with a wet plop. Then it turned gently on the water. Somewhere over the darkened curve of the world the sun and moon were pulling; and the film of water on the earth planet was held, bulging slightly on one side while the solid core turned. The great wave of the tide moved further along the island and the water lifted. Softly, surrounded by a fringe of inquisitive bright creatures, itself a silver shape beneath the steadfast constellations, Simon's dead body moved out towards the open sea.[22]

In the film, we once again hear the *Kyrie Eleison*, but this time as an extradiegetic comment melodiously sung by the same white voices we heard in the opening. The prayer takes us towards the vision of Simon's transfigured body, covered with silver light and floating in a luminous sea. Then, 'turned gently on the water', it slowly drifts out of the frame. For a few seconds we are left in

---

21   Golding, p. 169.
22   Golding, p. 170.

front of a black screen, still listening to the prayer's song, 'Lord, have mercy', and upon whose notes the illuminated sea water reappears — mercifully indeed — lingering on the screen and literally translating Golding's redeeming light, briefly shining into the heart of darkness.

More than any other character in the film, Piggy is the very image of the boy we had in mind while reading the novel. He 'arrived by magic through the post', recalls Peter Brook,

> — a sticky *Just William* on lined paper, 'Dear Sir, I am fat and wear spectacles', and a crumpled photograph that made us cry with delight. It was Piggy, come to life in Camberley — the unique boy himself, conceived ten years before, at the very moment that Golding was wrestling with the birth of the novel.[23]

In the film, Piggy's spectacles, both a symbol of his intellectual power and his physical vulnerability, become an essential leitmotif of his tragic trajectory as a victim of Jack's brutality. Thus, the sequence in which Jack brutally seizes Piggy's spectacles in order to light the fire literally translates the corresponding scene in the novel, but then goes on to further develop it through a backlit close-up of Jack holding the lenses against the sunlight, followed by an image of Piggy, blinded and awkwardly moving a hand before his eyes ('Jus' blurs, that's all. Hardly see my hand')[24]. It is through this backlit image, which suddenly disturbs the viewer's vision, that the film establishes an immediate and unconscious association with Piggy's vulnerability.

This sequence is symbolically juxtaposed to a passage of the story in which we see Jack brutally smacking Piggy's face and breaking his spectacles. Both sequences involve a fire: in the first one, it has been made as a rescue signal; in the second one, it has gone out, forgotten by Jack and his party who have gone hunting. In the first sequence Jack is still wearing his uniform shirt and has a clean face; in the second he's almost naked and his face is painted. In the novel, between the two passages a highly symbolic event has occurred:

---

23   Brook, p. 195.
24   Golding, p. 40.

Jack planned his new face. He made one cheek and one eye-socket white, then rubbed red over the other half of his face and slashed a black bar of charcoal across from right ear to left jaw. [...] He knelt, holding the shell of water. A rounded patch of sunlight fell on his face and a brightness appeared in the depths of the water. He looked in astonishment, no longer at himself but at an awesome stranger. [...] He began to dance and his laughter became a bloodthirsty snarling. He capered towards Bill and the mask was a thing on its own, behind which Jack hid, liberated from shame and self-consciousness.[25]

We never actually see that crucial moment on the screen, but in the second sequence the painted Jack is indeed 'liberated from shame and self-consciousness'. Whatever had restrained his hand in front of the piglet is gone, and his loathing of Piggy becomes a violent urge that has to be released. The film's elision of the symbolic moment in which Jack paints his face has the effect of focusing his violence directly on Piggy, making it more realistically tangible. As with Simon in the exploration sequence, it is on Piggy that the film puts its emphasis here, showing a close-up of him wearing the broken spectacles — another image from Golding's story that has become an icon.

---

25   Golding, p. 66.

Hugh Edwards (Piggy)

Piggy's spectacles appear again towards the end of the story, when Jack and two of his hunters attack the few kids who have remained in the huts on the beach. As in the novel, we hear the hunters' voices whispering in the night, 'Piggy, Piggy... Where are you, Piggy? We come to get you...', and then we see them attacking the huts. In the novel, Piggy thinks that Jack's purpose must be to steal the shell, the symbolic object of Ralph's democratic rule, which was held by anyone who wanted to speak in the assemblies. But Jack is not interested in such an obsolete object within his new totalitarian order: 'They didn't come for the conch,' says Piggy after the attack, 'They came for something else. Ralph — what am I going to do?'[26] A few lines later, at the end of the chapter, we see the three hunters trotting on the beach. Leading them, Jack has become 'the Chief': 'He was a chief now in truth; and he made stabbing motions with his spear. From his left hand dangled Piggy's broken glasses.' (186). In the film Jack also mimics Piggy by wearing his spectacles and walking with an imaginary protruding stomach. That parody makes him

26 Golding, p. 186.

a less commanding and more childish figure than he was in the corresponding scene in the novel, but this further increases the grim effect of the entire sequence. It is just a game, of course, like their whispering in the night, but Jack has taken the power, he is the pig hunter and Piggy has been definitively robbed of his sight: 'Ralph — what am I going to do?'.

Piggy's destiny was indeed written from the beginning — in his nickname and his spectacles — and in the following sequences we witness its tragic realization. From above, we see him grasping the mountain rocks leading to Jack's new headquarters, presided over by screaming painted kids. Looking up at them with blinded squinted eyes, Piggy's weakness is clear, but despite everything he gets to his feet and, holding the shell, delivers his final speech: 'Which is better to be — a pack of painted savages like you are, or sensible, like Ralph is? Which is better — to have rules and agree, or to hunt and kill?'. Overhead meanwhile, Roger (Jack's sadistic lieutenant) levers an enormous rock from the mountain and, as if answering in the worst possible way Piggy's appeal to reason, strikes him, precipitating his body into the sea below. Here, we are reminded of the first expedition, when three boys happily pushed a massive rock down into the sea. Also, we obviously think of Simon's death, compared to which this second murder appears indeed as an anticlimax. There is no ecstasy in the act of murder, here, just Roger's emotionless expression, Jack's astonished look and the silent disconcertment of the painted boys. And Piggy's body is just a dead body, floating facedown in the water. Piggy dies without having reached Simon's dark truth, the real reason 'why it's no go […] why things are what they are' (158). He dies believing in the good values of the lost world of civilization, without understanding that even the adults in the outside world have forgotten them, choosing 'to hunt and kill' rather than 'to have rules and agree'.

In Brook's version, Piggy's character indeed crystallizes the deceptive nostalgic bond with civilization. (Ironically, Piggy is the only one who does not really belong to that upper-class world shown in the film's opening). 'Like a crowd of kids,' he sighs at the beginning of the film, observing the boys who excitedly run off to light their first fire. The 'martyred expression of a parent who has to keep up with the senseless ebullience of the children'[27] stiffly reproduced by the young actor and the stereotyped adultness of his words produce a somewhat comic effect, which makes us smile empathically with Piggy's character. Later on, when the older kids go up the mountain to see the 'beast' and he is left in charge of the little ones, Brook integrates an entirely original sequence, his only major addition to the novel's narrative. Hugh Edwards, the boy who plays Piggy, is seated in front of the children and tells them a story about his actual hometown, Camberley, and how it came to be named that way. It begins with the difficulty of getting letters delivered to a town originally called Cambridgetown, a toponym akin to the better-known Cambridge. Within the attentive silence of the audience, Piggy's pedantic narrative becomes a wonderfully absorbing bedtime story, because the problem presented by those undelivered letters deeply resounds with the tragic situation that the lost children are actually facing. Thus, the solution eventually offered by Piggy's story — the transformation of 'Cambridgetown' into 'Camberley' and the letters that are at last delivered — produces a soothing happy-ending, both for the children as well as for the viewer. 'So dignified and poignant is the scene,' writes Jackson Burgess, 'that I couldn't help feeling that any species represented by Piggy [...] cannot finally be brought low by its Jacks.'[28] Yet, no matter how reasonable and dignified Piggy appears in sequences such as these, Brook's adaptation also carefully takes note of his limitations, relying on that same deceptive belief in the salvific values of civilization. As in the novel, Piggy refuses to acknowledge Simon's murder: 'It was dark. There was that — that bloody dance. There was lightning and thunder and rain. We were sacred!'. And even, with the very hypocritical voice of bourgeois respectability: 'It was an accident. He was batty, he asked for it'.

---

27   Golding, p. 38.
28   Jackson Burgess, 'Lord of the Flies', *Film Quarterly*, 17:2 (1963–1964), p. 32.

In both the novel and the film, Jack, Simon and Piggy are realistic figures that, however, seem to carry with them the weight of a destiny that has already been written, inscribed within their own personalities. Ralph's character instead is more contradictory and pliable, less burdened by a defined symbolic role. Among Golding's main characters, he's the only one who possesses the features of a proper novel's hero and, in fact, in the end he will be the boy who survives — having learned the island's dark lesson and bearing its weight back into the world: 'You'll get back to where you came from,'[29] Simon tells him.

He 'might make a boxer, as far as width and heaviness of shoulders went, but there was a mildness about his mouth and eyes that proclaimed no devil':[30] Ralph is a natural-born hero and he is the elected leader, because of 'his size, and attractive appearance' (19) and also because he's the one who first blew into the shell, gathering the children together on the beach. Nonetheless, it is Piggy who explains to him how to use the shell, and Piggy again who always knows what has to be done, while Ralph experiences frequent attention lapses in which he suddenly loses contact with reality and retreats into a dream world. At first excited by the wonders of a desert island without adults, he soon grows aware of the urgency to be rescued and he generally behaves according to that priority. He's a good, generous boy, but he betrays Piggy's confidence, revealing to the entire assembly the humiliating nickname that he had been explicitly asked to keep secret, causing 'a storm of laughter' (17), 'a closed circuit of sympathy with Piggy outside' (18), and by doing so somehow contributes to writing Piggy's destiny. At the same time, he is capable of remorse and apologizes for the pain that he has inflicted; he's also the only one who is able and willing to protect Piggy from Jack's violent contempt. Ralph is instinctively drawn to Jack's adventurous nature, generously offering him the hunters' leadership, and they share happy moments of excitement and friendship. Nevertheless, he also knows when and how to stand up against him. With all

---

29   Golding, p. 121.
30   Golding, p. 5.

the others, except Piggy, he participates in the bloody circle that killed Simon (and Brook's camera takes care to make him fully recognizable in the night sequences), yet he is the only one who explicitly calls it a murder, fully acknowledging his own responsibility. Neither a victim nor a bully nor a saint, Ralph is just a normal, decent kid with whom it is easy to identify. In the film, Ralph's character is extremely faithful to the novel's 'normal' hero. Essential to the story's development, he's often present on the screen. But contrary to the other main characters there are no iconic images of him, as if his undetermined nature refused to be captured and fixed by the camera. After Piggy's murder, Ralph becomes the next designated victim of Jack's tribe. Both in the novel and in the film we witness his frantic escape through the forest, pursued by 'the desperate ululation' advancing 'like a jagged fringe of menace', and we finally see him stumbling, 'rolling over and over in the warm sand, crouching with arm up to ward off, trying to cry for mercy' (222).

> He staggered to his feet, tensed for more terrors, and looked up at a huge peaked cap. It was a white-topped cap, and above the green shade of the peak was a crown, and an anchor, gold foliage. He saw white drill, epaulettes, a revolver, a row of gilt buttons down the front of a uniform.[31]

Suddenly, the presence of an adult reveals the restricted vision that the novel has imposed upon its reader: 'A naval officer stood on the sand, looking down at Ralph in wary astonishment' (222). Through Ralph's gaze, slowly moving upwards from the officer's white socks, Brook translates the novel's shift. Then, following the adult's glance, we see the island in flames and the staggering figures of the naked boys on the beach. 'One of them came close to the officer and looked up. 'I'm, I'm —'.[32] It is Percival Wemys Madison, one of the little children, whom we have seen before. In the film, he appears in the beginning, among the group that gathers after the sounding of the conch shell, neatly attired in

---

31   Golding, p. 222.
32   Golding, p. 223.

his school uniform and scrupulously pronouncing his name and address. Later on, we see him again in another assembly, by then almost naked and with long hair, vainly trying to remember 'the incantation of his address':[33] 'Percival Wemys Madison, The Vicarage, Harcourt St. Anthony, Hants, telephone, telephone, tele —'. That incantation, which Brook had momentarily restored through Piggy's voice narrating the happy story of Camberley, is now entirely forgotten as we see little Percival looking up at the officer, silently moving his lips, 'I'm, I'm —', and then turning his gaze around, looking back at an unintelligible world.

Kent Fletcher (Percival)

The officer looks away, and following his gaze the camera shows us Jack's and Roger's painted figures, with flames burning behind them. They look small and thin, very different from the fierce, menacing figures to which Brook's images had gotten us used to seeing. The entire sequence unfolds in silence. Then, the military march that we have heard since the choir's arrival

33   Golding, p. 102.

resumes, while the camera shows us a cutter on the shore with some other men in white uniforms looking towards the beach. Just then, Ralph's back appears in the frame and, as in the novel, a semi-subjective shot frees the viewer's gaze from the adult's point of view, giving it back to Ralph.

> Ralph looked at him (the officer) dumbly. For a moment he had a fleeting picture of the strange glamour that had once invested the beaches. But the island was scorched up like dead wood — Simon was dead — and Jack had... The tears began to flow and sobs shook him. [...] with filthy body, matted hair, and unwiped nose, Ralph wept for the end of innocence, the darkness of man's heart, and the fall through the air of the true, wise friend called Piggy.[34]

In the film, nobody explains to us what Ralph's thoughts are nor what is he weeping for. Everything is left to the two long close-ups of his dirty face looking straight at us with tears running down his cheeks.

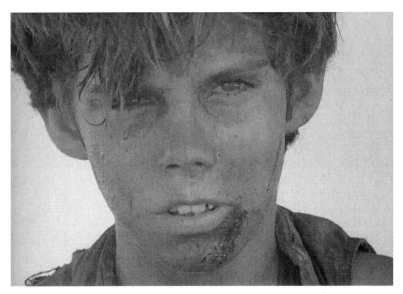

James Aubrey (Ralph)

34   Golding, pp. 224–225.

Then he bows his head and disappears from the screen. We are reminded here of Simon's close-up looking at the slaughter of the pig and then bowing his head, but Ralph's image is devoid of that beautiful, symbolic stillness that had imprinted Simon's face in the viewer's mind. At the end of the adventure, Ralph has completed his initiation path, reaching a full awareness of mankind's inner evil as Simon had done before him. Ralph's knowledge, however, hasn't come to him as a spiritual epiphany, but through his painful material experience. He might weep 'for the end of innocence' and 'the darkness of man's heart', but here he simply appears as an exhausted, traumatized boy who weeps for something simpler and more tangible than that — perhaps 'the fall through the air of the true, wise friend called Piggy' (225). A last frame, onto which the closing credits roll, shows the beach and the palm trees enveloped by dark smoke while the military march recovers the sound of the children's voices: *Kyrie Eleison.*

After Peter Brook's film, *Lord of the Flies* has known only one other adaptation, and a bad one, entirely missing the point.[35] Perhaps, for all its cinematic qualities, Golding's writing is not so easily approachable by a real camera, as it is almost too straightforward to reproduce its visual narrative by simplifying it and leaving no place for invention. And maybe, the encounter between Peter Brook's cinematic reality and William Golding's realism was so stunning that it has made it difficult to imagine another way to recreate the essence of the novel for the screen. Brook's film and Golding's novel are indeed so organically complementary that they have become part of a single, extended, and maybe definitive text, where Golding's voice glows beside Brook's cinematic images, both truly 'incandescent and furious'.

---

35   *Lord of the Flies*, directed by Harry Hook (Columbia Pictures, 1990).

Bibliography

Bloom, Harold (ed.), *William Golding's* Lord of the Flies (New York: Infobase Publishing, 2008).

Brook, Peter, *The Shifting Point. Forty years of theatrical exploration. 1946–1987* (London: Methuen Drama, 1989 [1987]).

Burgess, Jackson, '*Lord of the Flies*', *Film Quarterly*, 17:2 (1963–1964), 31–32.

Dessem, Matthew, '#43: Lord of the Flies', in *Lord of the Flies* (New York: The Criterion Collection, 2013).

Golding, William, *Lord of the Flies* (London: Faber & Faber, 2000 [1954]).

Hodson, Leighton, *William Golding* (New York: Capricorn Books, 1969).

Hynes, Samuel, *William Golding* (New York–London: Columbia University Press, 1964).

King, Stephen, 'Introduction', in William Golding, *Lord of the Flies* (London: Faber & Faber, 2014).

Kinkead-Weekes, Mark and I. Gregor, *William Golding: A Critical Study* (London: Faber & Faber, 1967).

Macnab, Geoffrey, '*Lord of the Flies*: Trouble in Paradise', in *Lord of the Flies* (New York: The Criterion Collection, 2013).

Oldsley, Bernard Stanley and S. Weintraub, *The Art of William Golding* (Bloomington–London: Indiana University Press, 1968).

Pemberton, Clive, *William Golding* (Harlow: Longmans, Green & Co., 1969).

Filmography

Brook, Peter, *Lord of the Flies* (British Lion, 1963).

Hook, Harry, *Lord of the Flies* (Columbia Pictures, 1990).

Rouch, Jean, *Les maîtres fous* (Les Films de la Pléiade, 1955).

SOUTH AFRICA'S NEW ARCHIVES. LITERATURE, PHOTOGRAPHY AND THE DIGITAL HUMANITIES

Carmen Concilio
(University of Turin)

Prologue: On Photography

This essay explores the idea that photo-essaysm is perhaps becoming a new, hybrid, interesting genre in our contemporary world. This might also be part of a revisionary process that questions the crisis of literature and the appearance of new genres, such as "creative non-fiction" together with journalism and quicker forms of writing as urgent responses to the immediacy of what happens in the present. Photography is certainly one of the most interesting media of our time which also offers new possibilities of intermediality if accompanied by texts. The instances here presented are meant as active agents in this debate and also as new forms of archives. This exploratory work is therefore a contribution to new literary genres and new semiotic codes, on mew media and new cultural phenomena.

The photograph representing 'Refugees from Zimbabwe sheltering in the Central Methodist Church on Pritchard Street, in the city. *22 March 2009*'[1] is half familiar, half unfamiliar. It represents the dis-composed bodies of refugees. They seem half alive, half dead in their exhausted rest or sleep. Some are crouched, some bent over, some laying, some retreating, some dressed, some not. Some of them hide their faces: against the daylight, against the camera, the viewers, the volunteers? There

---

1   David Goldblatt, *TJ Johannesburg Photographs 1848–2010* (Rome: Contrasto, 2010), p. 315.
See also: https://www.theguardian.com/world/gallery/2010/nov/25/david-goldblatt-southafrica-photography, accessed December 7, 2016.

are women (few), young men (the majority), boys (numerous). Some are on the floor, half fallen, some on benches. These are church benches. That is unfamiliar: to see so many contorted bodies lying one against the other, fittingly arranged as if in a puzzle, inside a church, as if the challenge had been how to cover every single inch left void. The space of the image/church is saturated with bodies, limbs, arms, legs, torsos, heads. Refugees and church stand as "*studium*" and "*punctum*" in Barthes's semiotic theory of photography.[2] The *punctum* is a "detail" that pricks the eye/I. In Goldblatt's photograph the church is that *punctum*.

The black and white photograph is a famous one, by the well-known South African photographer David Goldblatt. The shot shows a downward perspective, a lateral view, parallel to the benches, from above, a god-like view of the central large amphitheatre. The black and white — plus all the shades of grey — is perfectly mastered to provide a view of humanity caught in our modern politics.[3] I agree with photojournalist Ferdinando Scianna, who claims that a photograph "shows" [*mostra*] and does not "demonstrate" [*dimostra*] a theory. Furthermore, he states that 'the ideological function of a photograph is engendered by the "text" that every image contains' (my translation).[4] The text is either the one the photographer ("*Operator*" in Barthes's semiotics) has in mind, or the one the interpreter ("*Spectator*") produces.

2   'It is not possible to posit a rule of connection between the *studium* and *punctum* (when it happens to be there). It is a matter of a co-presence. In order to perceive the *punctum* [...] I should receive it right here in my eyes. Very often the *punctum* is a "detail", i.e., a partial object. Yet, the *punctum* shows no preference for morality or good taste: the *punctum* can be ill-bred.' Roland Barthes, *Camera Lucida* (New York: Farrar Straus and Gireaux, 1981), pp. 42–46.

3   'The fundamental categorial pair of Western politics is not that of friend/ enemy but that of bare life/political existence, *zoë/bios*, exclusion/ inclusion.' Giorgio Agamben, *Homo Sacer. Sovereign Power and Bare Life*, trans. by Daniel Heller-Roazen (Stanford: Stanford University Press, 1998), p. 8.

4   Ferdinando Scianna, *Etica e fotogiornalismo* (Milan: Electa, 2010), pp. 9–10.

The picture speaks another language, too: of care and cure; charity, piety, hospitality, rescue, safety, shelter, arrivals. What are they doing there? They are sleeping off their bad dreams of real life. They are exerting their right to aspire. Images and photographs do tell stories, or at least they contain stories and in order to unleash them, words are needed. Thus, here comes the story:

> The compassion of a Protestant church [...] not evidenced by the Catholics, the Jews, the Muslims in their religious establishments, had sheltered refugee immigrants from countries in conflict around this one's borders since the influx started, Christianity appropriate to the circumstances of the times. [...] The church turned dormitory flowed over to the pavement where people slept like corpses under any old shroud on scavenged cardboard.

This is a passage from Nadine Gordimer's last novel *No Time Like the Present* (2012).[5] Here, Nadine Gordimer speaks of 'the red-brick dignity of the old Methodist church. The entrance façade of the Magistrates' Court, ignored, obscured by a clutter of occupant people' (191).

In this case, Goldblatt's image and Gordimer's words do converge in one textuality. They echo each other and resonate in tune, to the point that Nadine Gordimer's text might well be a perfect caption to Goldblatt's photograph.[6] These are 'People come from Zimbabwe, where you can die slowly, because your brothers take everything from you, that's the Mugabe way, for themselves' (195). And now, South Africa — in spite of this temporary hospitality — is not keen on admitting: 'these brothers who let us operate from their countries in the Struggle' (195). This is the accusation against the ex-activists and veterans of the Umkhonto, the radical and military branch of the African National Congress, who are now reluctant to take positions about

---

5   Nadine Gordimer, *No Time Like the Present* (New York: Farrar Straus & Giroux, 2012), p. 191.
6   Goldblatt's dedication in his photo-album reads: 'For Nadine Gordimer, Lionel Abrahams and Barney Simon'.

the newly-arrived migrants. Their aspiration to be admitted into a new life, a new country, is not necessarily met with favour.

Clearly, to Gordimer this is a case of afrophobia, not only on the part of whites but also on the part of black people:

> afrophobia — [...] A society that through the strategies of apartheid colonialism has impoverished blacks materially and has gone on to do so psychologically. It has managed to convince black south afrikans [sic] that their souls are not their own and that they are in fact, not Afrikan [sic]. That is, black South Africans [sic] fear/attack fellow Afrikans [sic] but serve white society with an ingratiating docility without compunction.[7]

More words add up to the same story:

> Now Father is in South Africa, working, but he never writes, never sends us money, never nothing. (22)
> My cousin Makhosi [...] After a while, he too went to South Africa. (23)
> I don't go to school anymore because all the teachers left to teach over in South Africa and Botswana and Namibia and them, where there's better money, but I haven't forgotten the things I learned. (31)
> Moshe went to South Africa a few days ago. (44)
> And last summer, she went to Khayelitsha in South Africa to teach at an orphanage. (176)
> And then, in another phone call, Aunt Fostalina's cousin NaSandi called to say her son, Tsepang, who was my age, had been eaten by a crocodile as he tried to cross the Limpopo River to South Africa. (203)
> Bastard finally went to South Africa.[8]

Darling is the narrating child voice of NoViolet Bulawayo's novel *We Need New Names* (2013). She names all the people, relatives and friends who slowly leave Zimbabwe and move

---

7   Thembinkosi Okonko, 'On Afrophobia', *The Johannesburg Salon*, 9 (2015), 32–33 (p. 33).
     See http://www.jwtc.org.za/the_salon/volume_9.htm, accessed December 7, 2016.
8   NoViolet Bulawayo, *We Need New Names* (London: Chatto & Windus, 2013), p. 284: page references quoted in the text are from this edition.

to South Africa. Some meet their death, some come back, only to die because they are affected by Aids. South Africa is not the Paradise they are all looking for. Bulawayo's words could also perfectly work as caption to Goldblatt's photograph of Zimbabwean refugees.

So far, words and images have been matched to circumscribe a historical mass migration from Zimbabwe to South Africa through its artistic representations. The works of art here considered are not immediately related to one another. Yet, if analysed in their reciprocal interceptions, they tell one and the same story of migrancy, of temporary homes and of aspiration.

There is still another chapter to the same story. It is a long and detailed journalistic chronicle, published by one of the most interesting and innovative on-line Journals in the field of Digital Humanities: *Johannesburg The Salon*. The article follows step by step the flows of Zimbabwean refugees from 2006 up to 2010. It is the story of hundreds of people to whom the Methodist church opened its doors and who participated each Friday night in a meeting where they were instructed on basic things like the use of toilets, rules and services:

> over 500 people are waiting for the meeting to start. Men with worn clothing walk in carrying flat cardboard boxes that will later be their beds. Women and children sit close to the front. The green carpet is frayed, many of the seats in the pews are broken and the lights are dim.[9]

Bishop Paul Verryn was cooperating with NGOS as *Médecins Sans Frontières*, who operated in the basement, and volunteers to secure sports activities, entertainments, adult education, computer training, sewing lessons and book-clubs. In the building there are special rooms for families, women with children and married couples. That explains why in Goldblatt's photo young black men

---

9   Christa Kuljian, 'Making the Invisible Visible: A Story of the Central Methodist Church', *The Johannesburg Salon*, 3 (2010), 36–43 (p. 36). Further page references will be quoted in the text.
See http://www.jwtc.org.za/the_salon/volume_3.htm, accessed December 7, 2016.

are the majority in the central amphitheatre. But soon the crowd overflows the church. They sleep in the street, along the nearby garage ramps. Soon, the neighbours start complaining about the chaos, the mess and poor hygienic conditions. The Church is sued in various court cases and so is the Bishop. City authorities provide toilets and evacuation plans: all ineffective.

> After the meeting, at about 9 pm, residents start putting their mats and blankets on the floor. Soon there's no place for your feet. One night, I left the meeting out of a side door and found myself in a dark passage, stepping around people's heads and their belongings. [...]
> Walking into the basement is a descent past bedding and hanging clothes. It is an informal settlement in a building. (36)

Most of the refugees were professionals: teachers, nurses, lecturers, artisans. Yet, in January 2008 the police raided the place. The church was vandalised, people were under arrest for days.

> Judge Sutherland of the High Court compared the police raid on the church 'to grotesque apartheid-era abuses of 20 years ago.'
> Researchers estimate that there are likely 600,000 to 650,000 Zimbabweans in Johannesburg. The Solidarity Peace Trust says Central Methodist is the 'highly visible tip of a huge iceberg of Zimbabweans in Central Johannesburg.' (37)

Not only refugees from Zimbabwe but also destitute South Africans lived for years in that church. Xenophobic violence and failed elections in Zimbabwe in 2008 provoked new fluxes of people into South Africa. 'By the end of 2008, the numbers living in the Church swelled to over 2,000 and people began sleeping outside the Church as well.' (42)

The city had no precise plans about refugees and even the state had neither projects nor a plan, nor framework within which to operate. The Church had to stand up to case after case for years, fighting the inadequacy of City measures. Another police raid occurred in 2009 while the Bishop was preaching against xenophobia. Among these ebbs and flows, with the Church sensing the crisis in Zimbabwe with larger or less numerous crowds of migrants according to the seriousness of poverty and inequality in both countries, Johannesburg inner city was put to the test and, with it, the entire South Africa. If the *punctum* — as Barthes claims — has metonymic power, the Church easily stands as a substitute for South Africa. And, if with Susan Sontag one could say that photographs are 'miniatures of reality',[10] Goldblatt's picture stands for a whole world of refugee camps.

The *Salon* article, too, might be a caption to David Goldblatt's photograph, which is much more than an artistic photo. It speaks also the language of failures: political, humanitarian, sanitary, collective. Also failure of Africans towards other Africans.

South Africa's Post-apartheid Archives between Photographs and Literature

In South Africa the passage to the twenty-first century has been characterized by the opening of an archive that was internationally not visible during the years of apartheid: photography. The London exhibition *Figures and Fictions* in 2011 stressed how the post-apartheid period coincides with the rise to prominence of photography in the contemporary international art world.[11]

In previous decades photographic reportage with a political content was of course widely practised in the country. The major force that had engendered this new international interest in photography is not exclusively the so-called "pictorial turn",[12] but rather a new, genuine approach to photography that takes into consideration also its interpolation with literary and narrative discourses. Exactly on this topic, Amitav Ghosh claims:

---

10   Susan Sontag, *On Photography* (Harmondsworth: Penguin, 1977), p. 4.
11   See http://www.vam.ac.uk/content/articles/f/figures-and-fictions-contemporary-south-african-photography/, accessed December 7, 2016.
12   W. J. T. Mitchell, 'The Pictorial Turn', in *Picture Theory* (Chicago: University of Chicago Press, 1994), pp. 11–34.

with the Internet we were suddenly back in a time when text and image could be twinned with as much facility as in an illuminated manuscript. It is surely no coincidence that images too began to seep back into the textual world of the novel; then came the rise of the graphic novel — and it soon began to be taken seriously.[13]

An exhibition of Alf Kumalo's photographs of the last fifty years was organized at the turn of the last century, in 1998. The South African curator was Santu Mofokeng, the Italian ones were Noris Lazzarini and Monica Fresco.

For some years now a project has been under way in Africa to make an inventory of all photo archives. A partnership between Africans and Westerners resulted in the Biennial Exhibition of African Photography taking place at Bamako (Mali) from 1994, an important occasion for updating the archive.[14]

In the same years, another seminal and ground-breaking work in the field of the interceptions between word and image was published: *blank___ Architecture, Apartheid and After* (1998) by Hilton Judin and Ivan Vladislavić. It is really a compendium in the Humanities, for it encompasses essays on sociology, architecture and urban planning both in cities and in suburban areas, maps, site plans, drawings, images, design, advertising, photographs and short narrative fictions. That collective work includes some photo series by several prominent South African photographers. To begin with, the photo series by Chris Ledochowski (1956),[15] *Rural in Urban*, portrays shots of life in the townships of Khayelitsha, Nyanga, Guguletu, Philippi, outside Cape Town.

We should remind ourselves that in 1990 J. M. Coetzee's novel *Age of Iron* named some of those townships (Guguletu,

---

13   Amitav Ghosh, *The Great Derangment. Climate Change and the Unthinkable* (Chicago: Chicago University Press, 2016), p. 84.

14   Noris Lazzarini, 'Where Are the Negatives', in *Alf Kumalo. South African Photographer*, ed. by Itala Vivan (Milan: Leonardo Arte, 1999), p. 26.

15   Chris Ledochowski worked on a project called *Cape Flats Details* (2003). He participated in the 50th Venice Biennale with an international project: *The Structure of Survival* (2003). See also http://www.ledochowski.eu/chris/biography.html, accessed December 7, 2016.

Langa and Nyanga) as places never visited by the whites and hardly ever covered in the news. In particular, Guguletu entered literary maps, internationally, through that novel by Coetzee and later through the novel by Sindiwe Magona, *Mother to Mother* (2000). These are two complementary works of fiction, which respectively provide views of Guguletu from the outside and from the inside.

In that same volume by Vladislavić, Santu Mofokeng (1956) proposes his photo series *Appropriated Spaces*, where he speaks of home as a fictional space, and of appropriation of spaces and places in order to inhabit homes physically as well as spiritually. For instance, home might be a simple headrest to the nomadic shepherd, while the religious congregations, as the ones he photographs, occupy public (urban) spaces and (rural) areas in order to perform their rituals as if they had found a proper home, sometimes in the middle of nowhere. This type of image works as a counterpoint to the refugees in Goldblatt's picture, who found a temporary home in the space of a proper church.

Then, Mark Lewis's photo series, quite differently, represents *Armed Responses*, that is to say, monuments and buildings, which materially reproduce a fortress-like frame of mind of obsessive and absolute self-defence and total control.

Following a thematic arrangement, the photo series by Themba Hadebe (1969), titled *The Inner City*, presents pictures of life in the streets of Joburg. Apart from buildings and urban infrastructures, black people and their activities in the market place or in informal shops are portrayed.

Angela Buckland (1962) proposes photos of the Steinkopf community centre:

> Built in 1978. It was designed by the architect Roelof Uytenbogaardt and was one of the first community buildings in the country. Steinkopf is a remote town in the Western Cape, 500 kilometres from Cape Town. It has 6,000 inhabitants.[16]

---

16   Ivan Vladislavić and Hilton Judin (eds.), *blank___Architecture, Apartheid and After* (Rotterdam: NAi Publishers, 1998), p. 344.

The residents, their sport activities in this aesthetically nice structure, live close to a residential area built on a landscape of red dust desert.

Jodi Bieber's photos of *Carletonville* give an idea of how whites live, and how blacks adapt to live in men- or women-only hostels. Besides, the Dutch Reformed Church in the last shot of the series stands as a mere symbol in itself.

Zwelethu Mthetwa (1960) introduces photos entitled *Environmental Portraits*. These are pictures of black people in the interiors of their shack-houses in the townships off Cape Town. Their simple but creative decorations, the colourful attempts at dignifying such poorly organised spaces, school uniforms, youngsters in various poses allow us to gain insights into the life of black South Africans, in the first years after the democratic elections.

The above mentioned series are not the only photographs in the volume, for each essay and almost every piece of creative writing is accompanied by photos and images and therefore the book as a whole becomes an extremely interesting example of photo-essaysm.

The volume, which is a precious document, creative and fascinating both in form and content, informative and dense with historical, factual and visual information, has the merit — in my view — of creating a platform in print on the state of the arts in South Africa. Many of the sociologists, anthropologists, architects, urban planners, artists, photographers, journalists and writers participated in that collective and joint project and, before and since then, have been publishing or exhibiting individually, becoming more and more internationally popular.

For instance Jodi Bieber and Santu Mofokeng have published their photo albums also with prestigious Italian publishers. Contrasto, based in Rome and Milan, published both Bieber's photo reportage *Between Dogs & Wolves. Growing up with South Africa* (2006), and Goldblatt's *TJ. Double Narratives* (2010). Santu Mofokeng is the winner of the International Photography Prize 2016, and published his volume of black and white photos with Skira in Milan: *A Silent Solitude. Photographs 1982–2011.*

Thus, the work of these photographers is slowly becoming more visible, known and available for study abroad.

Moreover, Jodi Bieber, Santu Mofokeng and Zwelethu Mthethwa were also invited to the London Exhibition in 2011, *Figures and Fictions*, together with David Goldblatt, and they were among the seventeen photographers selected to represent the new developments of South African photography from 2000 to 2010. This was a composite project, in which each artist followed a thematic perspective: the positioning of the body/bodies in real life as well as in cultural productions was one of the main issues at stake in the so-called Rainbow Nation.

With this premise, it is not surprising that Ivan Vladislavić went back to photography in his writing career, insofar as he saw in narrative a natural complement to images. This brought him to work with Goldblatt and to write a novel, *Double Negative* (2010), to accompany the photographic project of *TJ*.

Double Negative has been praised elegantly and with pointedness by Teju Cole, New Yorker-Nigerian author, who is also a very successful photographer.[17] No better comment could be provided to Vladislavić's artwork. Teju Cole explains the meaning of "double negative":

> A metaphor is semantic. A double negative, on the other hand, is syntactical: two negations together in a sentence usually lead to an affirmation (in the wrong places, they could be merely an intensified negation). But a double negative, in the sense of two wrongs making a right, is a form of strategic longwindedness. To use two terms of negation to say that something is 'not unlike' something else is not the same as saying it is like that thing. Double negatives register instances of self-cancelling misdirection. They are about doubt, the productive and counterproductive aspects of doubt, the pitching ground, the listing figure, and the little gap between intention and effect.[18]

---

17   Teju Cole, *Open City* (London: Faber & Faber, 2011); Teju Cole, *Punto d'ombra* (Rome: Contrasto, 2016); Teju Cole, *Every Day Is for the Thief* (London: Faber & Faber, 2014).

18   Teju Cole, 'Introduction', in Ivan Vladislavić, *Double Negative* (London–New York: AndOtherStories, 2013), p. 13.

It might be correct to understand this definition under the influence of Derrida's idea of the workings of *différance* as an on-going deferral of meanings. A double negative would be, therefore, a continuously postponed arrival at a specific meaning. The meaning of "double negative" is also inquired into by Johan Jacobs, who adapts the metaphor to explain the status of double exile in which Neville, the protagonist of *Double Negative*, finds himself:

> Most importantly, photography provides Vladislavić's narrative with the concept of the double narrative. In photography, a positive image is a normal image and a negative image is a total inversion of a positive image, in which light areas appear dark and vice versa. When a negative image is created from a negative image, however, a positive image results — like multiplying two negative numbers in mathematics. Similarly, in rhetoric a double negative is an affirmative constructed from two negatives — for example 'Neville is never not ironic'. [...] Neville presents his own story, from Johannesburg to London and back again, as a double negative and the reader is invited into his narrative construct of mutually cancelling ironies to bring the diasporic subject at its centre more fully into view.[19]

This reading of the double negative metaphor as rooted in the diasporic conscience of the narrator as an 'image of the returned exile developed in relation to its absences — the lost ground of exile' is certainly convincing, particularly if attached to the serial photographs Neville takes of "thresholders": people frozen and framed while leaning against their gates. These people are no longer inside nor completely outside, they are caught in a limbo, by the shots of the "Prodigal son", by now a middle-aged photographer, who is now becoming famous as an artist in the South Africa of 2009 and in the digital world.

This view is anticipated and corroborated by what Teju Cole's adds on the same topic:

---

19 Johan U. Jacobs, *Diaspora and Identity in South African Fiction* (Pietermaritzburg: University of Kwa-Zulu Natal Press, 2016), pp. 247–248.

There is an echo of 'double negative' in the term given to a photographic negative that has been exposed twice before it is developed: a 'double exposure'. In a double exposure, two instances of light, two photographic events, are registered in a single frame. Nev's return to the places he visited with Auerbach, and his superimposition of two sets of memories on a single location in Johannesburg, are a kind of double exposure, too.[20]

However, I think that "double negative" might have a rather more allegorical meaning, if referred to the relationship between the novel and the photo-album as art-works, and not specifically to the novel's (anti)hero. The two art-works fit in with each other only fictionally, and are only loosely interrelated. Together they work precisely like a double exposure, like one of those double dia-projectors with fading effects. They shed light on one another only imprecisely, creating what I would call, following W. J. T. Mitchell, an exercise in multimediality, a photographic essay,[21] in spite of the fact that the text by Vladislavić is fiction.[22] One of the definitions that fits into the two artists' project is that there is a 'sort of photo essay whose text is concerned, not just with the subject matter in common between the two media, but with the way in which the media address that subject matter.'[23] Vladislavić's narrative reflects precisely "on the scene of production" of the photographer's images.

---

20 Teju Cole, 'Introduction', p. 14.
21 W. J. T. Mitchell examines four case studies of photo-essays: Agee and Evan's *Let Us Now Praise Famous Men*, Roland Barthes's *Camera Lucida*, Malek Alloula's *The Colonial Harem*, Edward Said and Jean Mohr's *After The Last Sky*. W. J. T. Mitchell, 'The Photographic Essay: Four Case Studies', in *Picture Theory*, pp. 281–322 (p. 289).
22 This definition might answer the question similarly asked by Stephen Clingman: 'David Goldblatt's and Ivan Vladislavić's *TJ/Double Negative* is valuable precisely where it is located at the intersection of documentary and invention, image and text, inside and outside views, the problematic play of subjectivities and viewing positions that both works, in their interactive and autonomous ways, evoke. Do we call this double production fiction or non-fiction? Does it matter? What matters occurs in the spaces, both within the two works and between them (2012: 56).' Quoted in Jacobs, *Diaspora and Identity*, p. 244.
23 Mitchell, *Picture Theory*, p. 286.

When Neville, the fictional Vladislavić, still a dropout from University, accompanies for one day the famous photographer Saul Auerbach, the fictional Goldblatt, on his photographic errands, he tells the readers, how the latter knocks at house doors and whispers a few words to the women who come to open, how he is easily accepted inside to take a portrait picture of them in their daily environment. He is proverbially calm, soft-spoken, patient and always waiting for the right light. That his fictional name is Saul, becoming Paul in the New Testament, the one who is struck by light on his way to Damascus, might be only a coincidence.

Yet, it is not only the quality of light (aesthetics) that marks Goldblatt's photos as art, but his own humanity (ethics), his manners, his persistence, his secrets ('He spoke to her from the doorway again, so softly I could not hear.' 68):

> The room felt even smaller inside than the view from outside suggested. Daylight, poking holes through the walls everywhere, drawing dotted lines along their seams, made the place seem temporary, like something you could tear up and scatter to the wind. Most of the space was taken by an iron bed on which the woman sat, nursing two infants; what remained was occupied by two tea chests lined with blankets, which evidently served as cradles, and a third chest standing on end and holding a Primus stove, a candlestick, plates and mugs, a medicine bottle.
>
> I know this because I have seen Auerbach's photographs. (69)

This is the ekphrastic description of the photograph provided by Neville, "redundant or inadequate", a kind of caption in words that mimics the proverbially longish captions by the real Goldblatt. Actually there is a missing part to the story, and it is the photographer who provides the missing bits: 'There were triplets, but one of them died. [...] They were burning the brazier in the room to keep warm this past winter. It's a miracle the others didn't suffocate too' (70). A portrait of the three babies is also within the frame of the picture, behind the mother's figure. Neville does not fail to notice this "picture-within-a-picture", this in-depth perspective, so that 'the third child, the dead one, irreplaceably absent in Auerbach's photograph, persists in that smaller frame like an echo' (72).

This image conflates the ideas of double negative and double exposure, together with all the binary oppositions that characterise photography: black and white, light and darkness, negative and positive, ghostly presences and real presences, depth and surface. Moreover, it tells the story of a family of five, who occupy a one-room shack at the rear of a house probably rented to students, where a silent death occurs while the authorities, the dwellers, the white society around them are utterly indifferent.

What is striking is that, in the third part of the novel, when Nev is back from London with a profession in commercial photography, he does the exact opposite of what his "master" had taught him. He asks the people out and shuts doors and gates behind them, before taking their pictures. He is not interested in the story that looms behind the walls. Rather, walls are by now his main obsession. It might be said that Auerbach's photographic technique is one of zooming-in. Or, "at-home photographic portraiture" as it is also labelled.[24] In contrast, Neville's technique consists in zooming-out. After all, photography is also always a matter of inclusion (what is in the frame) and exclusion (what is left out).

The zooming-in attitude of the photographer is proved years later over a last visit, when Neville is shown the picture of a man:

'It's Joel Setshedi.'
A serious young man in a collar and tie, perched on the end of a desk in a panelled office. He is holding a framed photograph of himself, and in this one he is smiling broadly.
'The smaller photograph is Amos,' Auerbach went on, 'the twin brother. It's the portrait that stood on his coffin at his funeral. He died a couple of years ago, of Aids I suspect [...] He works for a bank [...] He's done bloody well for himself, if you think where he started out, and he has his mother to thank. Veronica's still alive, by the way, [...] in Limpopo. I'm going to photograph her too one of these days.[25]

---

24   Sontag, *On Photography*, p. 57.
25   Vladislavić, *Double Negative*, p. 236.

Auerbach tracks down or keeps track of the people he has immortalized, through their life and through generations, and the *mise-en-abyme*, the "picture-within-the-picture" is always present.

In spite of the challenge Neville launches to us readers, inviting us to look for the image of Veronica 'you can look it up on the internet (71)', — an action that does not take us anywhere, actually — it is possible to identify in Goldblatt's photographs those who are only faintly similar to the one mentioned. In contrast, the image under the name of Mrs Ditton might be identifiable with one of Goldblatt's images in the book: 'A woman in her parlour, Bezuidenhout Valley, November 1973', included in the section *1970s City + Suburbs.*[26]

Curiously enough, fragment n. 27 of Vladislavić's novel *Portrait with Keys. The City of Johannesburg unlocked*, resembles one of Goldblatt's photos in *TJ*: 'On the sidewalk: silencers fitted while you wait. Esselen Street, Hillbrow. 13 January 2001' (274). The suggestion of this *déjà-vu* comes from the novel's passage mentioning 'exhaust pipes and baffles dangling like the day's catch on a line strung between two bluegums. A flattened cardboard carton — FIVE ROSES QUALITY TEE'.[27]

Moreover, Goldblatt chose for the cover of his photo-album a shot with an African couple, proudly posing with an old plate shield in their hands still carrying the initials TJ, meaning Transvaal Johannesburg, ('She said to him, "You be the driver and I'll be the madam," then they picked up the fender and posed, Hillbrow. 1975' — thus runs the caption). In the preface, *About TJ*, Goldblatt himself explains: 'Today, the Transvaal is a fading construct; Johannesburg's boundaries have been redrawn and it is now part of Gauteng Province, and TJ is no longer to be seen on our roads.' This feeling of nostalgia is mirrored in a comic passage of stories: *Villa Toscana*, where the protagonist is trapped at the entrance of a severely guarded and gated community and is found guilty of having the wrong plate number:

---

26   Goldblatt, *TJ*, p. 203.
27   Ivan Vladislavić, *Portrait with Keys: The City of Johannesburg Unlocked* (New York: W.W. Norton & Company, 2009), p. 46.

The guard took the clipboard and went around to the back of the car to check the numberplate [...] writing laboriously. [...]

'Sorry sir, you've got the wrong number.' As if they were speaking on the telephone.

'I forgot. I changed to GP plates just last week.'[28]

The man is "repelled at the ramparts" for still being identified by the TJ plate. This and the previous examples testify that not only *Double Negative*, but all of Vladislavić's latest literary urban errands, both fictions and non-fictions, are very similar to Goldblatt's photographic errands. Their wandering and attentive gaze seem to work almost in unison and their works are full of suggestive echoes, resonances and imperfect mirroring.[29]

As a final consideration on *Double Negative*, it must be said that the pedagogic apprenticeship Neville was given seems to have produced its fruits, but the capacity of looking at, and recognising urban and natural details comes from a game he used to play as a child while in the car with his father. He had to shut his eyes and guess where they were driving to. Only fragments blinked at through an impossible perspective could be of help. It is also interesting to notice that what he had learned in the past with the professional photographer was practised as a game, too, with that temporary substitute father figure. In the company of a third man, a British journalist, the three of them spotted a house from the top of a hill and then they drove down to the place to take a picture of the dwellers. Chance and light were therefore called into action in order to produce the photograph. Moreover, in the novel, as well as in reality photography has also a pedagogic and ludic quality as an art form.

---

28 Ivan Vladislavić, 'Villa Toscana', in *The Exploded View* (London: Random House, 2004), pp. 8–9.

29 'Before starting *Double Negative*, I had experience of working alongside visual artists and with photographers — in fact some of the work in *Portrait with Keys* (2006) appeared in David's catalogue 51 Years (2001).' Bronwyn Law-Voiljoen, 'TJ & Double Negative. Interview with David Goldblatt and Ivan Vladislavić', in *Marginal Spaces: Reading Ivan Vladislavić*, ed. by Gerald Gaylard (Johannesburg: Wits University Press, 2011), pp. 340–57.

The main principles of a photographic essay are based on the assumption that

> 'the photographs are not illustrative. They and the text, are coequal, mutually independent, and fully collaborative.' [...] each medium being given a "book" of its own, each equally free of admixture with the other.[30]

As in Edward Said and Jean Mohr's photographic essay which aims at showing 'Palestinians through Palestinian eyes', for Goldblatt and Vladislavić, too, the 'dialogical relation of text and image is collaborative [...] a cooperative endeavour by two like-minded and highly talented professionals, writer and photographer'.[31] Goldblatt and Vladislavić are two like-minded and highly talented professionals, moved by almost telepathic correspondence, or singular affinities.

The New Archives: Orchestras and The Music Lesson

The last, small-size photograph — in comparison to all the others — in Goldblatt's photoalbum portrays a class of children playing the violin. This is 'The children's class of the African Music and Drama Association, Orlando High School, Soweto. November 1972' (316).

The picture is a-typical for that time, a time of troubles. The image clashes dramatically with the Soweto massacre involving school children in 1976. Still the potentiality of music education is all there in that picture, in the composed postures of those serious children, their closed eyes, their rigid left shoulder, their bows all bent in the same direction and with the same inclination.

In terms of time/tense, this photo is a "future-in-the-past" kind of proposition, an anterior future, a signifier for future educational achievements. In post-apartheid South Africa, as elsewhere, school orchestras, as well as local and national adults' orchestras,

---

30   Mitchell, *Picture Theory*, pp. 290–292.
31   Mitchell, *Picture Theory*, p. 312.

have become a must. As sign of empowerment, investments in education at all levels have promoted music to the fore.

Nadine Gordimer was among the first to foresee the growing importance of orchestras, of the training and career of professional musicians, when she wrote a short story whose core was marital betrayal: *The First Sense* (2006).

Bach, Mozart, Hindemith, Cage, Stockhausen, and Glass were no longer regarded in the performance world patronizingly as music that blacks neither enjoyed nor understood. The national orchestra, which was his base — while his prestige meant that he could absent himself whenever he was invited to festivals or to join a string ensemble on tour — had a black trombonist and a young second violinist with African braids that fell about her ebony neck as she wielded her bow.[32]

In *Hundred Papers* (2008), Liels Jobson — a poet, musician and photographer — seems to have inherited Gordimer's special talent for shorter fiction, yet pushing the genre to the extreme of writing stories of half a page only. These prose poems or flash fictions — (pp/ff) as they are labelled — mimic photographic shots, lighting — as if with a flash — moments in people's life. However, tone and content are what strongly characterize Liels's short fictions: the shock they produce in the reader. In dealing with post 1994 South Africa, the stories speak of liberation, which is by no means political, it is erotic, amoral, excessive. Her ministories are parables of cynicism, depravity, unleashed desire, unbelievable appetites. The country seems prey to a frenzy, which makes Liels Jobson a *maudit* poet of the twenty-first century, a "naughty" exposer of subjects wich might be considered to be disreputable, taboo, marginal.[33]

Among her recurrent topics, she, too, explores music classes for children, now flourishing like mushrooms everywhere in the country. Only, in her lapidary style, she makes us discover that

---

32   First published in *The New Yorker*, December 18, 2006.
      See http://shortstories.about.com/od/ContemporaryStories/fl/Analysis-of-
      The-First-Sense-by-Nadine-Gordimer.htm, accessed December 7, 2016.
33   See Sontag on Diane Arbus, p. 113.

some of those children are predestined: not to a bright career as musicians, but to an early death by Aids.

Thus her work, both in content and in style — the focus on children and the exceptional brevity — is more easily connected with the art of photography than to a specific literary genre or current, if not webliterature or twitterature.

Jody Bieber's photos of stray, street children, abandoned and abused, or orphaned because of Aids, for instance, or Santu Mofokeng's series of photos entitled *Child headed households*, portraying orphans who live on their own in shacks are the closest complement to Liels Jobsons's texts and words than anything else in literature. Once again photographs and literary narratives converge to shed light on very specific realities of life in the New South Africa. The two media seem to be allied nowadays to better reproduce reality, and it is not by coincidence that Jobson is a photographer, too. Her quick gaze hits like lightning and what readers suddenly see is neither nice, nor reassuring.

Post-apartheid South Africa's Digital Humanities and Web Archives

The Web is the new way in which South Africa has entered the twenty-first century. And once again Ivan Vladislavić has registered that moment. The last of the three chapters of his novel *Double Negative* is about the digital age, when photos are no longer "taken", but are "made" through the use of photoshop. The protagonist is a person still without a google profile, but one day he is interviewed by a blogger who produces

> A bit of experimental fiction […] in a dozen pieces with headings like "Motion Pictures" and "Stills" and there's a quote from some Frenchman and a paragraph in italics. She says you're a man of your time: disaffected without being disengaged. (241)

In 1999 the Johannesburg Workshop on Theory and Criticism (JWTC) was inaugurated: a project in the field of the Humanities rooted in the Web and including a yearly one-week conference with major scholars such as Achille Mbembe, Jean and John Comaroff and many others; an on-line journal, *The Johannesburg Salon*, and a web-platform with a blog for exchanging research projects, and current debates. This new and modern project has become a firm reference in todays' Johannesburg cultural life, like a lighthouse shining from the South. I see this project as a second step in what Vladislavić attempted with his volume on architectures, including literary ones: the dialogue between anthropologists, sociologists, urban planners, architects, historians, writers, journalists, photographers. Only, the head of this project is Achille Mbembe, a historian originally from Camerun, in cooperation with a group of colleagues who make a point of producing a new "Theory from the South".

In line with this idea, a project was launched at the University of Johannesburg with the VIADUCT 2015 Platform, hosted by the Visual Identities in Art and Design Research Centre (VIAD). A team of researchers and artists started questioning the statute of archives from a theoretical point of view: their being one of the defining characteristics of the modern era; their being dialogic insofar as they engage both producers and receivers; their being places of production, control, circulation of information; their being counter-archives located in the digital realm. The questioning of the institution and machinery of archives goes hand in hand with the questioning of identities, subjectivities and "positionalities". One of the major concerns in the new South Africa is actually the positioning of the self/selves, of the artist/s within the Rainbow Nation. Interestingly, the VIAD's team sees the new lens-based and new media technologies (termed 'photographies') as rhizomatic. They created a digital platform for conferences, exhibitions, publications, that is, a space for crucial and innovative debates in the contemporary world of digital humanities and archival practices, particularly for the use of photography:

> The photographic archive functions as a lens through which to explore how the production, collation, presentation and dissemination of

individual images in the form of a collective might have a bearing on the ways in which photographic images are represented, received and read.[34]

At the same time, the Web project by the three photographers Sean Metelerkamp, Sipho Mpongo and Wikus de Wet, entitled *Twenty Journey* is also a new archive, to a certain extent a complement to the Johannesburg Workshop. *Born free*, *Land* and *Idiosyncrasies* are their main subjects. The Gallery Commune.1 in Cape Town, from August 18 to September 3, 2015, exhibited 45 of their photographs, taken while touring the country by caravan — 24,000 km across South Africa.

First of all, the strength of this project is in its cooperative approach, hinting at the necessity of comparing one's own visual/ visionary perspective with that of others. Second, the alternation of images and words, travel-impression poems, confirms that photo-essayism is maybe becoming a new, powerful, hybrid genre, maybe the genre of the twenty-first century, on the border between the visual image and the written word. Third, the project was born as an archive rooted in the present, yet meant for the future and not excluding the past altogether. Both *The Johannesburg Salon*, with its chronicles of our contemporary times, its collective intellectual vanguard, its analysis of the cultural trends in South Africa, and the *Twenty Journey* project, with its travel journal, visual impact and narrative aspiration are archives of and for the future.

The colour pictures do not differ substantially from the ones of the photographers previously mentioned in this essay. What is new is however the mixing of still images, video interviews, texts which are both narrative and poetic. The medium of expression is the same: photography itself. This time, however, the digital prevails with overtly bright colours, the use of a digicam for interviews and the posting on the Web as a form of exhibition. The interviews are quite explicit in expressing what apartheid has left in its wake and in illustrating the new meanings of being African nowadays in South Africa.

---

34   Leora Farber, 'Archival adresses: photographies, practices, positionalities.'
     See http://www.viad.co.za/publication-critical-artsvol-29-s1-2015/,
     accessed December 8, 2016.

Another example of this type is the work of the British photographer Jason Larkin (1979),[35] who lived for two years in South Africa from 2011 to 2013 and produced a series of photographs called *Waiting*. In this photo-album he portrayed people hiding in the shade in order to protect themselves from the summer sun and waiting in the streets of Johannesburg. They might be waiting for ever for public transport, for a lift, or for someone who could offer a job and pick them up or accompany them back home; what strikes, however, is the act of waiting as time-consuming. Those who stand waiting for hours are mainly blacks, for whites normally have cars. These are really photos of inequality and social injustice, implicitly showing that inefficient services, urban zoning, enormous distances to the working places are still legacies of the apartheid era.

Larkin also participated in a second project that is described on the Web as follows:

> *Platinum* is a mini-publication by photographer Jason Larkin and writer Jack Shenker. It examines the Marikana massacre and the physical and political context of the communities of South Africa's platinum mining industry. Breaking with traditional photobook format, *Platinum* combines large-format posters and an incisive, wide-ranging essay that is available both in English and Xhosa. This timeous publication explores the build up to and the implications of one of the most critical events in South Africa's recent history. Half of the print run of *Platinum* has been distributed for free to activists, political groups, and various communities across the mining region of Rustenburg and Gauteng, South Africa.[36]

This work shows a social concern and speaks of the responsibility of the artist in our present time.[37] The police shooting between 30 and 40 people during a prolonged strike and

---

35   See http://www.huckmagazine.com/art-and-culture/photography-2/ photographer-jason-larkin-unpicks-south-africas-complex-present/, accessed December 7, 2016.

36   See http://jasonlarkin.co.uk/publications/platinum-3/#text, accessed December 7, 2016.

37   Annalisa Oboe, 'Returning Images: Mandela, Marikana and the Rugged Road to the Future', *Altre Modernità*, 12 (2014), 1–14. See http://riviste. unimi.it/index.php/AMonline/issue/view/604, accessed December 7, 2016.

exhausting negotiations in 2012 at the platinum mine in Marikana, like the police ride at the Methodist Church in Johannesburg and the court cases against the refugees from Zimbabwe previously mentioned are cases in which South Africa seems to have fallen back into the worst apartheid years.[38]

In the specific case the work of photographer and journalist Jason Larkin is in his own words 'an exercise with audience engagement'. Yet, all the projects here mentioned and presented claim civil responsibility, which is another aspect of photo-esseysm as *art engagé*.

There are commentators who criticise Sebastiao Salgado, for he "uses" the poor to make good photos. Yet, people who come out from his exhibitions always discuss lively the themes he immortalises: migration, exploitation, destitution. And no matter how his techniques might be aesthetically classic, mastered and cleverly moving, as for their documentary value they respond to the criteria of ethical journalism and not to those of art Exhibition and market laws.[39]

The same type of criticism was expressed against Mofokeng when someone wrote in an exhibition comment book that he was 'making money from blacks!' Santu Mofokeng speaks of the responsibility of the photographer: 'I had not thought about my own responsibility in the continuing, contentious struggle over the representation of my country's history.' The commentator, Simon Njami adds:

> being a photographer does not mean simply turning up in places filled with good intentions and rendering justice. [...] This is where responsibility enters the game. It's not a question of doing things only for yourself or for the cultured and detached public who go to galleries

---

38   'Through mobilisation the political environment throughout these mining communities has changed dramatically since the massacre. Yet formal mining institutions have yet to make any serious adjustments to the lives of thousands of families who live and work in an environment dominated by the infrastructure of power.' See: http://www.huckmagazine.com/art-and-culture/photography-2/photographer-jason-larkin-unpicks-south-africas-complex-present/, accessed December 7, 2016.

39   Scianna, *Etica e fotogiornalismo*, p. 35.

and museums, but to place them in a broader context, within a political, social, and in this case, also racial awareness.[40]

One way of taking responsibility was for Santu Mofokeng to research into photographs of black South African families taken at the beginning of the twentieth century: studio photos. Once again, the matter was how to salvage those archives. Most of the authors of those archives had left no trace in the history of national photography. This activity gave life to his photo series *The Black Photo Album: 1890–1950*.[41] This project of retrieval from the past might be paired with J. M. Coetzee's nostalgic look at Mona de Beer's book enentitled *A Vision of the Past* (1992), showing pictures taken in the early twentieth century, with the perfection such early techniques allowed and granted.[42] As a conclusion, what can be noticed is that a comprehensive history of South African photography is still missing — from its very early beginnings ('Photography came to South Africa in the 1840s, not long after its invention'),[43] to nowadays' achievements. Also taking into consideration that inclusion of South African photography in European publications is almost negligible, with the exception of specialized publications on/by individual artists. This field may prove a challenge for scholars in order to create an all-comprehensive archive.[44]

---

40   Simon Njami, *A Silent Solitude*, p. 18.

41   Santu Mofokeng, *A Silent Solitude*, pp. 214–217.

42   'A photograph of 1900 today would be more likely to move us because it is a photograph taken in 1900. [...] Time eventually positions most photographs, even the most amateurish, at the level of art.' Sontag, *On Photography*, p. 21.

43   J. M. Coetzee, 'Photographs of South Africa', in *Stranger Shores. Essays 1986–1999* (London: Vintage, 2002), pp. 344–350 (p. 344).

44   See for instance A. D. Bensusan, *Silver Images: A History of Photography in South Africa* (Cape Town: Howard Timmins, 1966) — quoted by J. M. Coetzee, p. 350, or *Anthology of African and Indian Ocean Photography* (Paris: Publications Éditions Blue Outremer, 1999) — including Mofokeng; or the thematic overview by Erin Haney, *Photography and Africa* (London: Reaktion Books, 2010).

Bibliography

Agamben, Giorgio, *Homo Sacer. Sovereign Power and Bare Life*, trans. by Daniel Heller-Roazen (Stanford: Stanford University Press, 1998).

Amitav, Ghosh, *The Great Derangement. Climate Change and the Unthinkable* (Chicago: Chicago University Press, 2016).

Barthes, Roland, *Camera Lucida* (New York: Farrar Straus and Gireaux, 1981).

Bieber, Jodi, *Between Dogs & Wolves. Growing up with South Africa* (Amsterdam: Mets & Schiltuitgevers, 2006).

_____, *Tra cani e lupi. Crescere con il Sudafrica* (Rome: Contrasto, 2006).

Bulawayo, NoViolet, *We Need New Names* (London: Chatto & Windus, 2013).

Coetzee, J. M., *Stranger Shores. Essays 1986–1999* (London: Vintage, 2002).

Goldblatt, David, and Vladislavić, Ivan, *TJ. Johannesburg Photographs 1948– 2010: Double Negative* (Rome: Contrasto, 2010).

Gordimer, Nadine, *No Time Like the Present* (New York: Farrar Straus & Giroux, 2012).

_____, 'The Second Sense', *The New Yorker*, December 18, 2006.

Gosh, Amitav, *The Great Derangment. Climate Change and the Unthinkable* (Chicago: Chicago University Press, 2016)

Jacobs, Johan U., *Diaspora and Identity in South African Fiction* (Pietermaritzburg: University of Kwa-Zulu Natal Press, 2016).

Jobson, Liels, *Hundred Papers* (Johannesburg: Botsotso Publishing, 2008).

Kuljian, Christa, 'Making the invisible visible: a story of the Central Methodist Church', *The Johannesburg Salon*, 3 (2010), 36–43.

Law-Voiljoen, Bronwyn, 'TJ & Double Negative. Interview with David Goldblatt and Ivan Vladislavić', in *Marginal Spaces: Reading Ivan Vladislavić*, ed. by Gerald Gaylard (Johannesburg: Wits University Press, 2011), pp. 340–357.

Mitchell, W. J. T., *Picture Theory* (Chicago: University of Chicago Press, 1994).

Mofokeng, Santu, *A Silent Solitude. Photographs 1982–2011*, ed. by Simon Njami (Milan: Skira, 2016).

Oboe, Annalisa, 'Returning Images: Mandela, Marikana and the Rugged Road to the Future', *Altre Modernità*, 12 (2014), 1–14.

Okonko, Thembinkosi, 'On Afrophobia', *The Johannesburg Salon*, 9 (2015), 32–33.

Scianna, Ferdinando, *Etica e fotogiornalismo* (Milan: Electa, 2010).

Sontag, Susan, *On Photography* (Harmondsworth: Penguin, 1977).

Vivan, Itala (ed.), *Alf Kumalo. A South African Photographer, transl. by Amedeo Poggi, Richard Sadler* (Milan: Leonardo Arte, 1999).

Vladislavić, Ivan, and Hilton, Judin (eds.), *blank___Architecture, Apartheid and After* (Rotterdam: NAi Publishers, 1998).

_____, *The Exploded View* (London: Random House, 2004).

_____, *Portrait with Keys. The City of Johannesburg Unlocked* (New York: W.W. Norton & Company, 2009).

_____, *Double Negative*, intr. by Teju Cole (New York: AndOtherStories, 2013).

Websites

http://www.huckmagazine.com/art-and-culture/photography-2/photographer-jason-larkin-unpicks-south-africas-complex-present/, accessed December 7, 2016.

http://www.jwtc.org.za/the_salon/volume_3.htm, accessed December 7, 2016.

http://www.jwtc.org.za/the_salon/volume_9.htm, accessed December 7, 2016.

http://jasonlarkin.co.uk/publications/platinum-3/#text, accessed December 7, 2016.

http://www.ledochowski.eu/chris/biography.html, accessed December 7, 2016.

https://www.theguardian.com/world/gallery/2010/nov/25/david-goldblatt-southafrica-photography, accessed December 7, 2016.

http://riviste.unimi.it/index.php/AMonline/issue/view/604, accessed December 7, 2016.

http://shortstories.about.com/od/ContemporaryStories/fl/Analysis-of-The-First-Sense-by-Nadine-Gordimer.htm, accessed December 7, 2016.

http://www.vam.ac.uk/content/articles/f/figures-and-fictions-contemporary-south-african-photography/, accessed December 7, 2016.

http://www.viad.co.za/publication-critical-artsvol-29-s1-2015/, accessed December 8, 2016.

COUNTER-CANONICAL AESTHETICS IN POSTCOLONIAL ITALIAN LITERATURE AND CINEMA

Pietro Deandrea
(University of Turin)

> *I want the migrant to become a*
> *'subject' in a multiple sense, to have a voice.*
> *I don't want the migrant to remain only an empty image.*
> John Akomfrah[1]

Migrant literature and cinema in Italy are usually presented as debunking mainstream Italian discourse. A distinguished critic like Derek Duncan, for instance, praises Graziella Parati's *Migration Italy* (2005) as a groundbreaking work which argues 'for the power of migrant cultural production to offer counter-narratives to the negative representations of migrants that have been hegemonic'.[2]

This article discusses some aesthetic strategies employed by postcolonial writers and filmmakers in Italy to produce counter-narrations of our present times. It first focuses on *Momodou*, a short story by the Wu Ming writers' collective, showing how its formal features such as structure, multifocality and long historical perspective may embody some counter-canonical facets of postcolonial Italian literature. Moving to cinema, I argue that Ermanno Olmi's *Il villaggio di cartone* (2011) conceives a fluidity of spaces that goes against the segregational spatial arrangements typical of Italian (post)colonialism and its artistic expressions. The same fluidity is developed to its extreme in a very different film, Gabriele Del Grande, Khaled Soliman Al Nassiry and Antonio Augugliaro's *Io sto con la sposa* (2014).

---

1   Cristina Piccino, 'L'immagine migrante' [interview with John Akomfrah], *Alias – Il manifesto*, 8 January 2011, 3. All translations into English from works in Italian are mine.
2   Derek Duncan, 'Italy's Postcolonial Cinema and Its Histories of Representation', *Italian Studies*, 63:2 (2008), 196.

At the same time, this movie brings to the fore a fluid mixture of languages, media and genres. The generic alternation between fiction and documentary in this film is then related to Daniele Gaglianone's *La mia classe* (2013), where these two dimensions clash and bring Gaglianone's filmmaking to a critical dilemma, a point of crisis. Finally, I argue that this ambivalence between the fictional and the real, in *Io sto con la sposa* and *La mia classe*, is indicative of a coexistence between visionary artistry and an urgent need for an active engagement with the realities of postcolonial Italy. I show how this call to action is shared by *Il villaggio di cartone*, too, in spite of its highly symbolic cinematic language.

This article is concluded by observing how all the works analyzed here, including Wu Ming's *Momodou*, are characterized by counter-canonical aesthetics insofar as they depart from naturalism to enhance their readers/spectators' critical awareness. It is only at this point that I trace analogies between the literary work and the films here considered, because I deliberately approach these two media separately, each in its unique aesthetic specificities, without over-stretching my comparative analysis.

Sandra Ponzanesi rightly points at the danger of overlooking the aesthetic peculiarities of postcolonial Italian texts, besides their political value[3] — in this article I attempt to keep her warning in mind. However, my formal analysis is also close to the role of Cultural Studies, described by Emanuele Monegato in its primary interest for power dynamics:

> to develop a deeper comprehension of the ways in which symbolic and cultural processes are connected to political, economic and social power, without considering the centrality of notions such as canon and aesthetics, or considering them to arrive at their deconstruction.[4]

3   Sandra Ponzanesi, 'La "svolta" postcoloniale negli Studi italiani: Prospettive europee', in *L'Italia postcoloniale*, ed. by Cristina Lombardi-Diop and Caterina Romeo (Florence and Milan: Le Monnier Università and Mondadori Education, 2014), p. 57.
4   'sviluppare una comprensione più profonda delle modalità con cui i processi simbolici e culturali sono connessi al potere politico, economico e sociale non contemplando la centralità di nozioni come canone e estetica, se non per arrivare a una loro decostruzione'; Emanuele Monegato, 'Studi culturali

We have an extremely different subjectivity
from the Italian mainstream.
(Igiaba Scego)[5]

Thanks to its unique combination of polysemic ambivalence and political urgency, postcolonial Italian literature can offer, as Valentina Dogao writes, a new subaltern perspective.[6] *Controcanone*, "counter-canon", is the significant title of Monica Venturini's monograph on colonial and postcolonial Italian writing.[7] Critics have concentrated on its counter-canonical function from various angles. Giuliana Benvenuti emphasizes its role of counter-history capable of recovering the voice of those who have been made voiceless.[8] In a similar vein, Gabriele Proglio takes the Indian Subaltern Studies' horizontal historiography to argue that writers such as Gabriella Ghermandi enforce practices of counter-narration, rewriting the past by having recourse to oral memories.[9] Other critics focus precisely on the issue of genre. They give prominence to an aesthetic straddling between genres, codes and narrative perspectives as constitutive of a counter-canonical role.[10]

---

e letterari. (Nuove) frontiere ideologiche', in *Introduzione ai Cultural Studies: UK, USA e paesi anglofoni*, ed. by Nicoletta Vallorani (Rome: Carocci, 2016), p. 67 (Monegato here references Stuart Hall's *Cultural Studies and Its Theoretical Legacies*, 1992).

5   'Noi abbiamo una soggettività molto diversa rispetto al mainstream italiano'. Camilla Valletti, 'Siamo tutti disgregati: L'italiano lingua di Petrarca e Celentano. Intervista a Igiaba Scego di Camilla Valletti', *L'indice dei libri del mese*, January 2016, 10.

6   Valentina Dogao, 'Ibridazioni postcoloniali e decostruzioni letterarie', in *Subalternità italiane: Percorsi di ricerca tra letteratura e storia*, ed. by Valeria Deplano, Lorenzo Mari, Gabriele Proglio (Ariccia (RM): Aracne, 2014), p. 45.

7   Monica Venturini, *Controcanone: Per una cartografia della scrittura coloniale e postcoloniale* (Rome: Aracne, 2010).

8   Giuliana Benvenuti, *Il romanzo neostorico italiano: Storia, memoria, narrazione* (Rome: Carocci, 2012), p. 7.

9   Gabriele Proglio, 'Subalternità e silenzi tra storia e letteratura: Modelli epistemologici e luoghi della contro-narrazione', in *Subalternità italiane: Percorsi di ricerca tra letteratura e storia*, pp. 85–88.

10   See Giulia Molinarolo, 'Per una nuova critica della letteratura italiana della migrazione: Questioni aperte', *CoSMo: Comparative Studies in*

I consider Wu Ming's short story *Momodou* (2008) as embodying all these features.[11] Its narration goes backwards in time, through short chapters numbered from thirteen to zero. In Chapter 13 a newspaper article informs that Momodou, a raving mad immigrant, tried to rape an African woman in a flat and then stabbed a *carabiniere* whose colleague shot Momodou to death. Kati, an old acquaintance of Momodou's family from their childhood in Gambia, wonders at the article's imprecisions, such as omitting the fact that the assaulted woman is Momodou's sister Yama — could Momodou's cantankerous character have possibly worsened to the point of trying to rape his own sister? In Chapter 12 Yama wakes up in a friend's house, still confused after the previous day's tragedy. Chapter 11 moves to the previous day, reporting the policemen's interrogation of Yama for the writing of their report on the incident: through their paternalistic and arrogant attitude, they manage to make her declare that Momodou might have kept a knife with him on his bed. Still going backwards, the following chapters reconstruct the phases of the incident in Yama and Momodou's flat: vice-brigadier Tajani hopes no one will mar his reconstruction of the events; Yama is locked in the police car while Tajani and his younger colleague Ciaravolo modify the crime scene for their needs, so that Tajani cuts Ciaravolo's arm with a kitchen knife to stage Momodou's aggression; Ciaravolo panicking after Tajani has shot Momodou, who was lying harmless on his bed ('after all your abusing at niggers, now you've killed one');[12] kitchen-bound Yama hearing a gunshot, but prevented from entering Momodou's bedroom; Yama, worried sick for Momodou's worsening depression, calls an ambulance first, then *carabinieri*; moments before being called to the flat, Tajani and Ciaravolo chat in a bar, with the former giving vent to his hatred for immigrants, jews and communists;

Modernism, 8 (Spring 2016), 164 (here Molinarolo references Venturini's *Controcanone* and Matteo Aria's *Cercando nel vuoto*, 2007).

11   Wu Ming, *Momodou*, in *Anatra all'arancia meccanica: Racconti 2000–2010* (Turin: Einaudi, 2011 [2008]).

12   'a furia di imprecare contro i negri, ne hai accoppato uno'; Wu Ming, p. 288.

Yama's memories of Momodou's lively character before their move to Italy and his months of solitude as a factory worker in northern Italy ('Small worlds with their closed gates; anyway, in the factory you're a colleague, but outside you're just a nigger.')[13]

At the end, Chapter 0 describes a scene from Momodou and Yama's carefree childhood, when he complained about other kids teasing him for his pelican-like double chin while Yama sisterly advised him 'then you must change the song';[14] at this point, within the same chapter, the narration moves to Tajani's childhood, to his admiration for his grandfather's military past in Africa and the child's concomitant wish 'to become a hero'.[15]

The reasons why I consider this 30-page-long story emblematic of the counter-canonical orientation of postcolonial Italian literature are at once political and aesthetic. Structure-wise, its upside-down structure exemplifies the need to overturn the rigidly hegemonic discourse oppressing migrants in contemporary Italy, represented by media and policing institutions. The Wu Ming writers' collective, following Yama's piece of advice, attempt to 'change the song' in order to change our perspective on reality.[16] Not by chance, this structural feature is compounded by a narratological one, given the story's many points of view:

---

13   'Piccoli mondi coi cancelli chiusi, e poi in fabbrica sei un collega, ma fuori sei solo un negro.'; Wu Ming, p. 297. Commenting on his film *The Nine Muses*, John Akomfrah noticed that solitude was the most frequently mentioned feeling expressed by migrants, in the archival material that he had sieved: 'This, too, is a universal condition, but in a migrant's life it becomes explicit: you are what you appear to be, your interior dimension is denied.'; Piccino, p. 3.

14   'allora devi cambiare la canzone'; Wu Ming, p. 299.

15   'diventare un eroe'; Wu Ming, p. 301. While trying to calm down his panicking colleague, he mentions this possibility of turning the tragedy to their advantage and thus become heroes; Ciaravolo's answer is 'I don't want to be a hero. I just want not to feel ashamed.' ('Non voglio essere un eroe. Voglio solo non dovermi vergognare.'); Wu Ming, p. 283.

16   One member of the collective, Wu Ming 1, declared in an interview that Momodou may be seen as a symbol of Italian subalterns, representing the voiceless who stand on the wrong side of history, the side which was made to succumb in the arena of public memory; Simone Brioni, 'Postcolonialismo, subalternità e *New Italian Epic*: Intervista con Wu Ming 1', in *Subalternità italiane: Percorsi di ricerca tra letteratura e*

the newspaper article, Kati, Yama, the *carabinieri*'s report and Tajani are only some of the narrative perspectives alternating in *Momodou*. This Genettian multiple focalization may be seen as indicative of postcolonial Italian literature's drive towards multiple identities, as noted by Rosanna Morace.[17]

Momodou ends with the description of how Tajani became imbued, as a child, with the nostalgic colonial heroism about Italy's military enterprise in Africa, which would implicitly lead to his racist attitudes and his instinctive shooting of a harmless, bed-ridden immigrant. Rather than with a narrative closure, then, the story is concluded by opening wide the issue of the displacement of the past which recurs so often in the scholarship on Italian colonialism.[18] I particularly agree with Alessandro Triulzi when he sees contemporary postcolonial encounters as 'a direct boost for refreshing (and transgressing) the amnesiac and, to some extent, still "silenced" colonial narrative in our country [...] to denounce the return of old colonial practices of explicit violence to perceived Others.'[19] This unearthing and denouncing function involves a pedagogical one, as Stuart Hall conceived of it: to tear the veil from racist theories which presents themselves as natural, in order to show them in their historical and social constructedness.[20]

---

storia, p. 286. I take this declaration as a fictional equivalent to Benvenuti's concept of counter-history reported above.

17   See Molinarolo, p. 162 (here Molinarolo references Rosanna Morace, *Letteratura-mondo italiana*, 2012).

18   See, for instance, Alessandro Triulzi, 'Displacing the Colonial Event: Hybrid Memories of Postcolonial Italy', in *National Belongings: Hybridity in Italian Colonial and Postcolonial Cultures*, ed. by Jacqueline Andall and Derek Duncan (Bern: Peter Lang, 2010), passim.

19   Alessandro Triulzi, 'Empowering Migrants' Voices and Agency in Postcolonial Italy', *Critical Interventions: Journal of African Art History and Visual Culture*, 10:1 (2016), 60–61. This is to be taken as a constitutive feature of postcolonialism, as Robert Young argues: 'In a sense postcolonialism has always been about the ongoing life of residues, living remains, lingering legacies.' Robert Young, 'Postcolonial Remains', *New Literary History*, 34:1 (2012), 21; quoted in Sandra Ponzanesi, 'On the Waterfront. Truth and Fiction in Postcolonial Cinema from the South of Europe', *Interventions: International Journal of Postcolonial Studies*, 18:2 (2016), 219.

20   Stuart Hall, 'Teaching Race', *Multiracial Education*, 9:1 (autumn 1980), 7–10.

*If cinema is to be conceptualized as the cultural crucible of Italian
national identity, it is legitimate to ask if its representations of the
migrant subject rework and expand narratives of national belongings?*
(Derek Duncan)[21]

*Do you believe that cinema can
bring about real change,
shift the way we look at things,
and change our perspectives?*
(Elena Korzhenevich)[22]

I now wish to move from literature to the medium of film.
As in the case of literature, my starting point is constituted
by Ponzanesi's highlighting of its aesthetic facets: 'the term
"postcolonial cinema" not only addresses the question of
mobility and uprooting, but also wider issues of visual
hegemony and aesthetic counter-discourses. [...] It also refers
to a specific mode of viewing, filming and interpreting.'[23]
Through the analysis of the films that I selected, I here identify
two types of counter-discourse related to the use of space and
to genre.

Spatial disruption is certainly one of the key elements in the
story of Ermanno Olmi's *Il villaggio di cartone* (*The Cardboard
Village*).[24] The film is completely set inside a church and its
adjacent rectory. At the beginning the building (presumably
deconsecrated) is emptied out of its objects by a group of workers,
to the dismay and anguish of the old priest who remains to live
there alone. The scene when the big crucifix is lowered down to be
removed is emphasized by alternating a visual perspective from
the top downwards and from the floor upwards; then the crucifix,
tied to a rope, is made to rotate around itself while descending. Its

21   Duncan, p. 195.
22   Elena Korzhenevich, 'Changing the Narrative of the World: Interview
     with Gabriele Del Grande and Dagmawi Yimer', *Critical Interventions:
     Journal of African Art History and Visual Culture*, 10:1 (2016), 106.
23   Ponzanesi, 'On the Waterfront', p. 220.
24   Ermanno Olmi, *Il villaggio di cartone: Diabasis*, Cinemaundici, RAI
     Cinema, 2011.

descent also shows that some liquid is dripping from it: the viewer is likely to trace the connection with the incessant raining heard from the outside and with the sea images of shipwrecks showing from the priest's television set, inserted by the film's editing in between the removal scenes. This connection anticipates the arrival of a group of undocumented African migrants escaping the authorities (helicopters are another incessant noise in the background).

Little by little, the old priest devotes himself and his church to helping these people, who build a precarious cardboard village around the pews as a temporary shelter. By doing so, he also clarifies some of his old doctrinary doubts, being more and more convinced about the importance of good deeds over faith. In spite of the pressure and threats exercised by the authorities, he does not relent until the migrants find a transport to a preferred country of destination.

Olmi declaredly intended to create an extremely stylized story, that he calls 'an apologue'.[25] As a consequence, some of its characters are highly symbolic: the terrorist, the peaceful and educated leader, the ex-prostitute and the Italian doctor who survived a concentration camp are sometimes engaged in profound discussions about the meaning of existence. Given the unrealistic frame of the story, the resulting effect might risk mythologizing the subalterns, as Enrica Capussotti wrote in 2009 about some Italian films that failed, in her opinion, to give a convincing voice to migrant characters.[26]

I will leave this issue open and turn to what I find most interesting for the scope of the present article — that is, the use of spaces. The ur-space of mainstream culture, home to that Christian religion so often trumpeted by far-right exponents as the epitome of Europe's most important values, undergoes a profound transformation. Olmi sees this as an inevitable consequence of a crisis of our contemporaneity, which is based

25   'Intervista a Ermanno Olmi', in *Il villaggio di cartone*, DVD extra.
26   Enrica Capussotti, 'Moveable Identitites: Migration, Subjectivity and Cinema in Contemporary Italy', *Modern Italy*, 14:1 (2009), 65–66.

on 'cardboard institutions, cardboard churches, cardboard people — a cardboard reality',[27] that is to say a society without solid values supporting it. Pointing to a different idea of society based on the Christian value of unconditional charity, this space is thus changed not only to a cardboard shelter, but also through other symbolic reconfigurations: the stoup is turned into a rain collector under the leaking roof; the best room of the rectory, last used for the bishop's visit, into a recovery shelter for a wounded migrant. After the initial high/low visual perspectives and now that Christ has symbolically descended from its heights, everything is reduced to ground level.

Although it may seem as excessively stylized and based on a paternalistic idea of charity, one should contextualize Olmi's reconfigurations within the frame of the segregation of spaces that characterized Italian colonial cinema, often concerned with the elision and re-affirmation of racial and spatial boundaries between Italian colonizers and colonized subjects.[28]

Another blatant disruption of postcolonial segregational boundaries is offered by Gabriele Del Grande, Khaled Soliman Al Nassiry and Antonio Augugliaro's *Io sto con la sposa* (*On the Bride's Side*, 2014).[29] The story of its creation has now reached a worldwide popularity: in the face of the thousands

---

27 'Intervista a Ermanno Olmi'.

28 Duncan, p. 197; Jacqueline Andall and Derek Duncan, 'Introduction: Hybridity in Italian Colonial and Postcolonial Culture', in Jacqueline Andall and Derek Duncan (eds.), *National Belongings: Hybridity in Italian Colonial and Postcolonial Cultures* (Bern: Peter Lang, 2010), pp. 3–7. As for postcolonial Italian literature destabilizing the architectural structure and signification of Italian cities, see Jennifer Burns, 'Language and Its Alternatives in Italophone Migrant Writing', in Jacqueline Andall and Derek Duncan (eds.), *National Belongings: Hybridity in Italian Colonial and Postcolonial Cultures* (Bern: Peter Lang, 2010), p. 138. For the transformation of urban environments in migrant European cinema, see Yosefa Loshitzky, *Screening Strangers: Migration and Diaspora in Contemporary European Cinema* (Bloomington and Indianapolis: Indiana University Press, 2010), pp. 45–76.

29 Gabriele Del Grande, Khaled Soliman Al Nassiry, Antonio Augugliaro, *Io sto con la sposa*, Gina Films and Doc Lab (plus 2617 crowdfunders), Italy–Palestine 2014 (www.iostoconlasposa.com).

of immigrants fleeing the Syrian war through sealed borders and dangerously smuggled into Italy, some friends decided to organize a fake wedding in order to take a group of Syrian and Palestinian–Syrian migrants to Sweden, their wished-for country of arrival. Who would ever dream of stopping and checking a wedding procession?[30] Between 14 and 18 November 2013, a mixed group of Italian and Middle Eastern wedding guests climbed through Ventimiglia's smugglers' old trekking path,[31] then drove more than 3000 kilometres through Marseille, Nancy, Luxembourg, Bochum and Copenhagen, finally taking the train to Malmo, Sweden. This three-day trick worked, and was also filmed by a cinema crew accompanying the group. Then came the post-production phase, with its unexpected success through a crowdfunding campaign which became viral, all the way to the film being presented at top cinema festivals throughout the world.[32]

The dialogues during their journey often touch upon the cruelties of the Syrian war and on the injustice of being trapped under the bombings without Western embassies offering help, the only alternative being to resort to smugglers and thus go through the fatal dangers of Mediterranean crossings.[33] While sharing

---

30   In a previous article on Italian new forms of slavery in anglophone literature and cinema, I identified the recurrent trope of the limbo — which signifies the paralyzing situation where many migrants find themselves — and a similar need to break out of it by transgressing the law; Pietro Deandrea, 'New Slaveries in Italy: Anglophone Perspectives', in *L'immagine dell'Italia nelle letterature angloamericane e postcoloniali*, ed. by Paolo Bertinetti (Turin: Trauben, 2014), pp. 78–81 (I here referenced Michael Winterbottom and Tony Grisoni's *In This World*, 2002, and David Yates and Abi Morgan's *Sex Traffic*, 2006).

31   The old Grimaldi superiore mountain path used to be crossed by clandestine Italian emigrants – yet another suggestion of how contemporary migrations can unearth similar (and not unrelated) phenomena from the past.

32   For further details on this incredible enterprise, see Gabriele Del Grande, *Storia di un matrimonio*, booklet accompanying the DVD of *Io sto con la sposa*, Real Cinema Feltrinelli, 2014, passim.

33   Del Grande, p. 17. Del Grande had spent some time as a reporter from the Syrian war front. Furthermore, he runs the blog *Fortress Europe*,

Olmi's utter disregard for the spatial boundaries imposed by the powers-that-be,[34] *Io sto con la sposa* is evidently a completely different film from many points of view. It narrates an actual (not simply artistic) spatial disruption resulting from an initiative of cultural activism, rather than from an artist's vision. In the light of this, and not least because of its inability to raise funds which led to the crowdfunding campaign, it could easily fall under the category of "guerrilla film-making" as theorized by Mariagiulia Grassilli:

> A sort of film-making whereby the filming itself is an act of resistance and therefore laden with political meaning: images are produced which are not "recognized" by the cultural establishment which assigns resources and funds within the national territory. This is even more the case when the film-maker is a clandestine or "irregular" film-maker,[35] when his/her personal status as a citizen (let alone a film-maker) is not recognized.[36]

Differently from Olmi's monolithically directorial creation and its dominant symbolic register, *Io sto con la sposa* mixes a great variety of languages, media and genres. Here lies the second counter-canonical aesthetics that I identify in postcolonial Italian cinema. *Io sto con la sposa* is composed of a mixture of Italian, Arabic and English, with a dominant presence of the Arabic of the migrants who occupy a central role in the story. Media-wise, it is also made of a mixture of dialogues, rap songs, wall writings and poetry readings.[37] Furthermore, its genre is

---

concerned with the victims of the various fronts of contemporary migrations (fortresseurope.blogspot.com).

34　Del Grande (p. 9) defines the final product as 'a new aesthetic of the frontier' ('una nuova estetica della frontiera').

35　In the case of *Io sto con la sposa*, it was some of the actors who were undocumented, and who constituted the main reason and the centre of this activist initiative.

36　Mariagiulia Grassilli, 'Migrant Cinema: Transnational and Guerrilla Practices of Film Production and Representation', *Journal of Ethnic and Migration Studies*, 34:8 (November 2008), 1244–45.

37　*Io sto con la sposa* may be related to Hamid Naficy's theorization of exilic and diasporic filmmaking (2001) that he calls 'accented cinema': in

multi-layered: viewers are faced with a real action (travelling and arriving in Sweden) masked by a fiction (the fake wedding); in turn, this fiction is narrated through a documentary style which declaredly eschews a docu-fiction approach[38] while at the same time revealing its own fictional nature by repeated references (both visual and spoken) to the presence of the working crew filming the actors.

At the bottom of it all, this generic complexity results from an aesthetic achievement which is in tune with the directors' purpose, as Del Grande explains when he comments on the media's coverage of immigration issues:

> Yet this media over-exposure does not move the debate one bit. On the contrary, it risks distorting the story. [...] Instead, we increasingly need more lengthy stories and more time to process the encounter with the human side of the story. And this function can be carried out only through cinema, literature, music, in other words, by art. And not only in the role of witness. [...] we need to dare to imagine a common future. And only art can help us in so visionary a task.[39]

This visionary effort was capable, after all, of stripping the veil off the absurdities of our current immigration policies: Del Grande

---

summarizing its characteristics, Ponzanesi mentions 'questions of belonging and identity (travel and journeys, borders and confinement, a nostalgic longing for "home"), by language use (multilingualism, orality, acousticity, accents and inflections), modes of production (interstitial, collective forms of production, multi-source funding and co-production)'; Sandra Ponzanesi, 'The Non-Places of Migrant Cinema in Europe', *Third Text*, 26:6 (2012), 676.

38 Del Grande, p. 8. Elsewhere, Del Grande declared that *Io sto con la sposa* is 'not a classic documentary film [...]. This probably helps attract an audience who would hardly approach a documentary film'; Korzhenevich, pp. 109–10. For a discussion of docudrama in Michael Winterbottom's films, see Loshitzky, pp. 120–23. For an analysis of the genres of docudrama and mockumentary, see Sissy Helff, 'Scapes of Refuge in Multicultural Britain: Representing Refugees in Digital Docudrama and Mockumentary', in *Multi-Ethnic Britain 2000+: New Perspectives in Literature, Film and the Arts*, ed. by Lars Eckstein and others (Amsterdam and New York: Rodopi, 2008), passim.

39 Korzhenevich, p. 109.

wonders at the fact that not only was he never taken to court for his blatant infringement of the law, but the film was invited to be publicly screened for the members of Magistratura Democratica and the European Parliament![40] In other words, this film demonstrates what Ermanno Olmi expressed through his symbols — the cardboard, evanescent foundations of our major institutions.

Before reflecting on the effects of this entangled co-existence of reality and fiction, I want to study another recent film based on an analogous generic complexity. From its very beginning, Daniele Gaglianone's *La mia classe* (*My Class*, 2013)[41] works on a double level: the dimension of fiction, where a teacher of Italian works with a heterogeneous class of adult migrants in Rome,[42] and the dimension of reality, thanks to which we are repeatedly shown the crew filming their lessons. This double level is extremely explicit from the very beginning, when each student cooperates with the crew for a sound check. The teacher, played by the popular Italian actor Valerio Mastandrea,[43] plays the double part of character/actor, so that we see him getting in and out of character (whenever he discusses the filming with the director, for example). The students, on the other hand, are the characters for whom these two levels tend to coincide: they are real migrants playing themselves, their real difficulties with the Italian language and with life in general (and this makes one wonder what amount of improvisation was allowed during the filming).

Much of the film is devoted to language classes where the topics at stake tend to focus on migrants' lives in Italy: for

40 Del Grande, p. 16.
41 Daniele Gaglianone, *La mia classe*, Axelotil Films, Kimerafilm, Relief and RAI Cinema, 2013.
42 *La mia classe* has been read as a contemporary version of Vittorio De Seta's masterpiece *Diario di un maestro* (*A teacher's diary*, 1973), which was centred on an inexperienced teacher and his class of underpriviliged proletarian students in Rome's periphery; see Michele Marangi, 'Volti nuovi attraverso la cinepresa: Come la patria del neorealismo ha raccontato l'immigrazione recente', *L'indice dei libri del mese*, January 2014, 8.
43 His remarkable sense of humour often counterbalances the gravity of the narrated events.

instance, one lesson concentrates on terms and expressions related to job-seeking, with discussions and rehearsed phone calls.[44] Not differently from *Io sto con la sposa*, then, *La mia classe* is constructed quite sophisticatedly: in scenes like this we have a play within a play within a play.

However, it is real migrants who enact all this. From linguistic topics and expressions related to their lives, the film moves to personal stories narrated by each student separately: some of them are so traumatized about their past ordeals that find it hard to speak them out. These are very unstructured "interviews", where the migrants are free to express themselves and the camera assumes the role of listener,[45] similarly to the listening attitude of cameras in *Io sto con la sposa*. Gaglianone's "school" looks very similar to a real experimental school of Italian for migrants in Rome, called Asinitas. There, as Alessandro Triulzi describes it,

> food and words would mix with the migrants' wounds and bereavements. Their dreams and hopes of deliverance were acknowledged and shared, and the broken words of their narrations provided the first drive towards learning the Italian language, which was taught starting from their very memories and silence.[46]

---

44   Obviously the lessons are not limited to these very practical topics. That would risk flattening these migrants to their state of need. There is also a long scene where the students listen to a long song about marginality, read and discuss its lyrics. The role of art to offer glimpses into beauty and complexity is something that Marco Carsetti deems essential for teaching to migrants; Marco Carsetti, 'L'alfabeto per imparare a pensare', *Gli asini: Educazione e intervento sociale*, III:11 (August–September 2012), 83.

45   See Alessandro Portelli's method of oral history in Martina Martignoni, 'Fuori dai confini dello spazio dello spazio della narrazione: Esperimenti di (in)visibilità', in *Subalternità italiane: Percorsi di ricerca tra letteratura e storia*, p. 131.

46   'cibo e parole si mescolavano ai lutti e alle ferite dei migranti, i cui sogni e le cui speranze di riscatto venivano riconosciute e condivise e le parole spezzate delle loro narrazioni fornivano i primi stimoli di apprendimento della lingua italiana insegnata a partire dai loro stessi ricordi e silenzi.' Alessandro Triulzi, 'Volti nascosti, storie rimosse. Voci a contrasto dell'Italia postcoloniale', in *L'Italia postcoloniale*, ed. by Cristina

In the film, it is worth repeating, all this is expressed through a swinging between the dimensions of reality and fiction. After one Egyptian student tells the teacher that his visa has expired, he is arrested in a public park for being undocumented; later, the same student is instructed by the director on how to act his suicide in a prison cell.

This character creates a stark contrast with another student, a sub-Saharan African called Issa. His visa, too, has expired, but we are shown a seeming irruption of reality into fiction — or, rather, an implosion of these two dimensions. Issa is very angry, and breaks into the school interrupting a lesson (and the filming of it), in spite of the crew's attempt to stop him.

When asked to go outside and talk about it calmly, he stubbornly states that he wants to remain in the classroom. Besides teacher and students, the classroom is now filled with the whole crew. A tense discussion starts between the director and the students. The director faces his own helplessness in this situation, torn between using it as a justification ('I am not a policeman') and feeling discouraged by it. The students implicitly accuse him of accepting the status quo even in the face of an unjust law: 'If tomorrow the same thing happens again to two of us, what will you do?', one of them asks him. Gaglianone's despondently replies 'I don't know'. Mastandrea, the actor playing the teacher, is equally pessimistic: 'And anyway, what we do is fucking useless.'[47] Is it worth to continue making this film, the protagonist and the director ask each other. In the end, a collective decision is taken to resume the shooting of the film, significantly starting with a dialogue about Issa, with the students saying that they are unaware of his whereabouts.

Lombardi-Diop and Caterina Romeo (Florence and Milan: Le Monnier Università and Mondadori Education, 2014), p. 137.

47 'Io non è che sono la polizia'; 'Ma se succede che dopodomani che capita, e altri due ragazzi non possono fare più il film perché gli scadrà il permesso di soggiorno, che fai?'; 'Non lo so'; 'E comunque quello che facciamo non serve a un cazzo' (Gaglianone).

For the aims of a cultural studies analysis, the distinction between
fiction and cinema of the real (...) can become an ancillary detail.
What interests a cultural studies perspective is the way in which
the text succeeds in placing at the centre of its representation the
problematisation of the Other's reality, and in studying his point of view.
(Nicoletta Vallorani)[48]

Cinema critics have often problematized the neat separation
between documentary and fiction.[49] In the field of postcolonial
cinema, Sandra Ponzanesi questions any attempt to compare
their efficaciousness and comes to a conclusion similar to the
one expressed by Vallorani's cultural studies angle in the above
epigraph, while slightly shifting the focus on viewers:

> The question of accountability moves from the epistemological
> towards the ethical. It is not whether these accounts, fictional or
> documentary, are 'more true' or 'more objective' in representing the
> migrant condition, but about how these cinematic representations *put in*
> *motion spectator and migrant subjectivities*.[50] (*emphasis mine*)

Constructed around a sophisticated interplay between fiction
and reality, *Io sto con la sposa* and *La mia classe* make Vallorani's
and Ponzanesi's claims even more significant. The most important
effect of that interplay, in my view, is double faced. On one
hand, their artistic sophistication expresses their effort to offer a
visionary picture of a common future (albeit extremely uncertain,
in the case of Gaglianone).

---

48   'Ai fini del lavoro culturalista, la distinzione tra cinema di finzione e
      cinema del reale […] può diventare un dato accessorio. Quel che interessa,
      dal punto di vista dell'analisi culturalista, è il modo in cui il testo riesce a
      porre al centro della rappresentazione la problematizzazione della realtà
      dell'Altro e a investigarne il punto di vista.' Nicoletta Vallorani, 'Immagini
      in movimento: Narrazione, cinema, mimesi e cultura', in *Introduzione ai*
      Cultural Studies: UK, USA e paesi anglofoni, ed. by Nicoletta Vallorani
      (Rome: Carocci, 2016), p. 186.
49   Vallorani, p. 185.
50   Ponzanesi, 'On the Waterfront', p. 232; here Ponzanesi studies Andrea
      Segre's *A sud di Lampedusa* (2006) and Gerardo Olivares's *14 kilómetros*
      (2007).

At the same time, the solid presence of reality act as reminder of a deeply perceived need for 'putting in motion' more active, filterless forms of involvement with the real.[51] The participants of *Io sto con la sposa* are constantly on the edge, given the risky task they are undertaking; the film's opening credits explicitly announce an act of disobedience, while the closing credits dedicate the film to 'our children [...] because at some time in their lives they'll have to choose which side they're on.' Quite clearly, a need to act frames the movie. For their part, the crew members of *La mia classe* face an ethical dilemma concerned with a similar option of civil disobedience.

Olmi's *Il villaggio di cartone*, too, in spite of its very different language, shares this call to praxis: not only is it centred on the priest's disobedience to immigration laws, but Olmi also declared that charity implies a complicity with those who suffer. Accordingly he chose, as the subtitle to his movie, the word *diabasis*, meaning 'word becoming action'.[52] Quite curiously, a revered maestro of Italian cinema like Olmi, three activists and artists from Italy and Palestina (Del Grande, Al Nassiry and Augugliaro) and one of the most distinguished Italian arthouse film directors (Gaglianone), from their different ideological perspectives and in different degrees, share an engagement with reality — or a striving for it.[53]

However, an earlier step should be taken into consideration, before active involvement is called into play. These complex entanglements of fiction and documentary, Olmi's extremely

---

51   In his reflections on postcolonial Italian cinema, Michele Marangi traces this tendency towards the documentation of reality to Italian *neorealismo*. Moreover, he praises contemporary filmmakers for their ability to mix powerful metaphors and documentary purposes, similarly to what I argue here; Marangi, p. 8.

52   'Intervista a Ermanno Olmi'.

53   In 2008 Mariagiulia Grassilli lamented the gap between Italian filmmakers, who produced patronizing films, often 'driven by a risky enthusiasm for the "Other"', and a still emerging production of migrant filmmakers telling their own stories in their own accents (Grassilli, pp. 1248–49). My overall impression, as this article shows, is that this gap has narrowed in recent years.

stylized vision, and even Wu Ming's narration *à rebours* all represent ways of departing from an unproblematic mimesis of reality and from the forms of cathartic self-identification that this mimesis can generate. From a Brechtian perspective, we should consider them as helping viewers acquire a sort of critical distance about the topic in question[54] — that is, migrants' lives in today's Italy.

(I wish to dedicate this article to Claudio Gorlier, in memory of his curiosity, often counter-canonical)

---

54   Helff (p. 289) sees a similar function in the explicit constructedness of the mockumentary genre.

Bibliography

Andall, Jacqueline, and Derek Duncan, 'Introduction: Hybridity in Italian Colonial and Postcolonial Culture', in *National Belongings: Hybridity in Italian Colonial and Postcolonial Cultures*, ed. by Jacqueline Andall and Derek Duncan (Bern: Peter Lang, 2010), pp. 1–19.

Aria, Matteo, *Cercando nel vuoto: La memoria perduta e ritrovata in Polinesia francese* (Pisa: Pacini, 2007).

Benvenuti, Giuliana, *Il romanzo neostorico italiano: Storia, memoria, narrazione* (Rome: Carocci, 2012).

Brioni, Simone, 'Postcolonialismo, subalternità e *New Italian Epic*: Intervista con Wu Ming 1', in *Subalternità italiane: Percorsi di ricerca tra letteratura e storia*, ed. by Valeria Deplano, Lorenzo Mari, Gabriele Proglio (Ariccia (RM): Aracne, 2014), pp. 275–91.

Burns, Jennifer, 'Language and Its Alternatives in Italophone Migrant Writing', in *National Belongings: Hybridity in Italian Colonial and Postcolonial Cultures*, ed. by Jacqueline Andall and Derek Duncan (Bern: Peter Lang, 2010), pp. 127–47.

Capussotti, Enrica, 'Moveable Identitites: Migration, Subjectivity and Cinema in Contemporary Italy', *Modern Italy*, 14:1 (2009), 55–68.

Carsetti, Marco, 'L'alfabeto per imparare a pensare', *Gli asini: Educazione e intervento sociale*, III:11 (August–September 2012), 73–89.

Deandrea, Pietro, 'New Slaveries in Italy: Anglophone Perspectives', in *L'immagine dell'Italia nelle letterature angloamericane e postcoloniali*, ed. by Paolo Bertinetti (Turin: Trauben, 2014), pp. 73–82.

Del Grande, Gabriele, Khaled Soliman Al Nassiry, Antonio Augugliaro, *Io sto con la sposa*, Gina Films and Doc Lab (plus 2617 crowdfunders), Italy–Palestine 2014 (www.iostoconlasposa.com).

Del Grande, Gabriele, *Storia di un matrimonio*, booklet accompanying the DVD of *Io sto con la sposa*, Real Cinema Feltrinelli, 2014.

Dogao, Valentina, 'Ibridazioni postcoloniali e decostruzioni letterarie', in *Subalternità italiane: Percorsi di ricerca tra letteratura e storia*, ed. by Valeria Deplano, Lorenzo Mari, Gabriele Proglio (Ariccia (RM): Aracne, 2014), pp. 29–45.

Duncan, Derek, 'Italy's Postcolonial Cinema and Its Histories of Representation', *Italian Studies*, 63:2 (2008), 195–211.

Gaglianone, Daniele, *La mia classe*, Axelotil Films, Kimerafilm, Relief and RAI Cinema, 2013.

Grassilli, Mariagiulia, 'Migrant Cinema: Transnational and Guerrilla Practices of Film Production and Representation', *Journal of Ethnic and Migration Studies*, 34:8 (November 2008), 1237–55.

Hall, Stuart, 'Teaching Race', *Multiracial Education*, 9:1 (autumn 1980), 3–13.

_____, 'Cultural Studies and Its Theoretical Legacies', in *Cultural Studies*, ed. by Lawrence Grossberg, Cary Nelson, Paula Treichler (London and New York: Routledge, 1992), pp. 277–94.

Helff, Sissy, 'Scapes of Refuge in Multicultural Britain: Representing Refugees in Digital Docudrama and Mockumentary', in *Multi-Ethnic Britain 2000+: New Perspectives in Literature, Film and the Arts*, ed. by Lars Eckstein, Barbara Korte, Eva Ulriche Pilker, Christoph Reinfandt (Amsterdam–New York: Rodopi, 2008), pp. 283–99.

Korzhenevich, Elena, 'Changing the Narrative of the World: Interview with Gabriele Del Grande and Dagmawi Yimer', *Critical Interventions: Journal of African Art History and Visual Culture*, 10:1 (2016), 107–14.

Loshitzky, Yosefa, *Screening Strangers: Migration and Diaspora in Contemporary European Cinema* (Bloomington–Indianapolis: Indiana University Press, 2010).

Marangi, Michele, 'Volti nuovi attraverso la cinepresa: Come la patria del neorealismo ha raccontato l'immigrazione recente', *L'indice dei libri del mese*, January 2014, 8.

Martignoni, Martina, 'Fuori dai confini dello spazio dello spazio della narrazione: Esperimenti di (in)visibilità', in *Subalternità italiane: Percorsi di ricerca tra letteratura e storia*, ed. by Valeria Deplano, Lorenzo Mari, Gabriele Proglio (eds.), (Ariccia (RM): Aracne, 2014), pp. 139–60.

Molinarolo, Giulia, 'Per una nuova critica della letteratura italiana della migrazione: Questioni aperte', *CoSMo: Comparative Studies in Modernism*, 8 (spring 2016), 157–72.

Monegato, Emanuele, 'Studi culturali e letterari: (Nuove) frontiere ideologiche', in *Introduzione ai Cultural Studies: UK, USA e paesi anglofoni*, ed. by Nicoletta Vallorani (Rome: Carocci, 2016), pp. 67–85.

Morace, Rosanna, *Letteratura-mondo italiana* (Pisa: ETS, 2012).

Naficy, Hamid, *An Accented Cinema: Exilic and Diasporic Filmmaking* (Princeton: Princeton University Press, 2001).

Olmi, Ermanno, *Il villaggio di cartone: Diabasis*, Cinemaundici, RAI Cinema, 2011 (including 'Intervista a Ermanno Olmi', DVD extra).

Parati, Graziella, *Migration Italy: The Art of Talking Back in a Destination Culture* (Toronto: University of Toronto Press, 2005).

Piccino, Cristina, 'L'immagine migrante' [interview with John Akomfrah], *Alias – Il manifesto*, 8 January 2011, 2–3.

Ponzanesi, Sandra, 'The Non-Places of Migrant Cinema in Europe', *Third Text*, 26:6 (2012), 675–90.

——————————, 'La "svolta" postcoloniale negli Studi italiani: Prospettive europee', in *L'Italia postcoloniale*, ed. by Cristina Lombardi-Diop and Caterina Romeo (Florence–Milan: Le Monnier Università and Mondadori Education, 2014), pp. 45–60.

——————————, 'On the Waterfront: Truth and Fiction in Postcolonial Cinema from the South of Europe', *Interventions: International Journal of Postcolonial Studies*, 18:2 (2016), 217–33.

Proglio, Gabriele, 'Subalternità e silenzi tra storia e letteratura: Modelli epistemologici e luoghi della contro-narrazione', in *Subalternità italiane: Percorsi di ricerca tra letteratura e storia*, ed. by Valeria Deplano, Lorenzo Mari, Gabriele Proglio (Ariccia (RM): Aracne, 2014), pp. 85–88.

Triulzi, Alessandro, 'Displacing the Colonial Event: Hybrid Memories of Postcolonial Italy', in *National Belongings: Hybridity in Italian Colonial and Postcolonial Cultures*, ed. by Jacqueline Andall and Derek Duncan (Bern: Peter Lang, 2010), pp. 23–40.

——————————, 'Volti nascosti, storie rimosse: Voci a contrasto dell'Italia postcoloniale', in *L'Italia postcoloniale*, ed. by Cristina Lombardi-Diop and Caterina Romeo (Florence–Milan: Le Monnier Università and Mondadori Education, 2014), pp. 135–47.

——————————, 'Empowering Migrants' Voices and Agency in Postcolonial Italy', *Critical Interventions: Journal of African Art History and Visual Culture*, 10:1 (2016), 58–70.

Valletti, Camilla, 'Siamo tutti disgregati: L'italiano lingua di Petrarca e Celentano. Intervista a Igiaba Scego di Camilla Valletti', *L'indice dei libri del mese*, January 2016, 10.

Vallorani, Nicoletta, 'Immagini in movimento: Narrazione, cinema, mimesi e cultura', in *Introduzione ai Cultural Studies: UK, USA e paesi anglofoni*, ed. by Nicoletta Vallorani (Rome: Carocci, 2016), pp. 179–96.

Venturini, Monica, *Controcànone: Per una cartografia della scrittura coloniale e postcoloniale italiana* (Rome: Aracne, 2010).

Wu Ming, *Momodou*, in *Anatra all'arancia meccanica: Racconti 2000–2010* (Turin: Einaudi, 2010 [2008]), pp. 269–301.

Young, Robert, 'Postcolonial Remains', *New Literary History*, 34:1 (2012), 19–42.

DEREK MAHON'S EXPERIMENTS IN EKPHRASIS

Irene De Angelis
(University of Turin)

Ekphrasis (sometimes also spelled ecphrasis) is a term derived from the ancient Greek noun ἔκφρασις, from ἔκφραζο ("recount, describe"), formed by the prefix ἐκ ("out") and the verb φράζειν ("to point out, explain"). Although in rhetoric it is often simply associated with a description in prose or poetry, in more recent times its use has been limited to the description of a work of visual art — either real or imagined.[1] It was Horace in his *Ars Poetica* (13 BC) who famously compared the two arts, coining the expression *ut pictura poesis* ("as is painting, so is poetry").[2] However, the earliest and most famous instance of ekphrasis is to be found in Book 18 of Homer's *Iliad*, in the long passage describing the shield made by Hephaestus and given to Achilles as a present from his mother. The description of the bas-relief in metal is so rich and elaborate that it is hardly credible: the shield with its formidable representation of constellations and great cities adds a dreamlike dimension to this part of the *Iliad*. A similar though shorter example can be found in Book I of Virgil's *Aeneid* (from line 450 onwards), in the account of the carvings on the temple Aeneas visits in Carthage, a visual narrative of some of the key moments in the Trojan War.

---

1   Poems describing music, cinema or dance might also be considered examples of ekphrasis, but they are outside the scope of this essay.
2   The notion that poetry and painting are alike had previously been expressed by Simonides of Keos (first recorded in Plutarch's *De gloria Athenensium* more than a century after *Ars Poetica*): '*Poema pictura loquens, pictura poema silens*' ('poetry is a speaking picture, painting a silent poetry').

Dante's *Purgatorio* Canto X offers another superb example of ekphrasis, in the description of the white marble low-relief sculptures on the side of the mountain, which depict scenes of Biblical humility. The episode when the Roman Emperor Trajan addresses the mother of a dead soldier is a work of visual art that beautifully portrays a verbal exchange: Dante speaks of '*esto visibile parlare*' (X.95), 'this visible speaking', pointing out that God's work is so realistic it defies the senses of the observer.[3]

As regards the Elizabethan Age, in Edmund Spenser's *Faerie Queene* Book 3 the good heroine Britomart is shown a set of tapestries depicting Jove's love affairs. These depictions repeat the stories Arachne waves in her competition with Minerva in Ovid's *Metamorphoses*. Ekphrasis is therefore associated not only with intermediality, but also with intertextuality.

After Milton, when epic-length poems disappear from the English language, ekphrasis is limited to shorter poems.[4] Some outstanding examples are Keats's "Ode on a Grecian Urn" or "On Seeing the Elgin Marbles"; Shelley's "On the Medusa of Leonardo da Vinci" and Browning's "My Last Duchess". William Blake and Dante Gabriel Rossetti are two cases of distinguished English-language poets who were also painters, and made illustrations to accompany their verses, or vice-versa. Blake's "The Tyger" and "Holy Thursday" were turned by the poet-painter into graphic renderings, while Rossetti is famous, among other works, for "The Blessed Damozel", which originated as a poem and was later turned into a painting.

In the 20th century, the emergence of photography and film contributed to create a shift from a culture of words to a culture of images. As Elizabeth Bergmann-Loizeaux documented in

---

3   According to Dante's *Weltanschauung*, in God's creation words and
     things made coincide, without any need for mediation. In his effort to
     describe God's work, which cannot be translated into human language,
     the poet "steals" the Creator's words in order to celebrate Him. It is the
     concept of the "ineffable", when words try to express what is indescribable
     or unutterable.
4   However, an example of a long poem is Byron's "Childe Harold's
     Pilgrimage".

her 2008 monograph, many crucial authors were involved in the poetic representation of visual art, from W. B. Yeats[5] and Marianne Moore[6] to Ted Hughes,[7] from W. H. Auden[8] and Wallace Stevens[9] to Elizabeth Bishop.[10] Derek Mahon is by no means the only contemporary Irish poet showing an interest in ekphrasis: recent examples include the late Seamus Heaney's "The Seed-Cutters", based on a painting by Breughel, or Michael Longley's poems inspired by Hokusai, Pierre Bonnard and Robert Mapplethorpe. Ciaran Carson's *Breaking News* (2003) comprises poetic responses to Goya, Géricault and Edward Hopper, while Paul Durcan has published two volumes of poetry inspired by the paintings in the National Gallery in Dublin (*Crazy About Women*, 1991), and the National Gallery in London (*Give Me Your Hand*, 1994). Irish women poets such as Paula Meehan, Medbh McGuckian and Sinéad Morrissey have also successfully experimented with ekphrasis. More recently, the volume *Metamorphosis: Poems Inspired by Titian* (2012) collects a series of poems on the myth of Actaeon and Diana, while *Lines of Vision. Irish Writers on Art* (2014) is an anthology of poetry commissioned by the National Gallery of Ireland. Mahon follows in this long and well-established tradition, standing out as a refined connoisseur of the visual arts and one of the most original voices of contemporary Ireland.

In his article on Derek Mahon's relationship with painting, Terence Brown defines him as 'a markedly visual poet, one who attends patiently, even contemplatively, to the look of things.'[11] Mahon's interest in the visual arts is strictly related to his search for the numinous and the transcendent in everyday life. His attention to detail goes hand in hand with his passion for the

---

5   See "Lapis Lazuli".

6   Two examples are "No Swan So Fine" and "Nine Peaches".

7   See "Cave Birds".

8   In "The Shield of Achilles" and "Musée des Beaux Arts".

9   See "Angel Between Two Paysans".

10   For instance "Large Bad Picture" and "Poem".

11   Terence Brown, *The Literature of Ireland: Culture and Criticism* (Cambridge: Cambridge University Press, 2010), p. 199.

secret life of objects, the "mute phenomena" that leave a trace
of our passage on earth. This essay focuses on three of Mahon's
picture poems or "visual epiphanies", in Terence Brown's words.
Two of them celebrate great figurative artists of the past, Paolo
Uccello and Pieter de Hooch, while the third is inspired by the
Belgian surrealist painter René Magritte. Despite the richness and
variety of these and other ekphrastic poems by Mahon, who has
also turned to abstract painting and photography for inspiration,
literary critics have largely neglected them. Apart from a few
articles (see Terence Brown 1994, reprinted 2010; Edna Longley
1994, which takes into consideration several Irish poets; and
Richard York 2002), the only two meaningful exceptions are
Hugh Haughton's references in *The Poetry of Derek Mahon*
(2007) and Jerzy Jarniewicz's 2013 full-length study. Moving
from Mahon's poetry of the 1980s to one of the poems from the
sequence "Art Notes", published in *Life on Earth* (2008), my
analysis will take into consideration three "case studies", which
were all inspired by figurative paintings and show how Mahon is
a keen observer of light.

"The Hunt by Night" – Uccello, 1465

Fig. 1 Paolo Uccello, *The Hunt by Night*, 1465, Ashmolean Museum, Oxford.

Although Derek Mahon had already written poems about Van Gogh and Munch, his interest in painting was increased by 'visits to galleries in London after his return from Northern Ireland.'[12] The poem was first included in *Courtyards in Delft* (1981) and later reprinted in *The Hunt by Night* (1982). It is subtitled "Uccello, 1465", and shows Mahon's renewed passion for art and artists. Like "The Battle of San Romano", "The Hunt" — as it is also known — exemplifies Uccello's mastery of linear perspective, which creates a sense of depth in his paintings (fig. 1). Here he uses it to evoke the excitement of the chase and to draw the viewer further into the darkness as the hunters, horses and hounds disappear into the trees. It is Uccello's last known work and one of the finest examples of Italian Renaissance painting in the Ashmolean Museum in Oxford. Art critics believe it was probably painted as a wall decoration for the home of a wealthy patron. It represents a brilliantly structured scene of motion and noise. Hounds leap, horses rear back and men seem to be calling out in a darkening forest. Above the horizon line, the trees seem to recede into the distance, whereas everything that is below the horizon converges on a central vanishing point. The artist also uses the huntsmen's spears, fallen tree trunks and patterned lines of foliage to point towards the vanishing point. His brilliant feeling for colour is shown by his Renaissance palette, and his use of red and green, once brightened by shades of gold, now faded, gives the painting a unique jewel-like quality.

Mahon's "The Hunt by Night" effectively renders the suspended atmosphere and the tension of Uccello's scene. The rhyme scheme *abccba* creates a regular pattern, which contributes to emphasise the sense of movement and the quickening pace of the action. The poem begins with 'Flickering shades, | Stick figures, lithe game, | Swift flights of bison in a cave',[13] a reference to the Lascaux cave paintings. Ernest Gombrich calls these pictures the earliest 'relics of that universal belief in the power of picture-making',[14] the belief that an animal "captured" in paint will help hunters succeed in their pursuit in real life. Mahon merges these Neolithic images with Uccello's virtuosic Renaissance landscape, and the 'Hunt' becomes a metaphor for his search for poetic images.

---

12 Hugh Haughton, *The Poetry of Derek Mahon* (Oxford: Oxford University Press, 2007), p. 81.

13 Derek Mahon, *New Collected Poems* (Oldcastle: The Gallery Press, 2011), p. 133. The collection will subsequently be referred to as *NCP*, in parenthesis in the text.

14 E. H. Gombrich, *The Story of Art* (London: Phaidon, 1972), p. 22.

At the same time, the reference to "shades" may be interpreted as an allusion to Plato's parable of the cave in *The Republic* (Book VII), associated with the idea of the material world as a shadow. In Plato's philosophy, art is 'a shadow of a shadow, a second order of representation, twice removed from the real',[15] and in Mahon's poem the animals painted on the wall of the cave are copies of copies of Platonic ideas. Critic Stan Smith claims that Mahon 'uses the Platonic myth of the cave to focus on the changing function of art, its historical transformation from utility to entertainment.'[16] In the second and third stanzas the poet speaks about a sort of "domestication" of hunting, changed "to courtly uses" for sheer enjoyment in the sophisticated "pageantry" of the Renaissance. Wild beasts are said to be 'tamed and framed', turned into 'harmless decorative elements of the coats of arms and heraldic badges.'[17] They are also defined as "rampant", both because they are ready to attack and because in the painting they take the poses regulated by heraldry.

The third and fourth stanzas are characterized by alliteration ("the *h*unting *h*orn", "the *gl*ade a*gl*ow", "*d*iuretic *d*epots", "*p*ungent *p*rey"), which increases the musicality of the verses. The greyhounds recede into the background, following the principles of perspective. Mahon describes the vanishing point in the middle of Uccello's painting, 'the point on the horizon at which all the parallel lines meet, towards which the forest recedes and where the hunted game disappear.'[18] In the central image of the poem there is a transition from hearing to seeing: the *cries* of the dog recede 'to a point | Masked by obscurities of paint', with a shift 'from the observable and the physical to the auditory and imaginary.'[19] The material base of the painting *obscures* rather

---

15   Jarniewicz, Jerzy, *Ekphrasis in the Poetry of Derek Mahon* (Piotrków Trybunalski: Naukowe Wydawnictwo Piotrkowskie przy Filii Uniwersytetu Jana Kochanowskiego, 2013), p. 70.

16   In *The Poetry of Derek Mahon*, ed. by Elmer Kennedy-Andrews (Gerrards Cross: Colin Smythe, 2002), pp. 268–69.

17   Jarniewicz, p. 73.

18   Ibid.

19   Jarniewicz, p. 74.

than reveals. Since the painterly representation is made dark and unintelligible, the poet invokes the sense of hearing, but the centre towards which the figures are moving remains invisible:

> as if our hunt by night,
> so very tense,
>
> so long pursued,
> in what dark cave begun
> and not yet done, were not the great
> adventure we suppose but some elaborate
> spectacle put on for fun
> and not for food.
> (*NCP*, 134)

The darkness of the painting, made such by time and history, calls to mind the darkness of the caves to which Mahon referred in the first stanza, whose image was superimposed over the *Quattrocento* painting. Uccello's work, which should belong to the realm of the timeless, is on the contrary set in the stream of time. However it is said that the hunt 'is not yet done', an expression which links this poem to "A Postcard from Berlin", where it is called 'a night-hunt with no end in view'. As Haughton suggests, the poem is a comment on the nature of art, and 'the hunter's hunt by night becomes a figure of the artist's hunt for forms in the dark',[20] which is never-ending.

The alliteration of the last two expressions of the poem ('for *f*un | and not for *f*ood') emphasises the conceptual opposition between entertainment and utility: originally, hunting was linked to the necessities of life, but subsequently it became an activity for sheer pleasure. Jarniewicz convincingly argues that, for Mahon,

> at the root of the human search for pleasure, elegance and entertainment, lies the original impulse of killing [...] But the ceremonies of killing, no longer necessary for life, are performed now as — beautiful, elegant, pleasurable — representations of old hunts, as (to quote Plato again) 'nothing but the shadows of the images'. (70)

---

20   Haughton, p. 182.

The "obscurities of paint", which mask the vanishing point of the painting, correspond to the obscure origins of hunting, and "man the maker", who is capable of producing splendid forms of art, originally killed for survival. That dark point towards which everything recedes — that "heart of darkness", to appropriate Conrad — is also, metaphorically, an expression of the difficulties experienced by poets when they approach the visual arts and try to make them speak.

"Courtyards in Delft" – Pieter de Hooch, 1659

Fig. 2 Pieter de Hooch, *The Courtyard of a House in Delft*,
The National Gallery of London.

This second ekphrastic poem was first published in the eponymous 1981 collection and was included the following year in *The Hunt by Night*. The painting that is said to have inspired it is titled *The Courtyard of a House in Delft* (fig. 2), one in a series of paintings completed by the Dutch artist during his stay in Delft (1652–60). Mahon saw it in the National Gallery in London, after his return there from Coleraine. It is set in an "elsewhere" that recalls home, painted by an artist who was insatiably hungry for reality.

The opening stanza describes a scene of everyday life, a habitable space characterised by "trim composure" (l. 8). A series of adjectives merges the aesthetic with the domestic: the poem speaks about "*Immaculate* masonry", "*House-proud*" 'wives | Of artisans' who pursue '*thrifty* lives | Among *scrubbed* yards, *modest* but *adequate*' (*NCP*, 96, *emphasis added*). These images call to mind Mahon's "Glengormley" and his origins, rooted in the Protestant ethos of working-class Belfast. A list of objects — a trademark of Mahon's poetry — defines the domestic rituals traditionally associated with women: 'Water tap, that broom and wooden pail' (l. 3). Women are the only protagonists of the painting: one is turning her gaze towards her little daughter, while the other is standing under an arched passageway, with her back to the observer. The life-style described in the poem is simple and transparent, with nothing to hide, while the "Oblique light" on the "Immaculate masonry" evokes an idea of virtuousness. At the same time, stillness dominates the scene with the image of the "Foliage" that "clings" to the unruffled trees (l. 8).

The second stanza changes the tone of the poem, introducing a description by negation of other genre paintings of the period: "No spinet-playing", 'No lewd fish, no fruit, no wide-eyed bird', no 'virgin | Listen[ing] to her seducer' (ll. 9–16). This series of absences define 'what we as viewers find missing',[21] the canonical themes of Dutch still lifes. Keith Tuma observes that 'women seated at the keyboard' were a subject beloved by Jan Vermeer, while the "dirty dog" may refer to Jan Steen's realistic depictions of everyday life.[22] There is a great difference between de Hooch's painting and those of his contemporaries, who included 'harmonies and disharmonies' (l. 10), 'violence and conflict, randomness and waste, dirt and intoxication'.[23] Nothing 'mars the chaste | Perfection' (ll. 14–5) of the scene described by

---

21   Jarniewicz, p. 102.
22   Keith Tuma, *Anthology of Twentieth-Century British and Irish Poetry* (New York: Oxford University Press, 2001), pp. 684–85.
23   Jarniewicz, p. 102.

Mahon: the adjective expresses an idea of purity and cleanliness, while the noun alludes to the lack of any weakness or mistake.

The third stanza casts light on a figure of seemingly secondary importance in the painting, "That girl with her back to us". The poet is attracted by her mysterious presence, and wonders whether she is waiting for the return of her lover. She will keep waiting 'till the painting disintegrates | And ruined dikes admit the esurient sea' (ll. 19–20). This apocalyptic scenario and the detail of the 'cracked | Outhouse door' introduce the theme of decay and the survival of works of art, since 'de Hooch's art [is] a form of secular engineering against the ravages of time.'[24] 'Yet this is life too', the poem continues, anticipating the reference to personal memory, which is central in the following verse: 'I lived there as a boy [...] I must be lying low in a room there | A strange child with a taste for verse' (ll 25, 29–30). The "strangeness" of Mahon's poetic vocation is associated with his early fascination with light, which dominates the central part of the fourth stanza and his memories of childhood ("the coal" is "Glittering", "late-afternoon lambency" defines the soft flickering quality of light, while "The ceiling" is reflected in a "radiant spoon", ll. 25–28).

The closing two lines move from the autobiographical to the historical: 'my hard-nosed companions dream of war | On parched *veldt* and field of rainswept *gorse*' (ll. 31–32, *emphasis added*). Painting freezes life, but when it is turned into words it acquires a temporal dimension. This is introduced in the poetic narrative by two nouns, "*veldt*" and "*gorse*". The former is an Afrikaaner word meaning South African grassland, while the latter signifies the prickly shrub typical of Ireland.[25] 'Veldt' suggests 'a condensed allusion to Dutch colonialism, connecting seventeenth-century Holland to South Africa', while 'gorse connects it to Northern Ireland, where William of Orange is still such an iconic presence.'[26] By alluding to the two colonial contexts, Mahon draws attention to the aggressive forces within a certain expansive Protestant culture,

---

24   Haughton, p. 160.
25   One of Michael Longley's collections is titled *Gorse Fires* (1991).
26   Haughton, p. 159.

which seem absent in de Hooch's painting. Yet they are there: 'the violence, the colonialism, the urge to dominate, suppress, wipe out, exterminate.'[27] These forces seem absent because they cannot be seen, as the painting veils any troubling signs of history. Jarniewicz aptly speaks about the silenced themes of the painting:

> The enclosed space speaks of the open territories overseas; the courtyard speaks of the veldt; the domesticity — of the political and the colonial; the feminine — of the masculine; the harmony and cleanliness — of violence; the broom — of the sword; the 'patience and meekness' [...] — of militant, expansive Protestantism. (106)

De Hooch's painting transcends the borders of a specific place,[28] and this is probably why Mahon titled his poem "Courtyards", in the plural. Alpatov comments that Dutch artists 'did not try to represent any manifestations of brutality, they did not try to reveal the urge to get rich and the desire for profit [...] they remained silent about the colonial conquests and had nothing to say about the lives of Dutch peasantry.'[29] In *The Hunt by Night* (1982) the poem had an additional stanza, which Mahon later excluded, where he openly expressed the sublimated violence in the image of the Maenads, the mad female followers of Dionysus, who are described as they 'Came smashing crockery, with fire and sword.' The stanza disrupts the harmonious atmosphere of the painting in a scene of fury and fire-and-sword apocalypse. Actually the expression "with fire and sword", possibly a reference to Henryk Sienkiewicz's historical novel about the seventeenth-century wars in the eastern Borderlands of Poland and Ukraine, extends the theme of colonialism and the clash of cultures. The crockery smashed by the Maenads is an allusion to the famous Delft pottery, which, resembling in refinement Chinese porcelain, may call to mind 'a tinkling of china | And tea into china' from "The

27 Jarniewicz, p. 105.
28 Peter C. Sutton, *Pieter de Hooch* (New Haven and London: Dulwich Picture Gallery, in association with Yale University Press, 1998), p. 32.
29 M. W. Alpatov, *Historia sztuki*, vol. II (Warszawa: Arkady, 1969), p. 178 in Jarniewicz, p. 107.

Snow Party". In that poem, too, there is a stark contrast between a displaced "home" and an "elsewhere" of violence. However, Mahon must have had second thoughts about the stanza and expunged it from all the subsequent versions of the poem. The initial promise of domestic serenity echoes with the unavoidable threats of history, and the discovery of Belfast in Delft is both comforting, because it gives the poet a sense of belonging, and unsettling, because home is not synonymous with safe shelter.

'Does the sunlit courtyard represent a benign childhood epiphany mirrored in a Dutch painting, or a claustrophobically tidy place the poet needed to escape from into art? Is it a haven against violence and disorder, or shaped by it?'[30] These questions are left open for the reader to answer, while the women in de Hooch's courtyard remain hieratically unperturbed, and light continues to fall on the same scene of domestic harmony.

"The Realm of Light" – René Magritte

Fig. 3 René Magritte, *L'empire des lumières*, 1954,
Musées Royaux des Beaux-Arts de Belgique, Brussels.

---

30   Haughton, p. 161.

The Empire of Lights (*L'empire des lumières*, fig. 3) is a theme that the Belgian Surrealist painter René Magritte explored many times in the 1950s, in no fewer than sixteen oil paintings and seven gouaches.[31] Although there are variants with more than one house and one streetlamp, and with the sky occupying almost three fourths of the canvas, the best-known versions are those with a single house, a single lamp and a tall tree. It seems plausible that Mahon had in mind the 1954 variant commissioned by the Musées Royaux des Beaux-Arts de Belgique. The painting shows a house with a tall tree in front of it, and part of the scene is reflected in a pond facing the building. There is light coming from a streetlamp at the centre of the painting, and from two windows on the second floor of the house, on the left, where the lights are on. The right side of the painting is dominated by darkness and the black shades of trees. Silence and peace are preponderant in the scene, but if we consider it more closely, what is most peculiar about it, is that above the house and the trees we see a bright blue *daytime* sky, scattered with fleecy white clouds. There is a sort of fracture running through the composition, because the light in the sky has no effect on the scene in the foreground. The scene in general recalls night; the sky, day. In her analysis of this work of art, Catherine Klingsöhr-Leroy astutely comments that 'Day and light collide but do not connect. They are part of the same world and yet are estranged. They are as different from one another as the states of wakefulness and sleep.'[32]

Mahon's poem inspired by Magritte is included in his "Art Notes" from *Life on Earth* (2008). The title the poet chooses "The Realm of Light" — is slightly different from that of the painting, in line with Mahon's constant tendency towards rewriting and revisions. Light is one of the main focuses of the composition, as it was in "Courtyards in Delft", but in this case the poem is about "perceptual uncertainty."[33] The first line opens with the expression "The picture shows", with the verb in the simple

---

31   Charly Herscovici et al., *Magritte Museum. Museum Guide* (Brussels: Editions Hazans, 2009), p. 142.

32   Catherine Kligsöhr-Leroy, *Surrealism* (London: Taschen, 2006), p. 68.

33   Jarniewicz, p. 146.

present indicative, followed by a list of elements that constitute the painting: "an aspen", "a house", "a lamp post", "shutters" and a "pond" (ll. 2–4). However, from the outset of the poem, the uncertainty mentioned earlier surfaces in the doubt voiced in the interrogative, "an aspen, is it" (l. 2), which anticipates the central issue of the poem, whether it is "dawn or dusk" (l. 3). The observer is trying to decode the visual image, re-encoding it in language. The result is pleasantly musical, as a consequence of the skilful use of alliteration: 'a house *c*alm and *c*lear | at *d*awn or *d*usk, a *l*amp post's yellow *l*ight | abuzz on *sh*utters and a *sh*ivering pond' (*NCP*, 300, *emphasis added*). This melodiousness emphasises the centrality of the sonic metaphor 'a light | abuzz', which gives voice to something that is mute. The description of the painting is further animated by a second metaphor, 'a shivering pond' (l. 4). These images reach beyond the limitations of the painting, while the tree and the roof are said to "aspire", to rise high, pointing upwards towards another sphere, beyond the moving clouds (l. 8). The gaze of the observer is therefore directed from the centre of the painting (with the tall tree) to the "shivering pond" below, and then unhurriedly upwards, towards the whiteness of the sky.

The second stanza moves from visual perception to deduction, as signalled by the shift from the indicative mood of the first stanza to the use of modals:

> It *must* be dusk, with the light almost gone,
> but view this picture with extreme distrust
> since what you see is the *trompe-l'oeil* of dream.
> It *might* be dusk, with the house almost dead;
> or is there somebody getting out of bed,
> the exhausted street light anxious for a rest,
> birds waking in the trees, the clouds astream
> in an invisible breeze? It *must* be dawn.
> (*NCP*, *emphasis added*)

As can be noticed, the stanza is articulated into four main 'deductions': the first, "It *must* be *dusk*", is followed by an admonishment to '*view* this picture with […] distrust'. On line 4 the same hypothesis is expressed for the second time with a greater degree of uncertainty and doubt: "It *might* be *dusk*". It should be noted that the adverb "almost" is repeated twice, in the first line where it is said that the light is "almost gone", and in the fourth line, where the house is defined as "almost dead". This lays further emphasis on the dimension of doubt, of something the observer sees, but cannot understand precisely. Line 5 of the same stanza introduces the third possibility, with the interrogative 'is there [...]?' In the closing line the observer advances a diametrically opposed hypothesis: "It *must* be *dawn*", which seems to be partly confirmed by the representation of the sky in the upper part of Magritte's painting.

The question, whether it is dusk or dawn, is left open for the reader/observer to define, and herein lies the magic of the surrealist painting Mahon has chosen for inspiration. Through Magritte's work, the poet challenges readers to 'view this picture with extreme distrust | since what you see is the *trompe-l'oeil* of dream' (ll. 2–3). The French term, literally meaning "deceives the eye", alludes to a style of painting in which objects are depicted with photographically realistic detail. Mahon, who is also a sophisticated connoisseur of photography, complicates the matter by associating this visual illusion with the dimension of dream. As Jarniewicz argues,

> 'the *trompe-l'oeil* of dream' [...] modifies the meaning of the French term so as to make it refer not to the illusion of reality (so great we do not notice this is art and we believe we are observing reality), but to the illusion of a dream [...]. [W]hen we look at the Realm (or the Empire) of Light we may suspend our disbelief and assume that we are really dreaming. (150)

What allows Magritte to achieve this effect is the polarity of darkness and brightness, the flat colour, the eerie lighting coming from one small source, and the black backdrop, which usually 'connotes something hidden.'[34] Mahon translates this oneiric dimension into words, inviting the reader/observer to linger in the

---

34   David Machin, *Introduction to Multimodal Analysis* (London: Bloomsbury, 2010), p. 61.

transitional state so dear to him — suspended between "here" and "there", day and night, dream and reality — in which his poetry finds its place *par excellence.*

Conclusion: "Too Many Poems about (Figurative) Pictures"?

In 1985, Mahon told Terence Brown he had 'written too many poems about pictures', adding that it was 'a very bad habit'.[35] Apropos this, Hugh Haughton commented that with "St. Eustace" in *Antarctica* (1986) Mahon had for the time being ended 'the "hunt" pursued in his ekphrastic poems.'[36] However, Mahon's instinctive attraction towards the visual arts persisted, compelling him to write new, exquisite "visual epiphanies", including the series "Art Notes" in *Life on Earth* (2008), of which "The Realm of Light" is also part. A possible future development of this essay will encompass an in-depth analysis of these poems, which offer fertile new ground for literary analysis, since there is still relatively little criticism available on the subject, and the artists whose work inspired the poems are as varied as George Braque or the American Edward Hopper, side by side with lesser-known names such as Anne Madden or Vivienne Roche. In more recent times, Mahon has been increasingly attracted towards abstract painting, a tendency that is evident not only in his "Art Notes", but also in his book covers after 2005, when *Harbour Lights* was published. This interest seems to go hand in hand with more frequent experiments in prose writing, rather than poetry: Mahon's *Selected Prose* (2012), for instance, includes an essay titled "Anne Madden: A Retrospective", followed by "The Mystery Intact", a series of reflections on photography — to mention but two. In even more recent times, in *Red Sails* (2014), a collection of prose excerpts that can be read as an autobiography in progress, Mahon writes about William Scott in "Pots and Pans",

---

35   Terence Brown, 'An Interview with Derek Mahon', *Poetry Ireland Review* 14 (1985), 11–19, p. 16.
36   Haughton, p. 190.

significantly choosing a reproduction of "Shapes and Shadows" (1962) for the book cover (see fig.). The same artist also features with his "Interior" (1958) on the cover of *New Selected Poems* (2016), Mahon's latest poetic enterprise. It can therefore be argued that, at least in the foreseeable future, the visual arts in their various forms will continue to nourish Mahon's creative imagination, thanks also partly to his exuberant Muse, the Irish visual artist Sarah Iremonger. Their current collaborative project on a children's book, with words by Mahon and illustrations by Iremonger, is soon to be published by The Gallery Press, and it is something that readers with an interest in the (unpredictable) relation between words and images are eagerly awaiting.

Bibliography

Alpatov, M. W., *Historia sztuki*, 2 vols. (Warszawa: Arkady, 1969).

Bergmann-Loizeaux, Elizabeth, *Twentieth-Century Poetry and the Visual Arts* (Cambridge: Cambridge University Press, 2008).

Brearton, Fran, and Alan Gillis (eds.), *The Oxford Handbook of Modern Irish Poetry* (Oxford: Oxford University Press, 2012).

Brown, Terence, 'An Interview with Derek Mahon', *Poetry Ireland Review*, 14 (1985), 11–19.

_____, 'Derek Mahon: The Poet and Painting', *Irish University Review*, Special Issue on Derek Mahon (Spring/Summer 1994), 38–50.

_____, *The Literature of Ireland. Culture and Criticism* (Cambridge: Cambridge University Press, 2010).

Carvalho Homem, Rui, "Private Relations': Selves, Poems, and Paintings – Durcan to Morrissey', in *The Oxford Handbook of Modern Irish Poetry*, ed. by Fran Brearton and Alan Gillis (Oxford: Oxford University Press, 2012), pp. 282–95.

Carson, Ciaran, *Breaking News* (Oldcastle: The Gallery Press, 2003).

Durcan, Paul, *Crazy About Women* (Dublin: The National Gallery of Ireland, 1991).

_____, *Give Me Your Hand* (London: Macmillan and National Gallery Publications, 1994).

Gombrich, E. H., *The Story of Art* (London: Phaidon, 1972).

Haughton, Hugh, *The Poetry of Derek Mahon* (Oxford: Oxford University Press, 2007).

Herscovici, Charly, et al., *Magritte Museum. Museum Guide* (Brussels: Editions Hazans, 2009).

Homer, *The Iliad*, trans. by Robert Fagles (London: Penguin, 1991).

Irish University Review, Special Issue on Derek Mahon, Spring/Summer 1994.

Jarniewicz, Jerzy, *Ekphrasis in the Poetry of Derek Mahon* (Piotrków Trybunalski: Naukowe Wydawnictwo Piotrkowskie przy Filii Uniwersytetu Jana Kochanowskiego, 2013).

Kennedy-Andrews, Elmer (ed.), *The Poetry of Derek Mahon* (Gerrards Cross: Colin Smythe, 2002).

Kligsöhr-Leroy, Catherine, *Surrealism* (London: Taschen, 2006).

Longley, Edna, *The Living Stream. Literature and Revisionism in Ireland* (Newcastle: Bloodaxe, 1994).

Longley, Michael, *Gorse Fires* (London: Secker and Warburg, 1991).

Machin, David, *Introduction to Multimodal Analysis* (London: Bloomsbury, 2010).

Mahon, Derek, *Courtyards in Delft* (Dublin: The Gallery Press, 1981).

_____, *Life on Earth* (Oldcastle: The Gallery Press, 2008).

_____, *New Collected Poems* (Oldcastle: The Gallery Press, 2011).

_____, *New Selected Poems* (Oldcastle: The Gallery Press, 2016).

_____, *Red Sails* (Oldcastle: The Gallery Press, 2014).

_____, *Selected Prose* (Oldcastle: The Gallery Press, 2012).

_____, *The Hunt by Night* (Oxford: Oxford University Press, 1982).

McLean, Janeth (ed.), *Lines of Vision. Irish Writers on Art* (London: Thames & Hudson, 2014).

Ovid, *Metamorphosis*, trans. by A. D. Melville (Oxford: Oxford University Press, 2008).

Penny, Nicholas (ed.), *Metamorphosis: Poems Inspired by Titian* (London: National Gallery Company, 2012).

Plato, *The Republic*, trans. by Desmond Lee (London: Penguin, 2007).

Reggiani, Enrico, *In attesa della vita. Introduzione alla poetica di Derek Mahon* (Milan: Vita e Pensiero, 1996).

Seree-Chaussinand, Christelle, "Bring Out Artists; Take Music, or The Calm Light of Dutch Interior Art …': Derek Mahon's Pictorial Poems', in *Interfaces: image, texte, langage* (Paris: Presses de l'Université de Bourgogne, 2010), pp. 217–30.

Sutton, Peter C., *Pieter de Hooch* (New Haven–London: Dulwich Picture Gallery, in association with Yale University Press, 1998).

Tuma, Keith, *Anthology of Twentieth-Century British and Irish Poetry* (New York: Oxford University Press, 2001).

York, Richard, 'Derek Mahon and the Visual Arts', in *The Poetry of Derek Mahon*, ed. by Elmer Kennedy-Andrews (Gerrards Cross: Colin Smythe, 2002), pp. 131–44.

A BRAND NEW STORY? FROM LITERARY CLASSIC TO GRAPHIC NOVEL: *THE PICTURE OF DORIAN GRAY* AND *DR. JEKYLL AND MR. HYDE*

Paola Della Valle
(University of Turin)

Graphic novels have increasingly featured in the scholarly practice and discourse in the past decade. Since the late 1980s they have grown considerably, both in sophistication and popularity, to the point that they have also deserved attention in higher education. Some scholars identify a decline in the dominance of exclusively text-based sources of information in modern society and exhort those involved in information literacy education to help the new generations acquire the skills and competencies needed to read through texts containing multiple modes of information, including visual texts. In their view, teachers and professional educators should provide the theoretical and practical means to form a "media literate person", that is, one who 'can decode, evaluate, analyse and produce both print and electronic media'.[1] Harris underlines that 'while few have questioned the fact that verbal and alphabetic literacies must be learned, a lack of sensitivity to (or fear of) images and visual texts has obscured the need for instruction in reading images'.[2] Among the visual media that could be profitably used in education, Jacobs has explicitly referred to comics (and by extension graphic novels) suggesting that 'by situating our thinking about comics, literacy, and education within a framework that views literacy as occurring

---

1   Steven Hoover, 'The Case for Graphic Novels', in *Communications in Information Literacy*, 5:2 (2012), p. 178. Hoover takes this definition from P. Aufderheide's report on the 1992 National Leadership Conference on Media Literacy.

2   Benjamin R. Harris, 'Visual Literacy Via Visual Means: Three Heuristics', in *Reference Services Review*, 34:2 (2006), p. 213.

in multiple modes, we can use comics to greater effectiveness in our teaching at all levels by helping us to arm students with the critical-literacy skills they need to negotiate diverse systems of meaning making'.[3]

The graphic novel can be considered as a complex and multi-layered text, as it relies on a synthesis between textual and visual information to create meaning, conveys a message or narrative, and follows a precise set of conventions which need to be decoded by readers. It is therefore particularly useful to develop "multimodal literacy", that is, the ability to understand the mechanism behind multimodal texts. The term "multimodal" is used by Cope and Kalantzis with reference to the way meaning is produced in today's globalized world:

> Meaning is made in ways that are increasingly multimodal — in which written-linguistic modes of meaning are part and parcel of visual, audio, and spatial patterns of meaning. [...] To find our way around this emerging world of meaning requires a new, multimodal literacy.[4]

Lisa Schade Eckert also encourages American teachers to include graphic novels in their literacy/literature curricula on the basis that they comply with the notion of "textual complexity" as required by CCSS.[5] American students, she adds, are often 'unsophisticated readers who are reading at "levels" far beneath that which is appropriate for their age or grade'.[6] Drawing on the works of Roland Barthes, Umberto Eco and Dorothy Parker, who 'were applying critical concepts to comics long before the

---

3   Dale Jacobs, 'More than Words: Comics as a Means of Teaching Multiple Literacies', in *English Journal*, 96:3 (January 2007), p. 21.

4   Bill Cope, Mary Kalantzis, 'Introduction' in Cope & Kalantzis (eds.) *Multiliteracies: Literacy Learning and the Design of Social Futures* (New York: Routledge, 2000), p. 5.

5   CCSS is the acronym for Common Core State Standards: the set of educational standards describing what students should know and be able to do in each subject in each grade. Since 2010 a number of US states have adopted the same standards for English and maths.

6   Lisa Schade Eckert, 'Protecting Pedagogical Choice: Theory, Graphic Novels, and Textual Complexity', *LAJM*, 29:1 (Fall 2013), p. 40.

term graphic novel became pedagogically provocative',[7] she argues that reading graphic novels does not mean looking at the illustrations that accompany a written text and is also more complex than code switching:

> Graphics add layers of signifiers to a semiotic system, and layers of complexity for the reader within a text. Instead of consisting of an unproblematic kind of "translation" from one semiotic mode to another, the images and text form a complex, interrelated semiotic system: a layered interaction of multiple semiotic systems within a text. Rather than simply adding another decoding task to enhance a text, the sequential art of a graphic novel multiplies the interpretive challenges and opportunities for analysis and interpretation.[8]

Reading a graphic novel is therefore a complex cognitive exercise that helps develop critical thinking as well as adding to information and visual literacy.

In this essay I will first trace the historical origin of the graphic novel, then I will summarize its main features and outline the technical aspects that need to be taken into account for a correct approach to this genre. Finally, I will analyse the graphic novel adaptations of two masterpieces of British literature: Wilde's *The Picture of Dorian Gray*, illustrated by I. N. J. Culbard and adapted by Ian Edginton (2008), and Stevenson's *Dr. Jekyll and Mr. Hyde*, illustrated and adapted by Andrzej Klimowski and Danusia Schejbal (2009). My aim is to decode their modalities of meaning making and apply the proper critical instruments in order to see what is lost and what is gained in the passage from original text to adaptation.

The domains of word and image have a long history of mutual migration and collaboration in literature, as testified by the past success of illustrated novels, probably the ancestors of today's graphic fictions. In tracing the evolution from illustrated novels

---

7   Schade Eckert, p. 41. She refers to R. Barthe's *The Rhetoric of Image* (1977), U. Eco's essay *The Myth of Superman* (1962), and D. Parker's letter 'A Mash Note to Crockett Johnson' published in *PM Magazine* (1943).

8   Schade Eckert, p. 42.

through comic strips and comic books up to graphic novels, Andrés Romero Jódar expresses his belief in the potentials of iconic genres, which seem to 'develop into a field directly related to literature' and show 'a complex relation to the transformation of Western culture'.[9] This conviction has been influenced by John Barth's stances on the exhaustion of the novel as a major art form and, conversely, the dynamism of the comic-book genre, as exposed in his two essays 'The Literature of Exhaustion' (1967) and 'The Literature of Replenishment' (1980). One may agree or not with this view, but there is no doubt that verbal-iconical productions are evolving steadily. The vitality of the graphic novel, in particular, is confirmed by the recent publication of the first book-length study devoted to this subject, *The Graphic Novel: An Introduction*, by Jan Baetens and Hugo Frey (2015).

Romero Jódar takes into consideration only those verbal-iconical genres that originated in the industrial production promoted by the advent of the printing press. The illustrated novel is the oldest of them. It consists of a '*closed frame written text* inside which some images (pictures, drawings...) are embedded'.[10] The meaning of an illustrated novel comes primarily from the written text, whereas the iconical aspect adds unnecessary information. Illustrations may show details that are not included in the verbal text or reinforce the content, repeating iconically what has already been uttered in words. They can also be considered as individual representations of the textual world according to one single reader: the artist. In this sense, the artist's signature somehow limits the readers' possible imaginative representations of the text. Many classics have appeared with illustrations by various artists, from the Bible to *The Divine Comedy* and *Don Quixote*.[11] There are also works originally

9   Andrés Romero Jódar, 'The Quest for a Place in Culture: The Verbal Iconical Production and the Evolution of Comic-Books towards Graphic Novels', *Estudios Ingleses de la Universidad Complutense*, 14 (2006), p. 95.

10   Romero Jódar, p. 97.

11   Among the most famous ones are Gustave Doré's illustrations of Dante's *Divine Comedy* and Cervantes' *Don Quixote* and Aubrey Beardsley's

conceived of as texts accompanied by images. Being the result of the combined effort of a writer and a specific artist, this type of illustrated novel is based on a unity that cannot be divided. Although verbal text and pictures are more closely related than in the other illustrated novels and the text cannot be actualized by new artists, the two components still do not interact.[12]

The next step in the evolution of the verbal-iconical genres is the comic strip, which started to appear in magazines and newspapers in the mid 19th century, sustained by the improvements of the printing press. It is formally made of 'one or several coordinated pictures (vignettes) usually humorous in tone and based on a slapstick effect or sudden dénouement, producing a final laughter/joke'.[13] In contrast to the illustrated novel, the iconic aspect prevails over the verbal one in terms of meaning producer. Historically, the third genre taken into consideration by Romero Jódar — comic books — began as compilations of comic strips, detached from magazines and newspapers. The first comic book worthy of note was issued in 1884: *Ally Sloper's Half Holiday* by Gilbert Daziel. A specific market developed around these works, prompting the rise of 'a new productive industry under the common name of comic-book creation'.[14] In 1954 comic books were given a formal definition by a US senate interim report on 'Comic Books and Juvenile Delinquency'. They were described as pamphlets of some 30-40 pages, including from three to five stories told in pictures with balloon captions and issued monthly, bimonthly, quarterly or sometimes as one-time publications.[15] Comic books departed from the humorous basis of the comic strip, gradually introducing other subjects related to crucial

---

illustrations of Wilde's *Salomé*.

12 Romero mentions Neil Gaiman's *Stardust* (with Charles Vess, 1997) and *The Dream Hunters* (with Yoshitaka Amano, 1999) as examples of this type of illustrated novel. Other two novels by Neil Gaiman and Dave McKean are considered by Romero as closer to graphic novel. *The Day I Swapped my Dad for Two Goldfish* (1997) and *The Wolves in the Walls* (2003). Romero Jódar, p. 98.

13 Romero Jódar, p. 99.

14 Romero Jódar, p. 100.

15 Romero Jódar, pp. 99–100.

issues of their time. It is no accident that the first superhero comic book, Superman, appeared at a time of worldwide uneasiness and social instability, one year before the outbreak of World War II in 1939. The superhero comic book has been in fact the mainstream of Anglo-American comics production up to the 1980s (after Superman, it featured Batman, Captain Marvel, Captain America, The Fantastic Four), providing a Manichean representation of the reality.[16] This uniformity in content was actually the result of the restrictions imposed by censorship. In the late 1940s an anti-comics crusade spread in the USA, due to the increasing rate of juvenile criminality. Comic books were accused of having a negative impact on adolescents because of their violent content and frequent references to sexuality. An intellectual often associated with this phenomenon is psychologist Fredric Wertham, whose articles and later extended study *The Seduction of the Innocent* (1954) influenced the public opinion and politicians, leading to the appointment of the senate committee that issued the above-mentioned report on the connection between the growing success of comics and the rise of youth delinquency. As a consequence, a self-regulation code was created in 1955, the Comics Code,[17] which was overcome only in the 1980s-90s, after comic books had increasingly become works of specific authors. This meant a 'transformation from market-oriented industry to more author-conscious productions' with authors such as Alan Moore, Art Spiegelman, and Frank Miller, to mention just a few.[18]

In the 1950s comics, however, were not always considered dangerous. The so-called "sequential art"[19] was being regularly used for educational and instructive purposes. Comics were

---

16   Romero Jódar, p. 101.
17   Jan Baetens and Hugo Frey, *The Graphic Novel: An Introduction* (Cambridge: Cambridge University Press, 2015), pp. 30–31.
18   Romero Jódar, p. 101.
19   Famous cartoonist Will Eisner (1917–2005) called comics and graphic novels "sequential art", which he described as 'a means of creative expression, a distinct discipline, an art and literary form that deals with the arrangement of pictures or images and words to narrate a story or dramatize an idea'. See W. Eisner, *Comics and Sequential Art* (Tamarac, Florida: Poorhouse Press, 1985), p. 5.

regularly published to draw younger readers into the world of classic literature. The famous *Classics Illustrated* series were an important genre of comics and they worked as a bridge toward serious literary fiction. The text-image art was also used in instruction manuals. Will Eisner (one of the future father figures of the graphic novel) worked on the illustrations of a guidebook for the American Army, concerning the utilisation of equipment. Comic strips were being used by Health Services and Park authorities to inform people on issues of safety.[20]

The 1950s were often regarded as a period of conservativism in graphic arts, but they were also the decade that produced the challenge to conservative dominance.[21] Baetens and Frey are sceptical on the impact of Pop Art's recuperation of comic strip images for the change in comics' fortune.[22] It certainly revived public interest in comics, but the two scholars believe that 'the post-Wertham resurrection of comics toward a more serious and engaging mode was probably underway before Pop Art's full ascendency. [...] Nonetheless, the Pop Art phenomenon did reposition how one can understand comics, and indeed all mass consumer products.'[23] According to Baetens and Frey, however, comics were 'changing from within'.[24] They point to the underground comix of the late 1960s as a major influence on the development and rise of the graphic novel in the late 1980s.

> What is important to recognise is that in the mid- to late 1960s, it was on university campuses [...] and in the radical districts of major urban spaces [...] that graphic narratives aimed at adults, and with little or no connection to superheroes (including pop and the post-pop variants) were first circulated, printed on the new off-set presses that facilitated self-publishing and small press endeavours. Robert Crumb,

---

20   Baetens, Frey, p. 39. *Classics Illustrated* is a comic book series featuring adaptations of literary classics such as *Moby Dick*, *Hamlet*, and *The Iliad*. Created by Albert Kanter, the series began publication in 1941 and finished its first run in 1971, producing 169 issues.
21   Baetens, Frey, p. 40.
22   Baetens, Frey, p. 41.
23   Ibid.
24   Ibid.

Gilbert Shelton, Kim Deitch, Jaxon, and Justin Green, among others, produced new amusing, sexually explicit, and often satirical strips in self-produced magazines or in supplements to student newspapers. Their work was self-conscious, sometimes quasi-autobiographical, and utterly irreverent. For them no topic was taboo.[25]

Baetens and Frey, quoting Charles Hatfield's *Alternative Comics: An Emerging Literature*, continue by asserting that 'the underground comix changed the pre-existing assumptions of what comics could achieve', both in subject and style, 'and laid the groundwork for the alternative comics and the breakthrough of the graphic novel'.[26] Autobiography, introspection and personal outlooks on life became the most common subjects. The underground community also demonstrated that 'artists could achieve success without being entangled in the formal comics industry' and comics did not have 'to be based on extended runs of serialised plots, either in a daily newspaper or weekly magazine',[27] paving the way for the longer form of the one-shot "novel".

After discussing the birth of the graphic novel as an evolution of the comic book, Romero Jódar also traces a major difference between these two genres using Mikhail Bakhtin's notion of "chronotope". The chronotope is 'the intrinsic connectedness of temporal and spatial relationships that are artistically expressed in literature'. According to the Russian formalist, the chronotope defines 'genre and generic distinctions',[28] for time is the primary category in literature and it is also the fourth dimension of space, in Einstein's terms. For example, he distinguishes three categories in the ancient Greek novel, which depend on three different chronotopes, to wit, three methods to fix time and space: the Greek Romance, the adventure novel of ordeal, and the ancient biography and autobiography. Romero Jódar associates the chronotope of the Greek Romance with the comic book and the chronotope of the

---

25   Baetens, Frey, p. 55.
26   Baetens, Frey, p. 56.
27   Ibid.
28   M. M. Bakhtin, *The Dialogic Imagination* (Austin, Texas: University of Texas Press, 1981), both quotations, p. 84 and p. 85.

Greek adventure novel with the graphic novel. In the Greek Romance and comic book characters remain essentially the same throughout the story: for all their exploits, their identity is unchanged. In fact, characters are not affected by the passing of time in comic books and their identities are static. Superman never makes decisions that would effect a turn of events in his life, like getting married. In his essay on Superman, Umberto Eco refers to comic strips as a typical product of mass literature, which is a formidable myth-making machine in today's mass society. Superman exemplifies a myth of the present. He needs to be a common man and live an ordinary life (otherwise the process of identification with the readers would not occur) but, at the same time, he must also be fixed in timeless immutability. His deeds are never seen in temporal continuity, because this would enact a representation of real time and would push Superman towards his death: he could no longer be a myth. So Superman is not given the possibility of development.[29]

By contrast, according to Romero Jódar the graphic novel relies on the chronotope of the adventure novel of ordeal, in which time 'leaves a deep and irradicable mark on the man himself as well as on his entire life.'[30] This category implies 'the metamorphosis of the character, the evolutionary process of an individual affected by the passing of time'.[31] Change is the most important element in this type. The revision of the superhero is one of the main topics of the graphic novel, which deals with themes suitable to an adult and mature readership. It can be defined a "novel in a graphic form" or, as Romero Jódar says, quoting Roger Sabin: 'lengthy comics in book form with a thematic unity'.[32] The graphic novel is a hybrid genre that uses the comics visual language and the novel literary narration. The stories narrated involve dynamic characters that develop and change, and a structural cohesion. The first graphic novel is commonly attributed to Will Eisner with *A Contact with God* (1978).

---

29 Umberto Eco, 'Il mito di Superman', in *Apocalittici e integrati* (Milan: Bompiani, 1964), p. 224.
30 Bakhtin, p. 116.
31 Romero Jódar, p. 104.
32 Romero Jódar, p. 105.

In the second section of their volume, entitled 'Forms', Baetens and Frey discuss the basic formal aspects of the graphic novel, starting from its vital properties: the panel (or frame) and the page layout.[33] The graphic novel is basically a story told by a multiplicity of panels, which are organized according to three levels or layers: the strip or tier (organized horizontally, vertically or both); the page (which can have a variety of sizes and formats); and the book (whose size and format can also vary considerably). This description is however not sufficient, because the contact between the frames is crucial. This can be sequential or more like a single picture. Panels must be read both one next to the other and all at once. The sequential organization is necessary in order to keep the story going. Non-sequential reading is inevitable, given the impossibility for the human eye to separate the panels from the page. This second type of organisation can be called "tabular" or "translinear" and aims at achieving an overall effect (for example a chromatic balance or alternation of action and stasis). Moreover, the grid-form page layout can be interrupted for aesthetic or diegetic purposes by a single-page frame or a double spread, made of a panel covering all the available space (two pages), including the margins of the book.

Baetens and Frey also underline that the relationship between the unit (image or panel) and the whole (strip, page, book) is never fixed or definitive but always shifting. Graphic novels were often serialised before being printed in book form. Furthermore, the publication business is such that between two editions formats can change quite dramatically. Graphic novels embody the notion of "differential texts" in modern multimedia society, that is, texts that exist in different material forms, with no single version as the definitive one. The migration of literary works from one form to another (the novel, verbal-iconic arts, visual arts and the cinema) may represent the cultural environment of the future.

The page layout of graphic novels can be analysed according to a system devised by Benoît Peeters and described by Baetens and

---

33   Baetens and Frey, pp. 103–187.

Frey in detail.[34] Peeters articulates a taxonomy based on the various relationships between two basic elements: narrative (the graphic novel as a storytelling) and composition (the visual patterns or tableau). Either forms can be dominant (at the automatic expense of the other) and the connection between narrative and composition can be either autonomous (no direct interaction between the two dimensions) or interdependent (both dimensions influence each other). Peteers indicates four modes of panel utilization:

1– the conventional (or regular) mode: narrative is dominant; the relationship between narrative and composition is of autonomy. This system has no visual ambition since storytelling is dominant and tends to repeat the same structure of panels/tiers independently of content, author or style. Regularity however does not mean lack of sophistication.

2– the decorative mode: visual properties are dominant; the relationship between narrative and composition is of autonomy. The narrator treats the page as a canvas, each page can have a different composition. This system is very artistic, but not the most frequent format in graphic novels, given the importance of narrative in this type of drawn literature.

3– the rhetorical mode: narrative is dominant; composition and narrative are interdependent. This is probably the most frequent mode. Panel and page, sizes and forms of the images, their distribution: all is in the service of the narrative. The narrative pre-exists and informs, selects, shapes the panel and page structures. This is probably the most frequent type in graphic novels.

4– the productive mode: visual properties are dominant, the relationship between composition and narrative is of interdependence. In this type, the organisation of the page dictates the narrative. The form of the page structure helps the author to invent a story, which becomes the consequence of a pre-existent structure.

Peeters invites to use this taxonomy in a non-doctrinarian way, remembering that the four categories are not mutually exclusive.

---

34   Benoît Peeters, "Four Conceptions of the Page" (1983). In Baetens, Frey, p. 107.

Certain panel structures obey to more than one mode and in certain cases it is not easy to distinguish between different modes. Nevertheless, this system will be of great use in the analysis of the two texts that I will take into consideration below, together with other two approaches, mentioned by Baetens and Frey. One is Thierry Groensteen's theory expounded in his *Systems of Comics*. Groensteen pays tribute to Peeters but also integrates Peeters' system with a model of analysis that takes into account the regularity or irregularity of the layout and if it is discrete (a literal translation from the French *discret*, here in the sense of non-ostentatious) or ostentatious. He then demonstrates that there is a complex interconnection between these alternatives, as regular layouts can be quite ostentatious and vice versa. A conventional, regular grid-like page layout and its "discreteness" can be dramatically disrupted each time something important takes place in the story. Moreover, a regular layout can be quite ostentatious in its fixity, which may have a great evocative power or implicate allusive references. Groensteen's theory merges with the other approach, by Charles Hatfield, in emphasising the interpretive input of the reader in addition to the strategy of the artist. In his *Alternative Comics: An Emerging Literature*, Hatfield makes a distinction between "single image" and "image-in-series", which constitute a graphic novel, whose creation results from the tension between "breakdown" (dividing a narrative into single images) and "closure" (the reverse process of reading through such images and inferring connections between them). The author's role is to organise a visual series and break down the narrative into images; the reader's task is to translate the series into a narrative sequence. Like Groensteen, Hatfield stresses the reader's position and activity as complementary to the author's.

After this excursus on the formal organisation of graphic novels, I will focus on the close analysis of two of them — *The Picture of Dorian Gray*, by Edgington and Culbard, and *Dr. Kekyll and Mr. Hyde* by Klimowski and Schejbal — using Peeters' taxonomy and the above-mentioned categories formulated by Groensteen and Hatfield. Although quite faithful to the original stories, each adaptation must enact necessary strategies of simplification of the literary texts that are however compensated and integrated by the complex visual apparatus. The original text is therefore transformed into a new interrelated semiotic system where images and words interact, and meaning is produced in different modes.

Both graphic novels are printed in a black-and-white 17x25cm book format. The role of narrative is dominant in panel structure and page layout, as expected in this form of drawn literature. Starting from *The Picture of Dorian Gray*, the authors use a "rhetorical mode" in panel utilization: narrative is dominant but interacts with graphic composition. The most common grid-form page layout consists of four or three horizontal tiers of panels, as on pages 18 and 19 (fig. 1).[35] The four-tier grid accelerates the rhythm of the narrative, illustrates action or intense dialogue, makes the plot advance. The three-tier grid, by using larger images, slows down the narrative and focalizes details. It includes close-ups on facial expressions and parts of the body, emphases on important objects, and descriptions of settings. This is a novel centred on the search of beauty, the worship of art, and the importance of sense-experience, so the reference to sight as a privileged sense is underlined by frequent close-ups on the eyes of the characters (fig. 2, p. 21). When characters expound their philosophical views there is a high density of speech in the balloons. Captions are used to convey temporal coordinates, reported speech or thought. There are also "silent" panels with no balloons or captions. They are used to stress a detail, a mood, an atmosphere or a consequence of previous actions.

Although this is the most frequent organization of the multi-panel pages, there are numerous exceptions. The irregularity of the tableau is striking and always in the service of the narrative. At one point (fig. 4, p. 85) the grid is divided into four panels of the same size: a visual effect to create a stasis. The page represents Dorian's escape to a sordid neighbourhood in search of opium. The four identical panels suggest the duration of the

---

35   Oscar Wilde, I. N. J. Culbard, Ian Edginton, *The Picture of Dorian Gray: A Graphic Novel* (London: Self Made Hero, 2008). Further page references, henceforth indicated in brackets in the text, are to this edition.

night trip on a carriage and Dorian's necessity to go to a far-away place, where nobody knows him. This is the only way for him to be free to experience any kind of sensations, without having to justify his behaviour or submit to people's moral judgement. Another irregular layout is for the "picture", given its importance in the story. It generally occupies an entire single-page frame (or covers over half a page in a double-frame page) and is displayed in its gradual degradation, reflecting Dorian's sinful life (fig. 2, p. 20; fig. 3, p. 125; fig. 5, p. 64). When Dorian first meets Sybil Vane, her image dressed in Juliet costume (fig. 6, p. 34) also occupies a large panel in a double-frame page. The big size of this image in the economy of the page reflects Sybil's importance as an actress in Dorian's imagination. Later in the story, she will never receive the same graphic attention again, a sign of Dorian's fading attention towards her, too. "Irregularity" tends therefore to be "ostentatious", in Groensteen's terms, marking changes, crucial events or relevant characters in the story.

In this graphic novel, however, panels have different sizes even within the prevalent types of grid forms (with three or four horizontal tiers of panels every page). Each tier, in fact, can include a single image or be divided into two images. Tiers can also differ in height considerably. This is typical of the rhetorical mode. The size of panels and page layout are absolutely functional to the necessities of the narrative. The complexity of Wilde's work has required many visual integrations in the graphic novel and a considerable amount of interaction between narrative and graphic composition. Moreover, the literary text is very long and the adaptation has also required some cuttings. Minor scenes and characters have been omitted, like the dinner at Lady Agatha's house in chapter III of Wilde's novel. Descriptive parts or highly philosophical dialogues have been cut out or considerably reduced. For example, chapter XI about Dorian's refined lifestyle and his search of precious objects from all over the world is basically absent. The influence of the so-called "yellow book" is not mentioned either, so Dorian's transformation into an aesthete is mainly due to Lord Henry's charismatic presence. A little amount of simplification has been necessary.

The simplification of the narrative is however compensated by particular visual effects. In the scene of the first encounter between Lord Henry Wotton and Dorian, on p. 13 (fig. 7), one of the four tiers of the grid is a very narrow strip representing a piano keyboard with Dorian's hands on it. This is Dorian's introduction to the reader, an evident allusion to his artistic sensibility: his being a fertile soil for Lord Henry's aesthetic doctrine. In Wilde's novel (at the beginning of chapter II) Dorian is first presented from the back, while he is sitting at the piano looking at music scores, but not playing. Dorian will play the piano only later in the story. The visual representation, on the other hand, anticipates a detail in a functional synthesis that illustrates the protagonist's personality but also graphically reproduces the effect of a keyboard. Another example of functional synthesis is after a few pages, when Lord Henry and Dorian move to Basil's garden. The drawings in the panels show them surrounded not only by flowers (as in Wilde's novel) but also by marble statues of young men, resembling Michelangelo's David or the Greek god Adonis (fig. 1, pp. 18–19). There is no mention of them in Wilde's text, but the graphic representation is obviously referring to Dorian as an aesthetic ideal for both Basil's painting and Henry's hedonistic philosophy. In the next chapter of Wilde's novel, Lord Henry will in fact think of him as an example of pure Greek beauty and will mention Michelangelo, too: 'Grace was his, and the white purity of boyhood, and beauty such as old Greek marbles kept for us. […] Was it not Buonarotti [*sic*] who had carved it in the coloured marbles of a sonnet-sequence?'[36]

Besides borrowing the image of Michelangelo's David from sculptural art, the graphic novel also appropriates some techniques of another visual medium: the cinema. The first conversation between Lord Henry and Dorian in Basil's garden, which inaugurates Dorian's "aesthetic education", is depicted with a four-tier grid of identical panels reproducing the zooming-

---

36 O. Wilde, *The Picture of Dorian Gray*, [1890], in *Plays, Prose Writings and Poems* (Dent, London and Melbourne: Everyman's Library, 1975), p. 100.

in of a camera movement, from a long shot to a close-up of the characters' faces (fig. 1, p. 18). The overall effect of the tabular organisation is to underline Dorian's growing interest in Lord Henry's speech and Lord Henry's growing influence on Dorian. Another example of film technique is at the end of the novel, when Dorian convinces James Vane (Sybil's brother) not to kill him thanks to his boyish appearance. Dorian argues that he is too young to be the man who caused Sybil's suicide eighteen years before. Then he stands up, walks away and slowly disappears in a typical fade-out effect of a film (fig. 8, pp. 92–93). The repetition of the same page layout, with a four-tier grid of identical panels, is "regular" but also "ostentatious" in its fixity, to use Groensteen's categories, and marks a crucial point in the novel. The readers' "closure" of these frames leads them to interpret Dorian's increasingly small figure disappearing in the background not only as a man escaping from danger but also as a person whose humanity is diminishing under the heavy burden of his corrupt soul.

The final two pages of the book juxtapose the dead Dorian — an old, twisted and hideous body devastated by evil — and the rejuvenated picture — an erect figure epitomising eternal beauty and youth. The irregular layout of two consecutive single-frame pages highlights the contrast and conveys a forceful moral ending (fig. 3, pp. 124–25).

As to the second graphic novel, the narrative is dominant and the development of the plot fully respected, even in the use of time devices like the flashbacks provided by Dr Lanyon's letter and Dr Jekyll's written confession. The first part of the novel (48 pages, approximately)[37] follows the "conventional mode" in panel utilization, that is, narrative and composition are independent. The layout of each page generally consists of a double-tier grid and each tier includes a single panel. The size of panels does not differ considerably (fig. 9, pp. 6–7). There are just very few

---

37 Stevenson, Klimowski, Schejbal, *Dr. Jekyll and Mr. Hyde* (New York and London: Sterling, 2009). Further page references, henceforth indicated in brackets in the text, are to this edition.

departures from this grid system, used for emphasis. For example, the first appearance of Mr Hyde to Mr Utterson is foregrounded by a large image that covers a single-panel page (fig. 10, p. 19). However, in the second part of the book, after Mr Utterson goes to Dr Jekyll's house on his butler's request (from p. 49 to the end, p. 121) and hears Hyde's voice coming from Jekyll's laboratory, the mode turns "rhetorical", that is, narrative and composition are in a relationship of continuous interaction. There are frequent double spreads, that is, the usual grid-form page layout is interrupted by an image that covers all the available space except for the margins of the book. These oversized images are meant to highlight crucial moments in the story, like the discovery of Hyde's body (fig. 11, pp. 58–59). Other irregular features are two consecutive and inter-connected single-panel pages, as those on pages 88 and 89 (fig. 12) to describe two parts of Hyde's body after his first transformation.

This passage from a rigid visual structure to a more flexible one, where composition serves the narrative, seems to result from a turn in the text's complexity that necessitates a wider range of graphic solutions and possibilities. If the first part of the story appears neat and ordered, the irregularity of the second part is definitely more dramatic. This also reflects Jekyll's growing physical and moral confusion, his loss of identity, his anguish for being unable to control the experiment. Somehow, the regular visual organization of the first pages reflects a world before the collapse of its certainties and unity.

Captions and balloons are used as in comic books (fig. 9, 10, 11). The authors use captions for narration and descriptions; speech balloons for dialogues, with tails indicating the speaker; and thought bubbles for the characters' thinking (cloud-like bubbles containing the text of the thought, with a chain of increasingly smaller circular bubbles leading to the character). The number of words in the balloons is generally limited. Stevenson's work is shorter and less verbose than Wilde's. Moreover, Klimowski and Schejbal's adaptation is mostly built around the action of the mystery thriller that informs the original novel. Only in the last part of the book, when Utterson reads

Jekyll's confession, speech balloons become more dense with writing: reported pieces from Jekyll's letter. Now the other aspects of Stevenson's multifaceted story arise (for example, the scientific, philosophical and moral implications) and are vigorously reinforced through the images.

The pictorial quality of this graphic novel is impressive. Some panels are real masterpieces of charcoal drawing. As the story proceeds, assuming increasingly mysterious and dramatic overtones, the drawing style becomes more and more intense: obscure and abstract in the form, and darker in the overall chromatic effect. Jekyll's moral drama is visible in the suffering expressions during his transformations (fig. 12). The images representing Jekyll and Hyde gradually become less clear, until distinctions between them are almost blurred. The last image of the novel, accompanying the final lines of Jekyll's confession and representing his eternal torment, is a highly evocative reference to Edvard Munch's famous painting: "The scream" (fig. 13). There are numerous artistic "quotations" in the authors' style. Group images (fig. 9, p. 7) are often reminiscent of Goya's famous "Pinturas Negras" (The Black Paintings) and the figure of Jekyll led by his studies 'toward the mystic and transcendental' (p. 82) recalls one of those angel-like flying figures in Chagall's paintings (fig. 14, p. 84). The striking contrast between light and shade, white and black evokes the paintings of Johan Heinrich Füssli, the visionary artist that called himself "the official painter of the Devil" and loved representing dreams and nightmares. Füssli was highly estimated by surrealist painters and considered a forerunner of expressionism. Finally, the appearance of Hyde in Utterson's dream on p. 16 (fig. 16), a disquieting figure drawing a curtain, reminds us of the geometrical figure appearing in Balthus's painting *La Chambre* and symbolizing the unconscious. All these references might derive from the formal artistic education of the authors, both coming from the Academy.[38]

---

38   Klimowski studied at the Saint Martin School of Art in London and at the Warsaw Academy of Fine Arts. Schejbal studied Fashion and Textiles at the Ealing School of Art and then stage design at the Warsaw Academy of Fine Arts.

Finally, a major iconic thread running through the book is the symbol of the double. The novel opens with a single-panel page showing a man, apparently asleep, next to a mirror reflecting a face that is not his own (fig. 15). Other mirrors appear in the novel as pieces of furniture in Jekyll's elegant house (pp. 24–25), in Hyde's apartment in Soho (p. 31), and in Jekyll's laboratory (pp. 59, 62–63, 92–93, 102). The other recurrent image utilised to suggest the theme of the double is the shadow, usually associated with Hyde. On their first encounter, Hyde's shadow appears to Utterson before his real body (fig. 10).

Klimowski and Schejbal's work is far removed from the usual drawing style of comic books and graphic novels. Their evocative artistic rendering of the story has a powerful impact on readers. Not only does it activate a non-sequential reading of every page (which stands on its own as an individual picture) and of the book (which can be overall seen as a piece of art). It also prompts a series of associations with the wider world of art, drawing on the readers' cultural "collective unconscious". The gap between the author's "breakdown" (breaking the narrative into single images) and the readers' "closure" (reading by connecting those images) is enriched with a multitude of inputs and references that go far beyond simple story-telling.

The close analysis of these graphic novel adaptations reveals complex texts that apply to the readers' imagination and cultural background and require multimodal skills to be penetrated, because their meanings are created in multiple ways. They are not just illustrations of previous "closed" texts. The personal style of the authors and the elaborate synthesis of verbal and iconic language make them original products in-between literature and art: the expression of a specific authorial voice, like that of a film director in a cult-movie or an artist in painting. Being cultural products that reflect the evolution of a society increasingly relying on iconic language for communicative purposes, they can also help us learn how to decode images. The value of the graphic novel, for children and adults alike, should therefore not be underestimated in education and the world of "high culture".

Bibliography

Baetens, Jan, 'Comic Strips and Constrained Writing' (2003), http://www. imageandnarrative.be/inarchive/graphicnovel/janbaetens_constrained.htm, accessed December 7, 2016.

Baetens, Jan, and Hugo Frey, *The Graphic Novel: An Introduction* (New York: Cambridge University Press, 2015).

Bakhtin, M. M., *The Dialogic Imagination* (Austin, Texas: University of Texas Press, 1981).

Cope, Bill, Mary Kalantzis, 'Introduction', in Cope & Kalantzis (eds.), *Multiliteracies: Literacy Learning and the Design of Social Futures* (New York: Routledge, 2000).

Eco, Umberto, *Apocalittici e integrati* (Milan: Bompiani, 2016 [1964]).

Eisner, Will, *Comics and Sequential Art* (Tamarac, Florida: Poorhouse Press, 1985).

Harris, Benjamin R., 'Visual Literacy Via Visual Means: Three Heuristics', *Reference Services Review*, 34:2 (2006), 213–221.

Hoover, Steven, 'The Case for Graphic Novels', *Communications in Information Literacy*, 5:2 (2012), 174–186.

Jacobs, Dale, 'More than Words: Comics as a Means of Teaching Multiple Literacies', *English Journal*, 96:3 (January 2007), 19–25.

Mitchell, W. J. T, 'Word and Image', in *Critical Terms for Art History*, ed. by Robert S. Nelson and Richard Shiff (Chicago: The University of Chicago Press, 2003).

Romero Jódar, Andrés, 'The Quest for a Place in Culture: The Verbal Iconical Production and the Evolution of Comic-Books towards Graphic Novels', *Estudios Ingleses de la Universidad Complutense*, 14 (2006), 93–110.

_____, 'Comic Books and Graphic Novels in their Generic Context. Towards a Definition and Classification of Narrative Iconical Texts', *Atlantis* (*Journal of Spanish Association of Anglo-American Studies*) 35:1 (June 2013), 117–35.

Schade Eckert, Lisa, 'Protecting Pedagogical Choice: Theory, Graphic Novels, and Textual Complexity', *LAJM* (*Language Arts Journal of Michigan*), 29:1 (Fall 2013), 40–3.

Schwarz, G., 'Expanding Literacies through Graphic Novels', *English Journal*, 95 (2006), 58–64.

_____, 'Media Literacy, Graphic Novels, and Social Issues', *Simile*, 7 (2007), 1–18.

Stevenson, R. L., *The Strange Case of Dr Jekyll and Mr Hyde and other stories* (Rapallo: Cideb, 1992).

_____, Andrzej Klimowski, Danusia Schejbal, *Dr. Jekyll and Mr. Hyde* (New York–London: Sterling, 2009).

Wilde, Oscar, *Plays, Prose Writings and Poems* (Dent–London–Melbourne: Everyman's Library, 1975).

Wilde, Oscar, I. N. J. Culbard, Ian Edginton, *The Picture of Dorian Gray: A Graphic Novel* (London: Self Made Hero, 2008).

Fig. 1

Fig. 2

Fig. 3

Fig. 4

Fig. 5

Fig. 6

Fig. 7

Fig. 8

Fig. 9

Fig. 10

Fig. 11

Fig. 12

Fig. 13

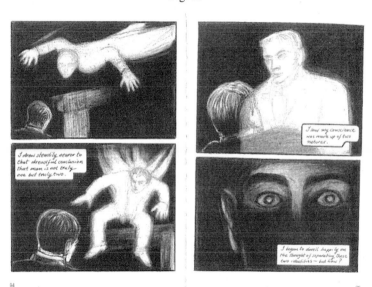

Fig. 14

Fig. 15

Fig. 16

PLAYING WITH SHADOWS: TIME, ABSENT PRESENCE, AND *THE WINTER'S TALE*

Lucia Folena
(University of Turin)

> Yet seemed it winter still, and, you away,
> As with your shadow I with these did play.[1]

> O absent presence! Stella is not here.[2]

> Writing *represents* (in every sense of the word) enjoyment.
> It plays enjoyment, renders it present and absent.[3]

> The 'world' of images does not reject the world of
> logic, quite the contrary. But it *plays* with it, which is to
> say, among other things, that it creates spaces there —
> in the sense that we speak of 'play' between the parts
> of a machine — spaces from which it draws its power,
> which offers itself there as the *power of the negative*.[4]

The Daughter of Time

The subtitle of Robert Greene's *Pandosto* (1588), the main source of *The Winter's Tale*, is *The Triumph of Time*. Since

---

1   Sonnet 98, ll. 13–14, in William Shakespeare, *The Sonnets*, ed. by J. Dover Wilson (Cambridge: Cambridge UP, 1969), p. 51. Subsequent references are to the same edition.
2   Philip Sidney, *Astrophil and Stella*, Sonnet 106, l.1, ed. by A. Pollard (London: David Stott, 1888), p. 146.
3   Jacques Derrida, *Of Grammatology* [1967], trans. by Gayatri Spivak (Baltimore: Johns Hopkins UP, 1997), p. 312. Italics in the text.
4   Georges Didi-Huberman, *Confronting Images: Questioning the Ends of a Certain History of Art*, trans. by John Goodman (University Park, Penn.: Pennsylvania State UP, 2005), [*Devant l'image: question posée aux fins d'une histoire de l'art*, 1990], p. 142. Italics in the text.

Petrarch's day[5] — and particularly in 16th-century England —,
the expression had taken on a new meaning, entering the semantic
and iconographic field of the representations of Truth. The full
title of Greene's tale explains its 'moral' by stating that in it there

> is discouvred by a pleasant Historie, that although by the meanes of
> sinister fortune, Truth may be concealed yet by Time in spight of fortune
> it is most manifestly reuealed. Pleasant for age to avoyde drowsie
> thoughts, profitable for youth to eschue other wanton pastimes, and
> bringing to both a desired content. *Temporis filia veritas.*[6]

In many of its visual and verbal renderings, the image of *Veritas filia
temporis* was a diachronic projection of another Renaissance topos,
that of *nuda Veritas* – the formula originating from Horace (*Odes*,
I.24) but the idea of embodying it in an actual icon being ascribable,
as Erwin Panofsky demonstrates in his *Studies in Iconology*,[7] to Leon
Battista Alberti's 1435–36 treatise *De pictura*. There the Florentine
humanist proposes, as a model for contemporary painters to imitate,
a lost allegorical work by the ancient Greek master Apelles entitled
Calumny, describing it on the basis of an account provided by Lucian.[8]
A misreading of the latter produces what becomes a recurrent, typical
feature of Renaissance allegories of Naked Truth: Alberti attributes
'shame', which Lucian attaches to the figure of Remorse in the same
painting, to Truth herself— 'una fanciulletta vergognosa e pudica', 'a
young girl, shameful and modest' — thus prompting an iconographic
association with the common representation of *Venus pudica*.[9] For,

---

5   In the *Trionfi* Time, the protagonist of the fifth poem, wipes out everything
     in the human world — love, chastity, death, fame — and is only defeated
     by Eternity.
6   *Pandosto: The Triumph of Time*, http://internetshakespeare.uvic.ca/
     Annex/DraftTxt/Pandosto/pandosto.html (June 2016).
7   Erwin Panofsky, *Studies in Iconology* [1939] (New York–London: Harper
     & Row, 1972), pp. 153 ff.
8   See Sara Agnoletto, 'La *Calunnia di Apelle*: recupero e riconversione ecfrastica
     del trattatello di Luciano in Occidente', *engramma*, 42, July–August 2005,
     http://www.engramma.it/eOS2/index.php?id_articolo=2288 (June 2016).
9   Alberti, *De pictura*, III.53, http://www.filosofico.net/albertidepictura.htm
     (March 2016); Eng. trans. by J. R. Spencer, *On Painting* (Westport:
     Greenwood Press, 1976), p. 91.

as Panofsky observes (159), 'while repentance implies a feeling of shame, Truth could not conceivably be "shamefaced and bashful" — were it not for her nudity'. This 'shamefaced' Truth appears clearly in one of the paintings inspired by Alberti, Botticelli's *Calumny of Apelles*, and bears a meaningful resemblance to the same painter's Venus rising from the sea.

Fig. 1. Sandro Botticelli, *La calunnia* (1496), detail. Florence, Uffizi

The nudity of Truth is obviously a representation of her simplicity and straightforwardness, and Renaissance iconologists stress the difference between this kind of univocal, unmediated self-manifestation and the constant need to dissemble and appear in borrowed wrappings that characterizes life in society, especially as far as the upper classes are concerned:

> Ignuda si rappresenta, per dinotare, che la simplicità gli è naturale, onde Euripide in Phaenissis, dice esser semplice il parlare della verità, né li fa bisogno di vane interpretationi; percioché ella per se sola è opportuna. Il medesimo dice Eschilo, & Seneca nell'epistola quinta, che la verità è semplice oratione, però si fa nuda, come habbiamo detto, & non deue hauere ornamento alcuno.[10]

---

10 Cesare Ripa, *Iconologia*, p. 499 of the 1603 version: 'She is represented naked to indicate that simplicity is natural to her. Hence Euripides in his *Phoenissae* says truth's speech to be simple and in no need of diverse

Fig. 2. Cesare Ripa, *Verità. Iconologia*, 1603 version, p. 500

The phrase *veritas filia temporis* may likewise be traced back to a Latin author — Aulus Gellius.[11] Originally, in fact, the images that the Renaissance derived from this saying took two different forms, which soon tended to reunite into one. The first had to do with a literal dis-closure — the eventual opening by Father Time of the dungeon or tomb that had previously kept the heavenly virgin hidden.

---

interpretations, since she is appropriate by herself. The same is said by Aeschylus, and by Seneca in his fifth epistle: that truth is simple speech. That is why she is drawn naked, as we said, and must wear no ornaments'. Facsimile, https://archive.org/details/iconologiaouerod00ripa (June 2016).

11   *Noctes atticae*, XII.11.7, where an unspecified earlier writer is indicated as the originator of this idea: 'Alius quidam veterum poetarum, cuius nomen mihi nunc memoriae non est, Veritatem Temporis filiam esse dixit', 'Another one of the old poets, whose name has escaped my memory at present, called Truth the daughter of Time'. Orig. and Eng. trans. by J. C. Rolfe (1927), http://penelope.uchicago.edu/Thayer/E/Roman/Texts/Gellius/home.html (June 2016).

Fig. 3. G. Whitney, *Veritas temporis filia*

The second took the notion of revelation back to its etymological meaning — the removal, again by Time, of the "veil" or covering under which his daughter had been previously forced to conceal her radiant beauty.[12]

---

12   The combination of the two is evident, for instance, in Carracci's painting (Fig. 5 below), where Truth is placed before the well where she had previously been imprisoned. The illustration above is from Geoffrey Whitney, *Choice of Emblemes*, Leyden, 1636 [1586], p. 4, under the heading *Veritas temporis filia*, and the explanatory lines run as follows: 'Three furies fell, which turne the worlde to ruthe, | Both Envie, Strife, and Slaunder, heare appeare, | In dungeon darke they longe inclosed truthe, | But Time at lengthe, did loose his daughter deare, | And setts alofte, that sacred ladie brighte, | Whoe things longe hidd, reveales, and bringes to lighte. | Thoughe strife make fier, thoughe Envie eate hir harte, | The innocent though Slaunder rente, and spoile: | Yet Time will comme, and take this ladies parte, | And breake her bandes, and bring her foes to foile. | Dispaire not then, thoughe truthe be hidden ofte, | Bycause at length, shee shall bee sett alofte'. Facsimile of the 1636 edition in the 1866 rpt., https://archive.org/details/whitneyschoicee00paragoog (Aug. 2016). A fundamental contribution to the study of the trope and icon of Truth as the Daughter of Time was provided by Fritz Saxl ('*Veritas filia temporis*', in *Philosophy and History: Essays Presented to Ernst Cassirer*, ed. by Raymond Klibansky and H. J. Paton, Oxford UP, 1938, pp. 197–222). The antagonistic third figure present in Marcolini's emblem below and in numerous later images of time revealing truth is generally identified as Calumny in Catholic contexts and often as Hypocrisy in Protestant renderings. On Father Time see also the homonymous chapter in Panofsky, pp. 69–94.

Fig. 4. Francesco Marcolini, *Veritas*. Printer's emblem, 1538,
devised in 1536 by Pietro Aretino

In the two centuries after Marcolini representations of Time
Revealing Truth were numberless, some made by illustrious
painters and sculptors such as Bronzino, Rubens, Poussin,
Bernini, and Le Moine.

Fig. 5. Annibale Carracci, *Allegory of Truth and Time*, detail (1584–85), London,
Hampton Court Royal Collection

The popularity of this image reached an apex with Giambattista
Tiepolo in the 1730s and '40s, after which, like many other
traditional allegories, it gradually disappeared from the visual arts.

Fig. 6. Giambattista Tiepolo, *La verità svelata dal tempo*, ca. 1745. Vicenza, Pinacoteca di Palazzo Chiericati

Significantly, in 16th-century England the slogan *Veritas temporis filia* was appropriated, in opposite perspectives, by the two queens who ascended the throne in the 1550s. Mary Tudor, who adopted it as her personal motto and had it inscribed in her seal and coins, aimed of course at suggesting her own embodying the definitive triumph of the true Catholic faith over her father's heretical Anglicanism. In what was undoubtedly a deliberate prologue to a swift and irreversible return to the Protestant creed, her half-sister Elizabeth let herself be greeted by the same allegory as part of the coronation ceremonies. The account of the pageants staged for her in the city on January 14th, 1559, records that there

was made artificiallye one hollowe place or cave, with doore and locke enclosed; oute of the whiche, a lyttle before the Quenes Hyghnes commynge thither, issued one personage, whose name was Tyme, apparaylled as an olde man, with a sythe in his hande, havynge wynges artificiallye made, leadinge a personage of lesser stature then himselfe, whiche was fynely and well apparaylled, all cladde in whyte silke, and directlye over her head was set her name and tytle, in Latin and Englyshe, *Temporis filia*, The Daughter of Tyme [. . .]. And on her brest was written her propre name, whiche was *Veritas*, Trueth, who helde a booke in her hande, upon the which was written, *Verbum Veritatis*, the

Woorde of Trueth. [. . . There] was cast a standynge for a childe, which should enterprete the same Pageant [. . . and] spake unto her Grace these woordes:

This olde man with the sythe, olde Father Tyme they call,
And her, his daughter Truth, which holdeth yonder boke,
Whom he out of his rocke hath brought forth to us all,
From whence for many yeres she durst not once out loke.
                                [. . .]
Now since that Time again his daughter Truth hath brought,
We trust, O worthy Quene, thou wilt this Truth embrace;
And since thou understandst the good estate and nought,
We trust wealth thou wilt plant, and barrenness displace.

But for to heale the sore, and cure that is not seene,
Which thing the boke of Truth doth teche in writing playn:
She doth present to thee the same, O worthy Quene,
For that, that words do flye, but writing doth remayn. [13]

The whole of Edmund Spenser's *Faerie Queene* (1590–96) is based on the notion of a truth which is still unavailable but exists and is waiting to manifest itself in its fullness. The first book, in particular, foregrounds this image, which surfaces directly in Prince Arthur's account of his past interrogations of Merlin:

Him oft and oft I askt in privitie
Of what loines and what lignage I did spring:
Whose aunswere bad me still assuréd bee,

---

13   'The Passage of Our Most Drad Soveraigne Lady Quene Elyzabeth
      through the Citie of London to Westminster the Daye before Her
      Coronacion', in *The Progresses and Public Processions of Queen
      Elizabeth*, ed. by John Nichols, 3 vols. (London: J. Nichols & Son, 1823),
      Vol. I, p. 50. Facs. available at https://archive.org/stream/progresses
      andpu01nichgoog#page/n104/mode/2up (Oct. 2016). Saxl synthesizes as
      follows: 'In the militant days of Henry VIII, the old motto served as a
      rally-cry of Protestantism. It was revived by Mary Tudor to sum up her
      joy in the triumph of Catholicism at her coronation. In Elizabeth's first
      public procession it reappears in a new and contrary significance. In less
      than twenty-five years it has reversed its meaning twice, and has been
      made the vehicle three times of strong emotion' (209).

That I was sonne and heire unto a king,
As time in her just terme the truth to light should bring.[14]

More importantly, Truth — absolute, theological truth as well as the historically true Church, the Protestant, in opposition to the fallacy and duplicity of Roman Catholicism — is the female protagonist of *Faerie Queene* I. Predictably enough, and reproducing another topos, her name is Una, while Duessa allegorizes her antagonist, false faith.[15] Both, for their own separate reasons — but also because of both of them not only being, but *representing* allegories —, hide their true selves under heavy clothes and cloaks. The disrobing of Duessa produces a ghastly vision:

> that witch they disaraid,
> And robd of royall robes, and purple pall,
> And ornaments that richly were displaid;
> Ne spared they to strip her naked all.
> Then when they had despoild her tire and call,
> Such as she was, their eyes might her behold,
> That her misshaped parts did them appall,
> A loathly, wrinckled hag, ill fauoured, old,
> Whose secret filth good manners biddeth not be told.
>
> [. . .]
>
> Which when the knights beheld, amazd they were,
> And wondred at so fowle deformed wight.
> Such then (said *Vna*) as she seemeth here,

---

14 I.ix.5.5–9; emphasis added. *Edmund Spenser's Poetry*, ed. by Hugh Maclean and Anne Lake Prescott (New York–London: Norton, 1993 [1968]), p. 107. Subsequent references are to the same edition, with page numbers in parentheses.

15 The allegorical construct of Oneness is of course intrinsically paradoxical, since by definition allegory, notably in its Spenserian ramifications, leads at least to a doubling, and potentially to an endless proliferation, of meanings and interpretations. The figure of revelation in Book I, as discussed below, functions as a mechanism for eventually re-compressing this plurality into a singular whole and regaining control over the semantic dispersion produced by the allegorical narrative.

> Such is the face of falshood, such the sight
> Of fowle *Duessa*, when her borrowed light
> Is laid away, and counterfesaunce knowne.
> Thus when they had the witch disrobed quight,
> And all her filthy features open showne,
> They let her goe at will, and wander wayes vnknowne.
>
> I.viii.46, 49 (105–106)

Una's final epiphany is the closest viable approximation to
the figure of *nuda veritas* — since utter nudity attributed to a
virginal figure in a narrative would appear shocking, but, more
to the point, because the conclusion of Book I proposes a further
deferral. Time has not yet accomplished its course; the male
protagonist, Redcrosse, is not yet the Saint George he knows he
will eventually be and must in the meantime spend a few more
years as a knight in the service of the Faerie Queene; a simple
betrothal must suffice to prefigure his final marriage to Truth;
the latter's full manifestation will have to wait until then. In the
interim, she is to content herself with wearing, like her counterpart
in Elizabeth's coronation pageant, a spotlessly white silken robe
the luminous simplicity of which forms a perfect frame to her
celestial features:

> As bright as doth the morning starre appeare
> Out of the East, with flaming lockes bedight,
> And to the world does bring long wished light;
> So faire and fresh that Lady shewd her selfe in sight.
>
> So faire and fresh, as freshest flowre in May;
> For she had layd her mournefull stole aside,
> And widow-like sad wimple throwne away,
> Wherewith her heauenly beautie she did hide,
> Whiles on her wearie iourney she did ride;
> And on her now a garment she did weare,
> All lilly white, withoutten spot, or pride,
> That seemd like silke and siluer wouen neare,
> But neither silke nor siluer therein did appeare.
>
> The blazing brightnesse of her beauties beame,
> And glorious light of her sunshyny face

To tell, were as to striue against the streame.
My ragged rimes are all too rude and bace,
Her heauenly lineaments for to enchace.
Ne wonder; for her owne deare loued knight,
All were she dayly with himselfe in place,
Did wonder much at her celestiall sight:
Oft had he seene her faire, but neuer so faire dight.

I.xii.21–23 (156)

As is suggested in these stanzas, such a blatant lack of closure — a structural and thematic trait of Spenser's romantic epic in its entirety — has not prevented Una from finally recovering, largely if not entirely, her postulated "plenitude". Now she is no longer just an allegory, or more generally a linguistic sign or visual image — an absence, a "figure" or a "shadow" hopelessly imprisoned in the dungeon of Representation and barred from any actual contact with Reality: a decentred object constantly pointing outside itself, elsewhere, to something which it "is" not — but has achieved a remarkable coincidence between "meaning" and "being"; now she

in her selfe-resemblance well beseene,
Did seeme, such as she was, a goodly maiden Queene.

I.xii.8.8–9 (153)

This self-centring corresponds to what iconologists recurrently represent by making their Truth hold a mirror to herself, 'pour monstrer qu'elle n'a point d'objet que soy-mesme', 'to show that she has no other object than herself'.[16] All other signs, whether linguistic or visual, invite those who observe them to divert their gazes from the images reflected in the mirrors they hold — or rather, *are* — to the concrete or abstract realities which produce those images. Truth, like a divine entity, arrests the gaze and detains it in its perfect circularity.

---

16   Cesare Ripa, *Iconologie* [Paris, 1644], French trans. by Jean Baudouin, facs. ed. by Stephen Orgel (New York–London: Garland, 1976), p. 145.

Fig. 7. *Truth Holding a Mirror to Herself*, in Ripa, *Iconologie*, Paris 1644, p. 144.

This process, however, can only come to completion when time reaches its maturity; in a global perspective, Father Time will only unveil Truth wholly and entirely at the instant of his own end, that is, when the human world enters the dimension of Eternity. The connection of the figure of Time Revealing Truth with the narrative of human history constructed by the sequence of books that composes the Christian Bible could not be more evident. Despite differences due to the canon of a certain Church — Catholic, Protestant, or Orthodox — including or excluding specific scriptural texts, the structure remains unaltered in all variants. The books which precede the last are either devoted to recounting more or less distant events of the past (Pentateuch, historical books, Gospels, Acts), or to wisdom and prophecy (from Job onwards in the Old Testament as well as the Epistles in the New). Even the prophetic books bear on a future — with regard to the moment of their coming into being — which is still located within the boundaries of historical time. The final text, contrariwise, opens up a window onto eternity, and it is appropriately known as Apocalypse or Revelation, that is, uncovering or discovery.

Consistency in allegorizing requires a narrative based on this model to remain as intrinsically unfinished — as "imperfect" —

as biblical time, and this is precisely what happens in the *Faerie Queene*. On the other hand, since the allegorical words and figures the text offers to its recipients are still "in the making", this can but result in a self-denying product, bound to render its own interpretation equally doubtful and defective, and to cast shadows on the author's creative omnipotence.[17] But self-denial is, after all, implicit in allegory as such — and ultimately in *all* language — even without considering relations with time. For an allegorical construct is, by definition and etymologically, intrinsically other than that which it represents, so much so that once its "meaning" is elucidated, it may be discarded as an empty shell; and this ontological absence is nothing else than an amplified version of the *manque-à-être* that characterizes language and semiotic systems in general. In any other object than God and Truth, "being" is inversely proportional to "signifying", inasmuch as the latter leads to transcend or traverse the object itself, which in extreme cases becomes a mere means of access to the former. At any rate, that the picture of a pipe is not a pipe — that the word "pipe" is not a pipe — has been clear to artists and writers from time immemorial, becoming a recurrent source of concern and grievance.[18] Read in this light, a conventional gesture of modesty like Spenser's avowal of inadequacy in the description of Una's splendour, 'My ragged rimes are all too rude and bace, | Her heauenly lineaments for to enchace',[19] takes on further implications. Like analogous declarations of impotence

---

17   In this perspective Spenser may be regarded as a precursor of much 17th-century literature, on the basis of a category formulated for the latter by Stanley Fish (*Self-Consuming Artifacts: The Experience of Seventeenth-Century Literature*, Berkeley–Los Angeles–London: University of California Press, 1974 [1972]).

18   See the paintings of René Magritte, in particular *La Trahison des images* (*Ceci n'est pas une pipe*), 1928–29; *La Clé des songes* (1927–30); *Le Miroir vivant* (1928); *Les Deux mystères* (1966). See also R. Magritte, 'Les Mots et les images', *La Révolution Surréaliste*, 15 Dec. 1929, pp. 32–33, http://gallica.bnf.fr/ark:/12148/bpt6k58451673/f39.image (May 2016); and M. Foucault, 'Ceci n'est pas une pipe', trans. by R. Howard, *October*, Vol. I (Spring, 1976), pp. 6–21.

19   *FQ* I.xii.23.4–5 (see above).

in the *Divine Comedy*, going beyond the "emptiness" of allegory it invests the ontological status of language as a whole and its inability to produce truth.

Figures of Delight

In the Christian history of the universe the word precedes the image, since it is the former that generates light, hence visibility, without which no image is even thinkable:

> In the beginning God created the heaven and the earth. And the earth was without form, and void; and darkness was upon the face of the deep. And the Spirit of God moved upon the face of the waters. And God said, Let there be light: and there was light. And God saw the light, that it was good: and God divided the light from the darkness.[20]

Five days later, in fact, the adventure of humankind is inaugurated by the production of images, once again announced by a verbal proclamation that seems to coincide with the creative act itself, since, in the absence of an interlocutor, it can only resound to provide the things created with form and function:

> And God said, Let us make man in our image, after our likeness: and let them have dominion over the fish of the sea, and over the fowl of the air, and over the cattle, and over all the earth, and over every creeping thing that creepeth upon the earth. So God created man in his own image, in the image of God created he him; male and female created he them. (Gen. 1.26–27).

John's Gospel goes back to this anteriority of the Word:

> In the beginning was the Word, and the Word was with God, and the Word was God.

---

20   Genesis 1.1–4, King James Version, http://quod.lib.umich.edu/cgi/k/kjv/ kjv-idx?type=DIV1&byte=1477 (July 2016). Subsequent references are to the same edition.

The Word became flesh and made his dwelling among us.[21]

In the Hebrew Bible "image" is *tselem*, "shadow, representation of substance, shade, resemblance, phantom, illusion", and the word for "likeness" is *demuth*, "shape, resemblance, similitude, similarity of features between spiritual and moral, or spiritual and physical".[22] Were the Gospels written in Hebrew, the term for "Word" in John 1 — Greek *Logos*, Latin *Verbum* — would be *Dabar*, in perfect keeping with the central role assigned to the Voice in Genesis 1. For the utterance of *dabar* produces far more than a mere series of signifying sounds and becomes itself "event" and "fulfilment" or "performance" of that which is said.[23] Hence, *dabar* represents the dream of the word that "means" and "is", or "makes be", at the same time, annulling the gap between representation and reality, "figure" and Truth.[24]

The notions of "image" and "likeness" are conveyed in the Septuagint by *eikon* and *homoiosis*,[25] in the Latin Vulgate by *imago* and *similitudo*.[26] Thus images — differently from the Biblical Word — come into existence inscribed with the interplay of presence and absence which characterizes their subsequent existence — they "are" and "are not" at the same time, just as Adam and Eve, while

---

21 John 1.1,14, King James Version, https://www.biblegateway.com/ (July 2016).

22 See http://biblehub.com/hebrew/6754.htm (July 2016); https://www.studylight.org/language-studies/hebrew-thoughts/index.cgi?a=592 (July 2016); http://www.ancient-hebrew.org/40_genesis1.html (July 2016).

23 Along with those shared with *logos* and *verbum*, *dabar* has, among others, the meanings of "command", "promise", "advice", "prophecy", "decision", "event "and "cause". See http://biblehub.com/hebrew/1697.htm (July 2016); http://www.midbar.net/blog/?p=2 (July 2016); http://www.morasha.it/riskin/riskin_d06chukkat.html (July 2016).

24 This 'full' language was imagined by numerous medieval and early modern intellectuals, notably John Milton, to be possible in the ultra-earthly context of heaven. See Lucia Folena, 'Dove fioriva l'eloquenza: Satana seduttore nel *Paradise Lost*', in *Retoriche del discorso amoroso nella letteratura in inglese*, ed. by Lucia Folena (Turin: Trauben, 2012), 119–48 (pp. 122–26).

25 Septuagint text, https://www.blueletterbible.org/lxx/gen/1/1/s_1001Septuagint (July 2016).

26 Vulgate text, http://www.vatican.va/archive/bible/nova_vulgata/documents/nova-vulgata_vt_genesis_lt.html (July 2016).

real, living human beings, bear in their physical and spiritual shapes the mark of their ontological lack, of their not being that which they re-present. And yet the self-same condition of an image being a defective replica of an unavailable original is a certification of the latter's actual presence, though in another place. Shadows and reflections in water or mirrors presuppose bodies and call them into being, as it were, while making their distance from them manifest.

The very etymology of *imago* associates the word with the notion of imitation,[27] condemning images from the start to such a status of difference and "belatedness". Even though most classical authors often use *imago* and *figura* as synonyms, the latter term — from *fingere*, originally "to form, mould, shape, forge, fashion, create"[28] — rather than the *écart* between absent original and present copy, foregrounds the interval between the maker and that which is made. Unlike an *imago*, a *figura* is not necessarily a reproduction of something already existing, but at the same time it is always and invariably a work of "art", a creation, whereas an *imago* may well have a "natural" origin, as happens with shadows and reflections in water.

Along with these, at least two other Latin terms related to the same semantic area deserve to be taken into consideration. *Signum*, in addition to a large number of other applications, most of which imply the same derivativeness as *imago*, is often used as an equivalent for the latter and for *figura*, and also means, more specifically, "statue". On the other hand, a *simulacrum* — Greek *eidolon* — does not point back to an original but takes its place: 'the simulacrum is never that which conceals the truth — it is the

---

27 See A. Ernout and A. Meillet, *Dictionnaire étymologique de la langue latine* (Paris: Klincksieck, 1994), p. 309. In the *Summa Theologiae* St Thomas Aquinas already stated: 'imago ab imitando dicitur', 'Image is derived from imitation' (1, quest. 35, art. 1, obj. 3). Orig. http://www.corpusthomisticum.org/sth1028.html; Eng. trans. http://www.sacred-texts.com/chr/aquinas/summa/sum039.htm (June 2016).

28 See the exhaustive analysis of the history of *figura* in Latin literature in Erich Auerbach, *'Figura'* [1938], in *Scenes from the Drama of European Literature*, trans. by Ralph Manheim (Minneapolis: Univ. of Minnesota Press, 1994), 11–76 (pp. 11–28).

truth which conceals that there is none. The simulacrum is true'.[29] In other terms, the 'simulacrum is not degraded copy, rather it contains a positive power which negates *both original and copy, both model and reproduction*'.[30]

An analogous distinction is at the core of Plato's devaluation of mimetic art, hopelessly entangled in a world of *eidola*, which it not only produces but re-produces, since the original it imitates is already a reduction of the real thing to a phantasm or an appearance.[31] The iconoclastic stance which contradistinguishes Hebraism and Islam and has recurrently characterized the Christian world — notably in its Puritan ramifications — is essentially due to the perception of the ease with which an *eikon* may turn into an *eidolon*, an *imago* into a *simulacrum*. Idolatry is the semiotico-moral mistake of ontologizing images, giving bodies to shadows and substances to appearances. And since, in the line of *contemptus mundi* which leads from Plato to Augustine, the whole material world is made up of appearances or *signa* of a true reality which is elsewhere, idolatry eventually coincides with the sin of *cupiditas*, the form of misdirected love which invests its objects with a "fullness" or "presence" they do not possess.[32]

---

29 'Le simulacre n'est jamais ce qui cache la vérité — c'est la vérité qui cache qu'il n'y en a pas. Le simulacre est vrai'. Jean Baudrillard, *Simulacres et simulation* (Paris: Galilée, 1981), p. 9; Eng. trans., 'Simulacra and Simulations', in *Selected Writings*, ed. by Mark Poster (Stanford: Stanford UP, 1988), 166–84 (p. 166).

30 Gilles Deleuze, 'Plato and the Simulacrum' [1969], trans. by Rosalind Krauss, *October*, Vol. 27 (Winter, 1983), 45–56 (p. 53). Italics in the text.

31 *Republic* X, 598–99, Eng. trans. by B. Jowett, http://classics.mit.edu/ Plato/republic.11.x.html (July 2016); Eng. trans. by Paul Shorey (Cambridge, Mass.: Harvard U. P.—London: Heinemann, 1969), http://www.perseus.tufts.edu/hopper/text?doc=Perseus%3Atext%3A199 9.01.0168%3Abook%3D10%3Asection%3D599a (July 2016). See Deleuze, pp. 47–51; Alan Silverman, 'Plato's Middle Period Metaphysics and Epistemology', http://plato.stanford.edu/entries/plato-metaphysics/ (July 2016).

32 See Francisco Benzoni, 'An Augustinian Understanding of Love in an Ecological Context', *Quodlibet*, Vol. 6, 3, July–September 2004, http:// www.quodlibet.net/articles/benzoni-love.shtml (Apr. 2012); Henry Chadwick, '*Frui–uti*', entry in *Augustinus-Lexicon*, Zentrum für

In the centuries which preceded the invention of modern psychology, the error of Narcissus was precisely idolatry, instead of self-love.[33] The point of Ovid's narrative in *Metamorphoses* III.339–510, according to its medieval and early modern readers, consisted in the protagonist's inability, before it was too late, to see the thing in the fountain as a mere duplicate, decentred from the tangible being which generated it. Ovid's word choice seems to support this view. While what Narcissus initially perceives is an *imago* (416–17),[34] his interpreting it as a self-standing reality capable of becoming an object of love turns it into a *simulacrum* (432), that is, a deceitful (*mendax*, 439) icon. Interestingly, his first reaction of wonder is so overwhelming as to freeze him into a marble statue ('e Pario formatum marmore signum', 419). Thus the body vanishes from the scene at both ends of the desiring gaze when the latter comes into being; in a sense, it will not reappear, its absence not even being eventually palliated by an outright metamorphosis. Rather than that, what the narrator recounts about Narcissus at the end of the story is a substitution: 'nusquam corpus erat', 'the body was nowhere', and what was found *in its place* ('pro corpore') was a flower (509–10).[35] The disembodiment of Narcissus is duplicated and amplified by that of Echo, which in fact begins before this final adventure — though she "is" still a body ('corpus adhuc [. . .] erat', 359) — when Juno severely mutilates her power of speech (356–69). After she is rejected, her misery causes her physical being to evaporate little

---

Augustinusforschung in Würzburg, 2004, www.kirchenserver.net/bwo/.../ fruiuti.htm (Apr. 2012). In a broader perspective, Owen Barfield's *Saving Appearances: A Study in Idolatry* [1957] (Middletown: Wesleyan U.P., 1988) remains very enlightening.

33   See Dante, *Paradiso* 3.10–18, where he is evoked as the one who mistook a shadow for an actual body; L. Vinge, *The Narcissus Theme in Western European Literature up to the Early 19th Century* (Lund: Gleerups, 1967).

34   More precisely, an *imago formae*, the image of a shape. The Latin original is quoted from Publio Ovidio Nasone, *Metamorfosi*, ed. by Piero Bernardini Marzolla (Turin: Einaudi, 1994 [1979]), pp. 108–16. Subsequent references are to the same edition.

35   See John Brenkman, 'Narcissus in the Text', *The Georgia Review*, 30, 2 (Summer, 1976), 293–327 (p. 326).

by little, until she is reduced to a voice and even her bones turn into rocks (393–401).[36]

Ovid's Pygmalion initially experiences a form of idolatry comparable to Narcissus', with the difference that it is he who has deliberately produced, with an art so exquisite that it denies its being art and appears as nature (X.252), the statue — *simulatus corpus* (253) or *simulacra puellae* (280) — that sets his desire alight.[37] Venus saves him from the despair of Absence by endowing the *signum* with the fullness of life. The conclusion literally reverses that of the former myth: 'corpus erat', 'it was a [real] body' (289). Narcissus is infected by the insubstantiality of his love-object to the point where he loses his own substance; Pygmalion succeeds — thanks to a divine intervention — in infusing into his artefact a "presence" equal to that which he possesses.

The Catholic tradition seems to have often regarded the separation between signs/symbols/images and their referents within the religious sphere as a disturbing fact — a temporary and escapable state of things which is occasionally susceptible of being overcome even in the world of appearances where humans are condemned to live. A very evident example of this is the doctrine of transubstantiation, with the dogma of the Real Presence through which bread and wine actually become flesh and blood. An analogous attempt to bridge the gap is attributable to the Fathers of the Church, from Tertullian onwards, who invented the figural or typological interpretation of the Scriptures, where the role of adumbrating divine truths is entrusted to factual things and living beings:

---

36 This is one of several Ovidian stories narrating the transformation of flesh into stone — the reverse of what happens to Pygmalion's masterpiece and to Hermione's effigy in *The Winter's Tale*.

37 Here the choice of *simulacrum*, as opposed to *signum*, *imago* or another synonym, may be due to this statue not pointing back to a tangible original — not attempting to reproduce the likeness of a specific woman — but endeavouring to transcend the physical world in order to attain a higher perfection.

Figural interpretation establishes a connection between two events or persons, the first of which signifies not only itself but also the second, while the second encompasses or fulfills the first. The two poles of the figure are separate in time, but both, being real events or figures, are within time, within the stream of historical life. Only the understanding of the two persons or events is a spiritual act, but this spiritual act deals with concrete events whether past, present, or future, and not with concepts or abstractions; these are quite secondary, since promise and fulfillment are real historical events, which have either happened in the incarnation of the Word, or will happen in the second coming.[38]

Thus, for instance, Moses delivering his people from Egypt is simultaneously an actual protagonist of past events and a prefiguration or foreshadowing of Christ delivering humankind from sin. By anchoring itself to historical fact, this kind of *figura*, or type, besides establishing a strong link of mutual presupposition between Old and New Testament, overcomes the intrinsic limitation of allegories — and images in general — whose "vehicles" and "tenors" are located on two irreparably distinct planes of reality. Contrary to what happened to transubstantiation, which numerous Protestant denominations, especially among the most radical ones, regarded as a variant of the idolatry attached to the worship of sacred icons and symbols, figural interpretation remained largely acceptable even from a Puritan stance;[39] it was commonly applied until the late 17th century at least. In a Catholic perspective this exegetical practice gives "body" and "presence" to that which would otherwise only re-present, reducing or annulling the gap between "being" and "meaning"; in a reformed one it foregrounds the "semiotic" nature of material reality as a whole — the fact that the latter is merely a forest or labyrinth of signs destined to disappear when the fullness of Truth manifests itself.

---

38   Auerbach, p. 53.
39   See for instance John Bunyan's self-defence for using "metaphors", i.e., allegories, in *The Pilgrim's Progress*: 'Solidity, indeed, becomes the Pen | Of him that writeth things Divine to men; | But must I needs want solidness, because | By Metaphors I speak; was not Gods Laws, | His Gospel-laws, in olden time held forth | By Types, Shadows and Metaphors?' ('The Author's *Apology* for his Book', ll. 107–12. Ed. by N. H. Keeble, Oxford, Oxford UP, 1988 [1678], p. 4).

The analogy between the figural bond and the image of Time Revealing Truth is evident. Both presuppose a diachronic process leading to the eventual disclosure, or actualisation, of something which had been there already, but in a hidden, latent, or potential form. Both function, so to speak, as embodied prophecies — conveyed through verbal or visual images rather than through declarations, but as obscure and hard to bring to light before the 'just terme', despite the support of competent interpretation, as authentic predictions.

The Power of the Negative

Absence is a central premise of the depiction of love in Elizabethan sonnet sequences. This has to do, of course, with the two principal traditions which contributed in shaping them — the literary one stemming from the Petrarchan model and the courtly philosophical one tracing back to Neoplatonism through the mediation of treatises and conduct books such as, first and foremost, Castiglione's *Courtier*. Obviously the moods generated in the loving persona by the beloved's distance — whether physical or spiritual and emotional — differ profoundly in the two traditions. In the former the poetical utterance typically vents the frustration and grief produced by the known unavailability of the love-object. The latter proclaims the bliss, the pure spiritual rapture, awaiting those who, transcending the physical and the individual, climb to the top of the stairway of love and enjoy the contemplation of the spiritual and universal.[40] Here the love-

---

40   This is how Castiglione's Pietro Bembo synthesizes the process: 'per la scala che nell'infimo grado tiene l'ombra di bellezza sensuale ascendiamo alla sublime stanzia ove abita la celeste, amabile e vera bellezza, che nei secreti penetrali di Dio sta nascosta, acciò che gli occhi profani veder non la possano; e quivi trovaremo felicissimo termine ai nostri desidèri, vero riposo nelle fatiche, certo rimedio nelle miserie, medicina saluberrima nelle infirmità, porto sicurissimo nelle turbide procelle del tempestoso mar di questa vita'. Baldassar Castiglione, *Il libro del Cortegiano*, IV. 69, ed. by Giulio Carnazzi (Milan: Rizzoli, 1994 [1987]), p. 331. In 1561 Thomas Hoby translated thus: 'let us clime up the stayers, which at the lowermost

object functions as an essential catalyst to initiate the ascent but must needs be surpassed and abandoned — like a deciphered sign or an interpreted allegory — in order for the process to be completed. In both perspectives, in sum, the beloved is always and inevitably "elsewhere".

Moreover, between the late Middle Ages and the 17th century love was almost universally believed to entail, in the process of its coming into being, the production of an image — a "double" or phantasm of the beloved which planted itself in the lover's heart, becoming an indispensable mediator of the emotional involvement.[41] From that moment onwards the lover's gaze was focussed directly on this reflection, which granted constant access to the contemplation of its source without ever lessening the awareness of its otherness from it. "Absent presence" had thus become an inescapable component of the representation of love in poetry as well as in numerous other textual and discursive productions.

Shakespeare's Sonnet 98 thematises this paradoxical condition. Petrarchan affliction and Platonic dematerialisation here concur in constructing a hyperbolic tribute to the Fair Youth, transfigured into a "place" and an Idea by the very first line, 'From you have I been absent in the spring', which reverses the usage of attributing absence to the spoken object rather than to the speaking subject ("my friend was absent" as opposed to "I was absent from my friend"), except when the latter is away from a locality ("I was absent from Rome"). Thus absence becomes a fall from the site of fullness and "being" identified with the Fair Youth into a world of signs that, however beautiful — as beautiful as spring flowers and birds' songs — can only point outside themselves, to the Presence they do not possess and yet presuppose:

---

stepp have the shadowe of sensuall beawty, to the high mansion place where the heavenlye, amiable and right beawtye dwelleth, which lyeth hid in the innermost secretes of God, least unhalowed eyes shoulde come to the syght of it: and there shall we fynde a most happye ende for our desires, true rest for oure travailes, certein remedye for myseryes, a most healthfull medycin for sickenesse, a most sure haven in the troublesome stormes of the tempestuous sea of this life' (*The Booke of the Courtyer*, http://www. luminarium.org/renascence-editions/courtier/courtier.html, March 2016).

41   See, e.g., *Cortegiano*, III.66 and IV.52.

They were but sweet, but figures of delight,
Drawn after you, you pattern of all those. (11–12)

The good season which turns even the gloomy god of melancholy into a merrymaker (4) is powerless against this metaphysical lack. No 'summer's story' can be told at the moment (7), but only a winter's tale (13), for the time of absence is still there:

HERMIONE [. . .] 'pray you sit by us,
And tell 's a tale.
MAMILLIUS Merry, or sad, shall 't be?
HERMIONE As merry as you will.
MAMILLIUS A sad tale's best for winter. I have one
Of sprites and goblins.[42]

Neither joy nor reality can be adequately staged in the half year when nature is dormant and the world suspended in the expectancy of the renewal of life and vegetation. Phantasms and nightmares invade the imagination and despondency establishes its seat in human minds and hearts. Proserpine seems lost, even though she is only hidden underground, like Truth before her "just terme"; she will manifest herself in her magnificence when cyclical time has accomplished another revolution:

And now the Goddesse Proserpine indifferently doth reigne
Above and underneath the Earth, and so doth she remaine
One halfe yeare with hir mother and the resdue with hir Feere.
Immediatly she altred is as well in outwarde cheere
As inwarde minde. For where hir looke might late before appeere
Sad even to Dis, hir countnance now is full of mirth and grace
Even like as Phebus having put the watrie cloudes to chace,
Doth shew himselfe a Conqueror with bright and shining face.[43]

---

42 *The Winter's Tale*, II.i.22–26. Ed. by J. H. P. Pafford (London: Arden, 2000 [1963]). Subsequent references are to the same edition.

43 Ovid, *Metamorphoses*, V.566–71, p. 202: 'nunc dea, regnorum numen commune duorum, | cum matre est totidem, totidem cum coniuge menses. | Vertitur extemplo facies et mentis et oris; | nam modo quae poterat Diti quoque maesta videri, | laeta deae frons est, ut sol, qui tectus aquosis | nubibus ante fuit, victis e nubibus exit'. Eng. trans. by Arthur Golding (London: W.

It seems very likely that the principal reason for Shakespeare's reversing the geography of *Pandosto* by opening and closing his play's action in Sicilia, instead of Bohemia, has to do with this mythical subtext — as extraneous to Greene's narrative, like the whole game of absence/presence, as it is fundamental here — which requires the final summer of plenitude brought about by the retrieval of Perdita and Hermione to be set in a land graced by the sun and a luxuriant flora, while the sixteen-year transition through winter is more appropriately placed in the cold climate of an imaginary Bohemia. Furthermore, it is precisely in Sicily that in Ovid's story the abduction of Proserpine by Dis, the god of the underworld, takes place.

Another major difference between this comedy and the novella that inspired it resides in Shakespeare's choice to make Time itself a character, taking Greene's generic and somewhat trite subtitle back to its philosophical implications. Time, designated as Chorus in the dramatis personae, takes the stage in IV.i with a monologue which occupies the whole scene and addresses the audience directly. In appearance he does not say anything particularly significant and is basically there to apologize for the play breaking the pseudo-Aristotelian theatrical convention of the unity of time by 'slid[ing] | O'er sixteen years, and leav[ing] the growth untried | Of that wide gap' (5–7). In fact, he is an essential agent of the transformations that the dramatic world of *The Winter's Tale* undergoes to attain the final epiphany, which requires a long and complex development. Besides, he is a perfect embodiment of the figure of the Discloser. Some kind of final revelation or recognition is indeed presupposed by many contemporary narrative as well as dramatic romances, but in this case, along with the coming to light of *the truth about* one or more of the characters involved, what is eventually unearthed, on one level, is *Truth itself* — absolute truth without qualifications.

In *Pandosto* the wronged queen, Bellaria, actually dies on hearing about her young son's sudden decease just after the

Seres, 1567), http://www.perseus.tufts.edu/hopper/text?doc=Perseus%3Ate
xt%3A1999.02.0074%3Abook%3D5%3Acard%3D487 (May 2015).

Oracle has proclaimed her innocence and a happy dénouement seems at hand despite the loss of her baby daughter. In *The Winter's Tale* Hermione's death, made known to Leontes and the courtiers by Paulina (III.ii.172–207), is in fact only the inaugural moment of a sixteen-year dormancy — the winter of absence — which is definitively concluded, after the lost child, Perdita, has been reinstated in her place and her marriage to prince Florizel enthusiastically welcomed by the two fathers, by the prodigy of the statue coming to life. In order for the metamorphosis to take place, solemn words have to be uttered and music must resound:

> PAULINA Music, awake her; strike! [*Music*]
> 'Tis time; descend, be stone no more; approach;
> Strike all that look upon with marvel. Come!
> I'll fill your grave up; stir, nay, come away:
> Bequeath to death your numbness; for from him
> Dear life redeems you. You perceive she stirs: [*Hermione comes down*]
> Start not; her actions shall be holy as
> You hear my spell is lawful. (V.iii.98–105)

Paulina's 'spell' thus shapes itself as *dabar*, the word that acts and "makes be", giving bodily existence and tangible presence to what was previously a mere re-presentation, the marker of an emptiness. Another instance of *dabar* in the play is proposed by the Oracle (III.ii.132–35), whose statement, like all prophecies awaiting their fulfilment, offers a clear example of the role of Time in the complete manifestation of Truth.[44]

Hermione, lost and found like her daughter Perdita, is at the same time Ceres, the bereft mother and universal civilizer,[45] and

---

44   Leonard Barkan establishes a correlation between oracle and statue: 'the appearance of the statue forms part of the same mysterious level in the play as the oracle: both are hidden from the audience (though in different ways), and both are connected to resolutions in the affairs of men that seem beyond their individual action. The statue itself appears in a kind of temple, and the events are described in terms of magic: both belong in the historical milieu of statues that come to life'. '"Living Sculptures": Ovid, Michelangelo, and *The Winter's Tale*', *ELH*, 48, 4 (Winter, 1981), 639–667 (p. 658).

45   In beginning her account of the loss and retrieval of Proserpine, the muse Calliope celebrates Ceres for teaching humans agriculture and being the

her child Proserpine in whose absence the physical world suffers the implacable harshness of an endless winter. Only when she returns to her original seat will the good season come to full bloom and the disorder and violence of the human community give way to gentler social practices. In sum, she is an incarnation of Truth, seen not, or not only, as a discursive condition or as the correspondence between an object and something external — "truthfulness" or "truth to . . ." — but as the metaphysical point of arrival of the unstoppable regression of signs, figures and shadows towards the origin of Being. As Una at the end of the first book of the *Faerie Queene* discards the heavy, mournful coverings which concealed her beauty, Hermione here eventually displays herself 'such as she was' — no longer under the borrowed semblance of a stone effigy. Time has let her remain hidden for sixteen years and now, in revealing her, he also manifests himself, for both statue and living body bear the inscriptions of his presence and power:

> LEONTES   [. . .]   But yet, Paulina,
> Hermione was not so much wrinkled, nothing
> So aged as this seems.
> POLIXENES   O, not by much.
> PAULINA So much the more our carver's excellence,
> Which lets go by some sixteen years and makes her
> As she lived now. (V.iii.27–32)

This writing on image and flesh, however illegible it may appear, is a piece of historiography — the chronicle of the interval between Hermione's supposed death and her comeback. She thus bears engraved on herself the entirety of her past existence, including the long phase of latency, which no further miracle has enabled her to 'slide o'er'. Like the spoken word that turns image into flesh in this final scene of the play, writing is an indispensable supplement to the visual, which, for all its immediacy and evocativeness, is largely immersed in the present, lifted out of the diachronic dimension and hence dispossessed of

---

first to provide them with the laws indispensable to lead a peaceful existence after the fall from the golden age (*Metamorphoses* V.341–43).

the mutability and the metamorphic potential intrinsic in corporal life. Paintings and sculptures require titles and captions which place them in appropriate contexts. Conversely, images need to prop up words by endowing them with an at least surrogate component of "presence" — the illusion that what is spoken about is actually there before the spectators' eyes.[46] And this is precisely what drama in general, and Shakespeare's drama in particular, with the self-awareness it displays, is all about.[47]

The rapport between actor and character, and, more in general, the connection between the fictive world created on stage and that which exists — or existed at a given moment in the past — outside it implies something else than the mere link between a "figure" or "shadow" and the "truth" that generates and validates it. Living beings can be images, as happens when they play other people's roles, but nevertheless they remain placed on the same level of "being" as the "actual" individuals they impersonate. Rather than a parallel with the figural bond — since no shortening of the distance from the Represented by virtue of time passing may be envisaged for an actor — this would suggest a similarity with the Biblical mirroring between the human creatures and their creator, were it not for the fact that in this case the creation involves only the superimposition of a signifying aspect on pre-existent, self-standing entities, and that the relationship it presupposes, rather than bilateral, is triangular, since what is reflected is not, or not primarily, the creator's face but a further reality.

---

46 In reference to words and images calling for mutual support, see for example Figs. 2, 3 and 7 above, as well as the whole tradition of emblem books, and that of "shaped" or "painted" poems such as George Herbert's 'The Altar' and 'Easter Wings'. A particularly enlightening and very ample study on this issue is Giovanni Pozzi's *La parola dipinta* (Milan: Adelphi, 1981).

47 In discussing V.ii, where the dialogues have the primary function of offering a synthetic account of numerous events that have taken place off-scene, Barkan comments: 'By withholding dramatic three-dimensionality Shakespeare is preparing us for a scene in which both three dimensional media of sculpture and drama come into their own. The speech-without-drama of this scene is contrasted by the statue-with-silence of the following scene. The verbal without the visual is empty, while the visual without the verbal is frozen. Only Shakespeare's medium can effect the marriage'.

The art of the playwright, at any rate, is akin to magic, as Shakespeare suggests repeatedly in *The Tempest* — where his "face" is indeed reflected in that of his protagonist Prospero — and in this sense it has a remarkable affinity not only with Paulina's conjuring but with the exceptional gift ascribed to Giulio Romano, the supposed author of Hermione's statue,

> a piece many years in doing and now newly performed by that rare Italian master, Julio Romano, who, had he himself eternity and could put breath into his work, would beguile Nature of her custom, so perfectly he is her ape; he so near to Hermione hath done Hermione that they say one would speak to her and stand in hope of answer. (V.ii.94–101)

As scholars have stressed recurrently, the choice of Giulio Romano, who is not remembered as a sculptor but as a first-rate painter and architect and a pioneer of mannerism, is probably due to the epitaph that Giorgio Vasari, in the first edition of his *Lives* (1550), records as having been inscribed on his tomb:

> VIDEBAT IVPPITER CORPORA SCVLPTA PICTAQVE
> SPIRARE, ET AEDES MORTALIVM AEQVARIER COELO
> IVLII VIRTVTE ROMANI. TVNC IRATVS,
> CONCILIO DIVORVM OMNIVM VOCATO,
> ILLVM E TERRIS SVSTVLIT, QVOD PATI NEQVIRET
> VINCI AVT AEQVARI AB HOMINE TERRIGENA.[48]

In this hypothetical epitaph, Giulio, in sum, embodies the myth of the artist who has appropriated the gods' power of creation, the only force capable of insufflating human shapes fashioned out of

---

48 'Jupiter saw sculpted and painted bodies breathe and mortals' buildings equal those in heaven thanks to the art of Giulio Romano. Then, in anger, having called all the gods to council, he removed him from the earth, because he could not bear to be surpassed or equalled by an earthly man'. Vasari, 'Vita di Giulio Romano, pittore et architetto', in *Le vite de' più eccellenti architetti, pittori, et scultori italiani* (Florence: Lorenzo Torrentino, 1550), https://it.wikisource.org/wiki/Le_vite_de%27_pi%C3%B9_eccellenti_pittori,_scultori_e_architettori_(1550)/Giulio_Romano (Sep. 2016). The revised edition (Florence: Giunti, 1568) suppresses these lines.

stone or drawn on coloured surfaces with the breath of life. His art is such that it reduces or annuls the distance between "meaning" and "being", "figure" and "truth", endowing with Presence that which would normally be condemned to remain an empty sign. The Third Gentleman who introduces him and his statue to his interlocutors in *The Winter's Tale* is remarkably less hyperbolic, however admiring, and denies him actual superhuman faculties. This artist, notwithstanding his excellence, is just a mortal, with no access to either eternity or the divine prerogative of giving life to inanimate matter. One is led to wonder whether these words may contain an allusion to a famous though somewhat obscure painting by Giulio, *The Allegory of Immortality*, made in Mantua in the 1520s. But the principal analogy between Romano's work and the statue of Hermione in Shakespeare's play might perhaps be offered by a little picture that a majority of experts attribute to the Italian artist — a work known as *Ceres, or Abundance*. Executed in 1516 for Bernardo Dovizi, cardinal Bibbiena — which explains the choice of a figure of abundance or *dovizia* and the presence of six eaves of wheat, the cardinal's emblem, in the deity's cornucopia — this panel was originally the wooden cover of a small devotional painting ascribable to the same hand and representing the Holy Family.[49] That the inscription at the bottom refers to Raphael as the author simply indicates that the two images were produced in the great master's atelier, and possibly under his direct supervision. That was where Giulio Romano — who was probably only seventeen in 1516 — was perfecting his skills[50] before moving to Mantua in 1524 to work for Duke Federico Gonzaga, for whom he created a number of memorable architectural and pictorial masterpieces, and notably erected and decorated the splendid Palazzo Te.

---

49 Basic information on this painting is provided by the Atlas of the Louvre at http://cartelfr.louvre.fr/cartelfr/visite?srv=car_not_frame& idNotice=13854 (Aug. 2016). See also https://fr.wikipedia.org/wiki/ C%C3%A9r%C3%A8s_(Rapha%C3%ABl) (Aug. 2016).

50 He inherited Raphael's studio in 1520 when the master died.

Fig. 8 Giulio Romano (att.), *Cérès ou L'Abondance* (ca. 1516),
oil on walnut panel. Paris, Musée du Louvre.

Though no sculptures by Giulio are known, this panel *represents*
a sculpture.[51] It is placed in a niche within the close-up of a palace
wall made into a *trompe-l'œil* by the impossibility of envisioning
the complete architectural structure to which it belongs and its
location. The subject seems as relevant as the choice of featuring
a statue instead of its hypothetical original, since, as was stressed
above, Ceres is at least indirectly evoked, in association with the
queen coming back to life, at the end of *The Winter's Tale*. In
addition, this female body is covered only by a thin veil that,
instead of hiding it, enhances its harmonic proportions, calling to
mind the figure of Truth and the idea of Revelation in the tradition
which the first book of the *Faerie Queene* also appeals to.

But the most fascinating thing about this painting is the combination
of the *trompe-l'œil* which frames the effigy of the goddess and the fact

---

51 The figure of Ceres might be modelled on an actual classical statue known
    as the *Aphrodite of Este*, originally in the possession of the Gonzagas and
    placed with other ancient sculptures in the *Loggia dei marmi* of Mantua's
    Ducal Palace by Giulio when he redecorated it. The *Aphrodite* is now in
    Vienna's Kunsthistorisches Museum.

that the latter is "twice removed" from reality — not being an image but *the image of an image*. The *trompe-l'œil* produces the illusion of a three-dimensional scene located in the same physical universe whence the spectator observes it; such an illusion is however contextually shattered by the evident, self-declared representational nature of the object offered to the gaze — an artefact, not a living being. And then one reminds oneself that the *trompe-l'œil* is, likewise, the pictorial reproduction of an artefact — the detail of a magnificent building. Human art, painting, duplicates human art, sculpture and architecture.

Following Magritte, one would be tempted to complete the picture with a caption, "This is not a statue",[52] which, by another coincidence, would also befit Hermione's staged effigy in *The Winter's Tale*, the pivot of a similar series of removals. For what Shakespeare's audience witnesses at that point is an actor playing, rather than directly a dramatic character — a figure —, the manufactured, sculptural imitation of that character — a figure's figure. From an intra-dramatic perspective, moreover, when enacting the statue Hermione is impersonating *herself* (through the mediation of her own image). That is, she is at the same time splitting her identity into representing "shadow" and represented "truth" — a dispersion reminiscent of allegorical doubling — and reconstructing her unity by turning herself into a mirror showing, not the replica of another being, as is the case with actors, but only and exclusively her own. Thus it is even before recovering her full bodily existence that, like Spenser's Una, she "seems such as she is", enclosed in the circularity characterizing that which "has no other object than itself". And if such a *mise en abyme* were not sufficiently mystifying, one might choose to consider the further level of complexity which the gender of the individual performing the role of the beautiful queen added to it in Shakespeare's day.

Reality disappears in these games of mutual reflections, or turns into the evanescent mirage of a faraway referent, so distant that one starts wondering if it has ever actually existed. Absent presence: *imagines nudas tenemus*.

---

52   Just as the statue itself, if it existed, might go under the heading "This is not Ceres".

Works Cited

Primary Sources

Alberti, Leon Battista, *De pictura*, http://www.filosofico.net/albertidepictura. htm (March 2016).
_____, *On Painting*, trans. by J. R. Spencer (Westport: Greenwood Press, 1976).
Aquinas, St Thomas, *Summa theologiae*, Latin text, http://www. corpusthomisticum.org/sth1028.html (June 2016).
_____, *Summa theologiae*, Eng. trans. http://www.sacred-texts.com/chr/aquinas/summa/sum039.htm (June 2016).
Aulus Gellius, *Noctes atticae*. Orig. and Eng. trans. by J. C. Rolfe (1927), http://penelope.uchicago.edu/Thayer/E/Roman/Texts/Gellius/home.html (June 2016).
Bible, Septuagint, https://www.blueletterbible.org/lxx/gen/1/1/s_1001 Septuagint (July 2016).
_____, Latin Vulgate, http://www.vatican.va/archive/bible/ nova_vulgata/documents/nova-vulgata_vt_genesis_lt.html (July 2016).
_____, King James, https://www.biblegateway.com/ (July 2016).
Bunyan, John, *The Pilgrim's Progress* [1678], ed. by N. H. Keeble (Oxford: Oxford UP, 1988).
Castiglione, Baldassar, *Il libro del Cortegiano*, ed. by Giulio Carnazzi (Milan: Rizzoli, 1994 [1987]).
_____, *The Booke of the Courtyer*, Eng. trans. by Thomas Hoby, http://www.luminarium.org/renascence-editions/courtier/courtier. html (March 2016).
Greene, Robert, *Pandosto: The Triumph of Time*, http://internetshakespeare. uvic.ca/Annex/DraftTxt/Pandosto/pandosto.html, (June 2016).
Nichols, John (ed.), *The Progresses and Public Processions of Queen Elizabeth*, 3 vols. (London: J. Nichols & Son, 1823). Facsimile, https://archive.org/ stream/progressesandpu01nichgoog#page/n104/mode/2up (Oct. 2016).
Ovid (Publius Ovidius Naso), *Metamorfosi*, ed. by Piero Bernardini Marzolla (Turin: Einaudi, 1994 [1979]).
_____, *Metamorphoses*, Eng. trans. by Arthur Golding (London: W. Seres, 1567), http://www.perseus.tufts.edu/hopper/text?doc=P erseus%3Atext%3A1999.02.0074%3Abook%3D5%3Acard%3D487 (May 2015).
Plato, *Republic*, Eng. trans. by B. Jowett, http://classics.mit.edu/Plato/ republic.11.x.html (July 2016).
____, Eng. trans. by Paul Shorey (Cambridge, Mass.: Harvard UP-London: Heinemann, 1969), http://www.perseus.tufts.edu/hopper/text?doc=Perseus%3Atext%3A1999. 01.0168%3Abook%3D10%3Asection%3D599a (July 2016).

Ripa, Cesare, *Iconologia*, 1603 version. Facsimile, https://archive.org/details/iconologiaouerod00ripa (June 2016).

_____, *Iconologie*, Paris 1644, French trans. by Jean Baudouin; facs. ed. by Stephen Orgel (New York–London: Garland, 1976).

Shakespeare, William, *The Sonnets*, ed. by J. Dover Wilson (Cambridge: Cambridge UP, 1969).

_____, *The Winter's Tale*, ed. by J. H. P. Pafford (London: Arden, 2000 [1963]).

Sidney, Philip, *Astrophil and Stella*, ed. by A. Pollard (London: David Stott, 1888).

Spenser, Edmund, *Poetry*, ed. by Hugh Maclean and Anne Lake Prescott (New York–London: Norton, 1993 [1968]).

Vasari, Giorgio, 'Vita di Giulio Romano, pittore et architetto', in *Le vite de' più eccellenti architetti, pittori, et scultori italiani* (Florence: Lorenzo Torrentino, 1550; revised ed., Florence: Giunti, 1568), https://it.wikisource.org/wiki/Le_vite_de%27_pi%C3%B9_eccellenti_pittori,_scultori_e_architettori_(1550)/Giulio_Romano (Sep. 2016).

Whitney, Geoffrey, *Choice of Emblems* [1586], 1866 rpt. of the 1636 Leyden edition, https://archive.org/details/whitneyschoicee00paragoog (Aug. 2016).

Secondary Sources

Agnoletto, Sara, 'La *Calunnia di Apelle*: recupero e riconversione ecfrastica del trattatello di Luciano in Occidente', *engramma*, 42, July–August 2005, http://www.engramma.it/eOS2/index.php?id_articolo=2288 (June 2016).

Auerbach, Erich, 'Figura' [1938], in *Scenes from the Drama of European Literature*, trans. by Ralph Manheim (Minneapolis: Univ. of Minnesota Press, 1994), 11–76.

Barfield, Owen, *Saving the Appearances: A Study in Idolatry* [1957] (Middletown: Wesleyan UP, 1988).

Barkan, Leonard, '"Living Sculptures": Ovid, Michelangelo, and *The Winter's Tale'*, *ELH*, 48, 4 (Winter, 1981), 639–667.

Baudrillard, Jean, *Simulacres et simulation* (Paris: Galilée, 1981).

_____, 'Simulacra and Simulations', in *Selected Writings*, ed. by Mark Poster (Stanford: Stanford UP, 1988), 166–84.

Benzoni, Francisco, 'An Augustinian Understanding of Love in an Ecological Context', *Quodlibet*, 6, 3, July–September 2004, http://www.quodlibet.net/articles/benzoni-love.shtml (Apr. 2012).

Brenkman, John, 'Narcissus in the Text', *The Georgia Review*, 30, 2 (Summer, 1976), 293–327.

Chadwick, Henry, '*Frui–uti*', entry in *Augustinus-Lexicon*, Zentrum für Augustinusforschung in Würzburg, 2004, www.kirchenserver.net/bwo/.../fruiuti.htm (Apr. 2012).

Deleuze, Gilles, 'Plato and the Simulacrum' [1969], trans. by Rosalind Krauss, *October*, 27 (Winter, 1983), 45–56.

Derrida, Jacques, *Of Grammatology* [1967], trans. by Gayatri Spivak (Baltimore: Johns Hopkins UP, 1997).

Didi-Huberman, Georges, *Confronting Images: Questioning the Ends of a Certain History of Art* [*Devant l'image: question posée aux fins d'une histoire de l'art*, 1990], trans. by John Goodman (University Park, Penn.: The Pennsylvania State UP, 2005).

Ernout, Alfred, and Alfred Meillet, *Dictionnaire étymologique de la langue latine* (Paris: Klincksieck, 1994 [1932]).

Fish, Stanley, *Self-Consuming Artifacts: The Experience of Seventeenth-Century Literature* (Berkeley–Los Angeles–London: University of California Press, 1974 [1972]).

Folena, Lucia, 'Dove fioriva l'eloquenza: Satana seduttore nel *Paradise Lost*', in *Retoriche del discorso amoroso nella letteratura in inglese*, ed. by Lucia Folena (Torino: Trauben, 2012), 119–48.

Foucault, Michel, *Ceci n'est pas une pipe*, trans. by R. Howard, *October*, I (Spring, 1976), 6–21.

Magritte, René, 'Les Mots et les images', *La Révolution Surréaliste*, 15 Dec. 1929, 32–33, http://gallica.bnf.fr/ark:/12148/bpt6k58451673/f39.image (May 2016).

Panofsky, Erwin, *Studies in Iconology* [1939] (New York–London: Harper & Row, 1972).

Pozzi, Giovanni, *La parola dipinta* (Milan: Adelphi, 1981).

Saxl, Fritz, '*Veritas filia temporis*', in *Philosophy and History: Essays Presented to Ernst Cassirer*, ed. by Raymond Klibansky and H. J. Paton (Oxford: Oxford UP, 1938), 197–222.

Silverman, Alan, 'Plato's Middle Period Metaphysics and Epistemology', http://plato.stanford.edu/entries/plato-metaphysics/ (July 2016).

Vinge, Louise, *The Narcissus Theme in Western European Literature up to the Early 19th Century* (Lund: Gleerups, 1967).

Web Resources

Cérès ou L'Abondance
http://cartelfr.louvre.fr/cartelfr/visite?srv=car_not_frame&idNotice=13854 (Aug. 2016).
https://fr.wikipedia.org/wiki/C%C3%A9r%C3%A8s_(Rapha%C3%ABl) (Aug. 2016).

Dabar
http://biblehub.com/hebrew/1697.htm (July 2016).
http://www.midbar.net/blog/?p=2 (July 2016).
http://www.morasha.it/riskin/riskin_d06chukkat.html (July 2016).

Plato, *Republic*
http://www.perseus.tufts.edu/hopper/text?doc=Perseus%3Atext%3A1999.01.
    0168%3Abook%3D10%3Asection%3D599a (July 2016).

Tselem
http://biblehub.com/hebrew/6754.htm (July 2016).
https://www.studylight.org/language-studies/hebrew-thoughts/index.
    cgi?a=592 (July 2016).
http://www.ancient-hebrew.org/40_genesis1.html (July 2016).

THE USE OF ANIMAL IMAGERY
IN TED HUGHES'S ANIMAL POEMS

Pier Paolo Piciucco
(University of Turin)

It is indeed remarkable that Ted Hughes, the poet who has so impressively written about animals and the animal world in the 20th century, was at the same time so fond of fishing as to deserve, according to a critic's humorous definition, the title of 'evangelist of fishing.'[1] Nor should one come to the hurried conclusion that Hughes was incoherent about his ways of conceiving art. On the contrary, Ted Hughes fostered an impressively vivid and dramatic visionary universe that is in line with his inclinations and interests in his everyday life. However, his perspective can reasonably be said to be quite different from the average view, so that his thought has been at times misconstrued.

Considerations about his artistic output apart, there has been little doubt about Hughes's fondness for animals in general. It is not a secret in fact that he was always captivated — or as he himself writes in *The Jaguar* 'mesmerized'[2] — by animals for their aptitude to manifest a particular form of wild energy that he always found irresistible. '[M]y interest in animals began when I began,'[3] overtly claims the poet in a book that collects a series of reflections and suggestions for students about the ways in which a poet follows the path of imagination towards the process of creative writing. Nevertheless, what at the beginning he simply calls 'interest' evolves into a major concern for him, a force he

---

1   Mark Wormald, 'Fishing for Ted', in *Ted Hughes: From Cambridge to Collected*, ed. by Mark Wormald, Neil Roberts, Terry Gifford (Basingstoke: Palgrave Macmillan, 2013), p. 119.
2   Ted Hughes, *Collected Poems*, ed. by Paul Keegan (London: Faber & Faber, 2003), p. 19.
3   Ted Hughes, *Poetry in the Making* (London: Faber & Faber, 1989), p. 15.

seeks direct identification with and that therefore develops into more than a mere passion. An anthropologist, a poet, an initiate into the world of magic practices and, essentially, a human being, Ted Hughes gradually steps into the animal world — that in his case may be said to be an instinctive dimension as well as, and most importantly, a personal projection — and strives to find identification with it. He mirrors himself in animals and studies them in order to spot common elements enabling him to intersect the two distinct natures: his human spirit and the animal soul. The material proof of his relentless pursuit of a common thread connecting man to animal is a striking element in his literary production: language. To an interviewer, he once explained that

> Since I spent my first seventeen or eighteen years constantly thinking about [animals] more or less, they became a language — a symbolic language which is also the language of my whole life. It was... part of the machinery of my mind from the beginning. They are a way of connecting all my deepest feelings together.[4]

And, needless to say, language — or the elaborate process that Danny O'Connor aptly calls 'Hughes's translation of animals into language'[5] — plays a pivotal role in Hughes's poems dealing with animal creatures. Even though it is hardly recognizable for a fixed register, this poetic voice has an amazing evocative power — and consequently it was criticized by some readers because of its excessive dramatic resonance — a passionate musicality and rhythm (particularly evident when recited aloud), an elaborate wording often playing on simultaneous levels of meaning, a loose sentence structure and a piquant, effective imagery. The resulting phrasing is a balanced mixture combining rational control with sharp and piercing animal instinct. A typical reader's reaction to the poems may also swing between tenderness and horror within a few lines. Gifford and Roberts are clearly not overstating its

---

4   Drue Heinz, 'Ted Hughes: The Art of Poetry LXXI', *Paris Review*, 134
     (1995), p. 81.
5   Danny O'Connor, *Ted Hughes and Trauma. Burning the Foxes*
     (Basingstoke: Palgrave Macmillan, 2016), p. 4.

intensity when they declare that in Ted Hughes's hands 'our language is both familiar and different from anything we had thought possible.'[6] Likewise, they reveal perceptiveness when they stress how it is the elaborate outcome of a complex work blending a number of distinct discursive levels together. 'Rhythm, syntax, imagery and repetition work together,'[7] they appropriately claim. It is therefore essential to analyse the language employed by Hughes in the animal poems in strict relation with the topic of the poems, because one of the main reasons of its recognizable and suggestive pathos lies in the interrelatedness of form and content.

What exactly Ted Hughes found alluring in animals, and why animal instinct and nature exerted such a magnetic attraction on him, has already been the subject of studies by a number of different scholars so that the present analysis cannot claim to offer an original interpretation to the case. Nonetheless, while other commentators have generally suggested a single explanation to the issue, sometimes offering very elaborate and sophisticated theories, I believe that Ted Hughes's intellectual proclivities, his cultural orientations and his commanding personality, all concur to offer an extremely complex picture of his captivating fascination for the animal world in general. Hence, I propose to explain his drive towards the animal dimension in terms of a combination of distinct factors, that may also overlap, mix and blur with one another at some point, but that originate from separate sources and respond to diverse premises. Digging into Ted Hughes's absorption in animals will further our discourse on his peculiar use of language, as well as offering us the chance to bring his personal adoption of animal imagery in his poems into focus.

If one has to open a debate on what Ted Hughes really meant as 'animal energy,' one cannot avoid starting by bringing one's attention to the topic of violence, if only that was the earliest widely-spread interpretation adopted by literary critics. In 1957,

---

6   Terry Gifford and Neil Roberts, *Ted Hughes: A Critical Study* (London: Faber & Faber, 1981), p. 11.

7   Gifford and Roberts, p. 43.

just after the first collection of poems had appeared, Edwin Muir
praised the 'admirable violence'[8] celebrated in these compositions,
and since then a long critical tradition has followed. The success
of this formula clearly owes to the striking, almost oxymoronic
contrast between the two terms, that readers more inclined to
evaluate literary texts in the light of an ethical code rejected.
However, it describes admirably the feelings after the reading of
The Jaguar, a poem that is a trademark of Hughes's poetic output
and that also brought the critic Dennis Walder to gently ironize
on the poet, described as 'a kind of Zoo Laureate.'[9] This is the
well-known story of a zoo-caged jaguar, the only captive animal
in the structure that shows verve and does not surrender to its
condition of imprisonment. After moving from cage to cage and
watching lifeless beasts that do not provoke emotions, the visitors
are suddenly 'mesmerized'[10] at the sight of a jaguar that restlessly
moves up and down the cage, seemingly threatening the crowds
in front of it with its blazing looks. Craig Robinson possibly has
this poem in mind when he writes that '[t]he nature poems of
the first volume seemed mostly to work at creating a sense of
awe at the power of the elements and animals. Awe remains an
appropriate word to use of *Lupercal,* but the poems now remind
us that awe includes horror.'[11] The poet shares with his readers a
kind of a sinister fascination for animals whose action is evidently
mischievous: in tune with these creatures, he seems to gloat at
their malice and for instance praises the pikes for their being
'killers from the eggs,'[12] or remains enthralled at a captive jaguar
who looks like a 'gangster' 'Muttering some mantra, some drum-
song of murder.'[13] One of the strategies employed by the poet in
order to celebrate violence is to lay stress on the animals' body
parts that are designed to eat, devour and kill such as teeth, jaws

---

8   Edwin Muir, 'Kinds of Poetry', *New Statesman*, 54 (28 September 1957).
9   Dennis Walder, *Ted Hughes* (Open: Open University Press, 1987), p. 4.
10   Ted Hughes, *Collected Poems*, p. 19.
11   Craig Robinson, *Ted Hughes as Shepherd of Being* (New York: Palgrave
     Macmillan, 1989), pp. 23–24.
12   Ted Hughes, *Collected Poems*, p. 84.
13   Ivi, p. 151.

and claws by way of comparing them with perfect mechanical instruments and/or weapons. It is for this reason that the jaguar's eyes are said to be 'drills' 'On a short fierce fuse,'[14] whereas later on, in its sequel, its body is compared to 'an engine.'[15] The same technique also recurs when the narrator describes the gnash of the pike's jaws as 'vice locks'[16] or when eulogizing the thrushes' sudden movements fascinated at 'this bullet and automatic | Purpose.'[17]

It is well-known that the animal that best epitomizes violence, even in a markedly arrogant and insolent way, is the protagonist of *Hawk Roosting*. The scornful raptor is both the protagonist and the narrator in this brief poem that relies on a limited, essential phrasing with the result that the spotlight remains fixed on the bird's self-complacence and tyrannical disposition. The hawk, that has been comprehensibly mistaken for a personification (or a caricature?) of Hitler, never actually kills but spends its time fantasizing about killing other animals. The awareness of its supremacy is such that it viciously claims 'I kill where I please because it is all mine,'[18] one of Hughes's most powerful verses. Yet, it feels comfortably sheltered in a permanently static situation that preserves its privilege: 'Nothing has changed since I began. | My eye has permitted no change,'[19] and by so claiming it shares a common element with the pike, in whose case the narrating voice celebrates 'The jaws' hooked clamp and fangs | Not to be changed at this date.'[20]

However, when confronted with the interpretations of his poems dealing with violent animals, Ted Hughes seemed more prone to consider this to be a wrong turn rather than a correct reading: 'Any form of violence — any form of vehement activity — invokes the bigger energy, the elemental power circuit of

---

14   Ivi, p. 19.
15   Ibid.
16   Ivi, p. 85.
17   Ivi, p. 82.
18   Ivi, p. 19.
19   Ibid.
20   Ivi, p. 85.

the Universe. Once the contact has been made — it becomes difficult to control.'[21] According to another credited interpretation of Hughes's poems, in fact, animals do not exactly occupy the centre of the stage but simply play a subsidiary role: Hughes's palpable attraction is not ultimately driving him to the animals but to the energy that animates them. In this perspective, animals would simply be pawns, moved by an uncompromising puppet-master, the law of nature, whose dictates and will remain out of range for living beings, and that Dennis Walder fittingly tags 'the ruthless predatoriness of nature.'[22]

A poem like *Hawk in the Rain*, for instance, provides an excellent example of this natural element in full sweep. The dramatic frame to the story presents a nightmarish scenario with an unnamed narrator absorbed in the view of a hawk 'effortlessly'[23] flying in the stormy sky at the moment in which he is gradually sinking into a farmland. The sense of awe for the bird of prey however is suddenly removed when the weather agents, called 'master- | Fulcrum of violence,'[24] smash the bird to the ground in a final description that rivals with a pulp fiction. Animal and natural energy in this composition clearly take distinct routes, showing, in addition, that the latter does not always, or not necessarily, work in favour of the former. Laura Webb makes an acute observation when she stresses that 'To Hughes, the cruelty of nature is a living, breathing, necessity, in which both humans and animals play their part.'[25]

It is within this context that Ted Hughes's austere dramatic vision shows its full potential: death — and, more to the point, a violent one — becomes a possible and a natural evolution to his story. From his perspective, death may also seem to be a part

---

21 Ekbert Faas, 'An Interview with Ted Hughes,' *Sydney Studies in English*, 2 (1976–77), p. 87.

22 Walder, p. 93.

23 Ted Hughes, *Collected Poems*, p. 19.

24 Ibid.

25 Laura Webb, 'Mythology, Mortality and Memorialization: Animal and Human Endurance in Hughes' Poetry?', in *Ted Hughes: From Cambridge to Collected*, ed. by Mark Wormald, Neil Roberts, Terry Gifford (Basingstoke: Palgrave Macmillan, 2013), p. 44.

of life, a sort of inescapable conclusive chapter, and that returns quite regularly in the animal poems. The trajectory 'from life to death' becomes a sort of a cliche in Hughes's poems and it also shapes *An Otter*, where the animal, 'neither fish nor beast,'[26] is initially described in full activity: after the reader has started sympathizing with it, the author briefly concludes the poem describing its violent death by means of a pack of hounds, in a surprising matter-of-fact way. *View of a Pig*, instead, inverts this order and illustrates a path 'from death to life.' It describes the narrator's feeling as he watches a 'less than lifeless'[27] pig that has just been killed, carried away on a wheelbarrow, and moves to compare its present state with what it once used to be when it 'was faster and nimbler than a cat.'[28] Of course, according to the details in the poem, it is evident that the animal has not met a natural death, but it has been slaughtered.

What is remarkable about Hughes's poems, and that proves the oneness of form and content in his poems, is that some of them also move toward an extinction point at the end. In a sense, not only are animals carried on a path 'from life to death' in these stories, but the rhetoric itself of these compositions adjusts itself to a rhythm that slowly exhausts its tempo as the conclusion — should one say the death? — of the work approaches. Stuart Hirschberg acutely detects a similar process shaping the writing of *The Bear*: 'Hughes conveys the bear's assimilation of everything ("his price is everything") by having each new stanza consist of one less line than the preceding stanza; the poem is, as it were, being devoured until nothing is left.'[29] *Pike*, a poem that has shocked many readers for its potentially apologetic message on cannibalism, may be said to be a further case in point. Following a first description of the fish in its natural context, three brief anecdotes are narrated. In the first one, three pikes appear in a glass fish bowl: 'Three we kept behind glass, | Jungled in weed:

---

26   Ted Hughes, *Collected Poems*, p. 79.
27   Ivi, p. 76.
28   Ibid.
29   Stuart Hirschberg, *Myth in the Poetry of Ted Hughes: a Guide to the Poems* (Dublin: Wolfhound, 1981), p. 36.

three inches, four, | And four and a half: red fry to them- | Suddenly there were two. Finally one | With a sag belly and the grin it was born with. | And indeed they spare nobody.'[30] The three-two-one countdown seems to be a pattern in this poem, because also the second story narrated focuses on two (battling) pikes. In the last episode, a single pike comes to the surface of a pond at night, exchanging a look with the child-narrator who is angling, and in this way it provides the surprising epiphanic conclusion in which the young fisherman identifies with the pike. The sense of an ending pervading the last lines of the poem is reinforced by the slowed-down pace conveyed by the diction in the concluding phrasing and culminating in a critical pause before the last word: 'Darkness beneath night's darkness had freed, | That rose slowly toward me, watching.'[31] This downshifting rhythm occurring at the conclusion of the poem also memorably characterises the end of *Second Glance at a Jaguar*, among others.

It is in fact true that the insatiable and rapacious essence of Mother Nature victimises non only men but also animals, and this fact emerges quite clearly in some of Hughes's verses, apart from *Hawk in the Rain*. In some situations, animals seem to be subject to a rule they cannot eschew, in particular in matter of voracity and ferocity. *Pike*, for instance, as well as celebrating the cannibal appetite of the fish, also seems to provide an explanation to this ferocious brutality, when the narrator argues that pikes do not kill for pleasure but simply because they are forced to by the law of nature. Speaking about their jaws, the poet explains that the pike has 'A life subdued to its instrument.'[32] Also the shark, in a parenthetical situation in the poem *Thrushes*, suffers from the same destiny: its greed may even reach a point when the activation of its uncontrolled energy turns into pure self-destructiveness: 'the shark's mouth | That hungers down the blood-smell even to a leak of its own | Side and devouring of itself.'[33] Be as it may, the sinister fascination for an uncontrolled form of energy

---

30   Ted Hughes, *Collected Poems*, p. 85.
31   Ivi, p. 86.
32   Ivi, p. 85.
33   Ivi, p. 82.

exerts a commanding allure on the poet who responds to it with passionate fervour. Steve Ely observes: 'Hughes is fascinated by the mysterious vitality of the universe he describes, and he takes a perverse pleasure in reminding readers of their physical and intellectual frailty in the face of an impenetrable and impersonal nature, red in tooth and claw.'[34]

Another interpretation of Ted Hughes's interest in animals arises from a statement that the poet himself delivered when interviewed in 1965 by John Horder. In this situation he claims that his 'poems are not about violence but vitality. Animals are not violent, they're so much more completely controlled than men,'[35] offering a satisfactory elucidation of the issue from a new perspective, as well as confirming how complex and unsatisfactory the process of translating the concept of violence from his imaginary realm may become. In a way, Hughes seems to stress that he remains mindless of the consequences of an energy's agency, if the release of that energy proves to be amazing: the two poems about the jaguar in the cage, among others, demonstrate the validity of such a theoretical premise. The first can be split into two main sections: initially, the zoo visitors watch the animals in the garden and remain somewhat disappointed. Tiger, lion and boa constrictor are predators that are supposed to stir strong reactions in a person and instead they lie dormant, their wildness totally dissolved. After the description of this scene in an apparently detached tone, the first half of the poem abruptly comes to a halt when the narrator suddenly shows his frustration at this view: the sight is so unimpressive that it would hardly give a fright to anyone and 'It might be painted on a nursery wall.'[36] In fact, people quickly move on and all gather in front of the cage with the jaguar, whose intimidating and enthralling energy alone makes the show. It is important to stress here that the jaguar's power is not only a means of capturing the zoo visitors' attention but it is the living force enabling the animal

---

34   Steve Ely, *Ted Hughes's South Yorkshire. Made in Mexborough* (Basingstoke: Palgrave Macmillan, 2015), pp. 149–50.
35   John Horder, 'Desk Poet', *The Guardian*, 23 March 1965, p. 9.
36   Ted Hughes, *Collected Poems*, p. 19.

to remain deaf in front of its state of imprisonment. Terry Gifford and Neil Roberts's comment that the jaguar 'is objectively caged but subjectively free'[37] again seems to be hitting the point. It is in this context that the display of energy (and of violence) may be equated to vitality. Ten years later the poet returns to this forceful image and writes *Second Glance at a Jaguar*, an evolution of the previous composition. In this second version of the poem dedicated to the caged wild beast, the zoo visitors have almost completely disappeared and only an apparently casual reference in the title shows their disguised presence. As for the other animals, no trace of them is left. The focus of the whole poem, from the first to the last word, remains stuck on the jaguar's fierce temper and the impeding sense of threat that any zoo visitor (and/ or reader) feels when confronted with its glance.

This interpretation widens our discourse to further and crucial areas of analysis. Associating the idea of the animal no longer with a negative concept such as violence, or potentially negative as it may become in Hughes's hands such as the Law of Nature, but with a positive kind of energy and vitality that celebrates the life principle in a raw form, makes the encounter between human and animal nature possible. We know that both Hughes's personal inclinations and his studies in anthropology have encouraged his way into shamanic practices. How far he practically went into them is not exactly clear but if one liked to make an idea about his level of knowledge in that field, his poems provide a considerable amount of material and reveal a significant familiarity with the subject. Briefly speaking, by way of an encounter between a human being — the shaman — and an animal — the animal helper — this kind of magic ensures that a symbiotic relationship is created between the two parts and the animal's inner energy is offered to the human being for a number of purposes. Still in vogue among primitive (and not) societies, it is believed to grant divination powers, to offer cures to particular illnesses, to disturbed states of mind and, more in general, to problems affecting a whole clan or society. In situations such as these, the shaman undertakes a journey into the underworld where

---

37   Gifford and Roberts, p. 64.

he is given the solution to the case: in order to cross the threshold of the supernatural dimension, and ensure that he has enough energies for his journey back, however, he needs the collaboration of a trusted animal that, by means of a magic transformation, donates the shaman its energy and endows him with the temporary superhuman powers he needs in order to accomplish the whole practice.

A critical theory with a great following owes to this magico-religious ritual Ted Hughes's passion for animals, and becomes a valuable key of interpretation in particular for all those poems in which a man and an animal feature. The (first) story of the zoo-visitor watching a jaguar restlessly walking inside a cage, for instance, enlarges the dimension of the previous interpretation by supplementing the whole context with important additional elements. This would actually be the story of a narrator frustrated by his inability to react to a contrary situation, metaphorically represented by his initial walking through the zoo cages where he only meets animals 'Fatigued with indolence.'[38] The encounter with the jaguar, his animal helper, would awaken in him his sense of freedom so that the predator's wild rage would be passed on to him. The images in the last stanza, insisting as they do on airiness and an achieved sense of independence, describe the acquired and final sense of liberty gained by the narrator as a consequence of his meeting with the jaguar. Stuart Hirschberg, the scholar who more than any other has clarified this path in Ted Hughes's creative world, explains the ways in which this magic practice may become useful in order to explain the poet's approach to the animal world.

> For Hughes, in his earliest animal poems, the process of writing the poem recreates the rite of blood brotherhood between the Shaman and his animal Helper. Whether hawk, bear, jaguar, or pike, among others, Hughes establishes a mystical alliance and 'exchanges blood' with his animal familiars. Hughes makes contact with a feral energy at the heart of the cosmos, mindless, luxuriant, capable of bringing death and revitalizing the dead, a terrible power to be both summoned and feared.[39]

---

38   Ted Hughes, *Collected Poems*, p. 19.
39   Hirschberg, p. 7.

One of the major elements introduced by Hughes's poetry when an encounter between a man and an animal via the shamanic practice is ensured regards the possibility of interpreting the animal as a metaphor of a liberating agency that, obviously, becomes particularly manifest in *The Jaguar*. Among other interpretive paths and allegorical explanations, at stake here is a terrific act of rebellion, symbolically represented by the jaguar's uncontrolled state of rage. The poem, which should be seen in its two constituent parts, as the mismatch between the dormant animals vs. the jaguar, or stillness vs. movement, can also be read in the alternation of repression vs. liberation, a drive whose engine is clearly embodied by the jaguar. The passionate and evocative conclusion of the poem stressing the newly-achieved sense of freedom on the part of the visitor-jaguar helps the reader understand how the first images, disguised behind an apparently flat tone, metaphorically allude to a claustrophobic and oppressive context. This particular key to the reading of the poem becomes still more important in view of the fact that this is the step in which the identification with the wild beast becomes revelatory. At this juncture, the comment by Gifford and Roberts seems particularly incisive: 'This is a poem that has excited many readers and repelled others. The reason for this is undoubtedly an awareness that the poet is in some sense identifying himself with the jaguar.'[40]

What the shamanic practice shows from the basis is that the duo man-animal does not match a system of equal forces together but an unbalanced combination, with the man profiting the most from the encounter. Man's mirroring process in the animal is looked for because it is equated to the state of perfection. Craig Robinson is correct in stressing that 'Hughes sought some human equivalent of what he admired in the animal world.'[41] The forces that these animals embody, rage for the jaguar, permanence for the bear, agility for the thrushes, and even cannibal instinct for the pike, in man's nature work in order to dismantle an entire

---

40   Gifford and Roberts, p. 64.
41   Robinson, p. 2.

psychic structure based on wrong principles. The change of state in man is never gradual but immediate: therefore, if animals do appear violent in Hughes's poems, this is not only due to their instincts but also to the forceful, sometimes brutal way in which their energy is employed in their interaction with man. Stuart Hirschberg's analysis dedicated to the issue has produced this insightful conclusion:

> Although based on shamanistic rites, these poems serve a personal, psychological function so that through violence, primitive contact with suppressed hatred and repressed aggression and even a kind of psychic self-mutilation, the sterile personality created by society is destroyed and the instinctual suppressed self can emerge liberated. In many cases, Hughes's need to liberate the forces symbolized by these animals is revealed in the fact that they are often shown constrained by situations and environments that limit them. The jaguar is caged, the bear is in hibernation, the hawk is seen at the end of a day of hunting. Hughes seeks, as did ancient shamans, an alignment with the unknown forces governing the universe. His work is a journey beyond the rational to the primitive depths of experience to liberate the self.[42]

Finally, the poem that best exemplifies the encounter between human and animal by the use of an esoteric method is *The Thought-Fox*, one of his most astonishing achievements. Described by Laura Webb as Hughes's 'ars poetica,'[43] by Dennis Walder 'one of his most characteristic and revealing poems,'[44] by Stephen Ennis 'a kind of signature piece,'[45] it narrates in the first person the story of an uninspired poet who faces his blank page, unable to write, in a starless night. It is midnight, however, the time when a new day replaces the old and — most importantly — the magic time in fairy tales when spells and witchcraft become possible. Through the window, the poet sees — or imagines he sees — a

---

42   Hirschberg, pp. 12–13.
43   Webb, p. 35.
44   Walder, p. 6.
45   Stephen Enniss, 'Self-Revelation, Self-Concealment & the Making of the Ted Hughes Archive', in *Ted Hughes: Alternative Horizons*, ed. by Joanny Moulin (London: Routledge, 2005), p. 55.

fox out in the wood that hesitantly and 'delicately'[46] walks toward
the lonely poet leaving footprints behind in 'the dark snow.'[47] The
interaction of the two subjects is soon established, so that while
the poet follows the fox, the animal approaches him, becoming
bigger and bigger in the artist's mind, until it suddenly leaps into
'the dark hole of the head.'[48] Shortly afterwards, the fox-image
— Ted Hughes calls it the thought-fox — vanishes but not its
magic effect, because the poem is written: in one of the very few
bright conclusions among the animal poems, Hughes reaches
the conclusion that 'The page is printed.' This poem, nicely
accounted for as Ted Hughes's 'self-mythologizing account of
writing a poem'[49] by Stephen Ennis, firmly creates the premises
for the interrelatedness of a complex network of opposite
elements that, because of the magic effect of art (or should one
say of a quick small animal?), find a harmonizing relationship:
all the dichotomies inside-outside, black-white, human-animal,
conscious-unconscious, movement-stillness on which the poem
creates its systematic texture reach a perfect state of balance in
the surprising — and surprisingly brief — conclusion. The poem,
that Ted Hughes claims is 'about a fox, obviously enough, but a
fox that is both a fox and not a fox,'[50] clearly describes a story that
has an esoteric and imaginary framework, placed as it is inside
the practice of shamanism. However, in this specific case it is not
evidently rage or violence, the predatory or killing instinct that
the speaking voice in the poem is after, but a form of a raw energy
helping him to accomplish the creative process. In other words,
The Thought-Fox might be a poem written by a shaman-poet and
by a fox-animal helper. Four-hands, one may be tempted to add.
The fox is the poem, as well as the poet's imagination. In *Poetry
in the Making*, Ted Hughes explains that as a child no other kind
of emotion could match a good catch when he went fishing or
hunting and *The Thought-Fox* as well as *Pike* in the final part

---

46   Ted Hughes, *Collected Poems*, p. 21.
47   Ibid.
48   Ibid.
49   Enniss, p. 54.
50   Hughes, *Poetry in the Making*, p. 20.

seem to re-create that feeling, albeit in two distinct situations. Roger Elkin while commenting *The Thought-Fox* returns to this point when he writes about 'Hughes's idea of writing poetry as akin to hunting animals.'[51]

In conclusion, this manifold cultural system of potential indications intends to be a further tribute to the weight of the literary production of Ted Hughes who, despite still having a good number of detractors, has already earned a steady collocation in the history of English poetry of the 20th century. Charged as it is with a number of concurrent cultural referents and personal stimuli, the whole output concerning his animal imagery appears to be a canvas with a multiple set of bizarre illustrations and a dazzling array of colours, some of them even apparently mismatching the rest. In my opinion, however, this also wishes to be a credit to the richness, intensity and fertility of a volcanic artistic mind and it strives to offer a reading as close as possible to the original message contained in the poems. At times, I must confess, I have even thought that providing only some five lines of interpretation might to be a little too narrow an explanation if compared with the explosive potential material available in Hughes's poems. In one of his typical turns from creator to critic, he explains the possible readings originated by the image of the jaguar in this way:

> A jaguar after all can be received in several different aspects... he is a beautiful, powerful nature spirit, he is a homicidal maniac, he is a supercharged piece of cosmic machinery, he is a symbol of man's baser nature shoved down into the id and growing cannibal murderous with deprivation, he is an ancient symbol of Dionysus since he is a leopard raised to the ninth power, he is a precise historical symbol to the bloody-minded Aztecs and so on. Or he is simply a demon... a lump of ectoplasm. A lump of astral energy.[52]

---

51 Roger Elkin, 'Neglected Auguries in Recklings', in *The Challenge of Ted Hughes*, ed. by Keith Sagar (London: St. Martin's Press, 1994), p. 14.
52 Faas, p. 86.

Bibliography

Elkin, Roger, 'Neglected Auguries in Recklings', in *The Challenge of Ted Hughes*, ed. by Keith Sagar (London: St. Martin's Press, 1994).

Enniss, Stephen, 'Self-Revelation, Self-Concealment & the Making of the Ted Hughes Archive', in *Ted Hughes: Alternative Horizons*, ed. by Joanny Moulin (London: Routledge, 2005).

Faas, Ekbert, 'An Interview with Ted Hughes', *Sydney Studies in English*, 2 (1976–77).

Gifford, Terry and Neil Roberts, *Ted Hughes: A Critical Study* (London: Faber & Faber, 1981).

Heinz, Drue, 'Ted Hughes: The Art of Poetry LXXI', *Paris Review*, 134 (1995).

Hirschberg, Stuart, *Myth in the Poetry of Ted Hughes: A Guide to the Poems* (Dublin: Wolfhound, 1981).

Horder, John, 'Desk Poet', *The Guardian*, 23 March 1965.

Hughes, Ted, *Collected Poems*, ed. by Paul Keepgan (London: Faber & Faber, 2003).

_____, *Poetry in the Making* (London: Faber & Faber, 1989).

Muir, Edwin, 'Kinds of Poetry', *New Statesman*, 54 (28 September 1957).

O'Connor, Danny, *Ted Hughes and Trauma. Burning the Foxes* (Basingstoke: Palgrave Macmillan, 2016).

Robinson, Craig, *Ted Hughes as Shepherd of Being* (New York: Palgrave Macmillan, 1989).

Steve, Ely, *Ted Hughes's South Yorkshire. Made in Mexborough* (Basingstoke: Palgrave Macmillan, 2015).

Walder, Dennis, *Ted Hughes* (Open: Open University Press, 1987).

Webb, Laura, 'Mythology, Mortality and Memorialization: Animal and Human Endurance in Hughes' Poetry', in *Ted Hughes: From Cambridge to Collected*, ed. by Mark Wormald, Neil Roberts and Terry Gifford (Basingstoke: Palgrave Macmillan, 2013).

Wormald, Mark, 'Fishing for Ted', in *Ted Hughes: From Cambridge to Collected*, ed. by Mark Wormald, Neil Roberts and Terry Gifford (Basingstoke: Palgrave Macmillan, 2013).

"DISTORTED SIMILARITY".
KAFKA'S PRESENCE IN BENJAMIN'S MIMETIC PRINCIPLE

Chiara Sandrin
(University of Turin)

Josef K., the main character of Kafka's novel *Der Proceß* [*The Trial*], comes to visit the painter Titorelli whose paintings of farmland landscapes are all identical: two faint trees, distant one to another, in a dark meadow with a multicolored sunset in the background. When they meet, the painter takes out from the bottom of the bed his art works which are all covered in dust. Josef K., in the urge of getting out from the oppressive attic where Titorelli is living, buys them all together and locks them in a drawer of his bank's office.[1]

Titorelli does not make a living from these landscape paintings, but by making portraits of judges commissioned by others. When Josef K. during his visit notices the picture that Titorelli is working on, he remembers that he saw a very similar painting in the office of the lawyer Huld. It was a very large canvas depicting a man dressed in a robe sitting on a very high chair.

Das Ungewöhnliche war, daß dieser Richter nicht in Ruhe und Würde dort saß, sondern den linken Arm fest an Rücken- und Seitenlehne drückte, den rechten Arm aber völlig frei hatte und nur mit der Hand die Seitenlehne umfasste, als wolle er im nächsten Augenblick mit einer heftigen und vielleicht empörten

---

1   On the definition of modernity as the relationship of what is new with what has always been in Titorelli's landscapes cfr. Walter Benjamin, 'Malerei, Jugendstil, Neuheit, Das Passagen-Werk', in *Gesammelte Schriften* (Frankfurt am Main: Suhrkamp, 1991) 5:2, p. 675 [Benjamin, *Painting, Jugendstil, Novelty. The Arcades Project*, trans. by Howard Eiland and Kevin McLaughlin (Cambridge–London: The Belknap Press, 1999) p. 544]. Cfr. also Barbara di Noi, 'Kafka e Karl Stauffer-Bern. Sul personaggio di Titorelli', *Studia Austriaca*, 20 (2012), 167–189.

Wendung aufspringen, um etwas entscheidendes zu sagen oder
gar das Urteil zu verkünden. Der Angeklagte war wohl zu Füssen
der Treppe zu denken, deren oberste, mit dem gelben Teppich
bedeckte Stufen noch auf dem Bilde zu sehen waren. „Vielleicht
ist das mein Richter", sagte K., und zeigte mit einem Finger auf
das Bild.

[The strange thing was that this judge wasn't sitting in calm
dignity, but instead had his left arm braced against the back and
arm of the chair, while his right arm was completely free, his
hand alone clutching the arm of the chair, as if he were about to
spring up any moment in a violent and perhaps wrathful outburst
to say something decisive or even pass judgment. The defendant
was probably to be thought of as at the foot of the stairs, the upper
steps of which, covered with a yellow carpet, could be seen in
the picture. 'Perhaps that's my judge,' said K. and pointed to the
picture.][2]

Leni, the servant that accompanied Josef K in the lawyer's
office, revealed him some details on how the judge in the painting
really looked like who actually was a very small person sitting on
a folded horse blanket on top of a kitchen stool.

The painting that Josef K. is now looking at in the painter's
studio is not oil colored, but it is weakly outlined with pastels.
With great difficulty Josef K. manages to see its true content:
even in this picture the judge seems to be standing up with an
intimidating look. Josef K.'s attention is rather drawn to a
towering figure standing in the back, regarding which he asks
the painter for an explanation who in the meantime was retracing
the outlines with a pastel: 'That is justice', Titorelli explains.
Josef K. recognizes the figure by the scale in her hand and by
the bandage covering her eyes, but notices that she has wings
on her ankles and that she is running. The painter then explains
that, in order to fulfil his client's request, he had to paint justice

---

2   Franz Kafka, *Der Proceß*, ed. by Malcom Pasley (Frankfurt am Main:
     Fischer, 1990), pp. 141–42.
     [Franz Kafka, *The Trial*, trans. by Breon Mitchell (New York: Schocken
     Books, 1998), p. 90].

and victory combined. But even in this case it is all made up. In the meanwhile the painter continues to work on his painting by adding a red shadow behind the judge's head together with some decorations.

Um die Figur der Gerechtigkeit aber blieb es bis auf eine unmerkliche Tönung hell, in dieser Helligkeit schien die Figur besonders vorzudringen, sie erinnerte kaum mehr an die Göttin der Gerechtigkeit, aber auch nicht an die des Sieges, sie sah jetzt vielmehr vollkommen wie die Göttin der Jagt aus.

[But, except for an imperceptible shading, brightness still surrounded the figure of Justice, and in this brightness the figure seemed to stand out strikingly; now it scarcely recalled the goddess of Justice, or even that of Victory, now it looked just like the goddess of the Hunt.][3]

The slow uncovering of the painting's true meaning reaches its peak when Josef K. recognizes what looks like the goddess of the Hunt, a figure that embodies the act of writing as tensity, an attack on the border, condensed in the two opposing moments of escape and pursuit that are identified with the predator and its prey, as one can read in a diary note left on the 9th of march 1922: „Das Pferd des Angreifers zum eigenen Ritt benützen. Einzige Möglichkeit. Aber was für Kräfte und Geschicklichkeiten verlangt das? Und wie spät ist es schon!" [Mount your attacker's horse and ride it yourself. The only possibility. But what strength and skill that requires! And how late it is already!][4]

In Josef K.'s interpretative act of the different layers of meaning of Titorelli's image it is possible to see clearly the special feature of Kafka's writing which is able to grasp a hidden truth in the brief alteration of things. It is a rich and deep deformation in which it is possible to distinguish the main features of the, „*entstellte*

---

3   Kafka, *Der Proceß*, p. 154 [Kafka, *The Trial*, p. 118].
4   Kafka, *Tagebücher: in der Fassung der Handschrift*, ed. by Hans Gerd Koch (Frankfurt am Main: Fischer, 1990), p. 910 [Kafka, *Diaries 1910–1923*, trans. by Joseph Kresh and Martin Greenberg (New York: Schocken Books, 1976), p. 377].

Ähnlichkeit", the distorted similarity — the alteration of the real where the fullness of the image of dream and memory translates into analogic form — that was crucial for Benjamin in his studies on language. The importance of the notion of „*entstellte Ähnlichkeit*"[5] emerges for the first time in his writings on Proust, where, by noting Proust's 'frenetic study and passionate cult' of the analogy, Benjamin shows how it reveals its true strength.

Nicht da, wo er sie in den Werken, Physiognomien oder Redeweisen, immer bestürzend, unvermutet aufdeckt [...]. Die Ähnlichkeit des Einen mit dem Andern, mit dem wir rechnen, die im Wachen uns beschäftigt, umspielt nur die tiefere der Traumwelt, in der, was vorgeht, nie identisch, sondern ähnlich: sich selber undurchschaubar ähnlich, auftaucht. [...] Und wie [die Kinder] sich selbst nicht ersättigen können, [...] die Tasche und was drin liegt, mit *einem* Griff in etwas Drittes zu verwandeln [...], so war Proust unersättlich, [...] das Ich mit einem Griffe zu entleeren, und immer wieder jenes Dritte: das Bild, das seine Neugier, nein, sein Heimweh stillte, einzubringen. Zerfetzt von Heimweh lag er auf dem Bett, Heimweh nach der im Stand der Ähnlichkeit entellten Welt, in der das Wahre surrealistische Gesicht des Daseins zum Durchbruch kommt.

[The true signs of its hegemony do not become obvious where he unexpectedly and startlingly uncovers similarities in actions, physiognomies, or speech mannerisms. The similarity of one thing to another which we are used to, which occupies us in a wakeful state, reflects only vaguely the deeper similarity of the dream world in which everything that happens appears not in identical but in similar guise, opaquely similar to itself. Children

---

5   Anja Lemke, *Gedächtnisräume des Selbst. Walter Benjamins "Berliner Kindheit um neunzehnhundert"* (Würzburg: Königshausen & Neumann, 2008), p. 73; Sigrid Weigel, *Entstellte Ähnlichkeit. Walter Benjamins theoretisches Schreiben* Frankfurt am Main: Fischer, 1997); Helmut Kaffenberger, *Denkfiguren des Dritten Raums? Walter Benjamins Theorie des Ähnlichen*, Claudia Breger and Tobias Döring (eds.), *Figuren der/des Dritten: Erkundungen kultureller Zwischenräume* (Amsterdam: Rodopi, 1998), p. 52.

know a symbol of this world: the stocking which has the structure of this dream world when, rolled up in the laundry hamper, it is a "bag" and a "present" at the same time. And just as children do not tire of quickly changing the bag and its contents into a third thing — namely, a stocking — Proust could not get his fill of emptying the dummy, his self, at one stroke in order to keep garnering that third thing, the image which satisfied his curiosity — indeed, assuaged his homesickness. He lay on his bed racked with homesickness, homesick for the world distorted in the state of similarity, a world in which the true surrealist face of existence breaks through.][6]

The short text *In der Sonne* [*In the sun*], written during his first stay in Ibiza the 15th of July 1932, two days before leaving the island, is of particular importance for the reconsideration of themes linked to language theory. *In der Sonne* has been considered as the „Kristallisationspunkt für die theoretisch-begriffliche Orientierung des Spätwerks" [The focal point for the theoretical and conceptual orientation of the late work][7] for its positioning in between the *Nordische See* cycle, composed between July and august 1930, and the script *Lehre vom Ähnlichen* [*Doctrine of the Similar*], that testify respectively the search for a new orientation and the attempt of materialistic reformulation of a theory of language.

The title, *In der Sonne*, should be read as a motto, as *inscriptio*, according to the connection of the form of Benjamin's *Denkbilder* to baroque emblems that can be already seen in the *Einbahnstraße* [*One-Way Street*].[8] The image related to this title is grasped under

---

6   Walter Benjamin, 'Zum Bilde Prousts', in *Gesammelte Schriften,* 2:1, pp. 313–314 [Walter Benjamin, 'On the Image of Proust', in *Selected Writings 2:1*, ed. by Michael W. Jennings, Howard Eiland, Gary Smith, trans. by Harry Zohn (Cambridge–London: Harvard University Press, 2005), p. 240].

7   Michael Bröcker, 'Sprache', in Michael Opitz, Erdmut Wizisla (eds.), *Benjamins Begriffe* (Frankfurt am Main: Suhrkamp, 2000), 2, p. 763.

8   Cfr. Dieter Sdun, *Benjamins Käfer. Untersuchungen zur bildlichen Sprache Walter Benjamins im Umkreis der "Einbahnstraße"* (Frankfurt am Main: Lang, 1994), pp. 104–115.

the sun, at about midday. That the reference to this time of the day should be related to Zarathustra's midday is proved by the *Denkbild* named *Kurze Schatten* [*Short Shadows*], the last of the series published under the same title in the "Kölnische Zeitung" in February 1933. After the description of the shadows that are nothing more than a thin black outline, before they quickly and silently disappear, hiding in their own mystery, here arrives in all of its bended and compressed fullness the time of Zarathustra, the thinker of life's midday, in the garden of summer. „Denn die Erkenntnis umreißt wie die Sonne auf der Höhe ihrer Bahn die Dinge am strengsten."[9]

Shadows, the objects' mystery hide in the sun's highest peak, at the height of knowledge. Exactly in the same way as the sun at its zenith, knowledge and wisdom define neatly the objects' outline, pushing their mystery within.[10] The other dwells, or hides, beyond this traced border is also this guarded secret inside the objects, where it is pushed back from the sun's brightness, from the power of knowledge.

The complex antagonism between knowledge and object, thought and image that is shown here is contained, as an instable synthesis, a "calm dialectic", in the term *Denk-Bild* [*Thought-Image*] that Benjamin uses from 1933 as the title his brief writings composed following the example of the ones collected in the *Einbahnstraße*.

By returning on the literary topos of the stroll, *In der Sonne* portrays an experience: the adventurous path of a traveller that crosses an unknown place. First, he observes the landscape with

---

9   Benjamin, *Gesammelte Schriften*, IV, 1, p. 428 [Benjamin, *Selected Writings*, 2:2, p. 272, trans. by Rodney Livingstone: "Short Shadows. Toward noon, shadows are no more than the sharp, black edges at the feet of things, preparing to retreat silently, unnoticed, into their burrow, into their secret. Then, in its compressed, cowering fullness, comes the hour of Zarathustra—the thinker in 'the noon of life,' in 'the summer garden.' For it is knowledge that gives objects their sharpest outline, like the sun at its zenith."]

10   Sdun, p. 92. Sdun and other interprets relate this *Denkbild* with Benjamin's definition of auratic knowledge and its relationship with the meridian and postmeridian light as the perception of proximity and distance.

the intent of reaching a kind of knowledge that is deeper than what can be achieved from a quick look: rather than a direct observation, a sensible experience, he is more interested in obtaining the knowledge contained in the names of the place in which he feels left out.

It can be read that every designation of a place is the sign of a law that governs the unique and unrepeatable encounter with the elements of that landscape, which are collected in a cryptic writing that is incomprehensible for the traveller.

Nevertheless, there is also who is able to understand that language that remains silent in the same way as the same collection of things contained in a landscape:

Aber der Bauer hat ja den Schlüssel der Chiffrenschrift. Er kennt die Namen. Dennoch ist es ihm nicht gegeben, über seinen Sitz etwas auszusagen. Sollten die Namen ihn wortkarg machen? Dann fällt die Fülle des Wortes nur dem zu, der das Wissen ohne die Namen hat, die Fülle des Schweigens aber dem, der nichts hat als sie?

[The farmer, however, has the key to this code. He knows their names. Yet it is not in his power to say anything about his domain. Is it that the names have made him taciturn? Would this mean that the cornucopia of language falls only to the man who has the knowledge without the names; and the cornucopia of silence, to the man who has nothing but the names?][11]

This excerpt ends with a "distance without name" in which all movements blend in a unique image.

In der Ferne zieht auf den Feldern zwischen Oliven- und Mandelbäume ein Wagen vorüber, aber geräuschlos, und wenn die Räder hinterm Lab verschwinden, so scheinen überlebensgroße Frauen, mit dem Gesicht ihm zugewandt, reglos durch das reglose Land zu wallen.

---

11   Benjamin, *In der Sonne, Gesammelte Schriften*, 4:1, p. 417 [Benjamin, *In the Sun, Selected Writings*, 2:2, p. 662, trans. by Rodney Livingstone].

[In the distance a cart trundles silently across the fields between the olive and almond trees; and when the wheels vanish behind the foliage, women, larger than life, their faces turned toward him, seem to float motionlessly through the motionless countryside.][12]

This quietness is not a sort of idealization of the dreamer-traveller, but it rather encloses the same experience described in the *Denkbild*, translated in language. The traveller who asks for the names is finally able to grasp them in their metamorphosis, in the fleeting transformation of the image where for one moment they are translated through fantasy. As a matter of fact, the exhausted traveller, when he is about to rest his body, attributes to fantasy a fundamental mediating role capable of transforming a familiar image in that unique alteration that makes it recognizable and foreign at the same time, thus producing an unknown but also definable third alterity.

Es ist ein Wechsel und Vertauschen; nichts bleibt und nichts verschwindet. Aus diesem Weben aber lösen mit einmal sich Namen, wortlos treten sie in den Schreitenden ein, und während seine Lippen sie formen, erkennt er sie. Sie tauchen auf, und was bedarf es länger dieser Landschaft? Auf jeder namenlosen Ferne drüben ziehen sie vorüber, ohne eine Spur zu hinterlassen. Namen der Inseln, die dem ersten Anblick wie Marmorgruppen aus dem Meer sich hoben, der Schroffen, die den Horizont schartig machten, der Sterne, die im Boot ihn überraschten, wenn sie im frühen Dunkel auf Posten treten.

[Things change, and trade places; nothing remains and nothing disappears. From all this activity, however, names suddenly emerge; wordlessly they enter the mind of the passer-by, and as his lips shape them, he recognizes them. They come to the surface. And what further need has he of this landscape? They drift past him on the nameless distant horizon, without leaving a trace. The names of islands that rose out of the sea like marble sculptures, of steep rocks whose craggy peaks broke up the sky,

---

12   Ibid., p. 420 [p. 665].

of stars that surprised him in the boat when they came on guard duty in the early darkness.][13]

Even if it maintains the main features of the *Über Sprache überhaupt und über die Sprache des Menschen* [*On Language as Such and on Language of Man*] written in 1916, the static and dynamic quality of the image in which the traveller's experience is condensed can be read as the *Enstellung*, the alteration or deformation of the image that, together with the immaterial resemblance, the non-sensible, will be at the very centre of Benjamin's last reflections on the themes of travelling.

Thanks to his considerations on the pre-modern ways in which the world was signified that emerged before any division between subject and object, signifier and meaning, essence and phenomena, Benjamin highlights the way in which this act of knowing is not founded on objectivity or on an outer observation, but by engaging the very net of correspondences that constitutes our world.

By considering the analogies between man and nature, Benjamin emphasizes the way man actively produces them with its mimetic capabilities, as in the case when dances can be linked to constellations in the sky.[14] And if, Benjamin emphatically shows how the ancient link between man and objects remains purely as a trace in the archive of *unsinnlich* and immaterial (or non-sensible) resemblences that constitutes both language and writing, it is important to note that this trace of the fundamental mimetic element is recognizable in its concreteness, in the materiality of language.

Benjamin's theory of mimetic faculty is meshed with a theory on reading in which the active and productive element is highlighted. The reader can respond to the feeling that is communicated to him

---

13   Ibid.
14   Wolfgang Bock, *Walter Benjamin. Die Rettung der Nacht. Sterne, Melancholie und Messianismus* (Bielefeld: Aisthesis, 2000); Marianne Schuller, 'Bilder. Schriften zum Gedächtnis. Freud, Warburg, Benjamin. Eine Konstellation', *Internationale Zeitschrift für Philosophie, Themenheft Walter Benjamin*, 1993, 2:1, 73–95.

by comprehending it in an act of re-elaboration that that cannot be reduced to a form of recognition, of an anamnestic kind, of an original content, but it is rather an active production of an analogy and in this sense an act of translating the image hidden in writing. Reading, in the same way as translation, tries to integrate, the mutual completion where the subjective and the objective meet.

Some pages of the *Berliner Kindheit* [*Berlin Childhood around 1900*] can be considered as an example of the possibilities of enrichment and enhancement of language through misconception, alteration or the deformation of images absorbed through language. In the same was as with childhood phantasies, the world can be seen in its altered, *enstellt*, transfigured appearance and in this way that ancient magic that characterizes the act of reading can emerge in a rapid and transitory moment on which Benjamin focuses in the last words of his text.

Quoting Hugo von Hofmannsthal, Benjamin observes:

„Was nie geschrieben wurde, lesen." Dies Lesen ist das älteste: das Lesen vor aller Sprache aus den Eingeweiden, den Sternen oder Tänzen. Später kamen Vermittlungsglieder eines neuen Lesens, Runen und Hieroglyphen in Gebrauch. Dia Annahme liegt nahe, daß dies die Stationen wurden, über welche jene mimetische Begabung, die einst das Fundament der okkulten Praxis gewesen ist, in Schrift und Sprache ihren Eingang fand. Dergestalt wäre die Sprache die höchste Stufe des mimetischen Verhaltens und das vollkommenste Archiv der unsinnlichen Ähnlichkeit: ein Medium, in welches ohne Rest die früheren Kräfte mimetischer Hervorbringung und Auffassung hingewandert sind, bis sie so weit gelangten, die der Magie zu liquidieren.

["To read what was never written." Such reading is the most ancient: reading prior to all languages, from entrails, the stars, or dances. Later the mediating link of a new kind of reading, of runes and hieroglyphs, came into use. It seems fair to suppose that these were the stages by which the mimetic gift, formerly the foundation of occult practices, gained admittance to writing and language. In this way, language may be seen as the highest level of mimetic behavior and the most complete archive of

nonsensuous similarity: a medium into which the earlier powers
of mimetic production and comprehension have passed without
residue, to the point where they have liquidated those of magic.][15]

Bibliography

Works by Walter Benjamin and Franz Kafka

Benjamin, Walter, *Gesammelte Schriften*, 7 vols., ed. by Rolf Tiedemann and
Hermann Schweppenhauser (Frankfurt am Main: Suhrkamp, 1991).
Kafka, Franz, *Der Proceß*, ed. by Malcom Pasley (Frankfurt am Main: Fischer,
1990).
_____, *Tagebücher: in der Fassung der Handschrift*, ed. by Hans Gerd
Koch (Frankfurt am Main: Fischer, 1990).

Books and Periodicals

Bock, Wolfgang, *Walter Benjamin. Die Rettung der Nacht. Sterne, Melancholie
und Messianismus* (Bielefeld: Aisthesis, 2000).
Bröcker, Michael, 'Sprache', in *Benjamins Begriffe*, ed. by Opitz, Michael,
Wizisla, Erdmut (Frankfurt am Main: Suhrkamp, 2000).
Kaffenberger, Helmut, *Denkfiguren des Dritten Raums? Walter Benjamins
Theorie des Ähnlichen*, in *Figuren der/des Dritten: Erkundungen kultureller
Zwischenräume*, ed. by Breger, Claudia, and Döring, Tobias (Amsterdam:
Rodopi, 1998).
Kemp, Wolfgang, 'Fernbilder, Benjamin und die Kunstwissenschaft', in *Walter
Benjamin im Kontext*, ed. by Lindner, Burkhardt (Königstein/Ts: Athenäum,
1985), pp. 224–57.
Kuhn, Hugo, 'Allegorie und Erzählstruktur', in *Formen und Funktionen der
Allegorie*, ed. by Haug, Walter (Stuttgart: Metzler, 1979).
Lemke, Anja, *Gedächtnisräume des Selbst. Walter Benjamins "Berliner
Kindheit um neunzehnhundert"* (Würzburg: Königshausen & Neumann,
2008).
Mitchell, William John Thomas, 'What Is an Image?', *New Literary History*,
15:3 (Spring 1984), 503–37.
Schuller, Marianne, *Bilder. Schriften zum Gedächtnis. Freud, Warburg,
Benjamin. Eine Konstellation, Internationale Zeitschrift für Philosophie*,
Themenheft Walter Benjamin, 1993, 2:1.

15　Benjamin, 'Über das mimetische Vermögen', in *Gesammelte Schriften*,
2:1, p. 213; [Benjamin, 'On the Mimetic Faculty', in *Selected Writings*,
2:2, p. 722, trans. by Edmund Jephcott].

Sdun, Dieter, *Benjamins Käfer. Untersuchungen zur bildlichen Sprache Walter Benjamins im Umkreis der "Einbahnstraße"* (Frankfurt am Main: Lang, 1994).

Weigel, Sigrid, *Entstellte Ähnlichkeit. Walter Benjamins theoretisches Schreiben* (Frankfurt am Main: Fischer, 1997).

WORD-IMAGE DIALOGIC IMAGINATION HYPOTHESIS FOR A COMPLEX AESTHETICS OF THE AUDIO-VERBAL-VISUAL

Chiara Simonigh
(University of Turin)

> In the experience of art we see the realization of an experience that really changes the one who makes it. This is a new way of presenting the problem of truth of that "comprehension" pursued by spiritual sciences.
>
> Hans Georg Gadamer, *Wahrheit und Methode*

> We are not really capable of comprehension, except at the cinema. This comprehension, which is so alive in imaginary life is what we lack in everyday life.
>
> Edgar Morin, *La Méthode 3. La connaissance de la connaissance*

Considered in the context of a complex aesthetics on which we will here try to propose some methodological hypotheses, the audiovisual media consist in an interrelationship of iconic and sound forms — dynamic images, sound (noise and music), spoken and written words. Evolving in time and space, these bring about a flow in which the author's and spectator's thought and sensibility appear to be subsumed, as if in a sort of dialogue, a single act of comprehension of the world and its changes.

In both the spectator's and the author's aesthetic experience, the dynamism of the iconic and sound forms of the audiovisual media gives rise to what Merleau-Ponty called a "temporal form"[1] which we could also designate as a *complex system* — from the Latin *complector*: I comprehend, I embrace, I conceive; from *cum*: together, and *plecto*: web; in other words, a heterogeneous, unitary, but at the same time multi-faceted whole, which cannot

---

1 See Maurice Merleau-Ponty, 'Le cinéma et la nouvelle psychologie', in Id. [1966], *Sens et non-sens*, (Paris: NRF-Gallimard, 1996).

be reduced to its single reciprocally connected elements and which produces the emergence of sense, triggering perception, sensibility and thought all at the same time. The continuous metamorphosis of iconic and sound forms — unfurling over time as acceleration, slowdown, suspension, rhythm, etc. — actually brings about a progressive and reciprocal transformation of their functions, their

> status and their meaning. This modifies the time and the space of the experience and comprehension,[2] effecting a mediation between the spheres of the perceptible and the conceivable, the phenomenal and the symbolic, the real and the imaginary.[3]

In over a century of history of media and post-media technologies (from cinema to television and from internet to wearable technology), the audiovisual media have effectively defined an aesthetic whose complexity derives not only from polymorphic and polyphonic interrelations — dynamically put in place by a vast heterogeneous range of materials: kinetic image, montage, written word, noise, sound, music, spoken word) — but also from the relationship that these interrelations in turn entail between different domains, namely that of *mythos* and that of *logos*.

Although the sphere of sound also plays a fundamental role, it is the image and the word that have been historically indicated as the primary agents, particularly in the field of cinema studies, which was the first of the audiovisual or audio-verbal-visual media to make a novel proposal on the old question of the

---

2   The space-time experienced in audiovisual media especially implies a cognitive and epistemic elaboration setting aside single perceptive stimuli and regarding the *complex system* of their reciprocal relationships, in terms defined by Erwin Panofsky as "dynamization of space" and reciprocally "spacialization of time" and by Gilles Deleuze as "image-movement" and "image-time". See Erwin Panofsky, *Three Essays on Style* (Cambridge–Massachusetts: Mit Press, 1997); Id., [1955], *Meaning in the Visual Arts* (London: Penguin, 1996); Gilles Deleuze, *L'image-mouvement* (Paris: Minuit, 1983); Id., *L'image-temps* (Paris: Minuit, 1985).

3   See, among others, Edgar Morin [1956], *Le cinéma ou l'homme imaginaire* (Paris: Minuit, 2013); Christian Metz, *Le signifiant imaginaire*, (Paris: Christian Bourgeois, 1993).

relationship between verbal and visual registers. It progressively institutionalized an authentic *image-word dialogic*, in other words a complementarity, an antagonism and a reciprocal and generative influence between the two elements.

The history of the aesthetic and theoretical debate on cinema has sometimes investigated the principles, functions and articulations of this dialogic, but it has more frequently privileged the study of one or other of its factors, generally to affirm singularity and independence, sometimes correlating the superiority of *mythos* over *logos* or vice-versa.

From the origins of silent films to the advent of talking cinema,[4] for example, the aesthetic specificity, dignity and autonomy of film

---

4   We must remember that the adjective "silent", used to define cinema at its origins, wrongly denotes the absence of sound (words, noises, soundtrack music), almost as if it were a sort of deficiency. It was introduced only after the invention and widespread use of the soundtrack, when — to go back to Robert Desnos's thoughts on the cinema — the average cinema-goer gradually went "deaf" because of the advancing "verbal-centrism" of the cinema. Effectively, however, the contemporary spectator's presumed "deafness" is due not so much to the word in itself but to how it is used in film. The cinema has been verbal-centrist since its birth through the quantity and functions of written captions and the words uttered by narrators and story-tellers. Before the advent of sound, they would read aloud the writings on the screen to a largely illiterate audience or they would explain the temporal, spatial, associative and cause/effect links between the projected sequences to spectators who had not yet learnt the founding principles and the aesthetic foundations of the new medium. In this sense, it could be said that the audio-verbal-visual was initiated as an aesthetic illusion with the very birth of cinema. Otherwise, just as there is a belief in the existence of a "silent" cinema, so it should be believed that a "blind" cinema may exist, with a so-to-speak Brownian motion of sounds — words, music, noises — that are completely indistinct and so non-interpretable, that cannot be referred to any specific situation and are consequently unintelligible and incapable of activating imagination and thought. It can easily be noted how, in this hypothetical Brownian motion, a single recognizable spoken or written word would be enough to set off the relationships of the imagination with memory, thought and sensation. See Barthelémy Amengual, *Clefs pour le cinéma* (Paris: Seghers, 1971); Michel Chion [1990], *L'audiovision. Son et image au cinéma* (Paris: Armand Colin, 2013); Id., *Un art sonore, le cinéma. Histoire, esthétique, poétique*, (Paris: Cahiers du Cinéma, 2003).

has often been affirmed in the name of its presumed iconocentrism and at the cost of a deliberate devaluation of the role played by both music and the written and spoken word. Consequently, there thus developed with the very birth of cinema (besides the spread of photography) the field of visual culture studies. They were somehow placed in the channel of theories that Croce had previously defined as "pure visibility", and starting from the pioneering research of artists and theorists like Béla Balász, László Moholy-Nagy and Jean Epstein, they were subsequently further explored through definitions of film like "visual spectacle" or "moving picture". Thanks to the contribution of historians and theorists of the figurative arts, gestaltists or iconologists, such as Rudolf Arhneim, Erwin Panofsky or Carlo Ludovico Ragghianti, among others, these studies somehow merged into the iconic turn or pictorial turn between the last years of the 20th century and the first of the 21st. These terms delineate a specialized and at the same time transdisciplinary field of inquiry into the consideration of static and dynamic images, which increasingly interests scholars of aesthetics, media, and also anthropology, sociology, psychology, cognitive sciences and neurosciences.[5]

If it is true that the speculative horizon of visual culture studies is rooted in an old tradition that includes, among others, Kant, Nietzsche, Husserl, Heidegger, Sartre, Merleau-Ponty, Wittgenstein and Lacan, and whose beginnings go back to the origins of western thought (from the Greek *theoria,* which echoes θεαομαι: I look, observe, contemplate), it is equally true that they are responsible for the reappraisal of an imaginal way of knowledge, historically a minority view or often expunged from the dominant direction of western thought and knowledge. In the

---

5   For a good summary on visual culture studies see Andrea Pinotti and Antonio Somaini (eds.), *Teorie dell'immagine* (Milan: Raffaello Cortina, 2009); Id., *Cultura visuale* (Turin: Einaudi, 2016). On iconocentrism in cinema studies see, among others, at least: Rudolf Arnheim [1957], *Film as Art* (University of California Press); Carlo Ludovico Ragghianti, *Arti della visione I. Cinema* (Turin: Einaudi, 1976); Id., *Arti della visione II. Spettacolo* (Turin: Einaudi, 1976); Erwin Panofsky, *Meaning in the Visual Arts*.

context of visual culture studies, reflection on cinema has also contributed to an unprecedented clarification of the ontological and gnoseological status of the image, which cannot be traced back to conceptual and predicate logic.

The identification of an expression of meaning that is not otherwise substitutable nor assimilable to extraneous logics has recently been applied to the static, dynamic and audiovisual or audio-verbal-visual image, also as a reaction to a cultural tradition which in the second half of the 20th century had almost been proposed as a hegemonic and transdisciplinary tendency through the linguistic turn codified by Rorty following studies by Peirce, Hjelmslev, Jakobson, Lotman, Greimas and others. Through subsequent derivations, such as the semiotic turn, the narrativist turn and the pragmatic turn, there was effectively a use of methods, concepts, principles and terminologies that were transferred from linguistic research to the sphere of the image per se and not just the audio-verbal-visual one. This resulted in the attribution of a forced verbal-centrism to the image and to its specific way of shaping and interpreting the world, thus disregarding the peculiarity of its own aesthetic-epistemic dimension. Saussure's distinction between *langue* and *parole* gave rise to an investigation into the audio-verbal-visual that was made by "difference" with regard to the verbal sign and aiming to include it in the sphere of *logos*. The semantic and structural discontinuity was admittedly pointed out, yet Metz, Pasolini, Barthes, Casetti, Bellour, Bordwell and others attributed to it specific "discursiveness", "syntax", "textuality", "narrativity", "statements", etc.[6]

Let us remember how the first and most notable contributions in the context of linguistics-based studies on the word-image

---

6   On the linguistic turn and its derivations in cinema studies see, among others, at least: Christian Metz, *Le signifiant imaginaire* (Paris: Christian Bourgois, 1993); Pier Paolo Pasolini [1972], *Empirismo Eretico* (Milan: Garzanti, 2000); Roland Barthes [1964], *Essais critiques* (Paris: Seuil, 1991); Roger Odin, *De la fiction* (Bruxelles: De Boeck, 2000); Francesco Casetti, *Dentro lo sguardo* (Milan: Bompiani, 1986); Raymond Bellour [1990], *L'Entre-Images: photo, cinéma, vidéo* (Paris: POL, 1999); David Bordwell, *Narration in the Fictional Film* (Madison: University of Wisconsin, 1985).

relationship in audio-verbal-visual media include Roland
Barthes's identification of verbal functions, under the categories
of "anchorage", where the first term — the word — intervenes
with its explanatory value towards the "fluctuating polysemy"
of the second — the image; and of "relay", when the first term
prepares and anticipates the temporal development of the second
or after the event recalls what has not been represented, in both
cases asserting its own evocative power. More generally, we can
remember how, essentially, some of the contributions from the
linguistic turn have opened up various sets of questions regarding
the history and status of the audio-verbal-visual media and the
presence of the word from the very start. The word has been
studied in the context of the audio-verbal-visual media through
the evolution of codes, forms of expression and significant
configurations, which have included a great many systems of
articulation: from captions to the proliferation of various vocal
styles, from dubbing to subtitles. Another set of questions
raised by linguistics-based studies concerns the typology of
temporal relations, whether synchronous or asynchronous,
given by montage within the same shot (vertical montage) or
between several shots (external or horizontal montage). These
are relations that together regard the issue of subjectivity and
identity, since they call into question the free play between the
presence and absence of the voice and/or body in audio-verbal-
visual sequences and the consequent total or partial "acousmetre"
theorized by Chion.[7]

In this framework of speculation, the most important set of
problems in the theory and aesthetics of audio-verbal-visual
media has been posed by both the linguistic turn and the iconic
turn and concerns the aesthetic-epistemic relationship implicit
in the image-word dialogic, with the relative implications for
comprehension. In such a context, it may be noted how the
first the linguistic turn and then the iconic turn seem to have
operated methodologically within an interdisciplinarity and

---

7   Michel Chion, *L'audiovision. Son et image au cinéma*; Id., *Un art sonore,
      le cinéma. Histoire, esthétique, poétique.*

a transdisciplinarity that are marked by hegemonic or in any case antagonistic approaches. Their most fruitful results seem to consist not so much in the primacy of *logos* over *mythos* or vice-versa, nor in the assimilation of the figural to the linguistic or vice-versa and not even in the identification of the iconic dimension exclusively with the visual reason, but rather in an analysis of the aesthetic-epistemic functions performed *jointly* by the word and the image in the audio-verbal-visual media. In other words, the word-image relationship has been more frequently analyzed from a dialectical perspective, namely as a synthetic development marked by negation, rather than a dialogical one, where the generative movement results from the reciprocal influence between complementary opposites in metamorphosis. Overcoming a phase of agonal interdisciplinarity or transdisciplinarity might, on one hand, limit hyperspecialization and reductionism, while on the other hand, it would permit the development of a research method able to generatively combine the contributions of different disciplines in a complex aesthetic dedicated to the system of audio-verbal-visual media in order to grasp the word-image dialogic. This, in fact, merely reproposes a *modus operandi* that unites sensibility and thought and that is found in the context of several disciplines: from psychology of perception to neuroscience, from aesthetics to epistomology.

As they interact, the word and the image of audio-verbal-visual media determine a union and a cooperation that unleashes a continuous and reciprocal transformation: the word passes through the image and changes its sense; crossed by the word, the image changes the word. A similar combination determines a semiotically heterogeneous system that is at the same time semantically unitary and in progress, in which the multidimensionality of the sense comes from a plurality of aspects of the sensible — including, incidentally, the concrete visual and auditory forms through which the word is transmitted.

In the context of developing a complex aesthetic, a first methodological hypothesis concerns the link between the aesthetic-epistemic unity and plurality of audio-verbal-visual media and the synaesthesia peculiar to it, which is unprecedented as it is dynamic. This synaesthetic *dynamis* is consubstantiated with a semantic coalescence: the impossibility of isolating in "pure" or "autonomous" sensitive data the single percepts of the author's and spectator's sensorial experience provokes a sense that is situated in a literally imperceptible transversal dimension and thus entrusted to the elaboration of the thought and the imagination and their respective inferences, inductions, deductions, associations, etc. We could define this type of thought as *trans-sensorial*, referring to the notion of "sensorial thought" formulated by Ejzenštejn, and to Chion's[8] "trans-sensorial perceptions."

The imperceptibility and therefore the absence or weakness of the visual and auditory perceptible has given rise to trans-sensorial thought, which, firstly through the imagination, emphatically completes the sense, literally moving it outside the audio-verbal-visual, elsewhere and other.

The imagination therefore underlies both the mediation between visible and invisible and audible and inaudible and the translation from the experience of the sensorium to the abstraction of thought. A long-lasting philosophical tradition, going at least from Kant to Heidegger, and from Sartre to Deleuze and beyond, has pointed out the multiple elaborative functions of the imagination, some of which need only be mentioned here. Besides conserving the traces of what is perceived and reproducing them even without sensorial stimuli, the imagination projects its own interpretative schemes and paradigms on perception and percepts, and thus, in a constant interrelation with perception, memory and language, it exercises a triple function, reproductive, creative and interactive. In particular, the imagination effects a mediation between sensorium and language, between *mythos* and *logos,* making them complementary, in that it links sensible configurations with a need that we might call "pre-linguistic" and that selects the most pertinent semantic possibilities, but without yet defining them. The need for language, necessarily brought forward in this

---

8   See Sergei Eisenstein, *Selected Works*, ed. by Richard Taylor, vols. I, II, III (London: Taurius, 2010).

indeterminate way, may subsequently operate following a double function: one more closely linked to the *logos*, which discriminate between semantic pertinences and impertinences, directing them towards known meanings and concepts, and one more rooted in the *mythos*, which can creatively regenerate the processes of perception and imagination, introducing new semantic and conceptual schemes.[9]

The imagination therefore performs its own mediatory function, intervening in the vast and dynamic sphere where there are numerous reciprocal relations between the principle of *mythos* and that of *logos,* or, to fall back on Edgar Morin's effective definitions, between analogical, symbolic and mythological thought and logical, rational, empirical thought.[10] In Morin's epistemology, the two types of thought are inserted in a complex dialogic not only because they are complementary yet at the same time antagonistic, but also in that each of them is partly incorporated in the other. This makes it clear why Merleau-Ponty glossed Kant's formulation according to which in knowledge imagination works to the benefit of the intellect, and was able to state how instead in the aesthetic dimension and specifically in cinema, the intellect works to the benefit of the imagination.[11]

From the aesthetic-epistemic perspective that we take here, the imagination, in relation to trans-sensorial thought, may be considered as a transmuter, which, through the action performed between the iconosphere and the verbal sphere, is able to bring into being potentially infinite quantities and qualities in the context of a third sphere, that of ideas or the noosphere, where *mythos* and *logos* intersect.

---

9   See among others Paul Ricœur, *La Métaphore vive* (Paris: Seuil, 1975); Emilio Garroni, *Immagine Linguaggio Figura* (Rome–Bari: Laterza, 2005); Id., *Creatività* (Macerata: Quodlibet, 2010); Pietro Montani, *Tecnologie della sensibilità* (Milan: Raffaello Cortina, 2014).

10   Edgar Morin [1986], *La Méthode 3. La Connaissance de la Connaissance* (Paris: Seuil, 2008); Id., *La Méthode 4. Les idées. Leur habitat, leur vie, leur mœurs, leur organisation* (Paris: Seuil, 1986); Id., *La Méthode 5. L'Humanité de l'Humanité. L'identité humaine* (Paris: Seuil, 2001); Id., *La Méthode 6. Éthique* (Paris: Seuil, 2004).

11   Maurice Merleau-Ponty, *Sens et non-sens* (Paris: NRF-Gallimard, 1996).

Indeed one of the expressive conventions of the aesthetics of audio-verbal-visual media — even beyond the various historical-cultural and aesthetic determinations, linked to genres, formats implicit in different media or devices — wants the expression of a precise meaning to be entrusted first to the resources of the imagination and, secondly, to be made explicit by the word, often the spoken word.

More rarely, the aesthetic-epistemic process happens the other way; whether due to the primary opening to the stimulus typical of the sensorium and the subsequent link with the imagination, which in turn the latter has with thought; or due to the direction of the ontogenetic and phylogenetic development of analogical, symbolic and mythological thought and of logical, rational, empirical thought.

When language intervenes after the event in the audio-verbal-visual media and further opens the polysemy of the image following original or novel possibilities, the word-image dialogic takes on a recursive loop structure, in which the reciprocal metamorphic influence between the iconic and sound forms takes place on the basis of the inter-retro-action between analogical, symbolic and mythological thought and logical, rational, empirical thought, mediated by the imagination.

In the audio-verbal-visual media, the imagination may determine a concurrence between the polysemy of the image and that of the word, indefinitely opening the semantic risk. This occurs more easily when the poetic dimension of the language is invoked, even independently of the use of poetry in the strictest sense of the word. In this case, the word-image dialogic intensifies the transmutation performed by the imagination between analogical, symbolic and mythological thought and logical, rational, empirical thought. When verbal tropes are accompanied by iconic tropes — *trópos*: translation —, the trans-sensorial thought intervenes, implying the exchange both from one sensorial sphere to another and from one semantic field to another, concrete/abstract, phenomenal/symbolic.[12]

---

12   On this point, see Paul Adams Sitney, *The Cinema Poetry* (New York–Oxford: Oxford University Press, 2015).

In this free play of exchanges of forms and meanings, we believe that there is to be found a particularly important potential, from both an aesthetic and an epistemic point of view. We shall now try to investigate the complex relationship between these two dimensions, as it is found in the audio-verbal-visual media, by means of the analysis of some extracts from works taken as *exempla*, first having duly given a brief terminological and methodological clarification.

If, on the one hand, it is clear that in the framework of this study, the aesthetic instance is meant in its original sense, deriving from αἴσθησις: "sensory perception", and going back to the Homeric *aiou* and *aisthou*, which means "I perceive", "I am breathless, I am trying to breathe"; on the other hand, it must be clarified that the epistemic dimension examined here concerns analogical, symbolic and mythological thought more than logical, rational, empirical thought. It is thus different from knowledge as understood in the scientific sphere, which, as is known, is defined as *comprehension* — from the Latin *cum-pre(he)ndĕre*, "take together": contain in itself, accept spiritually, account for something.

The meaning given to comprehension here refers, in particular, to a sort of subjective knowledge, which, in Gadamer's hermeneutic terms, represents an "experience of truth" that changes one who undergoes it.[13] In this sense, comprehension refers to the notions of *Verstehen* and *Einfühlung*, originally studied by German historicism and Husserlian phenomenology. However, it does not only concern the empathic-imaginative simulation used between subjects to obtain theoretical and practical inferences on the other — as traditionally happened and happens in studies developed by Dilthey, Simmel, Wittgenstein and Collingwood onwards; it rather concerns, *in extenso*, being introduced into an occurrence in which a particular sense emerges.

Moreover, comprehension is taken here in its two-fold and hierarchical articulation — just as it is conceived in the perspective of Morin's complex epistemology.

---

13   See Hans Georg Gadamer [1960], *Wahrheit und Methode* (Tubingen: Mohr, 2010).

At a first level, which we could define as *fundamental comprehension*, in the dialogic between analogical, symbolic, mythological thought and logical, rational, empirical thought, the first of the two thoughts is preponderant. What is particularly important at this level of comprehension is the psychological processes of identification, projection and transfer, which derive from perceptive, sensorial, emotional and affective solicitation. Particularly in the context of aesthetics, thanks to the use of the imagination, these may concern human beings and other beings of the cosmos, guaranteeing a deep involvement of the sensibility and an intense aesthetic participation, though always accompanied by an awareness of the distinction between the real and its aesthetic representation.[14] To quote Gadamer's words: 'He who comprehends is already always in an event in which a particular sense asserts itself'.[15]

A first example of fundamental comprehension may be found at the beginning of the film *Der Himmel über Berlin* (*Wings of Desire*, 1987) by Wim Wenders, which shows the image of a man writing on a sheet of paper some words from the poem *Als das Kind Kind war* (*When the Child was a Child*, 1987)[16] by Peter Handke — a well-known Austrian novelist, poet, dramatist and screenwriter —, recited by a voice-over as a sort of nursery rhyme:

---

14   On this point see Edgar Morin, *Le cinéma ou l'homme imaginaire*.

15   Hans Georg Gadamer, *Wahrheit und Methode*, p. 558.

16   Here is the part of the poem *Song on Childhood* which was composed for the film and is recited in it several times: 'When the child was a child, | It walked with its arms swinging, | wanted the brook to be a river, | the river to be a torrent, | and this puddle to be the sea. | When the child was a child, | it didn't know that it was a child, | everything was soulful, | and all souls were one. | When the child was a child, | it had no opinion about anything, | had no habits, || it often sat | cross-legged, | took off running, | had a cowlick in its hair, | and made no faces when photographed. | When the child | was a child, | It was the time for these questions: || Why am I me, and why not you? | Why am I here, and why not there? | When did time begin, and where does space end? | Is life under the sun not just a dream? | Is what I see and hear and smell | not just an illusion of a world before the world? | Given the facts of evil and people. | does evil really exist? | How can it | be that I, who I am, | didn't exist before I came to be, || and that, someday, I, who I am, | will no longer be who I am?'.

When the child was a child, | It walked with its arms swinging, | wanted the brook to be a river, | the river to be a torrent, | and this puddle to be the sea. | When the child was a child, | it didn't know that it was a child, | everything was soulful, | and all souls were one. | When the child was a child, | it had no opinion about anything, | had no habits, || it often sat | cross-legged, | took off running, | had a cowlick in its hair, | and made no faces when photographed.

The voice-over goes on reciting, even over the images of the opening credits until it is replaced by music, over which there first appears a dynamic aerial view of some city blocks, and subsequently the figure of a man standing on a ledge who is looking down and on whose shoulders there are wings that appear and disappear in double exposure. The image shows what the man was presumably looking at below, namely the coming and going of the crowd, in which stands out a motionless little girl who seems to be looking up towards the man, who, however, has disappeared from the image, letting us glimpse the ledge of the bell-tower where he was before. Then we have the image of a little girl on a bus, who, looking up presumably at the man on the ledge, says to her friend: 'Look!'

In this audio-verbal-visual sequence, the poem fulfills the task of defining the relationship with the world peculiar to childhood, assimilating it to what follows in the film, first by the children, who are the only ones to perceive the symbolic presence of the angels, and then by the angels, the only ones able to grasp the inner life of the human beings and listen to their thoughts. That, in fact, is what the following sequence shows, where there is the image of a man walking in the street carrying a baby in a sling, while a new voice-over says: 'The delight of lifting one's head out here in the open'. On these words an image opens up of a bird circling among the clouds and the voice-over adds: 'On seeing the colors, in all men's eyes, enlightened by the sun'. From this moment of the film, images follow each other of different urban contexts, with children, adolescents or adults in the centre, all accompanied in the same way by their various voice-overs, which express their thoughts in the form of a fragmentary and poetic interior monologue. In this way, even in the heterogeneity of fleetingly presented situations and characters, it will be possible to reach a profound comprehension of each of them, their experience, their fears, aspirations, needs, frustrations, etc., implementing as many psychological processes of identification, projection and transfer and using trans-sensorial thought creatively — as happens in the sequence just described, where the vision of the bird's flight in the sky and the evocation in words of the light in the people's eyes appear to merge together in a sense of freedom and fullness.

We can select another particularly effective example of solicitation of fundamental comprehension through word-image dialogic in Andrey Tarkovsky's autobiographical work *Zerkalo* (*The Mirror*, 1975). The author's subjectivity is expressed in the non-chronological dramatic structure, which uses a sort of stream of consciousness to interlace and mix various levels of representation — childhood memories, oneirism, historical memory, present reality — with citations of his own films and paintings by Brueghel and Vermeer, as well as in the literary-style introspection, which is entrusted to poetry and uses, among others, the recitative „Und siehe da, der Vorhang im Tempel..." taken from the *Johannes Passion* by Johan Sebastian Bach, or the opening words of Dante's *Divina Commedia*. The voice-over by Andrey's brother Arseny Tarkovsky — who is known to have been one of the most important Russian poets of the 20th century — recites the poem *Pervye svidanija* (*First meetings*, 1962)[17] in a sequence of the film during which childhood memory

---

17   Arseny Tarkovsky, *First Meetings*, 1962, in Andrey Tarkovsky, A *Sculpting in Time* (Austin: University of Texas, 2003): 'We celebrated every moment | Of our meetings as epiphanies, | Just we two in all the world. | Bolder, lighter than a bird's wing, | You hurtled like vertigo | Down the stairs, leading | Through moist lilac to your realm | Beyond the mirror. | When night fell, grace was given me, | The sanctuary gates were opened, | Shining in the darkness | Nakedness bowed slowly; | Waking up, I said: | "God bless you!", knowing it | To be daring: you slept, | The lilac leaned towards you from the table | To touch your eyelids with its universal blue, | Those eyelids brushed with blue | Were peaceful, and your hand was warm. | And in the crystal I saw pulsing rivers, | Smoke-wreathed hills, and glimmering seas; | Holding in your palm that crystal sphere, | You slumbered on the throne, | And — God be praised! — you belonged to me. | Awaking, you transformed | The humdrum dictionary of humans |

merges with the actual present through a montage constituting the word-image dialogic. The daytime image of a woman who first observes a man walking away across a meadow and then in turn walks slowly through a wood towards home is accompanied with the lines: 'We celebrated every moment | Of our meetings as epiphanies | Just we two in all the world. | Bolder, lighter than a bird's wing, | You hurtled like vertigo | Down the stairs, leading | Through moist lilac to your realm | Beyond the mirror'. On the word "mirror", the image of a little boy, in a farmyard at dusk, appears first to observe the previous scene and then to walk away, exiting from the shot and letting us glimpse his semi-naked little sister left sleeping on the ground and their mother who bends down and picks her up. The scene is accompanied with the words: 'When night fell, | grace was given me, | The sanctuary gates were opened, | Shining in the darkness | Nakedness bowed slowly'. At this point the image-word dialogic becomes more complex not only due to the verbal-visual resonance between the darkness of the scene and the expression "When night fell", but above all due to the interior and semantic resonance between the gesture of the mother that appears in the image and that of the lover evoked in the poem: they mirror each other in the sense of love and giving that both express, albeit in different ways. The close-up image of Aleksey eating together with his sister and slowly placing a handful of sugar on a cat's head is linked by analogous exterior and semantic symmetry to the profanation of the gesture of baptism, evoked by the lines: 'Waking up, I said: | "God bless you!", knowing it | To be daring'.

In this sequence, the word-image dialogic is structured on deep semantic echoes, which symmetrically reflect the specularity of

---

Till speech was full and running over | With resounding strength, and the word you | Revealed its new meaning: it meant king. | Everything in the world was different, | Even the simplest things — the jug, the basin — | When stratified and solid water | Stood between us, like a guard. | We were led to who knows where. | Before us opened up, in mirage, | Towns constructed out of wonder, | Mint leaves spread themselves beneath our feet, | Birds came on the journey with us, | Fish leapt in greeting from the river, | And the sky unfurled above… | While behind us all the time went fate, | A madman brandishing a razor'.

two of the levels of representation — childhood memories and actual present —, in which the same situation is symbolically mirrored: the abandonment by Oleg, the protagonist's father and *alter ego* of the author, Aleksey, of his wife, Maria, and the abandonment by Aleksey of his wife, Natalia. It is no accident that the parts of the protagonist's mother and wife are played by the same actor (Margarita Terekhova); this enriches the sequence and the whole film with emotional-affective ambivalences and semantic ambiguities, which are very effective in soliciting what Wittgenstein defined "resonance"[18] of comprehension, or in our terms, of fundamental comprehension, developed with regard to the deep psychology of the author and his *alter ego* Aleksey. In fact, this sequence shows how the combination of polysemy of the image and of the word may render the concrete/abstract, phenomenal/symbolic translation complex and creative, by using a recursive loop structure to intensify the transmutation achieved by the imagination between analogical, symbolic and mythological thought and logical, rational and empirical thought.

At a higher level of comprehension, which we could define as *complex comprehension*, logical, rational, empirical thought proves to be pre-eminent in the dialogic with analogical, symbolic and mythological thought. This pre-eminence does not exclude but is indeed essential to the deep involvement of sensibility that occurs in fundamental comprehension and that is, as it were, incorporated and assimilated so as to be overcome in its contingent aspects and particular expressions and to allow a wider and higher understanding. In fact, what Morin defined as "meta-point of view" intervenes in complex comprehension; this is a point of view on a point of view, which offers the opportunity to activate a two-fold observation of the real. As is typical of fundamental comprehension, this is immersed in the specific definitions of the real and maintains the psychological processes of identification, projection and transfer, and *at the same time*, it withdraws from the previous one and includes it in a wider

---

18   Ludwig Wittgenstein, *Philosophical Investigations: Critical Essays* (Lanham: Rowman and Littlefield, 2006).

overview so as to grasp the general or universal meaning. One of the main outcomes of complex comprehension, which derives from the use of the meta-point of view and explains the pre-eminence it gives to logical, rational and empirical thought, consists in the possibility of developing not only reflexivity but also self-reflexivity and hence self-criticism: to the "experience of truth", which is already implied by fundamental comprehension, is thus added, in complex comprehension, a potential transformation of the one who understands.

In the scene of milk and strawberries at sunset, taken from the film *Det sjunde inseglet* (*The Seventh Seal*, 1957), in a few moments the image-word dialogic, moving to the symbolic, opens unexpected opportunities for complex comprehension. The characters of the work symbolize the three stages of the human being, according to Kierkegaard's concept: the Juggler represents the aesthetic stage; the Squire, the ethical stage; the Knight, the religious stage. To these is added Death, who appears several times to the Knight, immersed in an existential and spiritual crisis. In the film, therefore, not only the characters, but also their actions and their words, are all taken in a sense that cannot be, as it were, literal, but symbolic, and in some scenes, it acquires a very wide significance, which, returning to Kierkegaard, could be defined existential. The scene in question offers exemplary evidence, in that it forcefully imposes on logical, rational, empirical thought the continuous transcendence of the levels of experience and interpretation that is typical of the meta-point of view. In this scene, the image shows all the characters — apart from Death — sitting in a meadow at dusk; the Juggler is murmuring and playing a sweet melody on his lute, while his wife is offering bowls of freshly milked milk and freshly picked wild strawberries to the Knight, who at first refuses them and earnestly, clasping his hands and interlacing his fingers, says: 'To believe is to suffer. It is like loving someone in the dark, who never answers'. The Juggler's wife then again offers the Knight the strawberries and milk and he finally accepts, smiling and adding: 'How unreal that in your company. It means nothing to me now'. The shot, which firstly just included the face of the Knight, the Juggler and his wife, now expands and, in an effect of chiaroscuro given by the light of the low setting sun, also shows the Squire and the cart on which Michael, the Juggler's son, is sleeping: 'I shall remember this hour of peace: the strawberries, the bowl of milk, your faces in the dusk, Michael asleep, Joseph with his lute. I shall remember our words'. The Knight again picks up the bowl full of milk and, after drinking, concludes: 'I shall bear this memory between my hands, as carefully as a bowl of fresh milk. And this will be a sign and a great content. Something to believe in'. The lyricism of the scene is given by the symbolic value of the word and the image, whose dialogic places both on a poetic level, independently of the fact that the text they recite does not belong to a poem. The image-word dialogic indeed strengthens the symbolic and poetic value that the two elements would have if taken individually. What is concretely shown and named — the milk, the strawberries and the dusk light — is symbolically taken in its wider semantic and existential value. In confirmation of this, there is, in particular, the coincidence between the image where the Knight drinks from the bowl held in his hands and the final words which refer to holding in the hands, keeping carefully and accepting a comforting truth in which to believe. If, on the one hand, it is thanks to the identification, projection and transfer with the Knight that it is possible to share the existential revelation he has obtained and make it one's own, on the other hand, it is by virtue of the meta-point of view obtained that it is possible to reach a complex comprehension on one's own way of experiencing life, as well as that of other human beings.

In the work *The Tree of Life* (2015) by Terrence Malick, the complex comprehension concerns the experience of life, probing the depth, vastness and mutability of human feeling and thought in the sphere of family love and the cycle of birth and death. It also concerns the relationship that all this has with nature and its processes of creation and destruction, order, disorder and metamorphosis. The image-word dialogic is conducted with a high degree of symbolism, by virtue of the semantic evocation, ambivalence and uncertainty that are imprinted on the subtraction, elision and essentiality of the iconic and verbal forms of expression.

'What are you thinking?' says Jack's voice-over, after he has apologized to his father on the phone after an argument, while he is going around his office, where there are other people. 'As I lost you?', adds Jack's voice-over, accompanied by a long shot of a tree near the office window, with sun rays filtering through its foliage. On the image of an ocean wave breaking loudly, the voice-over continues: 'I departed'. On the words 'I forgot you' Jack appears with his face in his hands that are wet with water from a puddle, in which his figure is reflected, now immersed in a rocky desert. In this sequence, the correspondence between the semantic ambiguity and the formal essentiality both of images and words places both elements on the side of the symbolic. The transformation of the subjects of the performance and of the contexts, as well as fragmentary laconism of the interior monologue, open the sense indefinitely, and by disorientating the fundamental comprehension with regard to the protagonist, solicit it to grasp his interior plurality: who is Jack addressing? His father who he was speaking to on the phone? His dead brother he was badmouthing to his father? Himself, as in an act of self-criticism? Or perhaps God, who was indirectly evoked at the start of the film? All these hypotheses remain plausible, validating various levels of interpretation, from the literal to the symbolic, since the images interlace reality with oneirism, in a sort of stream of consciousness, which includes childhood memories right from the start of the film. The iconic and verbal polysemy is thus moved to the highest degree, intensifying the concrete/abstract, phenomenal/symbolic relationship and powerfully invoking the imagination. Shortly after this sequence, the image of Jack's mother as a young woman appears, as she walks in a wood with a distressed expression on her face and observes the rays of the sun through the foliage of the trees. On this image, the woman's voice-over bursts out: 'Oh, God! Why?' On these words, a long series of images starts off, showing the metamorphic dynamism of forms, colors, lights of planets, stars, galaxies, deserts, volcanoes, oceans, rivers, rocks, plants, animals, and puts next to them that of cells, blood vessels and some organs of the body of a mother and human fetus. In a continuous and flowing passage from macroscopy to microscopy, from the cosmos to the human microcosmos, from phylogenesis to ontogenesis, the movement of life appears in its metamorphic multiplicity and unity, thanks to combinations and fusions or confusions of images which bring out the similarity or repetition of the same elements or processes. Jack's mother's words maintain semantic uncertainty in that they first seem to be an exclamation of grief for Jack's brother's premature death, which Jack had evoked on the phone to his father; subsequently, with the start of the images of the life of the cosmos and of man, they appear as the expression of stupor at existence itself, in its various forms and manifestations. With the words: 'Oh, God! Why?', what only seemed to be a flashback with Jack's childhood memories of his brother's death becomes also a sort of flashback on the history of life in the cosmos, with a transition from the point of view, which first was to be found in the singularity of an existence, and subsequently becomes a meta-point of view extending out of all proportion towards the horizons of the many-sided unity of lives. Around these same words, not only is the thematization of death interlaced with that of life, but the birth of all beings, and not only humans, observed in their similarity, opens up the question of the possibility of a single divine creation. The aesthetic-epistemic relationship between concrete/abstract, phenomenal/symbolic is here structured in a semantic-metamorphic recursive loop and seems thus to move towards a relationship between immanence and transcendence.

From the fundamental comprehension concerning the subjectivity of Jack and his mother, caught in their existential anxieties, we thus reach a complex comprehension, which regards the subjectivity of all beings in similar vital processes. Reflexivity and self-reflexivity, forcefully provoked, are moved towards an interrogative on the relationship between human existence and other existences and between oneself and the cosmos.

This and many other audio-verbal-visual works, besides the ones examined here, show how the aesthetic experience, being a subjective participation in the metamorphosis of sound and verbal iconic forms, may epistemically experience the world and itself as an ongoing experience, from which potentially arises the question on one's own or other's being, and maybe action, too.

PART TWO

VISUAL AND VERBAL PLAY IN BARBARA HODGSON'S *THE LIVES OF SHADOWS*

Maja Duranovic
(University of Turin)

Complex connections between visual and verbal elements, their meanings and their messages have always been of great interest to psychologists, sociologists, literary and cultural critics, such as Walter Benjamin, Roland Barthes, William Edward Burghardt Dubois, and Susan Sontag, and in recent times especially to visual artists, critics and researchers in media and visual studies. With the birth of digital photography connections between visual and verbal elements have become more complex and so has the interpretation of their meanings and interactions.

The interesting novel by Barbara Hodgson, *The Lives of Shadows*,[1] (2004) is set in the Middle East, in Damascus, Syria. It describes the period between the First World War (1915—18) and the Second World War (1938–45), with occasional comments on the bombings of Damascus in 1925. The narrative is enriched with old photographs, postcards, maps, architectural drawings, old newspaper articles, and pages with Arabic script and calligraphy. This perfect combination results in a visually stunning experience to readers of *The Lives of Shadows*. Its pages and artistic quality, in varying shades of sepia, lead the reader to a time before French Syria was ravaged by world wars. The plot involves a distinct combination of historical narrative, mystery, ghost story, and a haunting love story. Its visual contents make it a specific artistic and architectural testimony.

---

1   Barbara Hodgson, *The Lives of Shadows* (Chronicle Books LLC, 2012 [2004]), (Amazon Digital Services, Inc., Kindle); (all visual materials and subsequent references will be taken from this edition and referenced in the form "Loc." followed by a page number).

Besides providing a summary of the novel, I propose to analyse the way in which visual materials and text are interconnected. Some photographs are singled out and further attention is drawn to illustrations and other visual materials which clarify mysteries and occasional temporal gaps to the reader. I then propose to discuss the way in which Hodgson incorporated a number of visual elements as evidential support to the story. Consequently, architectural drawings help the reader's imagination and facilitate a visual reconstruction of the descriptions provided by the narrators. I finally intend to show how some of Barthes's ideas on photography surface in Hodgson's novel.

The novel is set in Damascus, Syria, between 1914 and 1945. The story follows the life of Julian Beaufort, a young Englishman who leaves his country and travels in the Middle East. His journey takes him to Damascus, which mesmerises him with its beauty, and his heart is taken by an amazing ancient palace, Bait Katib, which dates back to the period of the Ottoman Empire. The building hides a peculiar feature: the history of the palace and of its inhabitants is written on its walls. The owners are a middle-aged couple, Nasim and Muna, who have no male heirs, but one daughter who will soon get married and leave home. Julian is totally enchanted with their home and he is such a good person that they decide to take him in to live with them and eventually they leave the house to him. He promises to continue the story of this home on the walls. He slowly learns Arabic and fully understands the scripts around him. The story starts in 'present-day' Damascus, that is, at the end of the Second World War in 1945, when Julian is forced to prove his ownership of Bait Katib palace or otherwise it will be taken from him. A series of mysterious events which involve the daughter of the first owner of the palace, named Asilah, occur. They are ghostly events, because she actually died in the bombing of Damascus in 1925, but Julian does not know this. He feels the strong presence of her spirit and he hopes, until the end of the novel, when he learns the truth, that she is still alive. Since he is not able to find the owner's title deed, he must write a detailed history of his possession in order to certify it. The story reveals not only the history of the house and the family but also the history of the city and of the people who live there. Grounded as it is in a real place and time and thanks to the architectural details it provides, the novel is characterised by a dreamy, even ghostly, evocation of lost worlds and people. It throws the reader back into history, so that he can learn something about that unfamiliar side of the war in Damascus.

Hodgson decided once again, similarly to what happens in her other novels, to play with the position of the narrators and with the interconnections between text and visual elements, carefully placing the visual elements so as to complete and complement the descriptions and ekphrases which the narrators produce. Most of the photographs of the city are shown before the actual part of the town or the characters' actions are described, as if to announce or anticipate the events that will take place. Several photographs from family albums are placed within the narrative but none has any caption, nor are they described before or after appearing in the text. The reader must understand the connections between specific parts of the novel and the photographs shown in order to fully appreciate Hodgson's technique in using photos.

In the novel there are three narrations which intertwine. They intertwine so smoothly that the reader, unless he pays close attention, does not notice any abrupt change. The first narrative thread is spun by the omniscient third-person narrator, who often describes the actions of Julian and Asilah and sometimes fills in the gaps between the other two narratives. The second narrative thread provides Julian's perspective on the past and on current events, which are described in the notebook that Julian wants to use as the proof of his ownership of Bait Katib. This narrative is marked by beautiful descriptions of physical objects, historical events and people from the past, and by the feeling of being haunted and watched. The third narrative thread is entrusted to Asilah's version of the story, history and events. It is contrasted with Julian's narration of the same events and it is marked by a subtler and more feminine tone. It is characterised by a nostalgic mood and often speaks about events unknown to Julian but necessary for him to complete the story of Bait Katib; it also manifests itself to express a point of view different from Julian's, that of an insider. Asilah's view of the events is written in Arabic. Her handwriting begins at the back of that same notebook in which Julian is writing his story. It seems that the presence of these last two narrative streams and these two separate perspectives is necessary for the complete understanding of the events and relations within the novel, and the story is complete only if both are taken into consideration.

Apart from the three narrative threads, a significant problem for the reader in understanding the events may be represented by the constant temporal leaps. The narrators speak about the present, in 1945, but they also occasionally just slip into the past to the 1920s or sometimes even to the period before the First World War. Thus, although the chapters are all named after the predominant narrator and are all dated according to the time at which Julian writes his notebook of ownership, namely during four days and nights at the end of May 1945, within each chapter it is possible to have several temporal leaps. Hodgson helps the reader by inserting photographs most of which show the state of the city or Bait Katib palace in the time of those events, thus helping the reader to understand the sequence of the events better.

Photographs as a Means of Transposing Memories and Ghosts

While narrating the story and documenting his days in Bait Katib, Julian often comments on the importance of those old photographs he finds in the house even after its destruction. They create connections with the past events he lived through, which become alive again in front of his eyes and in his memory. Several characters who highly influenced Julian's life are described in great detail; however their photographs never appear in the novel, either because they were destroyed in bombings and fires, or because they were torn apart, or the faces were cut off from them.

Julian makes an interesting observation while remembering his life during the war years, when he was injured and then forced to leave Damascus. He spent a few years recuperating in a hospital and fell in love with a nurse who was taking care of him. He noticed that with the disappearance of the photographs most of his memories blurred and faded away; there was not much left and some other memories occupied their place.

> There were also some photographs — of a nurse I was sweet on while recuperating. Trouble was, though she was game for a fling, when it came to marriage she preferred a chap who didn't have bits of metal in his brain. I don't blame her; my sole achievement, after two years on the mend, had been the knitting of a scarf. Not to mention that I bored her to tears with all my blather about Damascus, which hardly struck her as a place to make a home. *When I tore up her photos, I had nothing left to tie me to the past except a few souvenirs saved from my earlier travels* (Loc. 726–730, *my emphasis*)

The novel opens with a sample from Julian's album which testifies to his travels in faraway countries. Before the narration starts there is a map of the Mediterranean and this photo:

Although in most cases there are no captions accompanying the photos, they are articulated within Julian's narration so as to provide the reader with clues and to help him identifying the people who appear in them. Sometimes, there is a year or a partially visible date; thus, the reader can place the photo in the correct temporal frame.

Another interesting photograph appears in the midst of Julian's descriptions of typical houses in Damascus and of the Bait Katib palace. He explains the way he senses a connection with the city and feels as if he has been living there all his life. It is not strange that after these descriptions the following photograph should appear:

As a matter of fact, the reader can assume that this is the photograph of the Bait Katib palace owners because they were the source of Julian's feeling of belonging to the place. They always made him feel comfortable and treated him almost as the son they never had. The second thing that makes the reader take the identity of the people in the photo for granted is a hidden clue behind it, the paper with musical notes. The couple who owned the house had always played the piano and sung together, and Julian remembers their music perfectly.

The second photo from Julian's album is of Ahmed, a person who always helped the family in Bait Katib and who remained in the palace after their death and later helped Julian. He is a faithful servant and a friend to Julian. The latter describes recurrently Ahmed's way of dressing, his appearance, and above all how he behaves and what he fears. However, almost until the end of the story there is no photo of him, and this is the only one contained in Hodgson's novel.

This photo appears at a key moment, just before Julian receives a court verdict about the ownership of his house. Before the picture is inserted, Julian describes the day on which Ahmed died in his sleep and his habit of wearing a special hat on Fridays, and thus one understands that he died on a Friday. It is just when the reader is prepared to accept the fact that there will be no photos of Ahmed that one suddenly shows up. It is the only one in the whole novel with a name and a date clearly written on it. It was taken in 1928 and examining it now in 1945 gives it the full meaning of a Barthesian 'return of the dead'. Ahmed becomes a ghost from the past that reminds Julian of many things and gives him a sense of responsibility in his striving to prove the ownership of the Bait Katib.

One of the most interesting and intriguing photos in the novel is definitely that of a faceless woman. It appears in the middle of the description of the Bait Katib palace without any hint as to her possible identity. It is only after Julian has lamented the fact of having found only one photo of Asilah that the reader realises whom this photo represents. The picture is faceless because the family's maid, Najwa, cut out Asilah's face in order to keep it as a memory of her lovely niece rather than leave it for Julian. The fact that the photo remains faceless deprives the reader of a visual image and leaves room for conjectures as to the realisation of Julian's ekphrastic description. Moreover, the fact that he actually speaks mostly of the impressions Asilah made on him and of the feelings she evoked matches with the fact that there is no detailed description of her face; all this leaves her character under the veil of mystery till the end of the novel. Julian calls her 'a shadow' and feels as if he was being observed by somebody that he is not able to see.

> So, I was alone that night, except for the powerful feeling of being watched. The next morning I attributed it to a subconscious awareness of Ahmed, but in time I knew it wasn't the only reason. The first days in the house were a roller-coaster ride of fear of the bombardments and joy with the house. Today, it's the joy that floods my memory (Loc. 685–688).

The only description of Asilah the reader finds and has to connect to this photograph appears after a number of pages:

> Asilah's hair long, black, wavy, though I had never seen it out of the knot she wore it in. It was, in truth, shoulder length, brown, straight, and full. Her nose had seemed to me broad and flat, as did her face, but her photo showed a narrow, straight nose and a face that was round and well-proportioned with a strong chin. She was relaxed as she looked at the camera, and though she wasn't smiling, highlights in her eyes betrayed good humor. Her large, dark eyes had been about the only thing I had remembered properly. She wore a dark dress that came to mid-calf, revealing thick, glossy stockings of the sort still fashionable here. Her brimmed hat was finished off with a veil that hung down her back. On her feet were patent leather shoes. (Loc. 1113–1121).

The description seems to have re-created a full image of Asilah, and just when the reader thinks he/she has finally visualised the image of this mysterious character, Julian reminds him/her that there are some things which are not visible to the objective of a photographic camera but are very important for those who want to reconstruct the memory of a person photographed. He also reminds the reader that a photograph may at times conceal or display falsely the aspects of somebody's character.

> The studio set was faintly visible in the background. *Missing were all those things that photographs don't show.* Like the quality of her skin. I picture it as rich and tanned, or perhaps I'm fooled by my memory of the warm August light. And the photograph hid her shyness (Loc. 1113–1121, *my emphasis)*

It is also quite complicated to connect the photo with the character because Julian seems to suggest that his impressions and recollections of her were quite different from what he saw in the photo. Furthermore, the photo seems to fail in representing important details about Asilah — details which remind him of her more than the photo itself. The latter is in fact unable to convey her complete being and all of Julian's memories of her.

Ghosts

The story is quite a ghostly one. As Barthes suggests, 'each photo represents the return of the dead'. In the case of this novel, the whole narrative develops around a character who seems to have really returned from the dead. Julian is under the constant impression of being watched and not being alone in the house: 'it's a very strong sensation of being close to a living, but invisible, being' (Loc. 810). Although he suspects that Asilah might actually be dead, he still hopes to see her alive. It looks as if his strong wish to see her again and the strong presence in him of memories of her have actually revived her ghost and brought her back from the past to his present. Since he returned to Bait Katib after his war experience and was cured for his wounds, and under the influence of Najwa's belief that Asilah was alive, Julian actually started thinking that this might be true, and he believes in her presence in the palace.

> I didn't believe that she had gone to Salhiyya or Beirut, as George suggested. It seemed clear to me, then, that she had been killed. Even so, I had Najwa clean her room and ready it for her return. Her presence was inexplicably strong, as if she were there with us. At first I dismissed this as sheer nonsense because, in spite of the many rooms, it just wasn't possible for someone to live there undetected. As time passed, however, I wasn't so sure. Now that I'm putting my thoughts to paper, I should pin down what gave me the idea that she was among us. Well, for a start, her door would be left open, when I know that Najwa always kept it closed. My alarm clock disappeared, and the replacement I bought vanished, too. Books would be left in the oddest places, especially my English/Arabic dictionary, which I would have remembered carrying around myself, because it was so heavy (Loc. 801–808).

Najwa cut off the face from the photograph in order to have it with her, and to be able to talk to Asilah. 'I want to fill my eyes with her face' (Loc. 1130), she is used to saying when Julian asks her for the explanation of what he considers an outrageous act. He remembers seeing Najwa putting two plates in the kitchen for lunch and speaking to the empty place at her table while eating her meal. He also remembers that he 'often hear[s] faint murmuring, and my spine tingled when I accidentally discovered that this sound had a word for it, zajal, a low hum made by jinns at night. I'm sure it's her' (Loc. 1132–1133). *Jinns* are believed to be ghosts or evil spirits that influence people's minds and actions; however, Julian believes Asilah can only be a good spirit. It seems that everyone except him has understood what happened to Asilah and what his role in the history of Bait Katib is. He was perplexed by Ahmed's reply when he expressed his feeling of being an intruder in the palace after his return. Ahmed said without any further thinking: 'You belong here [. . .]. You give the shadows life'. He now comments: 'As I write this down, I wonder if I've been looking for Asilah in all the wrong places' (Loc. 1170–1172).

It is quite interesting to think about Asilah's role as a ghost in this novel. In that capacity, she seems to be trapped in time and space in her own home with the assignment to reveal unknown parts of the story and of history, and her memories are necessary to complete Julian's report on the past years of Bait Katib. Her stories do not appear in the news or news reports, especially not in the French ones. They tell about ordinary people who are affected by the war and are innocent victims. She seems to be trying to fulfil her mission of helping Julian to keep the house to himself and 'in the family' in compliance with her father's last wish.

On the one hand, she seeks justice for the ownership of her house, and strives to reveal the real truth about the bombing and destruction of Damascus. On the other hand, it seems she unleashes the hidden emotions she has always had for Julian, and enables him to understand his own feelings for her, which he has been hiding and suppressing for such a long time.

Evidence: Photographs, House, Documents and Written Words

In the introduction to her essay *On Photography*,[2] Susan Sontag describes one of the fundamental postulates of photography, that

---

2   Susan Sontag, *On Photography* (London: Penguin Modern Classics, 2008).

is, "to furnish evidence. Something we hear about but doubt, seems proven when we're shown a photo of it" (5). John Berger echoes Sontag's thoughts in his book, *About Looking*:[3] 'photographs are relics of the past, traces of what has happened' (57). Indeed, they are traces of what has happened but the whole story beyond them is revealed only in the narrative.

If we consider the number of photographs featuring people and those that show the city or reproduce documents, we can see that the last two prevail in the novel. In my opinion, Hodgson may have made this choice not only in order to document Julian's and Asilah's testimonies about their own lives and destinies, but also in order to show how the city of Damascus looked previously and how it was destroyed in brutal bombings. The photographs of the city, unlike those that show people, follow the course of the narrative and provide a certain visual impression of Julian's or the other narrators' descriptions of life in that environment.

At first Julian explains how he fell in love with this city, why it was so mesmerising for him, and how Bait Katib enchanted him so as to make him think of buying it and later do so really and become its owner.

> But by the time I'd sailed in a felucca to Aswan, trekked by camel across the Sinai to Petra, and ridden with a caravan into Damascus, I knew that my love for the East was different from the others', even though I followed their well-trodden path. I belonged to this part of the world. I felt it with every nerve, every instinct. Any attempt to live elsewhere would have been a sham. It wasn't an esoteric yearning but, rather, an emotion that hits you when the rhythm and temperament in a certain place matches your own to a degree that you've never experienced before. Within the enduring, sepia-toned walls of Damascus especially, I envisioned a place for myself with such clarity that leaving threatened to break my heart (Loc. 106–110).

Along with his explanations and descriptions of the town the following photographs appear:

---

3   John Berger, *About Looking* (New York: Pantheon books: Writers and Readers, 1982).

While examining these photographs Julian recalls how beautiful, vivid, hasty and colourful the city of Damascus was, with gorgeous gardens and palaces and cheerful people. The reader can see the way buildings in the old and new part of the town looked, the way people were dressed and the places where they spent their free time. With the war and the destruction of the city, the streets, according to Julian and Asilah, became deserted, and those who stayed in the city, utterly scared, locked themselves in their houses and were afraid to go out. Most of the shops were closed and only gradually did some reopen to sell essentials and to be shut again when an attack was announced.

> She smiled at Julian's description of Damascus, its narrow streets, the beautiful houses, and of her own home, Bait Katib. But her smile disappeared at his account of the war. "I had no idea," she murmured. She shivered when she read of his arrival in Damascus. His words brought back the terror of October 1925, when the bombs fell and the buildings round her caught fire (Loc. 359–362).

After beautiful Damascus has been bombed and the war has started the photos also change in order to complement the narration and give a visual perspective to the words that relate the actions. The city is in ruins and the houses half destroyed or burnt down in fires. The people in the pictures no longer smile or appear in a relaxed mood as they did previously. They hurry to reach their homes before another attack, if they still have homes. There are numerous soldiers around town in trenches or improvised barricades. Contrary to what happens to the images of people, almost all the photos of places in the novel are identified either by a name or by a date, some even by both.

Julian writes about the situation that he found upon his return to Damascus:

> Much had changed. A broad boulevard now paralleled the Barada River, and military vehicles were squeezing out donkeys, carts, and pedestrians. There were many new buildings. Heading north toward the river, we passed one of them, an oddly becoming European/Arabian concoction. I pointed to it. "Gare du Hijaz," the driver said. "For the train to Mecca," he added. At the approach of a truckload of soldiers, he abruptly turned off the street. When the truck went by, he backed up and we resumed our way. To my puzzled look, he patted the steering wheel. "I keep her, insh'allah," he said. I gathered that the army was requisitioning private citizens' cars (Loc. 267–272).

It is interesting to notice that most of the narration and all actions in the novel are concentrated on the house, the palace Bait Katib. This house is a symbol of the destinies of people in Damascus and of the city itself; it is a representation of its art and architecture, and it is a representation and a witness of the lives of its inhabitants. Julian is convinced that the house has more to say than any photographs he has of its previous owners — his friends and once-new family, Nasim, Muna and Asilah — and that it testifies to their lives and their habits. The house seems to be a collection of snapshots and reflections of their existences.

> Intriguing, too, were the many cupboards, *each perfect snapshots* of Nasim, Muna, and Asilah, for all of their effects — clothing, jewellery, books, musical instruments, *bric-à-brac* — had been left, as though their owners would return any minute (Loc. 691–693).(*my emphasis*)

The most important thought for Julian during his absence from Damascus and while he was travelling back to the city was the state of his beloved house and the destiny of his friends and of the people who had accepted him as if he had been their son. His accounts of his dreams and talks with other wounded people and nurses in the hospital clearly manifest his overwhelming wish to return to Syria. On his arrival in Damascus, Julian is pleased to find the palace still standing, with some damages but in a condition good enough for renovation, and not long after his arrival he makes numerous drawings and plans on how to reconstruct it all.

> Once inside, I was relieved to find that the house was very much intact, apart from a ghastly hole in the courtyard wall and another, smaller one in the wall of the second-story summer reception salon. There was also a partially collapsed roof in the room I had slept in eleven years ago and blown-out windows on three sides of the house. Some objects had fallen off shelves but not as many as one might expect. I don't remember much about the rest of that day. A lively crowd gathered, but otherwise the house was empty. I had assumed — hoped — the family would be there, even though I knew both Nasim and Muna had passed away. As for Asilah, it appeared that she had been living there but had vanished a short time (Loc. 672–678).

He engages Ahmed to help him rebuild the wall, fix the roof, and try to renovate the house as quickly as possible in order for it to look the way it used to. The two men make a lot of efforts to repair the house and Julian feels they are getting some 'additional' help from the 'shadow'.

> Ahmed and I filled in holes blown out by mortar fire, temporarily propped up the fallen-in roof, replaced the windows, weather-proofed the roof with new straw and mud, and managed to close the main door. But I could never bring myself to repair the damage just outside that door. The bullet marks were a kind of memorial, though I wasn't really clear about it at the time. Now I know why I preserved them (Loc. 787–791).

Julian describes buildings and ornaments that were symbols of Middle Eastern architecture. He is proud of the beauty that Bait Katib represented and was extremely sad when he heard of its destruction during the war bombings. He and Asilah in their accounts often speak about the way windows and walls looked and about how the yard was taken care of, and evoke the doors and the ornaments that were carved above their top rails, all things that made the building one of the architectural beauties of the city.

Bait Katib palace and its yard as well as the part of the house that has been destroyed are beautifully described by both Asilah and

Julian. The latter's descriptions focus mostly on the architectural details, the ornaments and the carvings. He remembers how the palace used to look and tries to imagine how it could be reconstructed. Asilah's descriptions have a more oneiric tone. When she enters the gardens of the palace and the space around the fountains, time in her descriptions seems to have been frozen at a moment in the past – one of those moments when they were all living happily in their city and in their palace and the gardens were full of plants and blooming flowers, differently from now when they are filled with rubble after the destruction. The reader is constrained to imagine the palace since almost until the end of the novel there are no images of it. The only visual materials which can help one in visualising the house interiors are Julian's drawings for the reconstruction:

Towards the end of the novel the reader becomes aware, with certainty, that there are two worlds and two temporal frames which intertwine. One is the present time of 1945 when Julian is trying to reconstruct the house and to prove his ownership and Asilah's spirit seems to help him. The other time frame is defined by Asilah's memories of the bombings in 1925 and by the accounts of the happy times before the destruction and her death that she writes in Arabic and backwards in the same notebook where Julian writes his own accounts in order to prove his ownership. Towards the end of the novel a collection of old photographs of the palace from the old family album appears to complete the visualisation of both accounts. All of these pictures show the beauty of the palace before its destruction, and complement the readers' mental images of it, constructed only on the basis of Julian's and Asilah's accounts.

A specific role in the novel is attributed to the displayed photos of the documents Julian has, needs or receives, which are connected with his ownership of Bait Katib. Hodgson uses these images of documents in order to emphasise the importance of the official records and papers that have vanished during the wars. She challenges ideas about the validity of photographs and official records by suggesting that Julian's personal account of the life and years spent in Damascus in his house might be as important as (or even more important than) the documents issued by the city council. The official papers Julian has in his possession are written in Arabic and French; this also reminds, or teaches, the reader about those portions of history and reality in which the protagonist lived at that time. One of the first visual elements which appear in the novel is a photograph of a letter Julian has received, the official statement that his house will be confiscated and transferred to Asilah's cousin. 'The first page summarized the claim and listed his name, Julian Beaufort, and his address: Bait Katib, Harat al-Hariqa, Damascus, Syria. He always marvelled that such a simple address sufficed in a city of more than a quarter million people' (Loc. 56–58). The photo shows that the envelope has been torn apart nervously to be opened. It also has the sign 'urgent' stamped on it, and after so many years it has come to Julian's door to remind him of the past, of his debts and of the people he lived with almost twenty years earlier. What had been urgent a long time ago arrives after almost twenty years, but now it is urgent for Julian to find all the documents because he only has four days to prove his ownership.

The second photographed document is actually Julian's identity certificate. It states his origin, as well as his citizenship and his current residence in Damascus. This document is important for Julian in his battle for ownership because Asilah's cousin is trying to prove that Julian as a foreigner does not deserve to be the owner of a palace in Syria.

Further on towards the end of the novel, a photograph of the most important document appears. This happens when Julian is totally exhausted from writing about his life in the last twenty years and trying to remember all the minute details about Bait Katib palace, the way it looked, the people he shared his life with while staying there and the reconstruction of the palace which he is planning to finish soon. This document is slipped into his hands by Asilah (or rather, at this point we know it is her spirit) while he is sleeping soundly and dreaming about the palace and how it used to be. It seems that documents, mere pieces of paper, do not mean much without the beautiful accounts written by Julian. In this way, Hodgson shows that documents and photographs are just a statistical collection of information and represent frozen moments in the course of history and in that of the actions in one's life. The author equalises the importance of the official records with that of the personal experience of people, by placing the documents after making Julian write down the whole story. Julian's account is as valuable as the certificates of ownership of Bait Katib.

Besides official documents, in her presentation of records
and data which should function as guarantees of truth, Hodgson
inserts a large number of newspaper clippings which date back to
the 1920s and 1930s. Almost all articles are in French and most
of them provide reports on the destruction of Damascus, Syria.
In this way, similarly to what many other authors have done, by
combining the newspaper articles with the personal testimonies of
those affected by the war, she tries to draw the readers' attention
to the necessity of not taking for granted the records and data they
find in the media every day. She also calls for the necessity of
hearing both sides of a story and most of all for the necessity of
appreciating and respecting ordinary people's destinies.

The final scene of what we can assume is the moment of Julian's death in a repeated bombing of Damascus and the neighbourhood of Hariga where Bait Katib is situated, is documented in the newspapers in Arabic and in French. The destruction of the most beautiful palace in the city and of that wonderful neighbourhood is reported quite coldly in the foreign papers. They claim that the only visible damage is the destruction of buildings and that no casualties have been reported. These are newspaper accounts and the reader is aware that they are not telling the truth, because Julian died under the bombing and was the victim of a missile. All this is reported on as an accidental action.

Bombs Hit Damascus

Friday, June 1st, 1945, Damascus: French forces bombarded Damascus from the evening of May 29th until noon the following day, in an effort to quell anti-French sentiment. The target was the Parliament building in the Salhiyya district. One missile was accidentally released over the Hariqa district, which had seen extensive damage in October 1925. *Reports indicate that it landed in a vacant property and that no lives were lost* (Loc. 1823–1833, *my emphasis*).

Suzanne Seed states: 'Photographs are an extension not just of our sight, but of our thought. Like human thought itself, they use displacement, metaphor, and analogy; they step back to give us perspective and orientation. They allow us to evolve'.[4] From her observations there emerges how the way of thinking about photography and about the relation between photography and text has changed. These two media of expression, visual and verbal, encourage the mind and the eye to evolve in a search for the new meanings which are created by their hybrid combination.

---

4   Suzanne Seed, 'The Viewless Womb', in *Multiple Views: Logan Grant Essays on Photography 1983–89*, ed. by Daniel Younger (Albuquerque: University of New Mexico Press, 1991), pp. 387–406 (p. 403).

Bibliography

Barthes, Roland, *Camera Lucida Reflections on Photography*, trans. by Richard Howard (New York: Hill and Wang, 1981).

_____, 'Rhetoric of the Image', in *Image, Music, Text,* ed. and trans. by Stephen Heath (London: Fontana Press, 1977), pp. 35–52.

Berger, John, *About Looking* (New York: Pantheon books: Writers and Readers, 1982).

_____, *Ways of Seeing* (London: Penguin Classics, 2008).

Dubois, Philippe, 'Photography Mise-en-Film: Autobiographical (Hi)stories and Psychic Apparatuses', in *Fugitive Images: From Photography to Video*, ed. by Patrice Petro (Bloomington–Indianapolis: Indiana University Press, 1995), pp. 152–172.

Hodgson, Barbara, *The Lives of Shadows* [2004] (Chronicle Books LLC, 2012; Amazon Digital Services, Inc, Kindle).

Horstkotte, Silke and Pedri, Nancy, 'Introduction: Photographic Interventions', *Poetics Today*, 29:1 (2008).

Seed, Suzanne, 'The Viewless Womb', in *Multiple Views: Logan Grant Essays on Photography 1983–89*, ed. by Daniel Younger (Albuquerque: University of New Mexico Press, 1991), pp. 397–406.

Sontag, Susan, *On photography* (London: Penguin Modern Classics, 2008).

TEJU COLE'S NARRATIVE THROUGH WORDS AND IMAGES

Maria Festa
(University of Turin)

Teju Cole is a writer, art historian, and photographer. He is the Distinguished Writer in Residence at Bard College and photography critic of the *New York Times Magazine*. He was born in the US in 1975 to Nigerian parents, and raised in Nigeria. He currently lives in Brooklyn. Cole is the author of four books: a novella, *Every Day is for the Thief* (2007); a novel, *Open City* (2011); a book of texts and photographs, *Punto d'Ombra* (2016); and a collection of essays on literature, art, travel, and politics, *Known and Strange Things* (2016). His photography has been exhibited in India, Iceland, and the US, published in a number of journals, and was the subject of a solo exhibition in Italy in the spring of 2016. Simultaneously with the Italian solo exhibition, Contrasto published Cole's photographs in *Punto d'Ombra*. The English version, *Blind Spot*, will be released in 2017.[1]

The Narrative Art

Renowned biologist Stephen Jay Gould contends that humankind's ability to use narration to give meaning to our lives is one of our species' most distinguishing features:

---

[1] The biographical information provided here comes from Teju Cole's official website: http://www.tejucole.com, accessed December 1, 2016.

> We are storytelling creatures and should have been named Homo narrator (or perhaps *Homo mendax* to acknowledge the misleading side of tale telling) rather than the often inappropriate *Homo sapiens*. The narrative mode comes naturally to us as a style for organizing thoughts and ideas.[2]

I would go further and suggest that 'the narrative mode', in addition to being a 'style for organizing thoughts and ideas', is also a means of communicating with the intent of bequeathing culture to following generations.

In his studies on oral tradition, historian and anthropologist Jan Vansina informs us that at the earliest stages of human communication accounts of events were conveyed by oral sounds from one individual to another or to a group, thus giving rise to oral traditions. Since then, accounts/stories have been marked by a set of very distinctive characteristics: they can be expressed in the form of news, eyewitness reports, hear-say or of reminiscences. Furthermore, inasmuch as we organize our individual daily life within societal groups, a record of events can be expressed also in the form of proverbs, rules, guidelines and regulations.[3]

Because of our predisposition to storytelling, the means and practice of recording events vary, multiply and always adapt themselves to local and historical circumstances. Alongside accounts appropriate for day-to-day or routine occasions, we have literary forms of narration, such as novels, which are more sophisticated instruments for conveying and sharing knowledge.

According to author and literary critic Margaret Anne Doody, the emergence of the specific literary narrative form we refer to as the novel is not a recent event as we are commonly inclined to believe: 'the Novel as a form of literature in the West has a continuous history of about two thousand years.'[4]

---

2   Stephen Jay Gould, 'So Near and Yet so Far', *The New York Review of Books*, 41, 18 (October 20, 1994), quoted in Remo Ceserani, *Guida allo studio della letteratura* (Rome–Bari: Laterza, 1999), p. 200.

3   Jan Vansina, *Oral Tradition as History* (London–Nairobi: James Currey-Heinemann Kenya, 1985), pp. 3–13.

4   Margaret Anne Doody, *The True Story of the Novel* (New Brunswick New Jersey: Rutgers University Press, 1996), p. 1.

If the art of writing can be traced back to the beginnings of human history, photography, on the other hand, was only invented in 1824 in France.[5] Because its arrival coincided with an increasingly interdependent 'world market [that had] given a cosmopolitan character to production and consumption',[6] this new technique of freezing and framing time soon spread throughout Europe. It was an unprecedented way of reproducing durable images and it created, for the first time in human civilisation, an extensive photographic record of an era. If attentively analysed, the black and white pictures of Victorian England, for example, reveal, in a new form, the values, attitudes and *modus vivendi* of a particular place and time. Through the act of interpreting photographs, of noticing the dichotomy between light and darkness, between what is familiar and what is remote, Edwardian England, according to historian David Gange, came to regard the Victorian period as a reverse image of itself:

> The Edwardians invented this image of the Victorians as their opposites, the "other" against which they defined themselves. [...] Where *we* nurture children, the Victorians exploited them; where *we* pursue equality in class and gender, the Victorians protected institutions that sustained inequality; where *we* are spontaneous, liberated, and funny, the Victorians were earnest, uptight, and humourless.[7] (*author's emphasis*)

The above extract provides an example of a comparative analysis based on images, and it shows how images, like words, are able to evoke impressions and opinions. As Roland Barthes states, photography faithfully preserves a moment eternally;

---

5   'The first photographic process — heliography — was invented around 1824 by Josheph Nicéphore Niépce.' http://www.photo-museum.org/, accessed November 15, 2016.

6   Karl Marx and Friedrich Engels, *Manifesto of the Communist Party* (Moscow: Progress Publishers, 1966 [1848]), p. 45. At the current time, the expressions coined by Marx have turned into "global market" and "globalisation".

7   David Gange, *The Victorians: A Beginner's Guide* (London: Oneworld Publications, 2016), p. 4.

photography 'says: *that, there it is, lo!*'[8] (*author's emphasis*).
As such, photography seems to be an irrefutable witness that
leaves no margin for discussion or doubt. This trust in the power
of photographs to tell the truth more faithfully than words or
subjective paintings, summarised by the popular saying "the
camera cannot lie", has not gone unchallenged. Barthes, for
instance, questions the authority of "photographic knowledge"
and discovers opportunities for analysing a photograph from
three different perspectives:

> I observed that a photograph can be the object of three practices (or
> of three emotions, or of three intentions): to do, to undergo, to look.
> The *Operator* is the Photographer. The *Spectator* is ourselves, all of us
> who glance through collections of photographs — in magazines and
> newspapers, in books, albums, archives... And the person or the thing
> photographed is the target, a referent, a kind of little simulacrum, any
> *eidolon* emitted by the object, which I should like to call the *Spectrum*
> of the photograph.[9] (*author's emphasis*)

As an intellectual with a wide spectrum of interests, Barthes is
also interested in literature, which he analyses through the lens of
semiotics.[10] Scholar Rick Rylance summarises Barthes's view of
literary works as follows:

---

8   Roland Barthes, *Camera Lucida: Reflections on Photography*, trans. by
     Richard Howard (London: Vintage classics, 1993 [1980]), pp. 4–5.
9   Barthes, *Camera Lucida – Reflections on Photography*, p. 9.
10   Daniel Chandler defines semiotics as the science of "the study of signs",
     although 'semiotics involves the study not only of what we refer to as
     "signs" in everyday speech, but of anything which 'stands for' something
     else. In a semiotic sense, signs take the form of words, images, sounds,
     gestures and objects.' Consequently, the meaning is represented by a
     relationship that links something materially present to something else that
     is absent. Daniel Chandler, *Semiotics: the Basics* (London–New York:
     Routledge, 2007 [2002]), p. 2.
     For the purpose of this essay, I make no distinction between the process of
     conferring meaning to words and the process of conferring meaning to
     photographs: while the *Spectator*/viewer looks at the photograph, the image
     arouses the *Spectator*'s emotions, reflections, ideas establishing, to a certain
     extent, cross references, connected to the *Spectator*'s private experience.
     Similar to words, photographs carry a referent and convey meanings.

> For Barthes [...] literature is essentially an activity of language that makes a work literary. But this formal language is powerfully underwritten by conventions, approved vocabularies, standards of 'taste', ranges of reference, and so forth, which shape its acceptable 'readability' in any period. Therefore, to be 'Literature' [...] writing needs to conform to prevailing standards of expression. 'Literature', therefore, is fundamentally an *institutional* use of language. [...] To thrive, authors need to advertise their literariness; their work must display the signs of 'Literature' which prevail in their period.[11] (*author's emphasis*)

Barthes's definition of 'Literature' is founded on a triadic model, like the pattern employed in his reflections on photography. Writing, just like photography, depends on three 'practices (or three emotions, or three intentions)': 'the activity of language', all the elements that 'shape its acceptable "readability" in any period' and the writer's personal 'style' detected in the use of language.

As far as the writer's personal style is concerned, Barthes argues that the process of phrasing originates in the body of the writer and in the writer's past and gradually becomes the very reflex of his/her art. A writer's personal style is in large part not an intention, but rather a spontaneous offshoot of personal experience and preferences, 'it is the writer's "thing", his glory and his prison, it is his solitude'.[12]

In this essay, I will analyse Teju Cole's work, focusing specifically on his efforts to blend literature and photography. In the field of literature, as with any artistic endeavour, authors express themselves through means that are available at the moment of their artistic production. We, writers and readers/"*spectators*",[13] live in an historical time where images prevail over words. In his narratives, Cole blends words and images, combining them to produce a different kind of narration where words and images

---

11　Rick Rylance, *Roland Barthes* (Hemel Hempstead: Harvester Wheatsheaf, 1994), pp. 9–10.

12　Roland Barthes, *Il grado zero della scrittura, seguito da Nuovi saggi critici*, [*Le degré zéro de l'écriture suivi de Nouveaux essais critiques*], trans. by Giuseppe Bartolucci and others (Turin: Einaudi, 2003 [1953]), p. 10.

13　According to Barthes's definition, "the *spectator*" is 'ourselves, all of us who glance through collections of photographs.'

have equal value and importance and jointly become the ground for critical thoughts and reflections.

The Social Media Approach

Both Cole and his readers inhabit a contemporary, rapidly changing, information technology reliant world. The content, the form and even publication and circulation of his work are affected by this reality. Cole's work, to paraphrase Barthes, displays (and, in my view, even expands) the signs of 'Literature', which prevail in our period. For Cole images, whether in the form of photographs or of the mental images produced in our minds during the act of reading, work in tandem to convey meaning. It is not surprising, then, given his interest in exploring a visual dimension of literature, that he has, from the very beginning of his career as a novelist, recognised the potential the World Wide Web offers for finding new models of creating content and distributing it:

> *Every Day is for the Thief* appeared online in January 2006, as a limited-edition experiment. I wrote one chapter each day. In effect, I was blogging on this weird project eight hours a day for an entire month. Months later, after I had erased the blog, a Nigerian publisher showed interest, and the project was edited and found a second life as a book. But, yes, I believe in life online, the way a person in 1910 might believe in aviation, or a person in 1455 might believe in movable type: with excitement and apprehension.[14]

The passage is part of an email-conversation between Cole and the Bosnian-born American writer Aleksandar Hemon. They exchange and share ideas, opinions and feelings on literature, photography and social networking sites. As for that, during their entire conversation as well as on other occasions, Cole gives evidence of his mixed feelings towards online social media and

---

14   Teju Cole, *Known and Strange Things* (New York: Random House, 2016), pp. 89–90.

social networking services. One first example is the oxymoron 'excitement and apprehension' employed to describe his response to the so-called "life online". Furthermore, his description of his daily routine — 'I was blogging on this weird project eight hours a day for an entire month' — suggests there is a tedious, regimented almost mechanical quality to the work that contradicts the spontaneous, inspiration driven notions we have of artistic output.

Later in the conversation he admits that 'if we ever find ourselves writing only for the present — which would essentially mean that tweeting is all we can do — I would feel absolutely defeated as a human being and a writer.'[15] Nevertheless, Cole does recognise the contribution of social media to the field of photography:

> To my surprise, I joined Instagram. I did it only for Pinkhassov's sake. I wanted to see his new images, see what a really good photographer could do with an iPhone. I wanted also to give Instagram a chance against my objections. I love new technologies as much as I am skeptical of them (I went almost straight from rotary phone to iPhone; I tend to hold out, and then I plunge).[16]

Despite his initial reservation detected in the phrase 'I tend to hold out, and then I plunge', Cole follows hundreds of Instagram accounts, and, up to the present moment, he has posted thousands of photographs that attract tens of thousands of followers.[17] In *Punto d'Ombra*, Cole also reflects on social media and his ambiguous attitude towards having an online audience for his work. At one point in the book, while discussing a photograph of a person, taken from the back, waiting for the green traffic light in New York, May 2015, he alludes to his unease: 'on Instagram, people, who see what you have seen, are called followers. The word has an unsettling quality to it.'[18]

---

15   Cole, *Known and Strange Things*, p. 91.
16   Cole, *Known and Strange Things*, pp. 155–156.
17   See https://www.instagram.com/_tejucole/, accessed December 12, 2016.
18   'Su Instagram quelli che vedono ciò che hai visto tu si chiamano followers, seguaci. La parola ha un che di inquietante.' In this essay, all the passages

In addition to his interest in photography, Cole is also a prolific writer, and some of his essays focus on the extended practice of viewing images on the computer screen. He reflects on services like Google Maps' Street View and Google Earth and how they allow us to view sites and places without going there in person:

> My parents live in Lagos, Nigeria. Sometimes, when I miss them or miss home, I go to Google Maps and trace the highway that leads from Lagos Island to our family's house in the northern part of the city. I find our street amid the complicated jumble of brown lines just east of the bus terminal. I can make out the shape of the house, the tree in front of it, the surrounding fence. I hover there, 'visiting' home.[19]

However, Cole is aware of the perils that the extraordinary and unprecedented abundance of images available to anybody can create. He has concerns surrounding unwanted surveillance, as well as misuses and abuses of information easily accessible at the click of a button. Cole shares with us his first reaction when Google Image Search appeared on the Internet 'I remember the first time I saw this, and what I felt: fear. I knew then that the monster had taken over.'[20]

The Internet with its aura of complex, cutting edge technology, along with its talk of algorithms and machine languages, is very much associated with science which in turn suggests the idea of something provable and true. Consequently, for the majority of us, everyday users/consumers of images saturated social media, the content we see online is often taken as unquestioned evidence of reality, which is to say online images convert virtual to real.

Images have an advantage over words in that they can be stored in the human brain more directly and are helpful in the process of remembering. Images can be more explanatory than words and sometimes they convey messages more directly and, unlike written texts, are less burdened with the viewer's need to look for a meaning "between the lines". The message is taken much

---

quoted from Italian texts are my translations. Teju Cole, *Punto d'Ombra*, trans. by Gioia Guerzoni (Rome: Contrasto, 2016), p. 206.

19   Cole, *Known and Strange Things*, p. 209.

20   Cole, *Known and Strange Things*, p. 184.

more at face value, with less critical distance, as in the case of photojournalism for instance. Nonetheless, if on the one hand, I agree to a great extent with Hemon when he states: 'the only way to have an organic connection with the past is by way of narration, while the knowledge of (as opposed to information about) history has to be shared in language',[21] on the other hand, given the power and directness of images mentioned earlier, I believe that 'information about history can be shared in' photographs as well.[22]

Photography is a recent discovery if compared to language and written words. However, despite its short existence, photography has been impacted by technological developments, from the invention of roll paper film at the end of the 19th century to the advent of digital photography in our time. These innovations have transformed the act of taking photographs into a fast, and extremely prolific, form of art. In an essay dedicated to the photographer Gueorgui Pinkhassov, Cole quotes Matt Pearce, a national reporter for the *Los Angeles Times* on the subject of digital photography and the idea of ease of use associated with it: 'never before have we so rampantly exercised the ability to capture the way the world really looks and then so gorgeously disfigured it.'[23] Apparently, in order to be part of history, everything and everybody has to be recorded through the technique of freezing time. The immense profusion of social media photography overwhelms us with images, and this (over)abundance of posts in social media, becomes synonymous with what Cole defines 'cheap images.'[24]

After this brief discussion of the use of images in the social media and of Cole's experimentation with form — though conforming 'to prevailing standards of expression' — in the next sections of this essay, I will discuss Cole's efforts to blend words and images in his works, or to combine them as he does in *Punto d'Ombra*, and how his narrative manners introduce new ways to give account of events.

---

21   Cole, *Known and Strange Things*, p. 81.
22   See the comparative analysis based on images with reference to Victorian England.
23   Cole, *Known and Strange Things*, p. 154.
24   Ibid.

Narrating through Words and Images

In the preface of *Known and Strange Things*, Cole talks about his writing interests:

> Through the work I was assigned at various papers and magazines, in response to various occasions and invitations, I was able to follow my nose and think through a wide variety of subjects. The area I returned to most often was photography. But literature, music, travel, and politics were also subjects in which I was deeply absorbed.[25]

Before the above-mentioned collection of essays, Cole wrote *Every Day is for the Thief*, *Open City*, and *Punto d'Ombra*, all dealing in varying degrees, with photography, music, travel and politics. His entire literary output is characterised by the 'subjects in which [he] was deeply absorbed' and, as a consequence, those subjects become a defining attribute of his writing, part of what makes the work ascribable to Teju Cole. Elsewhere, Cole explains how delving into a topic is also an exploration of himself: 'through the act of writing, I was able to find out what I knew about these things, what I was able to know, and where the limits of knowing lay.'[26] To the author, 'the act of writing' seems to be the agency of testing and widening his personal knowledge, which is then transmitted to us, as readers of his work. These subjects he is attracted to and absorbed by constitute what Barthes defines as the writer's personal style, that is to say something linked with Cole's past and detectable in his use of language.

This process of exploration and realization is evident in *Every Day is for the Thief*. In this novella the unnamed narrator is an aspiring young Nigerian writer who goes home to Lagos for a short visit after 15 years living in New York where he studies medicine. At first, the bustling Nigerian capital seems unconducive to writing, to accessing the means of discovery and especially self-discovery afforded by what Cole describes as the 'act of writing':

---

25   Cole, *Known and Strange Things*, pp. xiv–xv.
26   Cole, *Known and Strange Things*, p. xv.

Writing is difficult, reading impossible. People are so exhausted after all the hassle of a normal Lagos day that, for the vast majority, mindless entertainment is preferable to any other kind. [...] By day's end, the mind is worn, the body ragged. The best I can manage is to take a few photographs. For the rest of the month, I neither read nor write.[27]

Although, the narrator describes Lagos as a city where 'the best [he] can manage is to take a few photographs', as he does wherever he goes in his travels, camera in hand, he ends up meeting people, exploring neighbourhoods and coming to the realisation that his dual Nigerian-American identity enables him to compare the complex realities of the two worlds. Photography, which is perceived by the young medical student as essentially a "mindless" activity, inferior to reading or writing, proves to be an extremely useful tool for gaining understanding of the world and ourselves. The events of the novella seem to challenge the young man's (and possibly Hemon's) belief in the supremacy of the written word over images/photography as a means of accessing knowledge. The narrator's journey (from New York to Lagos and back to New York) along with his daily trips within the city (by public transport, by car and on foot) form small narrations each one comprising a chapter. The narrative can be compared to a photographic film, or even to a developed print film provided with transparent negatives with the light and dark areas inverted to their respective complementary colours. In each negative, a new recount of events is visible/readable. The developed print film is interrupted nineteen times as to permit the possibility of cut-ins, specifically, black and white photographs, that somehow complement the fragmented stories. This personal perspective of the narrative has been shaped by the depiction of the unnamed narrator, both as a traveller and a wanderer, who often seems to consider his camera, like an extension of himself.

In one of the chapters he becomes interested in a stranger on a bus reading a book:

---

27   Teju Cole, *Every Day is for the Thief* (Croydon: Faber & Faber, 2014 [2007]), p. 68.

The bus comes to a stop. She disembarks, at Obalende, with her book, and quickly vanishes into the bookless crowd. Just like that, she is gone. Gone, but seared into my mind still. That woman, evanescent as an image made with the lens wide open.[28]

In this recollection of seeing a woman with a book, the phrase 'bookless crowd' underscores the incongruity of one person with a book in a population of non-readers. This idea of the majority, i.e. the crowd, who do not care about books, reinforces one of the narrator's statements that 'the Nigerian literacy rate is low, estimated at fifty-seven percent. [...] It is a hostile environment for the life of the mind.'[29] Nonetheless, against the odds in this book-averse metropolis, he sees a 'mysterious woman' reading a book by Michael Ondaatje. She captures his attention and curiosity. Presumably, she shares his interest in literature, and inextricably, he 'hunger[s] for conversation.'[30] Eventually, this time, the image of the fading target is impressed on the narrator's memory and not on a piece of paper.

Another example of blending words with images emerges in the last frame/chapter of the novella. The narrator is in New York, even though his 'body is still responding to the difference in time zone',[31] his mind returns back to Lagos where he 'alone wander[s] with no particular aim.'[32] The roaming leads him to a carpentry consortium where 'as far as [he] can see, is coffins. [...] Only coffins.'[33] The circumstance of the moment functions as a magnet for the narrator/photographer's eye:

I want to take the little camera out of my pocket and capture the scene. But I am afraid. Afraid that the carpenters, rapt in their meditative task, will look up at me; afraid that I will bind to film what is intended only for the memory, what is meant only for a sidelong glance followed by forgetting.[34]

---

28 Cole, *Every Day is for the Thief*, p. 43.
29 Cole, *Every Day is for the Thief*, p. 42.
30 Cole, *Every Day is for the Thief*, p. 43.
31 Cole, *Every Day is for the Thief*, p. 158.
32 Cole, *Every Day is for the Thief*, p. 159.
33 Cole, *Every Day is for the Thief*, p. 160.
34 Cole, *Every Day is for the Thief*, pp. 160–161.

On this occasion, the camera emerges as an extension of the narrator, the two forming a single entity. His instinct to register the moment is stronger than the negative feeling that those containers of corpses may convey. However, on second thoughts, his concern that the camera would intrude on the quiet concentration of the workers, and thus corrupt the moment he was hoping to capture, makes the narrator refrain from filming.

The image of the object associated with death reminds me of Barthes's description of photography as 'a relation to "spectacle" [which] adds to it that rather terrible thing which is there in every photograph: the return of the dead.'[35] If on the one hand, the target of the photograph receives immortality as it is fixed exactly as it was in a specific moment, on the other hand, the shutter's click captures the target's life and puts an end to it. This is the dark side of photography, but, it has to be emphasised that photography is characterised by dichotomies: darkness and light, black and white, life and death, momentary and timeless, speed and stillness, private and public, analogical and digital.

The narration of events through the employment of words related to photography is more evident in the novel *Open City*:

> Photography seemed to me, as I stood there in the white gallery with its rows of pictures and its press of murmuring spectators, an uncanny art like no other. One moment, in all of history, was captured, but the moment before and after it disappeared into the onrush of time; only that selected moment itself was privileged, saved, for no other reason than its having picked out by the camera's eye.[36]

These thoughts belong to Julius, the *flâneur* and main character of *Open City*. The unnamed narrator of *Every Day is for the Thief* and Julius have quite a few things in common: they are young Nigerians who live in New York, they study medicine, they wander along the streets of the city in which they find themselves; both are passionately interested in literature, music and history.

---

35   Barthes, *Camera Lucida: Reflections on Photography*, p. 9.
36   Teju Cole, *Open City* (London: Faber & Faber, 2012 [2011]), p. 152.

The novel *Open City* is not intersected with photographs. This time, Cole relies on the semantic power of words employed to narrate events. Moreover, it seems that, through the written word, he wants to offer a different approach to photography. This approach requires the reader's eye and mind to function as a camera. Like the device containing a photosensitive surface that records images through a lens, the eye and the mind prove a stimulus to the reader's imagination and impress the scenario on his/her memory individually and privately. Julius's walk through Brussels is a good illustration of Cole's ability to evoke images in the reader's mind through poetic language while, simultaneously, accurately describing a physical, geographical location:

> I went to the Musées Royaux des Beaux-Arts [...] I stepped outside again, [...] I simply wandered aimlessly, through the Egmont Park and its morose gallery of bronze statues, [...] down to Place de la Chapelle. The cathedral there was like the streaked hull of a sunken ship, and the few people around it were tiny and drab, like midges. [...] rain was lashing the land. It fell heavily all over the Portuguese district, on the shrine to Pessoa and on Casa Botelho. [...] It fell on the bronze head of Leopold II at his monument, on Cluadel at his, on the flagstones of the Palais Royal. The rain kept coming down, on the battlefield of Waterloo at the outskirts of the city, the Lion's Mound, the Ardennes, [...] on Ypres and the huddled white crosses dotting Flanders fields, the turbulent channel, the impossibly cold sea to the north, on Denmark, France and Germany.[37]

Julius aimless wandering offers us a tour of Brussels along with other European countries that are shrouded in history. He informs us about the past and provides artistic and architectural details. The cathedral as a 'sunken ship' may be a reference to Belgian as well as European colonial past in Africa and the rain that 'was lashing the land' democratically seems to avenge the victims from colonialism to World War II falling indistinctly on all territories and architectonic symbols of local history.

---

37   Cole, *Open City*, pp. 116–146.

Another common trait that defines both Julius and the unnamed narrator, and which is often associated with the work of writers and photographers, is their solitude. The two characters are lone travellers, spending most of their time alone, thinking, observing, taking photographs. The act of writing, like the act of reading as well as the act of photographing, is likewise a solitary activity where the individual is alone with the text, absorbing ideas, thinking, taking mental notes.

Early on in *Camera Lucida*, Barthes reflects on the state of being alone or remote from others when examining a photograph:

> One day, quite some time ago, I happened on a photograph of Napoleon's youngest brother, Jerome, taken in 1852. And I realized then, with an amazement I have not been able to lessen since: "I am looking at the eyes that looked at the Emperor." Sometimes I would mention this amazement, but since no one seemed to share it, nor even to understand it (life consists of these little touches of solitude), I forgot about it.[38]

Barthes's poetic observation that 'life consists of these little touches of solitude' encapsulates many people's emotional experience of and connection with a work of art as uniquely theirs, private and often difficult to communicate to other individuals. Evidence of these solitary emotions is given, for instance, in the quick vanishing of Michael Ondaatje's mysterious reader in *Every Day is for the Thief*: 'gone, but seared into my mind still', and in the conceptualisation of photography as 'an uncanny art like no other', in *Open City*, when Julius is 'in the white gallery with its rows of pictures and its press of murmuring spectators.' In this example, there is also a parallel with photography: 'the white gallery' suggests a dark room where the film extracted from the camera exposes its row of frames.

Moreover, Cole's employment of the adjective 'uncanny', redirects me, once again, to Barthes and his intellectual definition of photography: 'we might say that Photography is unclassifiable. [...] The first thing I found was this. What the Photograph reproduces to infinity has occurred only once: the

---

38   Barthes, *Camera Lucida: Reflections on Photography*, p. 3.

Photograph mechanically repeats what could never be repeated existentially.'[39] In addition, through Julius's reflection, Cole paraphrases Barthes's definition of photography as 'one moment in all of history.'

Cole seems to embrace both Barthes's view of photography and Hemon's assertion that 'the knowledge of [...] history has to be shared in language.' History is a central concern of his novel regardless of whether his texts include photographs or not. *Open City*, which relies solely on words to carry the narrative, is a novel almost entirely about history. Through narration, Cole establishes 'an organic connection with the past' as perceived, for instance, in the words Julius employs to recount his visit to the Negro Burial Ground, in the Civic Center section of Lower Manhattan in New York City:

> And yet, the Negro Burial Ground was no mass grave: each body had been buried singly, according to whichever rite it was that, outside the city walls, the blacks had been at liberty to practice. The security island near the monument was unmanned. I stepped across the cordon, and into the grassy plot. Bending down, I lifted a stone from the grass and, as I did so, *a pain shot through the back of my left hand.*[40] (*my emphasis*)

This site, besides being a reminder of the largest colonial-era cemetery for people of African descent, represents also one of the dichotomies that characterise photography: life and death. Today, 'most of the burial ground [i]s now under office buildings, shops, streets, diners, pharmacies, all the endless hum of quotidian commerce and government.'[41] Nonetheless, in his wandering (physically and intellectually) Julius informs us about the local past of slave trade and slavery providing historical details, dates and figures. Readers find themselves immersed in the past and cannot help but notice a parallel between an act of violence Julius suffers at the hands of criminals and the brutal history of West Africa. As a matter of fact, during one of his wanderings, Julius is the victim of an aggression:

---

39   Barthes, *Camera Lucida: Reflections on Photography*, p. 4.
40   Cole, *Open City*, p. 222.
41   Cole, *Open City*, p. 220.

We were in the day's last light, and the street was largely in shadow. [...] in the middle of [a] thought [...] I felt the first blow on my shoulder. [...] They began to kick me all over — shins, back, arms — a quick preplanned choreography. [...] a man on the ground being beaten. [...] The boys continued to laugh, and one of them stepped on my hand one last time, especially hard. The world darkened.[42]

The pain in the left hand is an aftermath of his being mugged, and 'what had felt like a minor bruise [...] seemed to have been a bruise of the bone'[43] that troubles him now and then. The pain becomes more intense on the same site where 'there had been interred the bodies of some fifteen to twenty thousand blacks, most of them slaves, but then the land had been built over and the people of the city had forgotten that it was a burial ground.'[44] Unlike photography, which 'mechanically repeats what could never be repeated existentially', history repeats itself and human beings, instead of learning from their ancestors' mistakes, seem to follow the same pattern repeatedly. One example is the violent behaviour that is intended to hurt or, even worse, kill that still occurs in New York, where 'violence for sport [i]s no strange thing in the city.'[45]

Another evidence of how literature and photography, as a form of narration and a means of passing down culture, are inextricably interwoven in *Open City* is palpable in Julius's thoughts about his work as a psychiatrist:

I had tried to give my friend an account of my evolving view of psychiatric practice. I told him that I *viewed* each patient *as a dark room*, and that, going into that room, in a session with the patient, I considered it *essential to be slow* and deliberate. [...] There is more *light* to work with in externally *visible* illnesses. [...] For the troubles of the mind, diagnosis is a trickier art, because even the strongest symptoms are sometimes not visible. [...] But what are we to do *when the lens through which the symptoms are viewed* is often, itself, symptomatic: the mind is *opaque* to itself, and it's hard to tell where, precisely, these areas of opacity are.[46] (*my emphasis*)

42 Cole, *Open City*, pp. 212–213.
43 Cole, *Open City*, p. 218.
44 Cole, *Open City*, p. 220.
45 Cole, *Open City*, p. 216.
46 Cole, *Open City*, p. 238.

To Julius, photography represents an essential component of his life to the point that he considers it a useful metaphor to help him in his psychiatric practice. He compares himself to a photographer and his patients to a dark room, i.e. a room where photographic materials (in this case the mental anguish expressed by his clients) can be processed either in complete darkness ('sometimes symptoms are not visible') or with a safe light. In order to process his patients' symptoms, time and patience become prerequisites. The occurrence of light is also crucial as, like a photographer, Julius has to be able to take advantage of its presence, and his professional skills have to be able to recognise, identify and use the light's revelatory characteristics. Moreover, to do so, the lens[47], or the figuration of the mind, has to be transparent otherwise the light, and its metaphoric associations with knowledge and understanding, cannot penetrate it.

In this metaphor, light can be interpreted as knowledge, and 'these areas of opacity', to which Julius alludes, allow me to introduce the last section of this essay focusing on *Punto d'Ombra*. I am of the opinion that, to some extent, this last work can be considered Cole's personal 'evolving view' of writing, both as a novelist and as a photographer. After all, has not photography, sometimes, been described as "writing with light"?

---

47   The noun "lens" has a double meaning: 'a ground or molded piece of glass, plastic, or other transparent material with opposite surfaces either or both of which are curved, by means of which light rays are refracted so that they converge or diverge to form an image' and 'the lens as a transparent, biconvex structure in the eye of a vertebrate or cephalopod that is located between the iris and the vitreous humor and focuses light rays entering through the pupil to form an image on the retina.' Entries in *Encyclopædia Britannica* https://www.britannica.com/, accessed December 18, 2016.

The Blind Spot

As mentioned earlier in this essay, *Punto d'Ombra* will be published outside Italy as *Blind Spot*. Cole first introduces the concept of the 'blind spot' through Julius's words in *Open City*:

> Ophthalmic science describes an area at the back of the bulb of the eye, the optic disk, where the million or so ganglia of the optic nerve exit the eye. It is precisely there, where too many of the neurons associated with vision are clustered, that the vision goes dead. [...] I recall explaining to my friend [...], I have felt that most of the work of psychiatrists in particular, [...] was a blind spot so broad that it had taken over most of the eye. What we knew [...] was so much less than what remained in darkness, and in this great limitation lay the appeal and frustration of the profession.[48]

Julius's preoccupation with these areas of darkness seems to reflect Cole's own curiosity about the lines demarcating the limits of his knowledge: Julius tests these limits through the practice of psychiatry, while Cole does it through the act of writing. The reflexive self-examination process characterises Cole's artistic production. In *Everyday is for the Thief*, Cole, through the narrator, shows that images are not inferior to narration, which appears to be a conclusion Cole has reached when he decided to include photographs in his writing in order to offer a more comprehensive view of Lagos and Nigeria. In *Open City*, through Julius, Cole develops an investigative process, in order to discover 'where [his] limits of knowing lay', that is symbolised by Julius's physical and mental wanderings in New York, Europe and Nigeria. The blind spot, which lies beyond the border of Julius's and Cole's understanding, is both a source of apprehension and attraction: it simultaneously conjures an instinctive fear of the unknown and the seductive promise of greater knowledge and self-understanding.

Cole's inquisitive nature can be detected in all his writings, and he reiterates his desire to broaden his knowledge at the end

---

48　Cole, *Open City*, pp. 238–239.

of *Punto d'Ombra*, where he provides reasons for his last work and summarises his thoughts in a question: 'at any instant I am intensely aware that looking is to see only a fraction of what is observed. Even in the most attentive eye there is a blind spot. What is missed?'[49]

According to Cole's words, *Punto d'Ombra* can be read as a personal map of the world that he has been able to outline as a result of his travels. To him, 'travelling is a privilege and a responsibility.' He argues that places are different as are life experiences that differentiate themselves depending on time and location, but human beings are equal on an emotional and psychological level and in his travels he constantly attempted to delineate these common traits that distinguish humankind. His camera functioned as an extension of his memory, and later when he looked at his travel-photographs he realised that, if on the one hand, his photographs are not ordinary pictures taken by a tourist on vacation, on the other hand, something seems to be missing in them.[50]

This idea of understanding a vacation as a moment to eternalise is well depicted, for instance, by Italo Calvino in one of his short stories, *The Adventures of a Photographer*:

> When spring comes, the city's inhabitants, [...] go out on Sundays [...]. And they photograph one another. They come back as happy as hunters [...]; they spend days waiting, with sweet anxiety, to see the developed pictures [...]. It is only when they have the photos before their eyes that they seem to take tangible possession of the day they spent, only then that the mountain stream, the movement of the child with his pail, the glint of the sun on the wife's legs take on the irrevocability of what has been and can no longer be doubted. Everything else can drown in the unreliable shadow of memory.[51]

---

49   'In ogni istante sono intensamente consapevole che guardare è vedere solo una frazione di ciò che si osserva. Anche nell'occhio più attento c'è un punto d'ombra. Cosa si perde?'; Cole, *Punto d'Ombra*, p. 229.

50   'Il viaggio è per me un privilegio e una responsabilità.' Cole, *Punto d'Ombra*, pp. 228–229.

51   Italo Calvino, 'The Adventures of a Photographer' (1955), in *Difficult Loves*, trans. by William Weaver, Archibald Colquhoun, Peggy Wright

This passage makes me think of memory and of the importance given to it by all of us. In my view, when it comes to remembering the unpleasant actions and events that occurred in the past (the past understood as History and consequently 'the time when we were not born'[52], but also the past related to the individual's own life), forgetting seems to be the general reaction. This happens, for instance, in the episode of the Negro Burial Ground site in *Open City*. Forgetting might be interpreted as a self-defence mechanism against suffering and pain; it seems to be the easiest way to move forward. Paradoxically, the majority of us strives both to remember the smallest details of particular days and moments in our lives,[53] and, as described in the above extract, 'to take tangible possession of the day [...] spent' somewhere away from home. Sure enough, this is the consequence of a choice, as the protagonist of Calvino's short story explains to us some lines later:

> A choice in the idyllic sense, apologetic, consolatory, at peace with nature, the fatherland, the family. Your choice isn't only photographic; it is a choice of life, which leads you to exclude dramatic conflicts, the knots of contradiction, the great tensions of will, passion, aversion. So you think you are saving yourselves from madness, but you are falling into mediocrity, into hebetude.[54]

The protagonist's reaction to this tendency of keeping a record of personal events and meaningless details may sound offensive. He undoubtedly expresses intense disdain and disapproval of the ordinary photographer, who falls 'into mediocrity, into hebetude', but, at the same time, that judgment belongs to a passionate individual who sees the larger potential and wants to take advantage of this powerful tool to understand the surrounding habitat.

(San Diego: Harcourt Brace Jovanovich, 1984), in *The Short Story and Photography 1880's–1980's A Critical Anthology*, ed. by Jane M. Rabb (Albuquerque: University of Mexico Press, 1998), p. 177.

52   Barthes, *Camera Lucida: Reflections on Photography*, p. 64.

53   I am referring to the actual tendency of taking selfies.

54   Calvino, *The Adventures of a Photographer*, p. 180.

A deep curiosity for the intercultural experience drives Cole to seek to understand the world through reading, travelling, writing and photography. He distances himself from the mainstream, popular understanding of photography and affirms it in *Punto d'Ombra* where he claims to dislike travel journals and to avoid places that have been defined as beautiful, exotic and breath-taking by tourist campaigns. He aims to produce the kind of image that would surely be rejected by any certified tourist organisations, which are more interested in glossy, sanitized images to entice potential tourists/clients. Cole aims to discover the substratum of the visible environment; he aims to go beyond the appearance.[55]

In *Punto d'Ombra*, Cole presents us with a sort of journal. This journal is a personal record of reflections with an unconventional slant, words introduce images that once gathered together evince a phenomenological perspective. Philosophically, phenomenology is a method of investigating the experience lived along with a reflexive approach to understand the lived world.[56] Cole's approach for understanding the lived world occurs with the juxtaposition of words and images. He considers photography 'inescapably a memorial art. It selects, out of the flow of time, a moment to be preserved, with the moments before and after falling away like sheer cliffs.'[57] In order to preserve the moment, he resorts to his camera which acts as a magnifier of memory, because according to Cole 'photography reveals what the photographer did not see at the moment of taking it.'[58] Thus, after the photograph is developed, the target is able to show to the "*spectator's*" eye all the surrounding details existing in the scene but belonging to a moment that has gone forever. Through Cole's retention of the image, the target is not at eye level but fixed from more complex angles offering, in return, different levels of interpretation, as it occurs with literary texts.

---

55   Cole, *Punto d'Ombra*, p. 188.
56   Edmund Gustav Albrecht Husserl, *Phänomenologie und Erkenntnistheorie, Fenomenologia e teoria della della conoscenza*, trans. by Paolo Volonté (Milan: R.C.S., 2000), pp. 161–167.
57   Cole, *Known and Strange Things*, p. 197.
58   'La fotografia rivela quello che il fotografo non aveva visto al momento dello scatto.' Cole, *Punto d'Ombra*, p. 124.

In *Punto d'Ombra*, the structure of the narration is similar, as above-mentioned, to a journal. Cole travelled during a span of time between 2012 and 2015 in almost every corner of the world. In his journal words and images are framed by a date. However, the events take more the shape of reflections and experiences rather than a personal record of occurrences, kept on a regular basis. During his wandering around the world, his main concern was to emphasise the common traits that equalise individuals on an emotional and psychological level.

In June 2015 he visited Capri, a famous Italian seaside location. From the window of his hotel room, Cole fixes in time a beautiful summer day. At a first sight, we see a nice view: the sea is quiet, cruise ships, yachts and boats harmoniously across it, the sun's rays reflect the summer colours on the water, lending the scene a feeling of warmth and calmness. It could be the perfect photograph to show to our friends who 'wish[ed] us a good trip' and suggested to 'take lots of pictures! [...] and we oblige them.'[59] However, Cole perceives a dark side in the striking landscape. Somehow, those vessels are associated with *The Iliad*, the ancient Greek epic poem attributed to Homer and set during the Trojan War. But, he also remembers the Irish writer Edna O'Brien's words: 'of these wonderful waters, we know they have death inside.'[60] Cole's association of ideas redirects me to the Mediterranean Sea as a container of corpses, whose origin goes back to ancient times, but in recent decades, human beings, who leave their troubled countries in search for a better place to live, have died in those 'wonderful waters'. The image of the Mediterranean Sea as a burial ground is, somehow, similar to the Negro Burial Ground in New York: both represent the coexistence of death and life as well as this universal feeling of general indifference.

Another photograph that emphasises the contradictions and the callous side of human nature is the mountain landscape taken in Muottas Murgal, Switzerland, July 2015. Cole informs us that it

---

59   Cole, *Known and Strange Things*, p. 176.
60   'Di queste meravigliose acque sappiamo che hanno dentro la morte.' Cole, *Punto d'Ombra*, p. 26.

was the site where, in the past, women, accused of having joined the devil, were cruelly executed. The apparent quietness evoked in the image is equated with the restfulness of a burial ground. The atmosphere of the past that surrounds the site is a powerful target that induces Cole to personify the image produced by his camera. The photograph seems to be made of flesh and blood, and the undissolved fragments of the past emerge from its skin.[61]

However, as the journal progresses, Cole continues to offer different perspectives of the same target. For instance, a shop window in Zurich, taken in September 2014, shows us earth globes on shelves, and for each globe, the visible side is set on a different location. Cole reflects on the thousands of steps made by individuals during their lives. He is referring to small daily routine movements, like moving from one room to another inside the house, or on the way to the subway station, or during a night stroll and so on. However, even those, who are not great walkers, at the end of their lives, can be said to have circumnavigated the earth more than once.[62]

The vision of different locations, side by side on a shelf, may be similar to the mental image that is impressed in the mind of a restless writer, who, under a phenomenological perspective, attempts to state his/her presence in the world. In the solitary moment devoted to writing, the individual engages himself/herself in a personal reflexive self-examination process, and in this kind of analysis the individual aims for a better understanding of his/her life. Self-education, as a means of understanding the real meaning of our existence, requires the intent and will to give up our judgement, our knowledge and what is already familiar in order to formulate a fresh judgment, to always see as if it were for the first time.[63]

This concept is illustrated in the photograph taken in Rhinecliff, NY, March 2015. The target is an opaque window which partially shows and reflects what is beyond or in front of the glass. Cole comments the image telling us about an eye ailment that made him temporarily sightless. During that time spent in darkness, he

61   Cole, *Punto d'Ombra*, p. 22.
62   Cole, *Punto d'Ombra*, p. 140.
63   Enzo Paci, *Diario Fenomenologico* (Milan: Bompiani, 1973 [1961]), p. 5.

realised that we easily take for granted our body and its capabilities, and we assign importance and meaning to its functions only when they fail. Moreover, due to his photographic attitude, he cannot help comparing his healing, as he slowly regains sight, to a film in a dark room during the development process, when the negative of the film shows its target little by little.[64]

The photographs discussed in this essay provide some examples of Cole's peculiar writing style which gives rise to diverse layers of interpretation and reading. His work is made of texts which span various locations and historical contexts. Moreover, his writing allows also to establish a close relationship between him, the author, and us, the readers of his work. Barthes argues that the process of phrasing 'originates in the body of the writer' and the philosopher Enzo Paci defines the act of writing as:

> there is no such thing as the word detached from the body. The written word does not exist: when we read it, we trace it back to its original incarnation, or to ourselves, if we are not able to imagine the living person who wrote it. The disembodied word, if it were possible, would not make sense.[65]

Both statements can be applied to Cole's writing. Cole's words, as well as his images, result from deep thoughts and self-examination and offer us a faithful reflection of himself. In his journal, he reflects on Maurice Merleau-Ponty's philosophical approach to life and concludes by expressing a desire to forever being able to put off the end of his journey, of his searching and discovering, a wish I myself would like to emulate: 'I keep postponing arriving at my destination. The destination is arriving at this perpetual postponing, in order to never reach the destination. I dream all day long. At night, I dream of wandering.'[66]

---

64 Cole, *Punto d'Ombra*, p. 162.
65 'La parola distaccata dal corpo non esiste. Non esiste la parola scritta: leggendo la riconduciamo alla sua originaria incarnazione, alla nostra, se non riusciamo a immaginare la persona viva che l'ha scritta. La parola disincarnata, se fosse possibile, non avrebbe senso.' Paci, *Diario Fenomenologico*, pp. 22–23.
66 'Continuo a rinviare il mio arrivo a destinazione. La destinazione è arrivare a questo rinvio perpetuo, per non raggiungere mai la destinazione.

Bibliography

Barthes, Roland, *Camera Lucida: Reflections on Photography*, trans. by Richard Howard (London: Vintage classics, 1993 [1980]).

—————————, *Il grado zero della scrittura, seguito da Nuovi saggi critici*, [*Le degré zéro de l'écriture suivi de Nouveaux essais critiques*], trans. by Giuseppe Bartolucci, Renzo Guidieri, Leonella Prato Caruso, Rosetta Loy Provera (Turin: Einaudi, 2003 [1953]).

Calvino, Italo, *The Adventures of a Photographer* [1955], in *Difficult Loves*, trans. by William Weaver, Archibald Colquhoun, Peggy Wright (San Diego: Harcourt Brace Jovanovich, 1984), in *The Short Story and Photography 1880's–1980's A Critical Anthology*, ed. by Jane M. Rabb (Albuquerque: University of Mexico Press, 1998).

Ceserani, Remo, *Guida allo studio della letteratura* (Rome–Bari: Laterza, 1999).

Chandler, Daniel, *Semiotics: The Basics* (London–New York: Routledge, 2007 [2002]).

Cole, Teju, *Every Day is for the Thief* (Croydon: Faber & Faber, 2014 [2007]).

—————, *Open City* (London: Faber & Faber, 2012 [2011]).

—————, *Punto d'Ombra*, trans. by Gioia Guerzoni (Rome: Contrasto, 2016).

—————, *Known and Strange Things* (New York: Random House, 2016).

Doody, Margaret Anne, *The True Story of the Novel* (New Brunswick, New Jersey: Rutgers University Press, 1996).

Gange, David, *The Victorians: A Beginner's Guide* (London: Oneworld Publications, 2016).

Gould, Stephen Jay, 'So Near and Yet so Far', *The New York Review of Books*, 41, 17 (October 20, 1994).

Husserl, Edmund Gustav Albrecht, *Fenomenologia e teoria della della conoscenza*, [*Phänomenologie und Erkenntnistheorie*], trans. by Paolo Volonté (Milan: R.C.S., 2000).

Marx, Karl and Engels, Friedrich, *Manifesto of the Communist Party* (Moscow: Progress Publishers, 1966 [1848]).

Paci, Enzo, *Diario Fenomenologico* (Milan: Bompiani, 1973 [1961]).

Rylance, Rick, *Roland Barthes* (Hemel Hempstead: Harvester Wheatsheaf, 1994).

Vansina, Jan, *Oral Tradition as History* (London–Nairobi: James Currey-Heinemann Kenya, 1985).

Sogno tutto il giorno. Di notte sogno di vagare.' Cole, *Punto d'Ombra*, p. 160.

Websites

https://www.britannica.com/, accessed December 18, 2016.
https://www.instagram.com/_tejucole/, accessed December 12, 2016.
http://www.photo-museum.org/, accessed November 15, 2016.
http://www.tejucole.com, accessed December 1, 2016.

THE WORD AS MASK.
A READING OF TOMMASO LANDOLFI'S
OTTAVIO DI SAINT-VINCENT

Alice Gardoncini
(University of Udine–Trieste)

> Landolfi non è uno che scagli la pietra e nasconda la
> mano; mostra anzi la mano, ma intenta ad altro gesto: quello,
> poniamo, di guardare l'orologio o di fare le ombre cinesi.[1]

Hoax and Metanarrative

The aim of this essay is to explore the relationship between
the word and the fictional concealment in the narrative work of
one of the most original — but, strangely, least known — Italian
authors of the 20th century, Tommaso Landolfi. This analysis
examines a single work by Landolfi, the long story *Ottavio di
Saint-Vincent*, which seems to have a particular relationship
with the whole narrative production of this author because of its
concern with metanarrative. The story of the poor poet Ottavio of
Saint-Vincent, who pretends to be a fictional duke conforming to
the duchess' wishes, surfaces more than once as a metaphor for
literary creation itself.

This work, as usual for Landolfi, was initially published in a
literary magazine — five instalments that appeared in *Il Mondo*[2]

---

1 Giacomo Debenedetti, 'Il "rouge et noir" di Landolfi', in *Intermezzo*
(Milan: il Saggiatore, 1963), pp. 215–38 (p. 224).

2 On *Il Mondo* (VIII, n. 52, 25th December 1956; IX, nn. 1, 2, 3, 4, respectively
del 1st January 1957, 8th January, 15th January, 22nd January) has been
published with the title *Ottavio l'impostore*, (on which reverberates Jean
Cocteau's *Thomas l'imposteur*); when it has been reissued in a single
volume it appears with epigraph, asterisks to separate the chapters and some
authors variations: cf. Tommaso Landolfi, *Opere I (1937–1959)*, ed. by
Idolina Landolfi, pref. by Carlo Bo (Milan: Rizzoli, 1991), p. 1035.

— and then, in January 1958, in a single edition with the reissue of *Le due zittelle*.[3] Written in Autumn 1956 in Pico, the story concerns an eccentric poet who presents himself from the first page as the poorest of the poor, 'misero dei miseri'.[4] The story takes place in Paris just before the French revolution: Ottavio walks alone at night in an ordinary street, wondering about his boredom and lack of money, and feeling a vague desire for suicide. The young poet has a strong presentiment that something is about to happen, and, indeed, something happens in the following scene. A melodious feminine voice, with a foreign accent, reaches him from the top of a terrace, declaring feelings that are similar to the poet's. Thus, he starts eavesdropping: he overhears, unseen, an important dialogue between a Russian duchess and a prince. The woman reports a strange fancy of hers: in order to escape boredom, she would like to find a poor desperate man, asleep on the street (drunk, she would relish), and to stage a hoax behind his back. She would kidnap him, carry him unconscious into her castle (court and wedding privileges included) and dupe him into believing that he is the duke. She and her whole entourage would pretend that they know him very well, tell him he had drunk too much 'vino di Sciampagna'[5] and that he therefore does not remember who he is. Ottavio seizes the chance and, with great presence of mind, he quickly prepares a "counter hoax", so as to be "accidentally" found by the duchess on her path. So begins the imposture of Ottavio, which will drag him in the middle of complex court intrigues and love interests. His performance of a fictional identity (which is known as fiction by the duchess and the other characters in the court) will reveal the lies of the duchess' three suitors, giving Ottavio a key role in the court's life.

This long story is emblematic of Landolfi's work in at least three ways. First, because of the peculiar language the author employs, which is why Montale stated that this prose 'sembra

---

3   Tommaso Landolfi, *Ottavio di Saint-Vincent: Preceduto da una ristampa di* Le due zittelle (Florence: Vallecchi, 1958).

4   Tommaso Landolfi, *Ottavio di Saint-Vincent* (Milan: Adelphi, 2000), p. 9. [This edition will be quoted from now on.]

5   Tommaso Landolfi, *Ottavio di Saint-Vincent*, p. 21.

scritta da un settecentesco traduttore di Shakespeare'.[6] Most of the features that make Landolfi's style so peculiar reside at the levels of morphology and lexicon, and are grounded in his very accurate research and work on the choice of terms, words, and expressions. The result is a language that has raised the interest of critics, starting from Oreste Macrì's essay[7] and up to more recent works, which have defined Landolfi's language as possessing a 'splendore quasi manieristico, ottocentesco o addirittura arcaizzante',[8] 'ricchezza senza pari',[9] 'lingua altra'.[10] The author tends to prefer the ancient word form instead of the current one (*strattagemma* instead of *stratagemma*, *tristo* instead of *triste*, *limosina* instead of *elemosina* and so on), opts for uncommon logical connectives, especially conjunctions (*vieppiù*, *giacché*, *al postutto*), and uses suffixes in an unconventional way (*vagol*ante, *penser*eccio).

The second reason why this short story can be considered as characteristic of Landolfi's prose is the large amount of metanarrative and intertextual features that it contains. One clear example is the aside in which Ottavio comments on the final dialogue between the duchess and her suitors:

'Eh no, vi è perfino del cattivo gusto qui: par d'essere a teatro, e in quale teatro!... Ma le risibili proclamazioni di codesti veri o falsi spasimanti, col loro bizzarro linguaggio, troppo somigliano alla mie di

6   Montale, Eugenio, 'Rien va', in *Il secondo mestiere. Prose (1920–1979)*, ed. by Giorgio Zampa, 2nd edn, 2 vols (Milan: Mondadori, 2006), vol. II (2006), pp. 2586–90 (p. 2586).

7   Oreste Macrì, *Tommaso Landolfi narratore, poeta, critico, artefice della lingua* (Florence: Le Lettere, 1990).

8   Maria Antonietta Grignani, '"L'espressione, la voce stessa ci tradiscono": Sulla lingua di Tommaso Landolfi', in *Un linguaggio dell'anima: atti della Giornata di studio su Tommaso Landolfi, Siena, 3 novembre 2004*, ed. by Idolina Landolfi and Antonio Prete (San Cesario di Lecce: Piero Manni, 2006), pp. 57–83.

9   Maurizio Dardano, 'Una "ricchezza senza pari": Per un'analisi della lingua di Tommaso Landolfi', in *Un linguaggio dell'anima: atti della Giornata di studio su Tommaso Landolfi, Siena, 3 novembre 2004*, pp. 11–51.

10   Paolo Zublena, *La lingua-pelle di Tommaso Landolfi* (Florence: Le Lettere, 2013).

pochi giorni addietro. Io qui mi vedo quasi riflesso, e non ne concepisco una grande idea di me medesimo.'[11]

Another example is Ottavio's reflection on that same scene during the night, in his bed:

> I personaggi di quella scena non erano... in che modo dirlo? veri. Non già che fosser mendaci o fallaci, che avessero, come si dice nei romanzi, l'eterna menzogna sulle labbra: no, erano proprio falsi e proprio loro. E neppur falsi, peggio...[12]

Ottavio's difficulty in finding a proper definition for the fictional status of the other characters reveals his own ambiguous position. On the one hand, he is a character among other characters, on the other, he represents an external metanarrative voice showing the deceptions of the court. It has been noticed that Ottavio's function here is to reveal the artificiality of the story: 'Ottavio serve a mostrare lo statuto finzionale del testo — incarna, meglio, l'*autocoscienza del testo in quanto tale*'.[13]

Together with metanarrative, intertextuality is an important related feature that makes this story an excellent sample of Landolfi's style. Many instances could be quoted to support this, because here Landolfi develops a contamination of different intertextual elements, while always referring to literary sources on various levels: plot, style, lexical choices. Critical interpretations, indeed, have found many connections and direct references in this story, the most evident being to Calderón's *Vida es sueño*; Ottavio seems to parody directly the plot of this famous play. A textual sign of Landolfi's conscious use of the play could be the following passage:

---

11   Landolfi, p. 74.
12   Ibid., p. 75.
13   Andrea Cortellessa, 'L'impostura di Ottavio: Prove per l'esercitazione di un "vero pezzo da concerto"', in *La «liquida vertigine»: Atti delle giornate di studio su Tommaso Landolfi. Prato, Convitto Nazionale Cicognini, 5–6 febbraio 1999*, ed. by Idolina Landolfi (Florence: Olschki, 2002), pp. 99–132 (p. 108).

non ci mancava altro che la duchessa sapesse che Ottavio sapeva e che
magari poi questi (ci si perdoni) sapesse che ella sapeva che lui sapeva,
perché tutta la farsa risultasse, diremo così, svuotata dall'interno.[14]

In these few lines, indeed, Sigismondo's words on his first
meeting with Rosaura reverberate: 'Pues muerte aquí te daré |
porque no sepas que sé | que sabes flaquezas mías'.[15]
The third and final feature I want to stress is the persistence
of the theme of the mask. An analysis of the plot reveals several
masking movements that interweave and overlie one another
in the story, creating the stratagem of imposture remembered
by the previous title of the short story (*Ottavio l'impostore*). To
summarise the impostures in the plot: first, the hoax organized by
the duchess against Ottavio, second, the "counter hoax" organized
by Ottavio against the duchess, and third the three different lies
spoken by the three suitors of the duchess, which are unmasked
and exposed by Ottavio's play-acting.

The Mask as Defamiliarization Strategy

On a closer inspection, it easy to notice that the features outlined
here — lexical, intertextual, and narrative — operate in a similar
way in the story: these masking procedures, instead of hiding
something, reveal the artificiality of the whole affair. This is what
masks do in Landolfi: they create defamiliarisation and distance
between reader and text.[16] This distance, which is easy to perceive
for the reader, is not located precisely in Ottavio's metanarrative
statements or in some reference to extrinsic texts: it lingers between
the lines, lending a feeling of mediation to the text. This impression

---

14   Landolfi, p. 34.
15   Pedro Calderón de la Barca, *La vida es sueño* (Madrid: Alianza, 2002), I,
     2, vv. 180–82.
16   This strategy is not far from Brecht's *Verfremdungseffekt* or from the
     priem ostranenije by Viktor Shklovsky. Although Landolfi did not
     theorize it directly, he knew formalist theory from his studies in Russian
     culture. For an articulate analysis of this topic cf. Valeria Pala, *Tommaso
     Landolfi traduttore di Gogol* (Rome: Bulzoni, 2009).

is perfectly described by the double metaphor ('music on music' and translation) in this note by Montale:

> Anche chi non avesse mai incontrato il personaggio ch'egli è non poteva sottrarsi, leggendo i suoi libri, dall'impressione ch'essi fossero frutto di un'arte costruita tenendo d'occhio altri modelli, qualcosa di molto vicino a quel che in termini musicali s'intende per musica al quadrato. Alla prova dei fatti si poteva poi constatare che nessuno dei modelli proposti reggeva e che Landolfi, magnifico traduttore dal russo e da altre lingue, quando scriveva in proprio non faceva altro che tradursi, tenendo nascosto in sé l'originale.[17]

The same general concept of mediation, expressed in different ways, is the common focus of three of the most important critical interpretations of this story. The first, by Giacomo Debenedetti, appeared in 1958, the second[18] is contained in the miscellaneous publication *Landolfi libro per libro*, and the third is by Andrea Cortellessa.[19] Debenedetti structures the second part of his *Il 'rouge et noir' di Landolfi*[20] around *Ottavio di Saint-Vincent*, which he highly appreciated. Debenedetti was among the jury of the Premio Viareggio in 1958, when the short story won the literary prize. Debenedetti begins his essay with what will be a *leitmotiv* of Landolfi criticism, that is, a complaint about the author's unsuccessful circulation among readers. Both Calvino's 1982 Anthology[21] and the already mentioned *Landolfi libro per libro*[22] are determined to create or stimulate a new generation of readers of Landolfi.

After summarizing the plot, Debenedetti reaches into the heart of the intertextual conundrum, regarding it from the beginning

---

17   Montale, p. 2586.
18   Leonardo Lattarulo, 'Ottavio di Saint-Vincent', in *Landolfi libro per libro*, ed. by Tarcisio Tarquini (Alatri: Hetea, 1988), pp. 103–10.
19   Cortellessa, pp. 99–132.
20   Debenedetti, pp. 215–238.
21   Italo Calvino, 'L'esattezza e il caso: Postfazione', in *Le più belle pagine di Tommaso Landolfi scelte da Italo Calvino* (Milan: Adelphi, 2001), pp. 549–63.
22   Walter Pedullà, 'Introduzione: La giovane critica e Tommaso Landolfi', in *Landolfi libro per libro*, ed. by Tarcisio Tarquini (Alatri: Hetea, 1988), pp. 11–13.

as unsolvable: his analysis of what he calls the list of literary precedents [*trafila dei precedenti*] takes on, in the case of Landolfi's story, the paradoxical aspect of a *mise en abyme*:

> Succede con Landolfi come a guardare la fotografia del signore, nella quale il signore tiene in mano una propria fotografia, e via di seguito, fino a un'ombra infinitesimale che sicuramente c'è, ma per vederla ci vuole il microscopio.[23]

In spite of this danger, Debenedetti does not give up and he identifies some precedents of Ottavio's plot (e.g. Pirandello's *Enrico VI* and Thomas Mann's *Bekenntnisse des Hochstaplers Felix Krull*). Then, however, he goes on reading the whole story on the basis of the dichotomy between earning [*guadagno*] — which is intended as a good action with inner self-approval — against winning [*vincita*] — which is intended as an illegitimate but necessary action aimed at going on living without working. Of the two, obviously, Ottavio can only obtain the latter, and his final sacrifice of winning is a proud atonement and a way to practice his preference for nothingness.[24]

The theme of parodic concealment resurfaces in the final part of Debenedetti's essay. What is more interesting than the story's actual precedents is how the entire process of exponentiation actually works in Landolfi's text.

> Si dice *pastiche*, ma poi i nomi dei maestri, nella loro precisa identità, risultano irreperibili. Il proprio di Landolfi, quella che in passato si sarebbe chiamata la sua serietà, consiste nel fare il *pastiche* di un *pastiche* immaginario.[25]

In the second essay here presented, the point is not *pastiche*, but parody in a narrower sense. According to Lattarulo, *Ottavio* is the perfect example of an intertextual text, and the most important reference here is Calderón's masterpiece.[26]

---

23 Debenedetti, p. 229.
24 Ibid., p. 235.
25 Ibid., p. 237.
26 Lattarulo, p. 105.

In this interpretation, the parody is for Landolfi a way to escape, an attempt to overcome the tragic through romance — such as in the paradoxical tragedy of *Landolfo VI di Benevento* and the lyricism of *Viola di morte*. This attempt is actually destined to fail, because 'la coscienza lucidissima [...] vuole ma non può morire a se stessa e [...] impedisce l'attuarsi di un vero processo di trasformazione'.[27] Thus, the parodic quality of this story is shown by both the will and the impossibility of 'credere davvero che noi siamo fatti della stessa materia dei sogni'.[28]

Parodic distance is also the starting point of the third essay, in which Cortellessa develops the reflections of previous critics, as if he wanted to further explore the infinite *mise en abyme* shown by Debenedetti in his image of the man with a photograph in his hands.

Cortellessa starts from the already quoted lines by Montale and Debenedetti, and goes on articulating a more specific examination of the list of precedents, adding more titles to those already quoted. Among these, for instance, we can find Hofmannsthal's *Rosenkavalier* (translated by Landolfi himself a dozen years before, but published in the series of books edited by Leone Traverso for Bompiani only in 1959)[29] and Jean Cocteau's *Thomas l'imposteur*.

Furthermore, Cortellessa develops very interesting considerations about what he calls the truth of masks: 'quella perversione spirituale che siamo soliti definire verità delle maschere'.[30] The scholar discusses hypotheses outside literary discourse, enlarging in this way the disciplinary field — this is the case of semiotic, speech act theory, Jankélévitch's and

---

27 Ibid., p. 107.
28 Ibid.
29 I also stress the connection between the names of Ottavio and "Octavian" in Hofmannsthal's *Rosenkavalier*. On Landolfi's translation of Hofmannsthal, cf. Mariagrazia Farina, 'Tommaso Landolfi e il "Bischeraccio della rosa", Hugo von Hofmannsthal tradotto dallo scrittore di Pico', *Italienisch*, 73 (2015), 57–77; and Andrea Landolfi, 'Il malinteso felice: Tommaso Landolfi traduttore di Hofmannsthal', *Studi germanici* n.s., 63 (2005), 459–71.
30 Cortellessa, p. 124.

Goffmann's thesis. Cortellessa confirm Calvino's well-known statement that from the standpoint of linguistic theory 'tutto quello che lui [Landolfi] dice in materia sembra d'una esattezza "scientifica" (come terminologia e come concetti) tale da poter far testo nel seminario universitario più aggiornato'.[31]

Finally, in the essay's conclusion, Cortellessa proposes a more classical thesis statement in the vein of traditional literary studies: *Ottavio* should be read (just like *Le due zittelle*) as a crisis work, and as such it should mark a caesura in the whole of Landolfi's oeuvre, thus modifying its periodization and interpretation.

Lzegherzogstvo's Mask

Although expressed in various ways — parody, *pastiche*, irony, self-translating or music on music — the strategy of defamiliarisation used in Landolfi's prose is at the centre of the various critics' analyses. Ottavio's imposture, analysed in terms of its acceptance of fiction/falsification [*finzione/falsificazione*] in Cortellessa's essay, could be read as a representation of literary fiction itself, or rather as a representation of representation. It is a fiction that both hides and reveals fiction itself.[32]

This macroscopic meta-device can also be recognized at the microscopic level of a single word. When Ottavio wakes up in the castle, in his ducal bedroom, the servants tell him who he is and explain why he does not remember anything. The name they give him is a very strange one:

---

31 Calvino, p. 556.
32 In Sara Bellotto, 'Le parole e la maschera: La poetica dell'occultamento in Tommaso Landolfi', *Studi di estetica*, s. III, XXIV, 14 (1996), 139–75 (p. 142) is suggested the hypothesis of 'un nascondimento classicistico intenzionale da parte dell'artista dei moventi creativi profondi mediante una lavorazione sapiente ed articolata del materiale linguistico'. Here the literary text is read as 'etimologicamente un "textus", ossia il prodotto di una tessitura [...]. Esso possiede la duplice proprietà di esibire se stesso e contemporaneamente rinviare ad altro, di essere opaco e trasparente insieme. Ed è su questi due versanti, il visibile e l'invisibile, l'evidente e il supposto, che Landolfi calcola i suoi "scherzi" letterari'.

'Vostra Grazia è il duca di Lzegherzogstvo.'
'Come avete detto?'
'Ho detto...'
'È inutile, un tal nome lo direte sempre voi per me, ché io non giungerò mai a pronunciarlo. E chi è codesto duca?'[33]

This fake identity doubles the mode of operation of the whole short story. The duchess and the duke are supposed to be Russian, so it would be natural for their names to be Russian as well. But this name "Lzegherzogstvo" — which Ottavio can barely pronounce or remember throughout the story — is not Russian at all, apart from some similarity in sound. It seems to be a conglomeration of broken Russian and random letters, but actually it conceals the word "Herzog", the German word for "duke". It is as if Ottavio were called "the duke of duke". "Lzegherzogstvo" is actually a mask-word: it hides the German word mocking Russian sounds.

Conclusion

In conclusion, and going back to the plot, we note that throughout the story Ottavio plays the role of a duke who does not exist for the benefit of people who know that this representation is fictional — the whole court knows about the duchess' pretence. The very fact that this fiction is known opens some unexpected possibilities and chances of unprecedented richness for Ottavio. As Debenedetti stresses, Ottavio could take advantage of this situation in order to get economic benefits, social privileges, and happiness. He refuses all of it. The proud and uncompromising ethics Ottavio shows in this situation may sound strange: he contemptuously refuses his various chances, squandering his win at gambling, and rejecting compromises. This is strange behaviour for a character who has done nothing but lie and pretend he is someone else. This ethical paradox can be resolved if Ottavio's fiction is thought of as a metaphor for literary fiction as such. There is no 'lying' in telling a story, and it may be that

---

33   Landolfi, p. 24.

Ottavio imitates this very act. In a style such as Landolfi's, with high levels of fiction, fantasy, anti-realism,[34] it is possible to find a strong ethical will to be faithful to the idea of truth — although this is defined negatively. This faithfulness prevents Ottavio from reaching a compromise with the other characters, who want him to put away his mask in order to gain money or social recognition. In a way, this mask is all Ottavio has; it is his true identity in this specific moment. When the story is over, he chooses to go back to what he had before, that is, a free and empty life that consists in 'procedere filosofando lungo il rigagnolo della strada', waiting for a new story to tell.

Bibliography

Bellotto, Sara, 'Le parole e la maschera: La poetica dell'occultamento in Tommaso Landolfi', *Studi di estetica*, III, XXIV, 14 (1996), 139–75.

Calderón de la Barca, Pedro, *La vida es sueño* (Madrid: Alianza, 2002).

Calvino, Italo, 'L'esattezza e il caso: Postfazione', in *Le più belle pagine di Tommaso Landolfi scelte da Italo Calvino* (Milan: Adelphi, 2001), pp. 549–63.

Cortellessa, Andrea, 'Landolfi 1929–1937: Sistema della parodia e dialettica del luogo comune', *Moderna*, IV, 1 (2004), 41–64.

—————————, 'L'impostura di Ottavio: Prove per l'esercitazione di un "vero pezzo da concerto"', in *La «liquida vertigine»: Atti delle giornate di studio su Tommaso Landolfi. Prato, Convitto Nazionale Cicognini, 5–6 febbraio 1999*, ed. by Idolina Landolfi (Florence: Olschki, 2002), pp. 99–132.

Dardano, Maurizio, 'Una "ricchezza senza pari". Per un'analisi della lingua di Tommaso Landolfi', in *Un linguaggio dell'anima: atti della Giornata di studio su Tommaso Landolfi, Siena, 3 novembre 2004*, ed. by Idolina Landolfi and Antonio Prete (San Cesario di Lecce: Piero Manni, 2006), pp. 11–51.

Debenedetti, Giacomo, 'Il "rouge et noir" di Landolfi', in *Intermezzo* (Milan: il Saggiatore, 1963), pp. 215–38.

Farina, Mariagrazia, 'Tommaso Landolfi e il "Bischeraccio della rosa", Hugo von Hofmannsthal tradotto dallo scrittore di Pico', *Italienisch*, 73 (2015), 57–77.

---

34 More about this interpretation in Beatrice Stasi, 'Sotto il mantello di Gogol: L'antirealismo di Tommaso Landolfi', in *La «liquida vertigine»: Atti delle giornate di studio su Tommaso Landolfi. Prato, Convitto Nazionale Cicognini, 5–6 febbraio 1999*, ed. by Idolina Landolfi (Florence: Olschki, 2002), pp. 67–90.

Grignani, Maria Antonietta, '"L'espressione, la voce stessa ci tradiscono": Sulla lingua di Tommaso Landolfi', in *Un linguaggio dell'anima: atti della Giornata di studio su Tommaso Landolfi, Siena, 3 novembre 2004*, ed. by Idolina Landolfi and Antonio Prete (San Cesario di Lecce: Piero Manni, 2006), pp. 57–83.

Landolfi, Andrea, 'Il malinteso felice: Tommaso Landolfi traduttore di Hofmannsthal', *Studi germanici* n.s., 63 (2005), 459–71.

Landolfi, Tommaso, *Ottavio di Saint-Vincent* (Milan: Adelphi, 2000).

——————————, *Opere I (1937–1959)*, ed. by Idolina Landolfi, pref. by di Carlo Bo (Milan: Rizzoli, 1991).

——————————, *Ottavio di Saint-Vincent; preceduto da una ristampa di Le due zittelle* (Florence: Vallecchi, 1958).

Lattarulo, Leonardo, 'Ottavio di Saint-Vincent', in *Landolfi libro per libro*, ed. by Tarcisio Tarquini (Alatri: Hetea, 1988), pp. 103–10.

Macrì, Oreste, *Tommaso Landolfi narratore, poeta, critico, artefice della lingua* (Florence: Le Lettere, 1990).

Montale, Eugenio, 'Rien va', in *Il secondo mestiere. Prose (1920–1979)*, ed. by Giorgio Zampa, 2nd edn, 2 vols. (Milan: Mondadori, 2006), pp. 2586–90.

Hofmannsthal, Hugo von, *Le nozze di Sobeide; Il cavaliere della rosa*, trans. by Tommaso Landolfi, ed. by Leone Traverso (Florence: Vallecchi, 1959).

Pala, Valeria, *Tommaso Landolfi traduttore di Gogol* (Rome: Bulzoni, 2009).

Secchieri, Filippo, *L'artificio naturale: Landolfi e i teatri della scrittura* (Rome: Bulzoni, 2006).

Pedullà, Walter, 'Introduzione. La giovane critica e Tommaso Landolfi', in *Landolfi libro per libro*, ed. by Tarcisio Tarquini (Alatri: Hetea, 1988), pp. 13–15.

Serafini, Francesca, 'Appunti linguistici sulla narrativa landolfiana', in *La «liquida vertigine»: Atti delle giornate di studio su Tommaso Landolfi. Prato, Convitto Nazionale Cicognini, 5–6 febbraio 1999*, ed. by Idolina Landolfi (Florence: Olschki, 2002), pp. 225–47.

Serra, Mauro, 'La magia del linguaggio tra nostalgia delle origini e riflessione metalinguistica nell'opera di Tommaso Landolfi', in *Un linguaggio dell'anima: atti della Giornata di studio su Tommaso Landolfi, Siena, 3 novembre 2004*, ed. by Idolina Landolfi and Antonio Prete (San Cesario di Lecce: Piero Manni, 2006), pp. 93–102.

Shklovsky, Viktor, 'Art as technique', in *Russian Formalist Criticism: Four Essays*, ed. by Lee T. Lemon, Marion J. Reis (Lincoln: University of Nebraska Press, 1965).

Stasi, Beatrice, 'Sotto il mantello di Gogol: L'antirealismo di Tommaso Landolfi', in *La «liquida vertigine»: Atti delle giornate di studio su Tommaso Landolfi. Prato, Convitto Nazionale Cicognini, 5–6 febbraio 1999*, ed. by Idolina Landolfi (Florence: Olschki, 2002), pp. 67–90.

Zublena, Paolo, *La lingua-pelle di Tommaso Landolfi* (Florence: Le Lettere, 2013).

'FROM ONE FACULTY TO ANOTHER': TEXT AND IMAGE IN ROBERT HOOKE'S *MICROGRAPHIA*

Alessio Mattana
(University of Leeds)

Introduction

Unprecedented in his ability with experiments, Robert Hooke (1635–1703) was at the centre of the English culture of the second half of the seventeenth century. The entry in the second edition of *The Oxford Companion to British History*, in its succinctness, provides a glimpse of his impact on the cultural life of his age:

> Hooke made the microscope well known as a scientific instrument, publishing his *Micrographia* in 1665. Its splendid engraving of the flea made a tremendous impression, and the book opened up a new world below the level of naked-eye observation. Previously, Hooke had worked with Robert Boyle on the air pump, and in 1662 had been appointed curator to the Royal Society, with the duty of performing experiments at the meetings. He was referee of Isaac Newton's first optical paper, and his critical comments made Newton his enemy. Hooke lectured on earthquakes, worked on pendulum clocks, toyed with something like a wave theory of light, and was a great, versatile, and controversial figure in the scientific revolution in England.[1]

In an age when the boundaries between natural philosophy and science were blurred, as were the ones between amateurish dabbling into experiments and professional examination of specimens, Hooke emerged as a new figure. A central philosophical and scientific personality like Robert Boyle — with whom (or *for* whom, being his clerk by that time) Hooke had built and manoeuvred the air-pump in

---

1   John Cannon, *The Oxford Companion to British History* (Oxford: Oxford University Press, 2009).

1661 — perceived himself as a gentleman, one that did not want to sacrifice his genteel status to become fully devoted to scientific work. In this respect, Boyle was perfectly aligned with Restoration culture. Differently from him, Hooke is by our standards better defined as a scientist. To do so we need to apply what Steven Shapin calls an 'unfortunate but not necessarily vicious' anachronism: in the second half of the seventeenth century English society did not 'automatically comprehend the role of experimental philosopher'.[2] There was no such thing as the scientist by job and Hooke could be said to have invented this professional and intellectual category. As Stephen Inwood remarked, given his official functions as 'Gresham professor of Geometry, Cutler Lecturer, Fellow and Curator of Experiments of the Royal Society', Hooke, 'in a world occupied almost entirely by "virtuosi", physicians, aristocratic dilettantes and gentleman scholars of independent means', established himself and was recognized *de facto* as 'England's first professional research scientist'.[3]

The extent of his eclectic interests, on the other hand, should make us wary of crystallizing his figure into that of the detached scientist exclusively interested in abstractions. As Lisa Jardine reminds us, Hooke was 'a multi-talented intellectual'; or, borrowing the concept from the Renaissance, a 'polymath' whose discoveries and inventions were 'acknowledged to be of lasting interest and importance'.[4] In a culture that in a few decades would see the emergence of the philosophy of Isaac Newton and an increasing professionalization of the scientific enterprise, Hooke represented the archetype of a figure oscillating between the two worlds of geometry — Descartes was a favourite reference of his — and experiment. Hooke's genius, as Michael Cooper observes, lies exactly in this ability 'on the one hand to design, make, and

2   Steven Shapin, 'Who Was Robert Hooke?', ed. by Michael Hunter and Simon Schaffer, in *Robert Hooke. New Studies* (Woodbridge: The Boydell Press, 1989), p. 253.

3   Stephen Inwood, *The Man Who Knew Too Much: The Strange and Inventive Life of Robert Hooke, 1635–1703* (London: Macmillan, 2002), p. 33.

4   Lisa Jardine, 'Robert Hooke: A Reputation Restored', ed. by Michael Cooper and Michael Cyril William Hunter, *Robert Hooke: Tercentennial Studies* (Farnham: Ashgate, 2006), p. 247.

use a microscope and on the other to discuss, to Boyle's profit, Euclid's *Elements* and the philosophy of Descartes'.[5]

This double dimension illuminates our understanding of *Micrographia*, arguably Hooke's most enduring contribution to the history of science. Not only, as the editor of the English 1938 edition writes, is the long-standing impact of *Micrographia* easily discernible in the importance assumed by microscopic observations in modern medicine, physics, astronomy, chemistry, mineralogy and engineering.[6] *Micrographia* was more immediately ground-breaking because, for the first time in Europe, an author undertook the task not only of enquiring over a large number of minute bodies but also, and more powerfully, of showing the results of the microscopic observations to the readers via a set of engravings that displayed a level of detail that was unprecedented for the age. This move enabled Hooke's readers to be finally engaged in a conversation about the mysterious world of the minute. The reaction of Samuel Pepys, who wrote in his diary that he 'sat up till 2 a-clock' to read *Micrographia*, in his opinion one of 'the most ingenious book[s]' of the time, provides a glance on just how striking the book proved to be for the learned community in late-seventeenth-century London.[7] The relevance and impressiveness of *Micrographia*, in the words of Allan Chapman, depended on its having inaugurated the tradition of 'visual communication in science' by conjoining 'an easy style that would have been accessible to any innumerate' with a series of thirty-eight engravings that depicted his microscopical observations at 'an unprecedented level of detail'.[8]

---

5   Jim Bennett, Michael Cooper, Michael Hunter and Lisa Jardine, *London's Leonardo – The Life and Work of Robert Hooke* (Oxford: Oxford University Press, 2003), p. 15.

6   Robert Hooke, *Micrographia, or, Some physiological descriptions of minute bodies made by magnifying glasses Preface*, ed. by R. T. Gunther (Oxford: Oxford University Press, 1938), p. vi.

7   R. C. Latham and W. Mathews (eds.), *The Diary of Samuel Pepys* (London: G. Bell and Sons, 1970–1976), 9 vols., vi, 18.

8   Allan Chapman, *England's Leonardo. Robert Hooke and the Seventeenth-Century Scientific Revolution* (Bristol and Philadelphia: Institute of Physics Publishing, 2005), p. 58.

In this contribution, I will investigate the relations between word and image in *Micrographia*. The topic has already been explored in two contributions by John T. Harwood (on *Micrographia*'s 'rhetoric of graphics', defined as the set of 'strategies for linking not only text and image but larger segments of text and images to make a broader argument about the mechanical philosophy') and Michael Aaron Dennis (on the establishment of what he terms 'discipline seeing', a practice by which Hooke translates his 'private experience into public knowledge').[9] In addition to this, I will claim that Hooke in *Micrographia* promoted a particular way of reading his text, one that challenges the dichotomy between descriptive and narrative modes that Svetlana Alpers, in *The Art of Describing*, argued was typical of the European culture of the seventeenth century. Hooke, contrary to what Alpers claims, required readers to actively conflate word and image in order to make sense of the microscopical phenomena of nature showed in his book.

The Fallibility of the Senses

Micrographia was not the first attempt to discuss microscopic observations in written form. As David Wootton notes, after Galileo constructed the first microscopes in 1625, a 'detailed account of a living being based on the use of a microscope' appeared in Italy in 1644.[10] Written by Giambattista Odierna, it was titled *L'Occhio della Mosca* (the fly's eye) and it focused on one living being only. A project similar to Hooke's enterprise was instead taking place by 1661, when Christopher Wren attempted to write an extensive and illustrated text about microscopical observations. Wren then moved on to other studies without completing it, and years later he advised

---

9   Michael Aaron Dennis, 'Graphic Understanding: Instruments and Interpretation in Robert Hooke's *Micrographia*', *Science in Context*, Vol. 3, n. 2, 309–364 (p. 323); John T. Harwood, 'Rhetoric and Graphics in *Micrographia*', Hunter and Schaffer, *Robert Hooke. New Studies*, pp. 121–122.

10   David Wootton, *Bad Medicine: Doctors Doing Harm Since Hippocrates* (Oxford: Oxford University Press, 2006), p. 110.

Hooke to take over his project. The preface to *Micrographia* clearly acknowledges this intellectual debt:

> I first set upon this Enterprise, yet still came to it with much Reluctancy, because I was to follow the footsteps of so eminent a Person as Dr. Wren, who was the first that attempted any thing of this nature; whose original draughts do now make one of the Ornaments of that great Collection of Rarities in the Kings Closet. [...] But at last, being assured both by Dr [John] Wilkins, and Dr. Wren himself, that he had given over his intentions of prosecuting it [...] I set upon this undertaking, and was not a little incourag'd to proceed in it, by the Honour that the Royal Society was pleas'd to favour me with, in approving of those draughts (which from time to time as I had an opportunity of describing) I presented to them.[11]

This passage was inserted as a necessary strategy of authentication. The acknowledgement implies that the data presented in *Micrographia* was validated by two respected Royal Society fellows like John Wilkins and Christopher Wren and officially authorized by the Royal Society itself, of which the frontispiece of the book bears the coat of arms and the *imprimatur*. As Simon Schaffer and Steven Shapin claim in *Leviathan and the Air-Pump*, the endorsement given by the two gentlemen and by the Royal Society would have the effect of bringing informed readers in England to easily trust Hooke's graphic and textual representations of the microscopical world.[12] It would be erroneous, however, to infer that asking his readers to accept unconditionally the veracity of the engravings and descriptions in *Micrographia* was Hooke's primary goal. The acknowledgment is inserted at the very end of the preface and Wren's effort is defined very precisely: his draughts, Hooke writes, ended up as a 'Collection of Rarities' for the king. This specification relates to what Lorraine Daston has identified as the collecting of 'deviating instances, such as the errors of nature,

---

11   Robert Hooke, *Micrographia, or, Some physiological descriptions of minute bodies made by magnifying glasses Preface* (London: 1665), p. xxvii.
12   Simon Schaffer and Steven Shapin, *Leviathan and the Air-Pump: Hobbes, Boyle, and the Experimental Life* (Princeton: Princeton University Press, 1985), p. 65.

or strange and monstrous objects, in which nature deviates and turns from her ordinary course', and it was an integral part of the Baconian project upon which the Royal Society was founded.[13] However, by the time the reader comes to this point of the preface, Hooke has already specified that *Micrographia* is not so much concerned with collecting rare specimens. Its anxiety rather lies in another Baconian strand, one less pursued by the practitioners of the Royal Society. As the first pages of the preface make clear, Hooke is interested in identifying the flaws innate in the act of seeing, in the processes by which such deficiencies alter our experience and comprehension, and in the solutions that could be applied to counterbalance them. Rather than asking for trust, Hooke demands attention and a touch of scepticism; the reader is to focus on the process by which 'bodies', natural and artificial, are seen *and* interpreted by an observer, and thus how they are represented. That is why, before discussing the improvements provided by the microscope, Hooke mentions a necessary preliminary step. In order to understand nature (and, thus, the contents of the book), the reader must take 'a watchfulness over the failings and an inlargement of the dominion, of the Senses'.[14] The issue was first framed by Lord Bacon who, in the *Novum Organum* (1620), defined the 'idols of the tribe' in this way:

> [T]he idols of the tribe are inherent in human nature and the very tribe or
> race of man; for man's sense is falsely asserted to be the standard of things;
> on the contrary, all the perceptions both of the senses and the mind bear
> reference to man and not to the universe, and the human mind resembles
> those uneven mirrors which impart their own properties to different
> objects, from which rays are emitted and distort and disfigure them.[15]

How does one read the Book of Nature — what Alpers defines as the idea that 'God creates by imprinting himself [...] in things'

---

13   Lorraine Daston, 'Marvelous Facts and Miraculous Evidence in Early
       Modern Europe', *Critical Inquiry*, vol. 18, 1, 93–124 (p. 111).
14   Hooke, *Micrographia*, p. v.
15   Sir Francis Bacon, *The Novum Organon, or a True Guide to the
       Interpretation of Nature,* trans. by G. W. Kitchin (Oxford: Oxford
       University Press, 1855), p. 12.

— if the human senses convey data to uneven mirrors that can only distort it?[16] This problem proves to be central in *Micrographia*. The great prerogative of Mankind 'above other Creatures', the very first sentence of Hooke's preface reads, is that 'we are not only able to behold the works of Nature' but that we also have 'the power of considering, comparing, altering, assisting, and improving them to various uses'. There is thus no such thing as pure seeing in humans. Compared to other beasts, their defining characteristic is that whatever they perceive is immediately interpreted and transformed into representation. Accordingly, the term used to define the acts of seeing presented in *Micrographia* is 'Observations', which is in the first occurrence of the preface paired with the more linguistic term 'Deductions'. Observation is thus employed by Hooke in its polysemous sense of seeing and saying; of capturing sensorial data and instantly produce an interpretation.[17]

The Deranging Potential of the Microscope

In Hooke's philosophy, the interweaving of perception and interpretation, of vision and representation, has two relevant and mutually dependent consequences. Capturing imperfect sensorial input, Hooke points out from the very first pages of the preface, brings about a chain effect that distorts the activity of memory and reason, since 'all the uncertainty, and mistakes of humane actions, proceed either from the narrowness and wandring of our Senses'. The imperfection of the human senses is a result of the fallen condition of man due to the original sin—what Hooke, with oxymoronic phrasing, defines as a 'deriv'd corruption, innate and born with him'.[18] However, and this is the second consequence, man has the power to rectify the operations of these three faculties by correcting the sensory input. *Micrographia* — far from being a mere collection of rarities — aims exactly at providing an aid

---

16   Svetlana Alpers, *The Art of Describing. Dutch Art in the Seventeenth Century* (Chicago: Chicago University Press, 1983), p. 93.
17   Hooke, *Micrographia* p. viii.
18   Ibid., p. iii.

to the senses and, by consequence, to the understanding. It does so by detailing the method of observation through glasses (the microscope specifically, but the telescope is mentioned as well) in order to promote an improvement of the senses that will make the correction of errors in judgment possible. The Baconian 'uneven mirrors' of men, in Hooke's philosophy, can be compensated for by magnifying glasses crafted through the art of man.

These glasses, which already show us the instructive and pleasurable 'secret workings of Nature', at a higher level of refinement might allow us to see:

> [t]he subtilty of the composition of Bodies, the structure of their parts, the various texture of their matter, the instruments and manner of their inward motions, and all the other possible appearances of things [...]; all which the ancient Peripateticks were content to comprehend in two general and (unless further explain'd) useless words of Matter and Form. From whence there may arise many admirable advantages, towards the increase of the Operative, and the Mechanick Knowledge, to which this Age seems so much inclined, because we may perhaps be inabled to discern all the secret workings of Nature, almost in the same manner as we do those that are the productions of Art, and are manag'd by Wheels, and Engines, and Springs, that were devised by humane Wit.[19]

In this instance of the nature-as-clockwork metaphor, Hooke argues that it is by the art that produced the lenses of the microscope that we can bridge the gap with nature. With improved sight fruit of technological advancement, humankind progressively tends toward the discovery that nature is an archetypical machine, a perfect model of the technology that man has lost in the Fall from Eden. The discussion over the putrefaction of natural bodies is one instance of this strategy: Hooke asks his reader to imagine this process by '[s]uppos[ing] a curious piece of Clock-work, that had had several motions and contrivances in it, which, when in order, would all have mov'd in their design'd methods and Periods'.[20]

---

19   Ibid., p. iv.
20   Ibid., p. 133.

Being nature mechanically contrived, it can be understood by mastering the mechanical arts. This is why the very first engraving presented by Hooke in *Micrographia* is one portraying the microscope, in order to familiarize the readers with the instrument of observation that will enhance the senses — an operation that Hooke calls 'the adding of artificial Organs to the natural'.[21] However, aware that the sudden perception of the level of detail in the depictions of (and by) the microscope might be bewildering for the reader-observer, Hooke uses textual descriptions to highlight the structure and workings of the image presented. The wordy depiction of the microscope — amounting to roughly nine hundred words — begins with the declarative, and apparently tautological sentence 'The Instrument is this', which is then punctuated by a number of index letters that refer to a set of small signs discernible inside the picture (see Figure 1). These cues are employed in order to provide orientation to the reader on how to build and use a microscope:

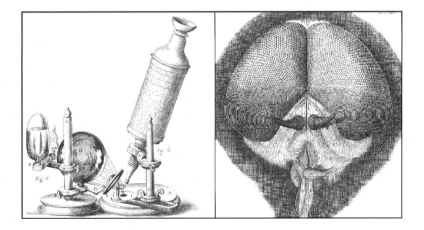

Figure 1. The microscope and the head of the fly. Copyright: Library of Congress.

---

21   Ibid., p. iii.

> The Instrument is this. I prepare a pretty capaceous Bolt-head AB, with a small stem about two foot and a half long DC; upon the end of this D I put on a small bended Glass, or brazen syphon DEF (open at D, E and F, but to be closed with cement at F and E, as occasion serves) whose stem F should be about six or eight inches long, but the bore of it not above half an inch diameter, and very even; these I fix very strongly together by the help of very hard Cement, and then fit the whole Glass ABCDEF into a long Board, or Frame, in such manner, that almost half the head AB may lye buried in a concave Hemisphere cut into the Board RS; then I place it so on the Board RS, as is exprest in the first figure of the first Scheme; and fix it very firm and steady in that posture [...].[22]

In addition to the index letters, Hooke walks his readers through the engraving by indicating the figure in each scheme. The schemes are often compounds of different samples or even different perspectives and they are systematically glossed upon.

Hooke employs this strategy because he recognizes that the unprecedented possibility of glancing into the (formerly) invisible world of the minute brings with it the risk of a displacement in the observer. Images seen through the microscope were so zoomed-in that they lost all sense of wholeness, showing unexpected particulars and patterns that might have disoriented the non-expert observer. '[E]very considerable Improvement of Telescopes or Microscopes', Hooke warns with navigational metaphor, produces 'new World and Terra-Incognita to our view'.[23] The question is not simply one of technical mastery. Microscopic observations could easily degenerate in an enquiry over the trivial, one that diverts the attention from more important philosophical and theological questions. The very size of the particulars seen through the microscope, Tita Chico underlines, typically brought microscopists from Hooke onwards to 'return again and again to a defense of the small, betraying a nervousness about its potentially trivial nature'.[24] As Christa Knellwolf adds, however, much more dangerous was the fact that

---

22 Ibid., p. x.
23 *Micrographia*, p. xvii.
24 Tita Chico, 'Minute Particulars: Microscopy and Eighteenth-Century Narrative', *Mosaic*, 39:2, 143–161 (p. 147).

microscopic observations were perceived to 'endanger the whole epistemological edifice because questions about perspective and dimension immediately challenged the possibility of a stable point of view'.[25] The unknown potential of these journeys through the lenses of the microscope would be discussed by John Locke in a passage from Book II, section xxiii of his *Essay Concerning Human Understanding* (1690). Were we to have a microscopic eyesight ('the most instructive of our senses'), Locke argues, we would be forced to deal with a dangerous consequence:

> It would bring him [the observer] nearer to discovering the texture and motion of the minute parts of corporeal things, and he would probably get ideas of the internal structures of many of them. But then he would be in a quite different world from other people: nothing would appear the same to him as to others; the visible ideas of everything would be different.[26]

Seventy years after *Micrographia* was published, Alexander Pope in his *Essay on Man* (1733) would still feel the actuality of this problem in perception. He scathingly quipped: 'Why has not man a microscopic eye? | For this plain reason, man is not a fly. | Say what the use, were finer optics giv'n, | T' inspect a mite, not comprehend the heav'n?'[27] The cohabitation in the final line of mite and heaven suggests that the recalibration in perception generated by the microscope brings with it the risk of a grotesque reversal in the order of nature. That is, art would not integrate but substitute nature, a point about which Margaret Cavendish was sceptical about in her 1666 critique of the microscope, and particularly of the observation of the eyes of a fly included in *Micrographia*. Art, Cavendish writes, 'produces most commonly hermaphroditical figures'. Therefore, she 'can hardly be perswaded to believe, that this Artificial Informer (I mean the Microscope) should be so true as it is generally thought'.[28]

---

25 Christa Knellwolf, 'Robert Hooke's *Micrographia* and the Aesthetics of Empiricism', *Seventeenth Century*, 16:1, 177–200 (p. 178).
26 John Locke, *An Essay Concerning Human Understanding* (London: 1753), p. 145.
27 Alexander Pope, *An Essay on Man* (London: 1733), p. 31.
28 Margaret Cavendish, *Observations upon Experimental Philosophy to which is Added, The Description of a New Blazing World* (London: 1666),

There is at least a passage in the preface to *Micrographia* that justifies the doubts raised by Locke, Pope and Cavendish. At the end of the preface, right before the beginning of the series of observations, Hooke expresses the wish, indeed the 'belief', that his efforts

> will be no more comparable to the Productions of many other Natural Philosophers, who are now every where busie about greater things; then my little Objects are to be compar'd to the greater and more beautiful Works of Nature, A Flea, a Mite, a Gnat, to an Horse, an Elephant, or a Lyon'.[29]

In the upside-down world of microscopy, a flea is as important as a horse — indeed, as big as a horse; and this was unmistakably expressed by the fact that *Micrographia* was originally published with large, foldable engravings of the insects represented, with the louse being devoted a fold-out page four times larger than the book (see figure 2). When Francisc Szekely writes that the zoomed-in image does not 'strike us as physically alien, because its shape is known to us from naked eye observations', he does not fully consider the subversive potential of an animal that, while familiar to man in its reduced size, could be obscurely tantalizing.[30]

Aware of this, on most occasions Hooke seeks to limit the risks derived by the deranging level of detail in the microscopic images. Throughout *Micrographia*, his concern is to restrain the dangerous potential of the images by written commentary that directs the readerly activity of observation. This is achieved by what Jordynn Jack calls a 'pedagogy of sight', a set of 'specific rhetorical strategies rhetors use to *teach* their readers how to see and interpret an image according to some kind of motivated program, whether scientific, religious, civic, or otherwise'.

---

   p. 24.
29   Hooke, *Micrographia*, p. xxviii.
30   Francisc Szekely, 'Unreliable Observers, Flawed Instruments, "Disciplined Viewings": Handling Specimens in Early Microscopy', *Parergon*, 28:1, 155–76 (p. 157).

Hooke, in this sense, conjoins word and image in order to show his readers not only *'what* to see' but also *'how* to see' the pictures of *Micrographia*.[31] He does so, mostly, by carefully selecting adjectives that help to qualify the image in object and thus reduce its deranging potential. The observation on the head of a fly (with the adjectives italicized by me) constitutes a case in point:

> I took a *large grey* Drone-Fly, that had a *large* head, but a *small* and *slender* body in proportion to it, and cutting off its head, I fix'd it with the forepart or face upwards upon my Object Plate (this I made choice of rather then the head of a *great blue* Fly, because my enquiry being now about the eyes, I found this Fly to have, first the *biggest* clusters of eyes in proportion to his head, of any *small* kind of Fly that I have yet seen, it being somewhat inclining towards the make of the *large* Dragon-Flies. Next, because there is a *greater* variety in the knobs or balls of each cluster, then is of any *small* Fly.) Then examining it according to my *usual* manner, by varying the degrees of light, and altering its position to each kinde of light, I drew that representation of it which is delineated in the 24. Scheme, and found these things to be as *plain* and *evident*, as *notable* and *pleasant*.[32]

Along with a linear writing style, Hooke makes use of adjectives belonging to the semantic spheres of size ('large', 'small', 'slender', 'biggest') and colour ('grey', 'blue'), so that the reader can connect Hooke's microscopical observation to basic perceptive categories. The textual apparatus, in these cases, is used to make the information provided by the microscope clear and conspicuous, graphical in the sense of 'well delineated'. As Howard Gest argues, the fact that seventeenth-century microscopists 'repeated their experiments several times, or that they re-read the results of others' experiments, is proof that they were already aware that the microscope was insufficiently equipped to label the acquired information as stable'.[33] Words,

---

31   Jordynn Jack, 'A Pedagogy of Sight: Microscopic Vision in Robert Hooke's *Micrographia*', *Quarterly Journal of Speech*, 95:2, 192–209 (p. 193).

32   Hooke, *Micrographia,* p. 175.

33   Howard Gest, 'The Remarkable Vision of Robert Hooke (1635–1703): First Observer of the Microbial World', *Perspectives in Biology and*

in this sense, are instruments that qualify and stabilise the raw information conveyed by the image.

At the same time, other adjectives are utilized in order to display and control the methodology of the microscopical observation — the *how* inherent in any observation. In the example of the fly, the specimen is examined 'in my usual manner' — that is, a number of times, under different perspectives and illuminations. As a result of this, a word-image 'representation' is obtained. At this point of the textual description, the object under observation has become 'plain' and 'evident', so that the reader's eye can move back to the picture (or to the microscope, if in possession of one) in search of the conspicuous features described by Hooke. Without these 'descriptive techniques', as Gest defines them, 'the images could remain beautiful and spectacular, but unrecognizable'.[34]

With the aid of the written glosses, instead, picture even acquired an aesthetical value. More precisely, Hooke's text follows the Horatian aesthetical value of being *utile* and *dulce*, 'notable' and 'pleasant'. The point was to be theorized upon in *A General Scheme, or Idea of the Present State of Natural Philosophy*, a posthumously published philosophical treatise. Oftentimes, we read in the long section titled 'Of the True Method of Building a Solid Philosophy, or of a Philosophical Algebra', 'much more may be expressed in a small Picture of the thing that can be done by a Description of the same thing in as many words as will fill a Sheet'. Therefore, Hooke explains, 'it will be often necessary to add the Pictures of those Observables that will not otherwise be so fully and sensibly exprest by Verbal Description', not in substitution of words but in conjunction with them. Pictures that only serve 'for Ornament or Pleasure' without providing instruction are instead to be excluded because of their being 'rather noxious than useful', *dulce* but not *utile*.[35]

Medicine, 48:2, 266–272 (p. 271).

34   Gest, 'Remarkable Vision', pp. 266–267.

35   Robert Hooke, *The Posthumous Works of Robert Hooke, M.D. S.R.S. containing his Cutlerian lectures, and other discourses.* ed. by Richard Waller (London: 1705), p. 64.

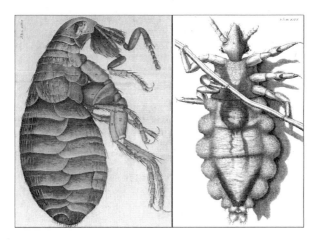

Figure 2. The flea and the louse. Copyright: Library of Congress.

The Imagistic Character of Hooke's Language

In what is probably the most quoted passage of the preface, Hooke claims that to achieve a reformation in our knowledge of nature and man, the only requirement on the part of the observer is 'a sincere Hand, and a faithful Eye', in order 'to examine, and to record, the things themselves as they appear'.[36] According to Alpers, 'Hooke's preface, from which this passage is taken, articulates the binding of the attentive or, as he calls it, faithful eye to the manual craft of the recording hand. He binds sight to crafted description'.[37] A sentence like this, however, when accurately analysed, discloses something different.

A feature that does not immediately stand out in the 'a sincere Hand, and a faithful Eye' formula is its metaphorical and metonymical nature. For all Hooke's claims of plainness in representation, a hand cannot literally be sincere, nor can an eye literally be faithful. Since the two adjectives rather refer to the moral stance of the observer-draughtsman, the hand and the eye are metonymical for the person who observes. The two organs are

---

36   Hooke, *Micrographia*, p. iv.
37   Alpers, *The Art of Describing*, p. 73.

mentioned as if detached, anatomized from the rest of the body
— much the same process that occurs when a natural body is
seen through the microscope, with instances provided in Schema
XXIII, the foot of the fly; and Schema XXIV, the eyes and head
of a fly; and Schema XXV, on the teeth of a snail). The hands
and eyes are isolated, given prominence and assigned moral
properties. These two organs are particularly important because
they are shared by two process that are different but that share a
similar order. Both the processes of reading-writing and seeing-
drawing move from sensory perception to representation.

Hooke's syntax, however, logically inverts the process of
perceiving and representing. Making use of the classical (and
sophisticated) rhetorical device called *hysteron proteron*, the hand
precedes the eye, and a prominence is thus attributed to the acts
of writing/drawing. The sincere hand and the faithful eye are
necessary, the passage goes on, in order 'to examine, and to record,
the things themselves as they appear'. By means of this *chiasmus*
(hand and eye/examine and record), the act of examining (with a
faithful eye) is incorporated within the wider enterprise of recording
(with a sincere hand) 'the things themselves as they appear'. In
this way, things are first seen in their raw, imagistic form ('as they
appear'); they are thus written about or drawn; and, finally, after
the conflation of word and image, they are to be observed again,
this time in order to be properly examined. This is not the only
possible interpretation of this ambiguous passage. If we admit no
chiasmus, the act of writing/drawing (with a sincere hand) becomes
associated with the examination of a natural phenomenon, whereas
the eye is in charge of recording. What remains valid, even in this
case, is that sensory perception is understood as an active process
that blends with the act of representing.

Passages like this, in their apparent simplicity, conceal a high
degree of conceptual indeterminacy. Alpers perceptively notes that
Hooke in a certain sense synthetizes the textual and visual mode
— he wants, Alpers writes, 'nature to be not only visible, but also
readable'.[38] It should be added that the readability of nature in
Hooke's sense implies the irreducible presence of ambiguity that

_____

38   Ibid., p. 93.

a description of nature that aims at being true cannot sacrifice. Therefore, figures of speech, rather than undermining, are employed in order to stimulate and harness the goal of describing what Hooke calls 'the new visible World'. Knellwolf argues that in *Micrographia* figures of speech, and metaphors particularly, have the specific function of expressing the 'blurred boundary between empirical observation and the projection of imaginary ideas'.[39] And indeed, as she underlines, of the two passages of the preface where a 'new World' is said to be visible only through the microscope, one passage 'talks about it as having been discovered and the other as having been produced'. As Knellwolf puts it,

> even while he calls for an unembellished mode of description, Hooke's language expresses ambivalence as to whether knowledge is like a real world that is being discovered or a fictional world that is being invented.[40]

A closer look at the preface might help us comprehend the rationale behind this use of language. The fallacies of the senses are to be compensated for by 'the real, the mechanical, the experimental philosophy', an approach that is apparently incompatible with the 'Philosophy of discourse and disputation'. In the continuation of this passage, however, Hooke specifies that the difference between the two lies in the latter dealing in the 'subtilty of [...] Deductions and Conclusions' not grounded by a correct sensory input. The usefulness of mechanical philosophy lies in its providing a reliable 'ground-work' for the senses, so that the successive elaborations through language, the 'deductions and conclusions', can rest upon reliable sensory input. The climax of this somewhat ambiguous conjoining of mechanical representation and linguistic elaboration is the conceptualization of God as a writer-engraver. The observation on the seeds of tyme (XXIX) is concluded by a statement on the features of natural bodies that (only seemingly) digresses over the fact that Adam, the first observer of nature, is the one who, prior to the original sin, could unambiguously interpret the characters written by 'the Creator'.

---

39   Knellwolf, 'Aesthetics of Empiricism', p. 177.
40   Ibid., p 185.

> Who knows but Adam might from some such contemplation, give
> names to all creatures? If at least his names had any significancy in
> them of the creatures nature on which he impos'd it; as many (upon
> what grounds I know not) have suppos'd: And who knows, but the
> Creator may, in those characters, have written and engraven many of
> his most mysterious designs and counsels, and given man a capacity,
> which, assisted with diligence and industry, may be able to read and
> understand them.[41]

The recovery of our senses through the microscope is thus a
restoration of our hermeneutic ability to interpret signs: when
sensory input is perfect, things and names, referent and signs, are
all perfectly matched. The postlapsarian condition has torn nature
and our systems of representation apart. These can be reunified only
through artistic efforts — the crafting of the microscopic lenses;
the elaboration of language and images — that are necessarily
hindered by the problems relative to our fallen condition. The
first observation in *Micrographia* is significantly devoted to this
problem of representation. What to the naked eye looks like a
small, black point of a printed Bible actually presents a number
of irregularities that appear only through the Microscope.[42] Art
strives to be identical to nature, but the recovery of the grace is a
long process that passes through technology advancement and an
improvement of all the five senses — a point upon which Hooke
speculates in the preface when he suggests further improvements
for the audition and olfaction.

The artistic-technological advancement, however, also passes
through the inclusion of words and images in a common articulated
semiotic system that can be employed to describe natural and
artificial artefacts. Differently from Henry Power's 1664 book
Experimental Philosophy — a series of verbal descriptions about
phenomena observed through the microscope containing only
three simplified images annexed — Hooke's *Micrographia* aims
at displaying an integral mixture of images and text. The very
title chosen by Hooke betrays this purpose. The Greek root of the

---

41   Hooke, *Micrographia*, p. 154.
42   Ibid., p. 1.

two words in *Micrographia* — μικρός meaning *small*, *minor* (but also *petty*, *lesser*) and γράφω meaning *to write* — has an active connection with the adjective *graphical*, about which Samuel Johnson, referring to Bacon's 1626 *Sylva Sylvarum*, would write in the 1755 *Dictionary* that it relates to something that is 'well delineated'. This meaning, as the *OED* confirms, by that time went hand-in-hand with 'skilled in drawing'.

As its subtitle reads, *Micrographia* is a book on 'some Physiological Descriptions of Minute Bodies Made by Magnifying Glasses with Observations and Inquiries thereupon', with a strong accent placed on the Horatian 'oculo' of the epigraph — what in the *Ars Poetica* would be otherwise phrased as the principle of *ut pictura poesis*. Hooke consciously uses the term description in the Latin sense of *descriptio*, meaning the drawing of a diagram or plan — a conjoining of word and image. Most importantly, *descriptio* was a classic rhetorical figure found in the *Rhetorica ad Herennium* (90 a.c. approximately), one of the most popular books on rhetoric during the Renaissance. *Descriptio* is somewhat synonymous with *enargia* — a term that, meaning 'vividness of presentation', was identified by Harwood as pivotal to *Micrographia*'s graphic rhetorics.[43] In the *Rhetorica ad Herennium, descriptio* is a specific figure that aims at 'a clear, lucid, and impressive exposition of the consequences of an act'. It is not simply about the act *per se*; it concerns the performative dimension of its interpretation as well.

Complementary to the *descriptio*, Hooke makes use of another rhetorical figure discussed in the *Rhetorica ad Herennium*. A *Demonstratio*, we read, occurs when an event is

> so described in words that the business seems to be enacted and the subject to pass vividly before our eyes. This we can effect by including what has preceded, followed, and accompanied the event itself, or by keeping steadily to its consequences or the attendant circumstances [...].[44]

---

43   Harwood, 'Graphic Rhetorics', p. 135.
44   Harry Caplan (ed. and trans. by), *Rhetorica ad Herennium* (Harvard: Harvard University Press, 1954), pp. 357, 405–407.

In Observation LVIII, titled 'Of a new Property in the Aire', Hooke discusses the phenomenon of the inflection of light. He reproduces richly detailed observations of the experiments he has just performed by specifying the conditions to replicate them. He then comments by asserting the validity of his hypothesis because of its having been demonstrated *ad oculum*:

> I could produce many more Examples and Experiments, to illustrate and prove this first Proposition, *viz.* that there is such a constitution of some bodies as will cause inflection. [...] But that, I presume, I have by this Example given proof sufficient (*viz. ocular demonstration*) to evince, that there is such a modulation, or bending of the rayes of light, as I have call'd *inflection*, differing both from *reflection*, and *refraction* (since they are both made in the superficies, this only in the middle); and likewise, that this is able or sufficient to produce the effects I have ascribed to it.[45]

By making use of these figures of thought, Hooke authenticates the images and findings of *Micrographia*, thus casting the book as an artificial replica of the microscopical world. *Micrographia* can thus be understood as an epistemological lens through which readers, invested with the active role of the experimenter, can observe nature in its microscopical appearance.

From this angle, *Micrographia* is less a text than a surrogate of the microscope. Hooke himself suggests this point by urging readers to employ it to question his own observations. In the preface, the reader who 'finds that I have ventur'd at any small Conjectures, at the causes of the things that I have observed', is invited not only 'to look, upon them only as doubtful Problems, and uncertain ghesses' but also to question them. If readers find Hooke's observation 'contradicted by the future Ocular Experiments of other and impartial Discoverers', they are to trust those other pairs of eyes and hands. In a final, seemingly paradoxical request, Hooke pleads his reader, once he has read *Micrographia*, 'not absolutely to rely upon these Observations of

---

45   Hooke, *Micrographia*, p. 221.

my eyes.'[46] This plead is essentially tantamount to asking readers to write their own personal micrographia in response to Hooke's text. Only by doing so will they have discovered the potentiality of Hooke's graphic-textual apparatus and, hence, assumed an active role as observers of nature.

---

46   Ibid., p. v.

Bibliography

Alpers, Svetlana, *The Art of Describing. Dutch Art in the Seventeenth Century* (Chicago: Chicago University Press, 1983).

Bacon, Sir Francis, *The Novum Organon, or a True Guide to the Interpretation of Nature*, trans. by G. W. Kitchin (Oxford: Oxford University Press, 1855).

Bennett, Jim, Michael Cooper, Michael Hunter and Lisa Jardine, *London's Leonardo – The Life and Work of Robert Hooke* (Oxford: Oxford University Press, 2003).

Cannon, John, *The Oxford Companion to British History* (Oxford: Oxford University Press, 2009).

Caplan, Harry (ed. and trans.), *Rhetorica ad Herennium* (Harvard: Harvard University Press, 1954).

Cavendish, Margaret, *Observations upon Experimental Philosophy to which is Added, The Description of a New Blazing World* (London: 1666).

Chapman, Allan, *England's Leonardo. Robert Hooke and the Seventeenth-Century Scientific Revolution* (Bristol and Philadelphia: Institute of Physics Publishing, 2005).

Chico, Tita, 'Minute Particulars: Microscopy and Eighteenth-Century Narrative', *Mosaic*, 39:2, 143–161.

Cooper, Michael and Michael Cyril William Hunter, *Robert Hooke: Tercentennial Studies* (Farnham: Ashgate, 2006).

Daston, Lorraine, 'Marvelous Facts and Miraculous Evidence in Early Modern Europe', *Critical Inquiry*, 18:1, 93–124.

Dennis, Michael Aaron, 'Graphic Understanding: Instruments and Interpretation in Robert Hooke's Micrographia', *Science in Context*, 3:2, 309–364.

Gest, Howard, 'The Remarkable Vision of Robert Hooke (1635–1703): First Observer of the Microbial World', *Perspectives in Biology and Medicine*, 48:2, 266–272.

Hooke, Robert, *Micrographia, or, Some physiological descriptions of minute bodies made by magnifying glasses Preface* (London: 1665).

_____, *Micrographia, or, Some physiological descriptions of minute bodies made by magnifying glasses Preface*, ed. by R. T. Gunther (Oxford: Oxford University Press, 1938).

_____, *The Posthumous Works of Robert Hooke, M.D. S.R.S. Containing his Cutlerian lectures, and Other Discourses*, ed. by Richard Waller (London: 1705).

Hunter, Michael and Simon Schaffer, *Robert Hooke. New Studies* (Woodbridge: The Boydell Press, 1989).

Inwood, Stephen, *The Man Who Knew Too Much: The Strange and Inventive Life of Robert Hooke, 1635–1703* (London: Macmillan, 2002).

Jack, Jordynn 'A Pedagogy of Sight: Microscopic Vision in Robert Hooke's Micrographia', *Quarterly Journal of Speech*, 95:2, 192–209.

Knellwolf, Christa, 'Robert Hooke's Micrographia and the Aesthetics of Empiricism', *Seventeenth Century*, 16:1, 177–200.

Latham, R. C. and W. Mathews (eds.), *The Diary of Samuel Pepys*, 9 vols. (London: G. Bell and Sons, 1970–1976).

Locke, John, *An Essay Concerning Human Understanding* (London: 1753).

Pope, Alexander, *An Essay on Man* (London: 1733).

Schaffer, Simon and Steven Shapin, *Leviathan and the Air-Pump: Hobbes, Boyle, and the Experimental Life* (Princeton: Princeton University Press, 1985).

Szekely, Francisc, 'Unreliable Observers, Flawed Instruments, "Disciplined Viewings": Handling Specimens in Early Microscopy', *Parergon*, 28:1, 155–76.

Wootton, David, *Bad Medicine: Doctors Doing Harm Since Hippocrates* (Oxford: Oxford University Press, 2006).

PORTRAYING MIGRATION IN CONTEMPORARY EUROPE: TWO COMPARATIVE APPROACHES

Part 1. Everywhere and Nowhere: Strategies of Refraction in Emmanuel Carrère's *Lettre à une calaisienne* and Gianfranco Rosi's *Fuocoammare*

Ilaria Oddenino
(University of Turin)

In his foundational volume of 1994, *The Location of Culture*, Homi Bhabha famously exposed the highly ambivalent nature of colonial discourse surrounding the colonised subject, one in which the tension between two coexisting, contradictory forces can never be fully resolved. If on the one hand the colonial subject is stigmatised as intrisically other and placed outside the borders of Western civilisation through the construction of stereotyping narratives of difference, on the other the same discourse inevitably encapsulates the colonised "other" within the borders of Western knowledge, where alterity is domesticated. To say it in Bhabha's words, 'colonial discourse produces the colonised as a social reality which is at once "other" and yet entirely knowable and visible' (H. Bhabha 1994, 70–71).

Replacing "colonised" with "migrant" offers an equally fitting account of public discourse around migration in contemporary Europe, an infinitely complex phenomenon too often reduced by (mass) media and political communication to simplistic, monolithic narratives in which the migrant "other" becomes a token, a repository for our fears, an instrument for propaganda. We know him and yet we do not, he is everywhere and yet he is nowhere, as Hanif Kureishi writes in his article:

The immigrant has become a contemporary passion in Europe, the vacant point around which ideals clash. Easily available as a token, existing everywhere and nowhere, he is talked about constantly. But in the current public conversation, this figure has not only migrated from one country to another, he has migrated from reality to the collective imagination where he has been transformed into a terrible fiction.[1]

No longer an individual, no longer part of reality, the migrant's existence is re-shaped in the collective imagination by the words and images through which his (fictional) existence is narrated. Following Kureishi, I have been using the personal pronoun "he", but the plural "they" would perhaps be more appropriate if we consider that most of the images crystallised in our imagination are of boats crammed with indistinct masses of people, and words like "hordes" or "floods" are now perceived as customary collocations accompanying, and defining, the noun "migrant". Images and words we are growing increasingly numb to, our eyes saturated to the point of blindness, or simply choosing to look elsewhere. However, or perhaps precisely because of this overexposure to narratives of out-of-focus collectivity, the picture that has become the symbol for the horrors of this new Middle Passage is that of one little Syrian boy, taken by Turkish press photographer Nilüfer Demir on 2 September 2015 on the Turkish shore near Bodrum.[2] It is true that, once seen, the still-frame of three-year-old Alan Kurdi, lying face down on the beach in his blue shorts, his palms turned upwards, can no longer be forgotten, and turning a blind eye becomes impossible. But the decision of many news organisations to show this image in mainstream media

---

1   Hanif Kureishi, 'The Migrant Has No Face, Status or Story', *The Guardian,* 30 May 2014. See https://www.theguardian.com/books/2014/may/30/ hanif-kureishi-migrant-immigration-1, accessed December 6, 2016.
2   'Nonstop imagery (television, streaming videos, movies) is our surround', writes Susan Sontag in her 2003 book on photography and warfare, 'but when it comes to remembering, the photograph has the deeper bite. Memory freeze-frames; its basic unit is the single image. In an era of information overload, the photograph provides a quick way of apprehending something and a compact way for memorizing it. The photograph is like a quotation, or a maxim, or a proverb'. Susan Sontag, *Regarding the Pain of Others* (New York: Farrar, Straus and Giroux, 2003), p. 22.

(with some notable exceptions, the BBC for example) inevitably poses a number of questions: what is legitimate to show? Where do we draw the line between testimony and spectacularisation? And when graphic, ob-scene pictures are not kept off scene, what do they make of us, the spectators? Are we witnesses, accomplices, or mere voyeurs?

In more general terms, the question of how to talk about migration has invested not only the media, but literature and the visual arts too. Again, it inevitably involves making conscious decisions as to what to represent and what to leave off scene, while at the same time offering exciting opportunities to challenge stereotypical perspectives and open alternative gateways into the kaleidoscope of the migratory experience. 'If the limits of the world are made by language' Kureishi writes paraphrasing Wittgenstein's famous quote, 'we need better words for all this'. We need a plurality of voices, we need languages that allow the complexity this delicate topic yearns for. My short essays, as well as Luisa Pellegrino's, offers a glimpse into some of the manifold ways in which literature, cinema, photography and the arts at large have engaged in an attempt to mould the limits of their individual languages to address the question of contemporary migration from Africa, through the Mediterranean, to Europe.

If for most of us this humanitarian emergency is always happening "elsewhere", the examples I am going to briefly explore concentrate on two places in which the encounter between the European "self" and the migrant "other" — an encounter between peripheral, marginal existences in both cases — is real, physical, it is "here". The first is Emmanuel Carrère's reportage on the French city of Calais, the second Gianfranco Rosi's 2016 documentary on the island of Lampedusa, *Fuocoammare*. Different in their intentions and tones, the two resort to a similar narrative strategy: they choose to focus on the everyday lives of the residents and let the experience of migration come alive by way of refraction. What emerges in the case of Carrère's piece is a powerful, thought-provoking account of the difficult relationship between the people of Calais and the inhabitants of the "Jungle", which soon proves to have little to do with the migrants themselves as it reflects an even more complicated relationship between the forlorn French periphery and the political centre. In the case of *Fuocoammare*, it begins with a beautiful, delicate observation of the life of a 12-year-old boy and a subtle reflection on the repressed unconscious invading our everyday life, and then shifts its focus to the daily work of the island's doctor, Pietro Bartolo, the film's moral centre, where the migrant, no longer a token, is given back his dignity as a person.

Emmanuel Carrère's reportage, originally commissioned by the French journal *Revue XXI*,[3] is a compelling piece of narrative nonfiction built around the traditional narrative framework of a mysterious letter sent to the author, in this case by a certain Marguerite Bonnefille. Disillusioned and defiant, she critiques the journalist's enterprise in a merciless condemn of the mediatic circus feeding off the city's misfortunes[4] and its constant failure to do any justice to the intricate reality of things. Throughout the reportage, Carrère establishes a dialogue with this (fictional) interlocutor, often candidly acknowledging his own limits and partiality of vision. The intention behind his piece is made clear from the very beginning: in a town so heavily connoted by the presence of the Jungle — the infamous migrant/refugee

---

3   *Revue XXI*, issue 34 (13 April 2016): 'Lettre à une Calaisienne'. The reportage was then published as *The Guardian*'s "long read" on 20 April 2016 with the title: 'That thing gnawing away at all of us: Calais and the shantytown on its doorsteps', trans. by Edward Gauvin. All quotations from the text are from *The Guardian*'s English translation. In Italy, the reportage was first published by 'la Lettura', *Corriere della Sera*, 17 April 2016, and then made into a book by Adelphi.

4   'No, not you, too! [...] We're fed up with the glitterati — pardon the term — coming to feed off Calais' misfortunes and treating the people stuck within its walls like lab rats. Mr Carrère, did you know that in the three years I've spent in this hole I've had at least one inquiry a week from people like you, people from outside who want to come and write, film, blab into a microphone about what they've seen, maybe thinking they can describe it better than everyone else, satisfying the need to add their personal commentary? I wonder: which traps will you fall into? What story are you looking for? One thing I know for sure: your venture will be a failure.' See http://www.revue21.fr/tous_les_numeros#n-34_lettre-a-une-calaisienne, accessed December 6, 2016.

encampment — Carrère chooses to turn his gaze to its resident, an approach received enthusiastically by the people in question: 'We can't stand the way whenever anyone talks about us, it's all they talk about. And we can't stand that whenever we talk, it's all we talk about too.' However, as the author himself concedes, not only is it impossible to talk about Calais without the Jungle ('How could you talk about 1942 Warsaw without its ghetto?' (Ibid.)), but it has become virtually impossible for the people of Calais not to (re)draw the contours of their identities in relation to 'that thing constantly gnawing away' at all of them,[5] that is to say not to position themselves on the "pro / anti" migrant spectrum.[6]

Set in a city so desperately involved, Carrère's reportage works as a mirror on different levels: on the one hand, it reflects and magnifies common reactions to migrants and migration flows everywhere, from the obstinate rationalisations of the "pro" migrant front, often downplaying the dangers for ideological reasons — an intellectual luxury that in Calais, however, not even they can afford[7] — to the simplifications and dreadful stereotypes of people like the "Angry Calaisians", so often exploited by certain media and political discourse. Emblematic in this sense is the widespread use of the word "Siberians", with which locals

---

5   'For some the issue is clear-cut, but for others, the worst part is not being able to get away from it, being forced at every turn to define themselves as "pro" or "anti-migrant". It's the Dreyfus affair all over again.' (Ibid.)

6   Carrère, however, warns his readers of how slippery these two concepts can be: 'Pro and anti-migrant are peculiar expressions. Pro-migrant doesn't really exist, in the sense that no one is in favour of having 7,000 wretched homeless people huddling in tents in the mud and cold at the gates of a city of 70,000. As for anti-migrant, in the extreme sense of people who scream, "Drown them!" or "Send them back!" — which often amounts to the same thing — well, they do exist. I've come across a few, but not that often.' (Ibid.)

7   'It's hard to tell how unsafe Calais really is. It depends on who you ask, but even people like my friends who are, for ideological reasons, apt to downplay the dangers, acknowledge that a climate of menace hangs over the town. The pro-migrants fear it, the anti-migrants hope for it, but everyone awaits the catastrophe that will become the tipping point: a Calaisian murders a migrant (that must have happened already, someone points out), or a migrant kills a Calaisian (that hasn't, not yet: we would know)'. (Ibid.)

refer to 'Syrians, along with the Kurds, Afghans, Eritreans, Sudanese, and everyone else now showing up by the thousands from the Middle East or East Africa, places shown daily on TV ripped apart by war'. The migrant has no face, status, or story, as Kureishi would say.

On the other, the simultaneously omnipresent and invisible migrant exposes the problems and contradictions lying at the very heart of contemporary Europe, in this case the French northernmost periphery: scarred by unemployment and social stagnation, symbol of a system's failure to manage migration, Calais becomes the ideal humus where despair and lack of perspectives can turn into hatred, where the marginalised of French society can direct their frustration towards this new perceived threat on their doorstep, people living on the edges of law and civilization potentially destabilising an already precarious order. The collision, here, is between margins, peripheric dwellers.[8]

As for the Jungle itself, Carrère honours his promise not to talk about it directly: even when he eventually does go into the camp, he emerges too overwhelmed to try and condense what he saw into a handful of paragraphs. All he tells us is that the Jungle 'is a nightmare of poverty and disease, terrible things happen there, like rape and revenge, its inhabitants aren't all peace-loving professionals, diligent students, and virtuous victims of political persecution — far from it.' However, he continues, 'something extraordinarily inspiring can also be witnessed there: the energy,

---

8   'The notion of marginality occupies a central premise in the discourse of
     the jungle: the migrants who congregate in these camps (while waiting to
     cross to the UK) are illegal bodies and hence marginal entities, the spaces
     they occupy are marginal lands within the town, and Calais itself is in a
     marginal zone on the edge of the Shengen area of free movement and on
     the sea border between continental Europe and the UK. [...] The proximity-
     distance framing provides a duality of subduing the suffering of the
     'other' while heightening the fear about the dissipation of order by casting
     the threat of physical violation as imminent in your backyard'. Anita
     Howarth and Yasmin Ibrahim, *Space and the Migrant Camps of Calais:
     Space-Making at the Margin*, in *Media, Margins and Civic Agency*, ed. by
     Thorsen Einar, Jackson Daniel, Savigny Heather and Alexander Jenny
     (New York: Palgrave MacMillan, 2015), p. 131.

the appetite for life that has driven these men and women on a long, perilous and heroic journey, on which Calais, despite its appearance as a dead end, is only a staging post.'

This is where the author finds his angle, in the stark contrast between the inertia afflicting the city[9] and the hunger for life that, in spite of everything, motivates these people to continue their journey. And this is what Banksy's mural on a concrete wall outside the camp — reminding us that Steve Jobs was the son of a Syrian refugee in America — stands for: 'Some migrants will die trying to get to Britain, and others will linger on the margins of Europe, enduring humiliation and poverty. But perhaps one Syrian or Afghan who braves a thousand dangers, makes it to Calais, and goes through hell in the Jungle, will eventually think of this as part of his life, a brief period of hardship in the journey towards fulfilling his dreams'.

Graffito di Bansky: Steve Jobs nel campo profughi di Calais.[10]

---

9   Marie Bonnefille writes: 'You come crashing to the ground when you realise this city just isn't working. That everyone's stuck: the bourgeois in their bubble, the morons in their towers, the politicians striking their poses, the razorwire professionals along the port road and the Channel tunnel.' Carrère, Ibid.

10   See http://www.repubblica.it/esteri/2015/12/11/foto/nuovo_graffito_di_banksy_steve_jobs_nel_campo_profughi_di_calais-129260745/1/#1, accessed December 6, 2016.

On the other hand, 'a white boy who has always lived off welfare in Beau Marais — his situation is less precarious but, in a way, more deeply mired, more irredeemable'. The author wonders if this contrast might be, at least partially, at least on an unconscious level, where much of the resentment originates. Gianfranco Rosi's *Fuocoammare*, winner of the Golden Bear at the 66th Berlin film festival and now nominated for the 2017 Academy Awards for best documentary, is an impressionistic, highly symbolic film shot over a period of 12 months in Lampedusa. In the past 20 years, the Sicilian island — Italy's southernmost outpost — has offered its shores to more than 400,000 people in this modern-day Middle Passage from Africa through the Mediterranean,[11] and has too often seen its waters turn into a liquid cemetery of migrants whose journey had come to a tragic end. Rosi's original choice of perspective is not too dissimilar from Carrère's: he wanted to concentrate on the people of Lampedusa and let their eyes bring all other stories to the scene. 'Lampedusa was always told by the media [...] through the lens of the migrant crisis', the director explains. 'And Lampedusa, the people living there, were somehow dismissed by this. So there was always a link with tragedy, with dead people. I wanted to switch the point of view and tell the story of the migrants through the eyes of the people of Lampedusa, and especially the eyes of Samuele.'[12]

The film's near-oxymoronic title, translated into English as *Fire at Sea*, refers to a traditional Sicilian wartime song about the

---

11   In the words of Cristina Lombardi-Diop: 'The circulation across the Mediterranean of African migrants, as well as their enslavement and trafficking, activates a parallel circulation of images and memories of the Atlantic Middle Passage. These spectral presences stand for a warning about contemporary forms of slavery and dehumanization, and constitute a trace of the cultural memory of the oceanic crossing.' Cristina Lombardi-Diop, *Ghosts of Memories, Spirits of Ancestors: Slavery, the Mediterranean and the Atlantic*, in *Recharting the Black Atlantic: Modern Cultures, Local Communities, Global Connections*, ed. by Annalisa Oboe and Anna Scacchi (New York: Routledge 2008), p. 163.

12   See interview http://www.theverge.com/2017/1/24/14371650/fire-at-sea-gianfranco-rosi-interview-academy-awards-documentary, accessed December 6, 2016.

bombing of an Italian ship near the island's coasts in 1943. The lyrics 'Chi focu a mmari ca c'è stasira' run 'What fire at sea there is tonight'. But in Italian the word "fuoco" also means "focus", and this is where the film's powerful symbolism unravels: it is about our struggle to adjust our lens and see things clearly, about how we push them to the margins of our conscience even when they are so near we could almost touch them; be it a defect in our empathy or a strategy for survival, even for the people of Lampedusa the migrant crisis can take the form of mirage in the background, a piece of news one absent-mindedly hears on the radio while going about the routine of their everyday life.[13]

A considerable portion of the documentary revolves around 12-year-old Samuele, born and raised on the island — Italy's most extreme border — and himself inhabiting the liminal space between childhood and adolescence. His life, which evokes a world of timeless traditions apparently detached from the contemporary humanitarian crisis, is at one point captured in the midst of a little personal crisis: Samuele suffers from shortness of breath and has a lazy eye compromising his vision. After a visit to the doctor and with a patch on his good eye, he has to slowly, patiently re-educate the other, in a strain towards a clarity of vision that we cannot help but associate to our very own lazy eyes and to what is happening around him — around all of us — only apparently off scene. And our breath, just like Samuele's, is too short to extinguish the fire that in the meantime has once again broken out in the middle of the sea, enflamed by yet another catastrophe that will, at best, occupy our consciousness like a

---

13 'Perché, in un certo senso, questo viaggio cinematografico bello e straziante è anche un film su una rimozione. Chiamiamolo anche un difetto di empatia della mente umana, che ci porta a non mettere a fuoco certe cose, certi naufragi, certi morti, se non come un miraggio, come il fuoco di Sant'Elmo dei marinai. Il titolo del film, *Fuocoammare*, racchiude tutte e due questi significati — miraggio e messa a fuoco — in un documentario che schiera più simboli, e crea più risonanze tematiche, di molti film di fiction.' Marshall, Lee, '*Fuocoammare* di Gianfranco Rosi è il più bel film visto alla Berlinale', *Internazionale*, 16 February 2016. See http://www.internazionale.it/opinione/lee-marshall/2016/02/21/fuocoammare-rosi-berlino, accessed December 6, 2016.

mere mirage. The character of Samuele, who never talks about the migrants, is where Rosi finds his voice: 'The most beautiful thing', he said, 'is that he has this incredible interior world that somehow was reflecting what I was looking for — my incapacity of telling the story of the migrants. Because also for me, it was very difficult to create a connection with that world'.

The character of Samuele in the film: *Fuocoammare.*

In a documentary portraying the juxtaposition of lives that never really touch, doctor Pietro Bartolo represents the only real, physical connection between the island's two worlds. With the same patience and empathy, he visits Samuele (symbol of the life the migrants are risking everything for) or a pregnant African woman just escaped from the sea and its flames. In these encounters, the migrant is nothing but a person, a patient, and Bartolo is nothing but a doctor. As A. O. Scott writes on the pages of the *New York Times*, 'he is the film's moral center of gravity, not a hero but heroically decent, someone for whom kindness is a habit and an instinct. This doctor can treat only one person at a time, and he tries to give each one — whether it's a well-fed schoolboy or a hungry, delirious refugee — the full benefit of his calm, good-humored attention'.

The men and women who have survived their journey are not only shown in their interaction with the doctor, but also in the delicate moments immediately following their arrival, while being assisted and identified, or playing a football match in near darkness or — in one of the film's most poignant scenes — trying to give voice to their story through a dense, desperate chant. However, Rosi also does 'take us through the gate of hell at one point, into a ship where dozens have died' That thirty-second sequence marks the end of his year-long filming: there was nothing left to add, his testimony had to be edited and leave the island.[14]

Bibliography

Bhabha, Homi, *The Location of Culture* (New York: Routledge, 1994).

Boille, Francesco, 'Fuocoammare raccontato da Gianfranco Rosi', *Internazionale*, 23 February 2016.

Carrère, Emmanuel, 'That Thing Gnawing Away at all of us: Calais and the Shantytown on its Doorsteps', *The Guardian*, 20 April 2016.

Howarth, Anita and Ibrahim, Yasmin, *Space and the Migrant Camps of Calais: Space-Making at the Margin*, in *Media, Margins and Civic Agency*, ed. by Thorsen Einar, Jackson Daniel, Savigny Heather and Alexander Jenny (New York: Palgrave MacMillan, 2015).

Kureishi, Hanif, 'The Migrant Has no Face, Status or Story', *The Guardian*, 30 May 2014.

Lombardi-Diop, Cristina, *Ghosts of Memories, Spirits of Ancestors: Slavery, the Mediterranean and the Atlantic*, in *Recharting the Black Atlantic: Modern Cultures, Local Communities, Global Connections*, ed. by Annalisa Oboe and Anna Scacchi (New York: Routledge, 2008).

Marshall, Lee, 'Fuocoammare di Gianfranco Rosi è il più bel film visto alla

---

14 'Chi fa un'inchiesta o un documentario va sempre a occuparsi del disastro, della catastrofe, il momento in cui accade. Io sono arrivato sull'isola con l'eco di un disastro, poi pian piano nel corso del tempo ho fatto il mio incontro con il disastro. E quando l'ho incontrato per me si è come chiuso il film. Ho detto: non posso più aggiungere nulla, adesso devo montarlo, devo consegnare questo materiale ad altri. Il film è una testimonianza'. Francesco Boille, '*Fuocoammare* raccontato da Gianfranco Rosi', *Internazionale,* 23 February 2016. See http://www.internazionale.it/opinione/francesco-boille/2016/02/23/fuocoammare-gianfranco-rosi-intervista, accessed December 6, 2016.

Berlinale', *Internazionale*, 16 February 2016.

Scott, Antony Oliver, *'Fire at Sea* Is Not the Documentary You'd Expect About the Migrant Crisis. It's Better', *The New York Times*, 20 Oct 2016.

Sontag, Susan, *Regarding the Pain of Others* (New York: Picador, 2003).

Turan, Kenneth, *'Fire at Sea* Is a Harrowing Look at the Everyday Horrors of the International Refugee Crisis', *Los Angeles Times*, 27 October 2016.

PORTRAYING MIGRATION IN CONTEMPORARY EUROPE: TWO COMPARATIVE APPROACHES

Part 2. No Country for Black Men

Luisa Pellegrino
(University of Turin)

> Wade in the water
> Wade in the water
> Children wade, in the water
> God's gonna trouble the water.
> Eva Cassidy

Images have always played a pivotal role in communication. In the last few years we have been literally assailed by pictures as far as media are concerned. Words have become less and less important, while images are increasingly used to tell stories. Moreover, the spread of social media and digital channels of information provide the opportunity to participate in the telling of stories.

We are hit more and more frequently — and even shockingly — by news on tragedies, happening all around the world and we are growing more and more accustomed to them. We focus our attention on an individual tragedy for a very short span of time. As we see a photograph, even one that might have been taken by a professional photographer, we only stop for a while on that image and on its content. We rarely spend time to analyse it, to dig into its meanings, trying to understand what happened before that picture was taken, or what will happen next. As Nathalie Applewhite, managing director of the Pulitzer Center, points out: 'New media is very significant in immediacy, but not totally in long term. It doesn't matter if there are a thousand cameras, it's the storytelling that's important. A photojournalist has to have an artistic vision that transcends superficial coverage. It's a different media space.'[1]

A common saying runs: "a picture can say a thousand words". Consequently, a photographer needs to find the right word / image. Barthes claims that a photographer — as well as a writer — needs to find a "*punctum*": 'In this habitually unary space, occasionally (but alas all too rarely) a "detail" attracts me. I feel that its mere presence changes my reading, that I am looking at a new photograph, marked in my eyes with a higher value. This "detail" is the *punctum*.' (Barthes, 1982: 43, *author's emphasis*)

We are witnessing a crisis that has lasted for over ten years in the Mediterranean and it has not yet found a solution. It still follows the same, tragic patterns. The Mediterranean is the world's deadliest migration route. According to Human Rights Watch:

> in 2014, at least 219,000 people made the crossing, up from 60,000 the previous year. According to the UN refugee agency United Nations High Commissioner for Refugees (UNHCR), 89,500 crossed in the first five months of 2015. The principal route has long been from North Africa across the central Mediterranean, but increasing numbers are now crossing the Aegean Sea (eastern Mediterranean) from Turkey to the Greek islands. The International Organization for Migration estimates that 22,400 migrants and asylum seekers have died since 2000 in attempts to reach the European Union, many of them at sea. Over 3,500 died at sea in 2014, making it the deadliest year on record. With at least 1,850 estimated deaths in the Mediterranean in the first five months of 2015.[2]

As unprecedented numbers of migrants are crossing the Mediterranean, their representation has also seen unprecedented coverage. Boats crowded with people and dead bodies fill up the pages of our newspapers and newscasts, as well as images

---

1   James Keller, 'Photojournalism in the Age of New Media', *The Atlantic,* April 4, 2014.
2   *The Mediterranean Migration Crisis*, www.hrw.org, accessed December 6, 2016.

of similarly crowded Italian CIE (centres for immigrations and expulsion) in desperate conditions. As said before, it is difficult to find a deep and complete report of what is happening. Trying to avoid the mainstream type of discourse on the Mediterranean, in this paper — as a follow up of Ilaria Oddenino's article — I will focus on two different uses of images and pictures, and on two different methodological approaches: an ethnographic and sociologic one, by taking into account the work *Asylum Seekers* by the collective Cesuralab, and a more poetic and surrealistic one, by analysing the short graphic novel *Mare Nostrum* by Fabio Visintin.

Asylum Seeker is a photo book on refugees and asylum seekers in Italy[3]. It is the result of a long photo-ethnographic research on asylum seekers who have reached Italy through the Mediterranean Sea. The work has been carried out by three professional photographers, Giovanni Diffidenti, Alessio Genovese, Alessandro Sala and two anthropologists, expert in forced migration, Barbara Pinelli and Luca Ciabarri. As the group points out:

An ethnographic approach has represented a distinctive element of this research project. Throughout the project, the concern for refugees and asylum seekers voices, what [sic] has inspired our work, have been [sic] at the core of our research and photographic activities. Narrative and visual data collection have been carried out in places attended by asylum seekers: places of arrivals and transit, refugee camps or provisional homes, regular and irregular workplaces, informal meeting places, public squares, train and bus stations located prevalently in Lombardia, Lazio and Sicilia.[4]

The book starts with a picture showing the arrival of a group of migrants in Augusta, Sicily. They are orderly arranged in rows. It is a sunny day, there is a boat in the background, probably belonging to the Coast Guard, and a white landscape surrounding them. The landscape is strikingly in contrast with the actual

3   It is possible to see it entirely online, on Cesuralab website http://www. cesura.it/ or within the project 'Dopo l'approdo' http://www.dopolapprodo. com/, accessed December 6, 2016.
4   See http://www.cesura.it/progettoDettaglio.php?pagineCod=2214810, accessed December 6, 2016.

situation. In the following picture we see seven black men in a row, getting off a boat. The first in the row is looking beyond us. He looks tired as shown by his eyes. In front of them there is a rescuer, dressed in white, with safety gloves and mask, as if he was in a surgery room. The guard looks quite science fictional, as if coming from outer space.

Migrants' arrival, Augusta, Sicily, Italy.

This picture tells us gently of something that will come later, that is to say, it tells us about the camp, the CIE, the provisional accommodation, and opens up to a biopolitical reading of the image of migrants, as pointed out also by Marta Cariello in her essay 'Il corpo critico: pensare ai limiti dell'Europa'.[5]

The rescuer's uniform tells us about distance, dehumanization and control on bodies. The next images on that same website tell of the migrants' everyday life. The migrants are portrayed while playing basket in a camp, crossing a wired border, living in provisional tents, attending a lesson in an open air school. It is interesting to see how in this work migrants are often represented in active moments: walking, moving, playing, avoiding their classic representation as victims, which can be realistic on the

---

5   Marta Cariello, 'Il corpo critico: pensare ai limiti dell'Europa', *From the European South*, 1 (2016), 35–41. See http://europeansouth. postcolonialitalia.it, accessed December 6, 2016.

one hand, while stereotypically representing migrants as passive bodies. The psychologist Cristiana Giordano, referring to the work of the psychoanalyst Fethi Benslama, points out that:

> in the sociology of migration, migrants are often portrayed as victims rather than agents. They are passively moved by the need to leave, attracted by the illusion of a wealthy north that alienates them from their cultures. This argument classifies all kinds of migration as banishment [...] and it completely effaces the question of desire: the desire to exit, to exile one's self from a context that may have become unbearable.[6]

The images of *Asylum Seekers*, even when representing human beings in their often difficult situations — living in tents, sleeping in schools — always provide an idea of them as agents.

Nevertheless, one of the most powerful images of the series is that of a cemetery in Pozzallo, in Sicily.

Pozzallo cemetery, Sicily, Italy.

Among the traditional graves of the columbarium there are those of migrants. Their names are written with spray, and they are identified only by numbers. They have no face, no flowers, no

6   Cristina Giordano, *Migrants in Translation: Caring and the Logics of Difference in Contemporary Italy* (Oakland: University of California Press, 2014), p. 65.

recognizable signs. Yet, it is sheer luck the fact that they might have found a burial ground. An interesting debate promoted by Radio3RAI, [7] one of the Italian public radio stations, demonstrated that a great part of the Italian population was against the recovery of migrants' bodies from the Mediterranean, because of the high cost of this operation. This can be a good example of people's reaction to the arrival of migrants: dehumanization and disregard of the "Others" just outside one's door. Here we witness the classical colonial discourse on subalternity that seems to survive through time and space.

Fabio Visintin's work *Mare Nostrum* starts with a completely different perspective: it avoids explanations and documentary narrations. We find ourselves in the middle of the Mediterranean Sea, while crows are "chatting" and looking at the floating bodies on the water surface. There is a man whose face is looking up at the sky: his gaze is void. 'Is this being dead?' he asks himself.

Fabio Visintin's *Mare Nostrum*

---

7   See http://lacittadiradio3.blog.rai.it/page/6/?s=migranti, accessed December 6, 2016.

The same question is tormenting a woman who is looking for her little daughter. She is asking for help to those who are safe somewhere along the coast. The woman needs to find her lost daughter, in the hope that death has not parted them for ever. These characters are all portrayed as half-sinking and in shades of light green. Their outlines are just sketched, they are airy figures in a dark sea which is soon going to swallow them up. Their words are solemn. They are on the lookout for other places, other gods, Olokun, the crocodile god of the sea and the river, Orun, the god of the sun and Osu the god of the moon.

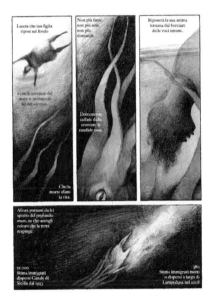

Fabio Visintin's *Mare Nostrum*

Their voices are in contrast with the almost grotesque and aggressive one of the boat pilot, who cannot do anything else but curse the migrants, as we can infer from the text. In the background nature seems to keep its own rhythm. Animals seem wiser than humans. Actually, all the human beings in the story are dead, their voices come as if from outer space, they can only be heard by the animals that are shocked by what they are witnessing. The crows which from time to time talk with the pilot, eventually fly away, disgusted by his story. Eventually, they will be killed by two hunters on the coast in the final scene of the novel. They will be killed just for fun, and the reader is left with a sense of hopelessness and despair.

The metaphor of animals, as in most classical fairy tales, helps give more strength and power to the message that the author wants to convey. That is, this is no country for migrants.

It is necessary to make one final consideration before concluding: the literary and artistic qualities that we have taken into consideration in relation to these works are indeed very much telling about human nature. Even if they imply anthropological, literary, metaphoric perspectives, text and image converge towards an iconic sameness. The reader is most probably caught by a sense of anger, helplessness and isolation. The two works — independent of their media — provide a powerful idea of what the journey across the Mediterranean — this contemporary epic — is like. However, there is silence all through the migrants' voices. The Italian weekly *Internazionale* tried to give voice to this silence, imitating what these two works have attempted, that is, giving voice to the migrants' points of view. More specifically the *Internazionale* website hosted a series of five short documentaries, now available online, called *Welcome to Italy,* where migrants talk about their experience of migration in their own language, and their voices are accompanied by drawings and documentary images. The authors' attempt at giving them the possibility to tell their own stories is clear, eventually they are staged by Italian "directors". Migrants, who are often faceless, who are even more often voiceless, cannot stand up, tell their stories without mediators. They cannot answer back. This is exactly where we, the mediators, fail.

However, something has started changing in the last few years: if on the one hand resentment and fear of the 'Other' affect large sectors of the Italian society, on the other hand, there is a stronger cultural exchange between the coasts of Africa and Italy, so much so, that Alessandra di Maio, drawing inspiration from Paul

Gilroy's *The Black Atlantic*, defined the Mediterranean area as 'Black Mediterranean': 'The term focuses on the proximity that exists, and has always existed, between Italy and Africa, separated [...] but also united by the Mediterranean [...] and documented in legends, myths, histories, even in culinary traditions, in visual arts, and religion.'[8] Artists, scholars, historians, novelists, filmmakers are rethinking Italy's relationship with Africa, 'linking the racialized economic and political subjugation of Southern Italy, Italy's own colonial entanglements in Africa, and forms of exclusion, racism, and violence waged against immigrants in Italy since the 1970s'.[9] This is just the beginning.

Bibliography

Barthes, Roland, *Camera Lucida* (London: Hill&Wang, 1982).

Cariello, Marta, 'Il corpo critico: pensare ai limiti dell'Europa', *From the European South*, 1 (2016), 35–41.

Ciabarri, Luca, and Pinelli, Barbara, *Dopo l'approdo* (Florence: Editpress, 2016).

Foucault, Michel, *Discipline & Punish: The Birth of the Prison* (New York: Vintage, Vintage; REP edition, 1995).

Giordano, Cristiana, *Migrants in Translation: Caring and the Logics of Difference in Contemporary Italy* (Oakland: University of California Press, 2014).

Visintin, Fabio, *Natali Neri e altre storie di guerra* (Rome: Comicout, 2014).

Articles

Amilla Hawthorne, 'Italian writer Igiaba Scego rewrites the Black Mediterranean', *Africa Is a Country*, October 14, 2015.

James Keller, 'Photojournalism in the Age of New Media', *The Atlantic,* April 4, 2014.

Web Sites

http://africasacountry.com/, accessed December 6, 2016.

---

8   Liminal Geographies, http://www.timothyraeymaekers.net/, accessed December 6, 2016.

9   Amilla Hawthorne, 'Italian writer Igiaba Scego rewrites the Black Mediterranean', in *Africa is a Country*, October 14, 2015. See http://africasacountry.com/, accessed December 6, 2016.

Liminal   Geographies,   http://www.timothyraeymaekers.net/,   accessed
    December 6, 2016.
Human Rights Watch, 'The Mediterranean Migration Crisis' www.hrw.org;
    www.cesura.it, accessed December 6, 2016.
http://www.internazionale.it/video/2016/05/12/hotspot-le-impronte-dei-
    migranti, accessed December 6, 2016.
http://lacittadiradio3.blog.rai.it/page/6/?s=migranti,   accessed   December   6,
    2016.
http://www.dopolapprodo.com/, accessed December 6, 2016.
http://www.theatlantic.com/technology/archive/2011/04/photojournalism-in-
    the-age-of-new-media/73083/, accessed December 6, 2016.
http://europeansouth.postcolonialitalia.it, accessed December 7, 2016.

Photo and Picture Credits

REPETITION AND VARIATION IN HITCHCOCK'S *THE 39 STEPS*

Nadia Priotti
(University of Turin)

If compared to the original, an adaptation is normally perceived as an inferior work, while 'the habitual reaction of conventional criticism to a literary adaptation [is reduced to] a judgement as to whether the adaptation has kept faith with the novel'.[1] Why is it so? Is 'coming first' to be considered a discriminating criterion to judge the value of a work and, as a consequence, fidelity to the original the fundamental element of evaluation for an adaptation?

Luckily, more recent approaches to adaptations have pointed out other relevant aspects that need to be taken into account, which are worth reporting as they have represented useful guidelines for this analysis. In particular, we want to refer to Linda Hutcheon's *A Theory of Adaptation*, a major work where the concept of adaptation is meant in a broad sense to include any production that derives from another work, be it a film or a videogame. Shifting the focus from the specificity of media to the different ways the public engages with stories — namely through the modes of telling, showing or interacting —, the writer advocates a different approach which privileges description rather than evaluation.

If the story itself becomes the core of the analysis, then an adaptation is perceived as an attempt to repeat stories that are considered relevant, with the introduction of variations due to a number of factors, from the changes in the context to the individual choices of the author. In this perspective, the adapter is seen in his double role of interpreter and creator, since 'what is involved in adapting can be a process of appropriation, of taking possession of another's story, and filtering it, in a sense,

---

1   John Ellis, 'The Literary Adaptation: an Introduction', *Screen*, 23.1 (1982), pp. 3–5, < doi: 10.1093/screen/23.1.3>, p. 3.

through one's own sensibility, interests, and talents'.[2] Therefore, it can be argued that the adapter's interpretation can shed light on the adapted work, as it helps us focus on the elements that are perceived as the kernel of the story or, in other words, on what makes the story worth retelling.

In the same way, the success of an adaptation is no longer evaluated in terms of fidelity to the original; an adaptation becomes effective if it manages to 'propagate the narrative for which it is a vehicle'[3] and as long as it is able to address effectively 'both knowing and unknowing audiences'.[4] As a matter of fact, the adaptation is not necessarily perceived as such, depending on whether the audience is familiar with the adapted work or not. An unknowing audience will therefore simply judge the adaptation as if it were an autonomous work, while a knowing audience will experience it in terms of intertextuality, detecting similarities and differences through the work of memory. However, this does not mean that the changes will necessarily be considered frustrating, as the pleasure in seeing an adaptation lies in a tension between repetition and change, ritual and surprise.[5]

Within this framework, the analysis of Alfred Hitchcock's adaptation of Buchan's novel *The Thirty-Nine Steps* becomes an interesting case study. It was in fact a breakthrough film, which won the director international recognition and the label of 'master of the thriller', but achieved by reinterpreting, adding and cutting the plot of the novel to fit the needs of film storytelling and to give prominence to messages the director felt urgent need to convey to the audience of the mid-thirties.

Considering the fact that Hitchcock had been given a fair amount of freedom in the choice of the subject for a new film, it is important to try to understand what reasons led him to

---

2   Linda Hutcheon, *A Theory of Adaptation* (New York–London: Routledge Taylor and Francis Group, 2006), p. 18.

3   Gary Bortolotti and Linda Hutcheon, 'On the Origin of Adaptations: Rethinking Fidelity Discourse and "Success" – Biologically', *New Literary History*, 38 (2007), 443–458, p. 452.

4   Hutcheon, p. 121.

5   See Hutcheon, pp. 1–32.

choose this specific novel.[6] First of all the choice is definitely a homage to one of Hitchcock's favourite writers, whose influence the director admitted being present in his works long before the shooting of *The 39 Steps*.[7] However, Hitchcock and Charles Bennett, responsible for the scriptwriting, were originally keener on adapting *Greenmantle*, in which the same main character is involved in a secret mission during the first world war. Opting for *The Thirty-Nine Steps* represented a practical advantage, since it 'was set entirely in England, while *Greenmantle* would have called for German and Turkish scenes', and therefore it 'could be shot almost entirely at Lime Grove'.[8] At the same time, it implied more changes to make it more appropriate for a film, as Hitchcock himself realized when he reread the book:

> When I did so, I received a shock. I had learned a lot about filmmaking in the fifteen-odd years that had elapsed [since my first reading]. Though I could still see the reason for my first enthusiasm — the book was full of action — I found that the story as it stood was not in the least suitable for the screen.[9]

---

6   It must be pointed out that Hitchcock was not particularly keen on adapting works which were considered 'classics', as he probably felt too much pressure to be faithful; following the experience of German expressionism, which had successfully adapted books considered *Trivialliteratur* to make good films, he willingly looked for inspiration within best-sellers of popular literature. With reference to this aspect, see Gosetti.

7   Hitchcock was certainly attracted by a feature of Buchan's novels, closely related to the effect of *suspense* he wished to create in the audience, namely a blending of adventure and realism; the writer defined such works as "shockers" — 'the romance where the incidents defy the probabilities, and march just inside the borders of the possible'. Hitchcock's fondness for Buchan is confirmed by the attempt to adapt, later in his career, another of his novels, *Three Hostages*, left unfinished. John Buchan, *The Thirty-Nine Steps*, in J. Buchan, *The Complete Richard Hannay* (Harmondsworth: Penguin Books, 1992), pp. 1–104, p. 2.

8   Patrick McGilligan, *Alfred Hitchcock: A Life in Darkness and Light* (New York: Harper Collins, 2010), p. 199, both quotations.

9   Ibid.

Since, as Hitchcock himself admitted, shooting a film meant above all telling a story,[10] he chose therefore to visualize what he perceived to be the fundamental elements of the novel, namely its hero, the adventure with the double-chase and the detailed description of the different settings, thus creating a scenario in which he could then introduce new elements.

With reference to the first of these elements, the hero, Buchan portrays Richard Hannay as a man born in Scotland but brought up in South Africa, who at the beginning of the novel looks bored with city life and craves for a bit of challenge in his life. Even if the reader is not given many details about him, he is presented as a man of action who embodies the values of the gentleman in his manliness, elegant behaviour and sense of humour; moreover, his being both British and part of the British Empire makes him, as Mark Glancy points out, one 'of the British Empire's literary heroes who are equally at home in a drawing room and in the wilds. They do not merely enjoy the fruits of civilization but actively defend civilization'.[11] Hannay's adventure is in fact described all through the novel as a personal struggle, in which he has to prove his innocence, as well as a mission for the sake of his own country. His patriotism becomes even more evident when he gets to know that Scudder has freed him from blame. He looks relieved, 'for I was now up against my country's enemies only, and not my country's law',[12] and yet he feels bound to carry on with his task, this time with the support of the authorities:

> Here was I, a very ordinary fellow, with no particular brains, and yet I was convinced that somehow I was needed to help this business through — that without me it would all go to blazes [...]. It seemed as if a voice kept speaking in my ear, telling me to be up and doing, or I would never sleep again.[13]

---

10   Francois Truffaut, *Il cinema secondo Hitchcock* (Milan: Nuova Pratiche, 1997), p. 84.
11   Mark Glancy, *The 39 Steps: A British Film Guide* (London–New York: I.B. Tauris, 2003), p. 11.
12   Buchan, p. 74.
13   Ibid., p. 79.

At the same time, as the above quotation shows, Richard Hannay is only an ordinary citizen, who finds himself involved in an adventure almost by chance. His reputation and values are no defence against the 'ever-present reality of evil, and the possibility of its breaking through into the most respectable lives'.[14] Hitchcock was definitely more fascinated by this second aspect of the character and by the sense of threat lying behind normality. The difficulty of discerning between good and bad, and therefore deciding whether to trust people or not, is relevant in both the film and the novel. Instead, the hero of the film seems to be more interested in proving his innocence, while the patriotic atmosphere of the novel leaves room to a more cynical view of man and of the world. In both cases, however, the writer and the film director aim at an identification of readers and audience with the protagonist from the very beginning: Buchan achieves this through a first person narration and by stating his innocence and moral values very early in the novel; Hitchcock obtains the same effect through subjective camerawork, where the focus on the protagonist's steps is a direct invitation to the watchers to put themselves in the protagonist's shoes and live his breathless adventure.

The process of identification with the protagonist also represents an invitation to the readers/audience to abandon temporarily their ordinary lives and accept to be entertained. Hannay's boredom in the early stages of the novel finds an end when he accepts to live the adventure, while the first sequence of the movie shows a man going to the music-hall, thus mirroring the public itself, looking for entertainment at the cinema.

The other element that is taken directly from the book is the theme of the double-chase, which really fascinated Hitchcock, so as to use it in other films as well. He said the situation, in which the protagonist finds himself pursued by villains but at the same time unable to go to the police, had two main purposes: on the one hand it created sympathy for the man who was escaping and,

---

14   Janet Adam Smith, *John Buchan: A Biography* (Oxford: Oxford University Press, 1965), p. 286.

at the same time, it made the story go on.[15] The double pursuit
in both works prevails over the espionage plot. Though Buchan
seems to be more detailed in the description of the secret goals of
the enemy, which is understandable considering that he was trying
to establish the *clichés* of a fairly new literary genre, it can be said
that in the novel and even more in the film 'all we really care about
on the outside is our hero on the run, not where he is running from
and what, if anything, he is running to [...], the chase itself is the
point'.[16] This can explain why very few people remember what
the espionage plot is about, not so much because the novel and the
film give different versions and the thirty-nine steps refer to two
different things — physical steps leading to the sea in one case
and the name of the secret organization in the other —, but mainly
because they get absorbed in the protagonist's escape.

Moreover, what is striking is the pace at which all this chase
takes place. The various episodes in the novel happen one after
the other in such a rapid succession as to make the reader overlook
how improbable some of the events are. In *John Buchan: a
biography*, Janet Adam Smith reports a letter written by T. E.
Lawrence in which he expresses his opinion on Buchan's style.
Even though he shows reservations about the writer's technique,
he admits that 'the books are like athletes racing: so clean-lined,
speedy, breathless' (280). This quality certainly accounts for the
success of the book, which made Buchan a best seller by 1916,
while the episodic structure proved particularly suitable for the
serialisation in *Blackwood's*. In *The 39 Steps*[17] the element of
speed is dominant again[18] and, thanks to the visual storytelling, it
is even accelerated: 'The scene in the flat fades out on Annabella's

---

15   Glancy, p. 14.
16   John Russell Taylor, *Hitch: The Life and Work of Alfred Hitchcock*
      (London–Boston: Faber & Faber, 1978), p. 129.
17   Hitchcock decided to use the number in figures for the title, a choice
      probably determined by the stronger visual impact; so, whenever the
      number is reported in this way, the reference is to the film.
18   When asked by Truffaut to comment on the film, Hitchcock identified its
      main quality in its speed, where an idea immediately follows another and
      everything is sacrificed to speed.
      Truffaut, p. 81.

last words — 'quickly, quickly, quickly' —, and these set the pace for the rest of the film. [...] The montage that follows [i.e. the escape from the flat to the station] offers a fine example of the way in which the film maintains its sense of pace and forward momentum. It lasts only fifty seconds'.[19] Also the sequence of episodes is used, even though they are not the same and the changes contribute a lot to the updating of the film, and becomes part of the director's aim 'for a brisk, disjointed effect, in which no time would be wasted on transitions: the film would simply move as quickly as possible from one thing to the next, with each episode dealt with almost as a self-sufficient short story'.[20]

The adventures Hannay goes through also imply movements in space and Hitchcock could certainly draw inspiration from the book. The novel is in fact rich in descriptive passages, especially of the Scottish landscapes Buchan knew so well, which are portrayed in minute detail, helping the reader visualize the scene. As Janet Adam Smith points out 'though Buchan may deal in stereotype and cliché for his characters, he delineates his landscapes as individually, as lovingly, as other novelists do their heroines' (285). The choice of the film director to send a troupe to Scotland for location footage seems to pay homage to the authenticity of the locales present in the book, even though Hitchcock's purpose was probably not a celebration of the beauty of the places but a way of introducing an element of dynamism and diversity in contrast with the rather static atmosphere of contemporary British cinema. Consistently with the atmosphere of the thriller, the open spaces of Scotland are not a place of quietness and peace, but, on the contrary, they can become a real trap.[21]

Apart from these elements, which are explicitly taken from the book, the film manages to reproduce another quality of the novel, described by Hitchcock as the 'understatement of highly dramatic

---

19   Glancy, p. 50.
20   Taylor, pp. 127–128.
21   With reference to this aspect, see the section entitled 'Open Spaces Claustrophobia', in William Hare, *Hitchcock and the Methods of Suspense* (Jefferson–London: Mc Farland, 2007), p. 16.

ideas',[22] achieved at times through a blending of suspense and humour. In the early phase of his escape, for example, Hannay reaches Scotland and, in a moment of high tension, describes his mood as that of 'a boy out for a spring holiday tramp, instead of a man of thirty-seven very much wanted by the police'.[23] A few pages later, then, the protagonist takes the chance of getting off the train, but after studying all the details to leave unseen at the right moment, he obtains exactly the opposite result:

> It would have been all right but for that infernal dog. Under the impression that I was decamping with its master's belonging, it started to bark, and all but got me by the trousers. This woke up the herd, who stood bawling at the carriage door in the belief that I had committed suicide [...]. Then from my shelter I peered back, and so the guard and several passengers gathered round the open carriage door and staring in my direction. I could not have made a more public departure if I had left with a bugler and a brass band.[24]

Hitchcock developed this quality even further through the introduction of sketches and brief dialogues of minor characters (with the contribution of Ian Hay), like the commercial travellers on the train, and above all by adding the romance plot which changes the tone of the film, mixing suspense and aspects of the comedy. The rendering of the understatement is not only related to humour, but it emerges from the presence of elements that are introduced and toned down all the time:

> There is wit but it is dry wit; there is romance but only in the most unsentimental terms; there is a hero but he is a reluctant one; there are fantastic adventures but they are portrayed within a world that seems almost defiantly normal and undisturbed.[25]

If so far the most relevant references to the novel have been pointed out, the film is rich in a number of details and echoes

---

22   Truffaut, p. 77.
23   Buchan, p. 23.
24   Ibid., p. 26.
25   Glancy, p. 103.

taken from the book and rearranged, from the menacing presence of the airplane and the reference to the music hall to the whistling of the protagonist, from the political speech to the photographic memory of the spy which recalls the extraordinary gift of Mr Memory, not to mention the variety of roles and disguises used by Hannay in his escape, one of which, the milkman, is the same. Therefore, it can be argued that the influence of the novel went far beyond what Hitchcock and all the people involved in the realization of the script were ready to admit.

However, if the similarities with Buchan's work represent more than the simple background for the film, the differences introduced seem to contribute to a higher degree of realism and, above all, manage to convey new messages that the filmmaker considered relevant in the context of 1936.

The most relevant novelty in the film is the introduction of female characters, both with lead roles and in minor ones. Apart from any other consideration, this choice represents fidelity to reality. In the novel, in fact, Hannay hardly ever meets women and, when this happens, they are generally represented as little more than shadows. The literary innkeeper lives with his grandmother, who never appears so that the protagonist gathers she is probably ill, the roadman lives on his own and so does Sir Walter. The only reported conversation of a woman is a brief complaint on the gyiard's behaviour on the train at the beginning of the escape, and even the woman who cures him when he falls ill is portrayed in a very superficial way. By contrast, in the film, Annabella and even more Pamela play two important roles, but the protagonist also meets some couples and the episode of the crofter's wife represents probably the most touching moment of *The 39 Steps*.

Annabella, the mysterious brunette spy, is presented from the very beginning as a woman full of initiative. She invites herself to Hannay's flat, and soon we get to know that she fired the gun at the music hall and that she is involved in a dangerous espionage case, an involvement which she will pay with her life. This mysterious 'dark lady' endowed with sex appeal contrasts with the character of the male protagonist who, at the beginning of the film, is characterized by passivity, showing no sexual interest towards the girl and being completely unable to defend her. As Glancy highlights, the shocked expression of Hannay with the corpse of the woman lying on him shows a moment of revelation and of awakening of the protagonist, who from this moment on will take an active role; the romance which follows represents thus a journey 'from a state of impotence and repressed desire towards a state of potency and sexual awakening' (16).

If some critics justify the presence of the romance as a convention which would have appealed more to the female audience and which would have enhanced the success of the film, it is also evident that Hitchcock used the romance plot to analyze the psychology of the character through Freudian references, much discussed among the filmmaker's friends,[26] and to deal more generally with the theme of sexual relationships.[27] The romance of Hannay and Pamela in fact parallels other couples, while different opinions of marriage appear in the film. On the one hand marriage is seen as an institution that puts an end to romance. The crofter's wife seems imprisoned by a mean husband obsessed by betrayal and by the temptations of evil; her trusting Hannay is therefore also a rebellion against her husband's way of thinking and in her final look we understand all her drama and resignation. Negative comments on marriage appear then in a comic vein for example through the words of the milkman, who helps Hannay on the ground of men's solidarity when the protagonist makes him believe that he is having an affair with a married woman.

Nevertheless, other couples show that relationships in marriage are not necessarily so superficial. Both the Jordans and the innkeepers seem to have a relationship very much based on the

---

26   Though Hitchcock's interest in psychoanalysis is generally mentioned with reference to the films produced after WWII, it is our opinion that some hints can be identified in *The 39 Steps* as well. In relation to the theme of psychoanalysis see Giorgio Gosetti, *Alfred Hitchcock* (Milan: Il Castoro, 1996), p. 24 and the already mentioned W. Hare, pp. 4–5.

27   See also Charles Barr's analysis of the sequence of the film in relation to the appearance of women and the development of Hannay's identity (154–156).

element of complicity. It is made clear in the film that Mrs Jordan is perfectly aware of her husband's involvement in espionage and she supports him, while the innkeepers' complicity seems to be grounded on a more romantic basis, which makes them defend the secret of what they suppose to be a couple in love. The audience is not allowed to know the kind of relationship Hannay and Pamela will build together, as the unconventional ending shows only two hands getting together with the handcuffs still hanging from Hannay's hand, but through the film the theme of marriage is definitely a dominant one and is closely related to the issue of trusting and betrayal which permeates all the human relationships in *The 39 Steps*.[28]

Another major difference between Buchan's work and Hitchcock's lies in the attempt to focus on elements that could better apply to a new context. The novel in fact reflects the atmosphere of the beginning of the first world war, in which evil can suddenly appear in people's ordinary lives, but Buchan's 'preoccupation with the 'thinness of civilization' is not a critique of British society or culture, but rather an acknowledgement that under extraordinary circumstances it could be undermined or destroyed'.[29] Moreover, the presence of the hero, who embodies chivalric values and who defends civilization making good win in the end, establishes a sense of order out of the chaos. The only criticism is towards the underestimation of the German menace. Sir Harry in his political speech describes it as 'a Tory invention' without which 'Germany and Britain would be fellow-workers in peace and reform',[30] while Hannay ironically depicts the easy acceptance of German people on the territory, when, talking about his enemy, he observes: 'Most likely he had letters from Cabinet Ministers saying he was to be given every facility for plotting against Britain. That's the sort of owlish way we run our politics in the Old Country'.[31]

---

28   See also Donald Spoto, *The Art of Alfred Hitchcock: Fifty Years of His Motion Pictures* (New York: Anchor Books Edition, 1992), p. 51.

29   Glancy, p. 18.

30   Buchan, p. 39, both quotations.

31   Ibid, p. 59.

Also the film hints at Germany as a potential foreign enemy, even though, due to censorship, it is never explicitly mentioned. The spies are in fact after the plans for a silent airplane engine, while in the novel there were plans showing how the British fleet would be disposed in case of war; this is not only a way of updating the story by introducing the strategic importance of air force in the 1930s, but, considering Germany was investing a great deal on this field, it identifies this country as a menace. In the same way the improvised speech of Hannay, considered by mistake a politician, and the easiness with which he manages to win the crowd's approval is likely to represent a worrying hint at Hitler's and Mussolini's orations and their successful impact. Finally, the choice of the actress, Lucie-Mannheim, a German actress who had left her country fleeing the Nazis, for the role of the foreign spy helping Britain is bound to be a further reference to the German threat.[32] The rapid rise of Nazism and the presence of German *émigrés* — with their own direct experiences — among the staff working at the studio may have generated in Hitchcock the urge for warning against the potential danger coming from this country.

However, the film director does not spare Britain a harsh judgement on its society, no longer generous and willing to help as the novel had shown. In the film there are various scenes of crowds that become violent all of a sudden, Hannay 'is more hindered than helped by those he meets, most of whom selfish and menacing',[33] as shown in the episode of the greedy crofter; even the police, the institution which is supposed to protect the citizen, appears brutal and more threatening than in the book.

It is on these grounds that some scholars — among whom Mark Glancy and Charles Barr[34] — strongly disagree with the idea of an apolitical aspect of *The 39 Steps*, as the film on the contrary manages to convey the awareness of international tensions as well as of the social unrest and disunity within the country notwithstanding the constraints of censorship. In this attempt

---

32   See Mc Gilligan, p. 201.
33   Glancy, p. 17.
34   See Charles Barr, *English Hitchcock* (Moffat: Cameron&Hollis, 1999).

to convey messages mainly in an indirect way, the cooperation with associate producer Ivor Montagu was crucial. He had in fact experience of the methods of the censors, he knew they expected films to be a form of light entertainment, but he also knew 'they were remarkably blind to implication and reacted only to the direct and overtly censorable'.[35]

The subtle method of implication is thus used in the film on more than one occasion to pass on messages. The real challenge to the audience comes at the end, when the people at the Palladium witness a murder on stage — of a man who is thus prevented from telling the truth —, but are distracted soon afterwards by the dancers' legs in the continuation of the show. The public of the film is invited to react in a different way and to pay attention to serious matters behind light entertainment, without being misled by diversions or wrong assumptions. This issue is in fact represented in the film through characters who fail to understand the complexity of reality because of their preconceived beliefs. The crofter thinks his wife is having an affair with Hannay because he is obsessed by the idea of betrayal; the milkman prefers the romantic version of Hannay's story rather than accept the explanation of the espionage plot; in the same way Pamela does not believe Hannay innocent, while Hannay trusts Professor Jordan, deceived by his appearance of confidence and respectability. The film therefore seems to invite the audience to see beyond appearance and awaken, just as the protagonist does when he understands that danger is part of his real life.

The analysis of the similarities and differences between the two works shows thus the extraordinary qualities of the adapter in reinterpreting certain themes in a new temporal context through a different medium. Though not the main focus of this essay, the film in fact is interesting if scrutinized within the framework of filmmaking technique, in which we find a great deal of experimentation, for example with sound, and the attempt to define characters suitable for the thriller, like the 'cool blonde' and the 'suave villain', together with various ways to achieve suspense.

---

35   Glancy, p. 24.

On the one hand, Hitchcock's interpretation of the book highlights some of Buchan's qualities as a writer; the film was in fact appreciated for the thrill, the fast pace, the changes of rhythm and the blending of light and dramatic moments, thus paying homage to some essential qualities of the structure of the novel, recognized by Buchan himself, who judged the film as superior to his work. At the same time, though, the success of the film in Britain and the *succès d'estime* it enjoyed in the United States, let alone the appreciation of experts in the long run — in 1999 the film reached the fourth place in the list of the 100 British films of the twentieth century in a survey conducted by the British Film Institute — show the positive response of the public for a product enjoyed both as an autonomous work and as an adaptation.

Since Hitchcock's work, *The Thirty-Nine Steps* has been further adapted [36] with reference both to the novel and to the film, with different degrees of fidelity to either product, thus showing an interest in the story which seems to have gained by what might be considered at first sight an 'unfaithful' adaptation. Let us then conclude with a quotation which perfectly fits *The 39 Steps* and reinforces the point of our analysis: 'an adaptation is not vampiric: it does not draw the life-blood from its source and leave it dying or dead, nor is it paler than the adapted work. It may, on the contrary, keep that prior work alive, giving it an after life it would never have had otherwise'.[37]

---

36   We refer here to the screen adaptations of 1959 by Ralph Thomas and of 1978 by Don Sharp, as well as to the TV adaptation directed by James Hawes and produced by the BBC in 2008. The novel was then adapted for the stage by Patrick Barlow with a fairly successful play which premiered in June 2005.

37   Hutcheon, p. 176.

Bibliography

Barr, Charles, *English Hitchcock* (Moffat: Cameron&Hollis, 1999).

Bortolotti Gary, Hutcheon Linda, 'On the Origin of Adaptations: Rethinking Fidelity Discourse and "Success" – Biologically', *New Literary History*, 38 (2007), 443–458.

Buchan, John, *The Thirty-Nine Steps*, in Buchan J., *The Complete Richard Hannay* (Harmondsworth: Penguin Books, 1992), pp. 1–104.

Ellis, John, 'The Literary Adaptation: an Introduction', *Screen*, 23:1 (1982), 3–5, < doi: 10.1093/screen/23.1.3>.

Glancy, Mark, The 39 Steps: *A British Film Guide* (London–New York: I.B.Tauris, 2003).

Gosetti, Giorgio, *Alfred Hitchcock* (Milan: Il Castoro, 1996).

Hare, William, *Hitchcock and the Methods of Suspense* (Jefferson–London: Mc Farland, 2007).

Hutcheon, Linda, *A Theory of Adaptation* (New York–London: Routledge Taylor and Francis Group, 2006).

McGilligan, Patrick, *Alfred Hitchcock: A Life in Darkness and Light* (New York: Harper Collins, 2010).

Smith, Janet Adam, *John Buchan: A Biography* (Oxford: Oxford University Press, 1965).

Spoto, Donald, *The Art of Alfred Hitchcock: Fifty Years of His Motion Pictures* (New York: Anchor Books Edition, 1992).

Taylor, John Russell, *Hitch: The Life and Work of Alfred Hitchcock* (London–Boston: Faber & Faber, 1978).

Truffaut, Francois, *Il cinema secondo Hitchcock* (Milan: Nuova Pratiche, 1997).

TALKING WALLS. (HI)STORIES OF WALLS IN IVAN VLADISLAVIĆ AND WILLIAM KENTRIDGE

Paola Quazzo
(University of Turin)

What is the stuff walls are made of? Bricks are too simple an answer. From the point of view of Ivan Vladislavić and William Kentridge a wall is almost never a wall. It can be a page, a screen, a mirror. Since the walls described by Vladislavić or decorated by Kentridge are built in metropolises, they also acquire the social and historical values that lay at the heart of a community. It is such interiority that the South African writer and the South African artist show by representing or using the walls of some of the cities they lived or worked in. The central city of their work is Johannesburg, where Kentridge and Vladislavić live, but others coexist that are closer to the Italian reader, such as Rome and Naples, which host some striking and innovative art works by William Kentridge. Following different artistic paths, the works of the two artists show thematic interconnections and share similar outlooks. Their discourse about urban space sheds light on the relationship between Africa and Europe, history, memory and art making. By juxtaposing their works, it emerges that for the two artists walls are part of a process of construction of private and collective memory as well as a means of reinventing public and private space, in the light of the impact that buildings and art have in the daily lives of city dwellers in huge metropolises.

Johannesburg has been the subject of numerous works in order to outline its peculiar character; see for instance the monumental work by Nuttal and Mbembe *The Elusive Metropolis* (2008), or *From Joburg to Jozi. Stories About Africa's Infamous City* by Holland and Roberts (2002). Johannesburg, or the 'afropolis', as Mbembe and Nuttal call it, has become one of the critical nodes of southern hemispheric capitalism and globalization. Its transition from 'racial city' to globalised metropolis, has acquired the symbolic power of representing not only South Africa's post-apartheid course but also African modernity. As many other towns in South Africa, the city physically carries the scars of apartheid in cement, because 'apartheid was expressed in bricks and mortar'.[1] Both apartheid and post-apartheid Johannesburg is a city of walls, as shown in David Goldblatt's photographies in *TJ Johannesburg Photographs 1948–2010 – Double Negative* (2010) or recounted in Vladislavić's *Portrait with Keys – Joburg & What-What* (2006):

> Johannesburg is a frontier city, a place of contested boundaries. Territory must be secured and defended or it will be lost. Today the contest is fierce and so the defences multiply. Walls replace fences, high walls replace low ones, even the highest walls acquire electrified wires and spikes. In the wealthier suburbs the pattern is to knock things flat and start all over. Around here people must make the most of what they've already got, and therefore the walls tend to grow by increments. A stone wall is heightened with prefab panels, a prefab wall is heightened with steel palisades, the palisades are topped with razor wire. Wooden pickets on top of the brick, ornate wrought-iron panels on top of plaster, blade wire on top of split poles. These piggyback walls (my own included) are nearly always ugly. But sometimes the whole ensemble achieves a degree of elaboration that becomes beautiful again, like a page in the *Homemaker's Fair* catalogue.[2]

Ivan Vladislavić is fascinated with the constant changing of the urban landscape in Johannesburg and how iconic places or buildings of the apartheid era either disappear or incorporate or hybridise with new constructions that reflect a new political establishment, a new society and new values. In *The Folly* (1993), *Propaganda by Monuments* (1996), *The Exploded View* (2004), *Portrait with Keys: Joburg & What-What* (2006), he

---

1   T. Garb, 'A Land of Signs', *Journal of Contemporary African Art*, 26, (Spring 2010), Nka publications, 9.
2   Ivan Vladislavić, *Portrait with Keys – Joburg & What-What* (Cape Town: Umuzi, 2006), p. 185.

investigates how people inhabit space in South Africa and how a political use of space affects people's lives. His work as editor also led him to contribute to several books about architecture, such as *Blank: Architecture, Apartheid and After* (1998) with Judin Hilton. However, in his narrative works, he mainly tackles problems and challenges in the city by adopting the point of view of individuals, especially in their everyday pursuits in 'the *local* network of labor and recreation [where] one can grasp how, within a grid of socio-economic constraints, these pursuits unfailingly establish relational tactics (a struggle for life), artistic creations (an aesthetic), and autonomous initiatives (an ethic)'.[3] Following De Certeau's classification, in Johannesburg Vladislavić has found walls that epitomise the tactics, the artistic initiatives and the ethics that the city's inhabitants put into practice in their daily life.

One of these walls is the protagonist of a short story entitled *Journal of a Wall*, included in Vladislavić's collection *Missing Persons* (1989), in which the narrator recounts the building of a wall under a series of (11) entries. One day the narrator sees the unloading of some packs of bricks just across the street, in his neighbour's garden. Later, he realises that his neighbour wants to build a wall in his front garden and he gets so excited that he feels he has to write a diary of the construction. Before that moment, he has never had any contact with his neighbour, but now he feels he can partake of his enterprise by observing and recording the work. As the work proceeds, the narrator's feelings are contrasting:

> I was surprised and hurt to discover that he had already started work without me.[4]
>
> Frankly, he was a disappointment to me.[5]

---

3   Michel de Certeau, *The Practice of Everyday Life* (Berkeley: University of California Press, 1985), p. IX.

4   Carmen Concilio, *The Wall as Signifier in Ivan Vladislavić*, ed. by Daria Tunca, Janet Wilson *Postcolonial Gateways and Walls* (Leiden–Boston: Brill Rodopi, 2017), p. 206.

5   Ibid., p. 27.

I admired that in him – his patience, his faith.[6]

I was alarmed when he came out just a few minutes later carrying a suitcase.[7]

I think I dislike him. […] The man has no imagination.[8]

I was mad as hell.[9]

I am no longer interested in them.[10]

The narrator's feelings swing from scepticism about the man's manual abilities to admiration for his constancy, from boredom and disillusion about his way of working, to ferocious anger when he finally realises that the man will build such a high wall that his house will be completely cut out from his neighbour's view. The irony gets its climax at the end of the story. After six months' work, Mr and Mrs Groenewald (this is the neighbours' name, as the narrator fortuitously found out), have a big party, from which the narrator is obviously excluded, and immediately afterwards they quickly sell their house and leave.

What makes this story remarkable is the voice of the narrator. The reader does not know much about him: he works, he sometimes drinks too much, he gets furiously angry at times. But the building of the wall completely absorbs him. His level of involvement overcomes mere curiosity and reaches obsession: he feels he is part of his neighbour's household (he notices his clothes, his pace, his wife's dresses and behaviour) so as to call his unidirectional interest 'our relationship'.[11] Therefore, it is no surprise that he defines the fact of being completely ignored by the Groenewalds 'a betrayal'[12]. Sometimes the reader may be led to believe that the narrator is slightly insane, considering his obsession for the wall, his excesses of rage and his impudent voyeuristic attitude towards the neighbours. However, there is no sense of madness in the narrative; on the contrary, humour

---

6   Ibid., p. 28.
7   Ibid., p. 31.
8   Ibid., p. 37.
9   Ibid., p. 41.
10   Ibid., p. 42.
11   Ibid., p. 38
12   Ibid., p. 42.

stems from the fact that the narrator is probably only a simpleton. His naivety is extraordinary: since the beginning of the wall, it has never come to his mind that the wall could mean separation, enclosure, distance. He wonders about the possibility of talking to the neighbours and he regrets not having started a friendship earlier on: 'I began to regret my reticence. They were nice people, I knew. He was solid and reliable and purposeful. She was quiet and sweet and sensitive. They were my kind of people. If only I had broken the ice earlier. Now there was so much ground to be made up'.[13] Unfortunately, they are not as he imagined. Throughout the story, the Groenewalds act as if the man does not exist: not only do they show no interest in him and pretend not noticing his presence, but they also act quite rudely when he finally approaches them with the excuse of asking for some sugar. However, the narrator blindly continues to see the positive aspect of the building:

> Yet, at the same time, even though they were unaware of it, we had so much in common. The wall. They knew it from one side, I knew it from the other. I began to see it not so much as a barrier between us, but as a meeting-point. It was the thin line between pieces in a puzzle, the frontier on which both pieces become intelligible.[14]

The wall is a 'meeting-point' between solitudes, or between human beings that share a sense of purposefulness. Building a wall can paradoxically mean openness, care and friendliness. The optimism of the narrator, which can be easily dismissed as naivety on his part, is actually explained when the reader learns that it is a time of great violence in South Africa. The recurring references to the news of riots in the townships set the story at the time of the apartheid:

> The news came on. It was Michael de Morgan. He told us there was unrest in the townships again. He showed us a funeral crowd being dispersed with tear-gas. A bus burned in the background. Then a camera

---

13   Ibid., p. 38.
14   Ibid., pp. 38–39.

in a moving car tracking along the naked faces of houses, and children peeling away from the vehicle like buck in the game reserve. A cloud of black smoke from a supermarket. Soldiers. Some people hurling bricks into the burning bus.[15]

While bricks are used as weapons in real life, in the narrator's imagination his neighbour's bricks may lay the foundation of a relationship, which overcomes the sickness that the news brings to him. Building a wall can then become an act of hope: 'I for one was finding the news depressing — full of death and destruction. Who would build amid these ruins?'[16]

The narrator seems to counterbalance his frustration with an impelling desire for commitment, which leads to two interconnected outcomes. Firstly, he is very concerned in recording every single moment of the construction, thus acting as a witness. His journal is more than a diary: it is a historical chronicle whose purpose is to document faithfully and in detail the enterprise. The wall and the journal will be both mementos of a precise time and space, a living record of history. Hence the second stance: the narrator creates a metaphorical relation between writing and building.

I should have foreseen it all. [...] If I had not been watching from behind the curtains in my lounge, like a spy, perhaps it would have been clear to me that *I was meant to be more than an observer*.[17]

[...] I finally realized what I had to do: I had to write it all down. I have laid my own foundations, and from now on *it will be brick for word, word for brick*.[18]

It's just a wall. That must be clear by now. Even a child could see it. And the words that go into it like bricks are as bland and heavy and worn as the metaphor itself. *He lays the last brick. But I have the last word*.[19]

---

15 Ibid., p. 24.
16 Ibid., p. 29.
17 Ibid., p. 23, (*my italics*).
18 Ibid., p. 34, (*my italics*).
19 Ibid., p. 43, (*my italics*).

Words win over buildings, but the latter remain as evidence of the words. And here the testimony of the enterprise is sad: 'The wall looked ashamed of himself'.[20] Any project aimed at segregating and humiliating human beings such as the one carried on by the architects of apartheid, openly denounces its cowardice by its mere existence. A wall may be either a barrier or a meeting point; nevertheless, it speaks of the tactics that two city neighbours can develop to face the challenges of the city. However, there are other tactics. As it has emerged so far, walls talk by their mere presence, but they can speak even more loudly when they carry signs on themselves. This is what happens in two other texts by Vladislavić. In *Portrait with Keys*, the building moment is overcome and the theme of art is introduced, with particular relevance to the function and value of art in a public open space. In the book, there are many fragments in which walls play a role, but two sequences stand out.

The first sequence of fragments (10, 40, 66) deals with a Ndebele mural. The narrator remembers when in the Nineties a neighbour of his had his garden wall painted by a Ndebele woman. As the narrator recalls, 'there was a fad for Ndebele painting at the time'.[21] Ndebele art is quite a recent phenomenon: it consists of abstract designs made of black lines and very bright colours, planned and painted by women on the walls of Ndebele houses or huts. The narrator comes to love the wall because, as in *Journal of a Wall*, it carries a message of hope: 'I thought it was bravely optimistic. It suited the early nineties perfectly: Africa was coming to the suburbs in the nicest possible way […]'.[22] His black friend Liz dislikes the mural because she thinks it is kitsch ('It's like that braai sauce people slosh over everything to give it an African flavour'),[23] but he challenges her notion of authenticity by arguing that it is difficult to say 'what will be regarded as "authentic" a generation from now'[24] and that Ndebele art is 'full of contemporary references' and 'it's constantly changing'.[25]

---

20   Ibid., p. 44.
21   Vladislavić, *Portrait with Keys – Joburg & What-What*, p. 24.
22   Ibid., p. 25.
23   Ibid.
24   Ibid.
25   Ibid.

The beautiful and big (six-seven metre long and two-metre high) mural will not live long. The reason of its defacing is not some racist graffiti sprayed over it, as the narrator fears, but the real estate market. Two or three years later, the narrator sees a man in overalls defacing the mural by applying a coat of yellow enamel. Either it is the first act of new owners or the advice of a real estate agent in order to sell the house more easily, the narrator considers it as an act of vandalism and he goes home 'with a heavy heart'.[26] The epilogue is in the last fragment, in which the narrator muses over the hidden Ndebele mural which still exists, though invisible. This leads him to reflect on the parallelism between *pentimento* in art and the writing of a memoir: 'The appearance of the original conception and the second thought, superimposed within the same frame, is a way of seeing and then seeing again'.[27] Walls, as an epitome of buildings and cities, preserve multiple layers of memory in concrete, which an acute gaze can detect. Such gaze is similar to the archaeologist's, because it is skilful enough to detect the object, it is perseverant in enquiring about it, and it can connect the object to time, space and society. Since the world is characterized by discontinuity, the focus is on small details to interrogate the whole picture. As argued by Deleuze and Guattari in *Anti-Oedipus*:

> We live today in the age of partial objects, bricks that have been shattered to bits, and leftovers. [...] We no longer believe in primordial totality that once existed or in a final totality that awaits us at some future date. [...] We believe only in totalities that are peripheral.[28]

At the same time, the narrator is well aware of the power of gaze. Just as in *Journal of a Wall*, the narrator feels that the process of selecting an ordinary object such as a wall, and transforming it into a piece of reading material which can be interpreted (seen and seen again) by the gaze of the onlooker is worth documentation.

---

26   Ibid., p. 26.
27   Ibid., p. 92.
28   Jill Deleuze and Felix Guattari, *Anti-Oedipus* (London: Continuum, 2004), pp. 45–46.

Long afterwards, it occurred to me that I might have documented the making of the mural. It would have been a wonderful photographic essay. Or, even better, a film. That intricate pattern, vibrant and complex as stained glass [...] spreading out, segment by segment, over a blank white wall. What a metaphor for the social transformation we were living through!
'If only you were a film-maker,' Minky said, 'or a photographer.'
'But I'm a writer, for Pete's sake, I could have spoken to the painter. I should have got her name, at least. I'm walking around with my eyes wide open, taking everything in like a vacuum cleaner, coughing bits of it out on paper. But I never bother to get the facts.'[29]

The ways of documenting suggested in the passage are those thought to be more objective and reliable: photography, filming and journalism. However, as already surfaced in *Journal of a Wall*, it is not a faithful day-by-day diary nor a piece of supposedly neutral form of representation that would suit the gaze of the looker and the complexity of the wall. The best way to render them is to give a very personal and subjective version of the event, by 'taking' it, chewing on it and 'coughing' or spitting it on paper, leaving the facts of distrustful official reports and privileging a symbolic representation of reality. In doing so, a wider sense of freedom can be attained. Besides, knowing that *pentimenti* will emerge sooner or later, thus fostering meditation on the past in a more personal and cogent way.

The second sequence about walls by Vladislavić consists of fragments 29 and 30 from *Portrait with Keys*. Jeff (Lok) tells the narrator about a project of his: 'a wall of remembrance'.[30] People from Johannesburg will be asked to give an object to the artist, who will enclose it in a transparent resin block which will be used as a brick to construct a wall. The objects can be anything:

we moved on to the likely numbers of everyday objects — key, coins, lapel badges, pencil sharpeners. Even later we worked through the conventional body parts — appendixes, gallstones, wisdom teeth — and the run-of-the-mill fetishes.[31]

29   Vladislavić, *Portrait with Keys – Joburg & What-What*, pp. 25–26.
30   Ibid., p. 46.
31   Ibid., p. 47.

The reader will never know if this extravagant project will be put into practice; the whole project sounds more like the dreamy outcome of a happy evening spent with friends and beer than a factual plan. However, it is interesting to highlight some ideas which the project entails. First, the reason behind it: 'The city is passing away, said Jeff, even as we speak, and everyone in it, including ourselves. We must build ourselves a memorial while there is still time'[32] and 'Let's say the whole initiative is aimed at those who wish to belong to it, who have an active desire to be commemorated'.[33] The wall is an attempt at fighting back time and the risk of oblivion by building something durable with an individual but also social and anthropological resonance.

Hence, the second important element in the text, that is, the recurring concern of the narrator with documentation:

> I had started out thinking this was one of those artistic projects that would be easier to realize on paper than in the real world. It had been on the tip of my tongue to offer to write it down, to work the idea up into a scrap of fiction, relieving Jeff of the responsibility of having to pretend that practical steps were necessary. But I came away convinced that the Great Wall of Jeff belonged in the city. I even had an eye on a patch of parkland in Bertrams for the construction site.[34]

The passage seems to suggest a certain distrust in literature, in particular fiction, to transmit the importance of the building project if compared to the real thing. This failure of words also reverberates in *Journal of a Wall* and in the Ndebele mural series, where the loss of faith in the project on the one part, and the lack of initiative on the other part, maim the grandness of the written report. However, this attitude appears to be more of a literary cliché because in fact the walls mentioned in the three texts are not visible but on paper, in the books published by the author and in the minds of his readers. Again, it is the writer, not the architect, who 'has the last word'.

---

32   Ibid., p. 46.
33   Ibid., p. 48.
34   Ibid.

Finally, it is worth considering the question of value in architecture as presented by Vladislavić. It is a reflection, which is implicit in *Journal of a Wall* and in the Ndebele mural series, but it surfaces here more clearly.

> 'Why a wall? Half the city has already vanished behind walls. Even a semi-transparent one can only make things worse. Why not something useful?'
> At which point there arose before my mind's eye a building [...] It was the Hyperama of Sentimental Value. I was walking along its shiny corridors, surrounded on all sides by a peculiarly impenetrable transparency, where objects hung suspended, attached by nothing but space to the names of the people who once loved them.[35]

In the passage the narrator tries to overcome the negative connotation that a wall has — meaning division, separation, silence —, as emerged in *Journal of a Wall* and in the Ndebele mural series, by imagining walls as building elements of a piece of architecture whose function is basically to preserve sentiments instead of ideas. It is the end of constructions which were propaganda monuments, that is, the result of ideology. Now, new buildings are needed that lay their foundations on 'sentimental values' which guarantee universality, yet denote subjectivity too.

There are walls that arouse sentimental values by being narrative. This is the case with William Kentridge's *Triumphs and Laments, a project for Rome* (2016). Inaugurated in April 2016, the project started several years before ('È la prima volta che lavoro in questo modo: ho concepito quest'opera dieci anni fa, e ora vive')[36] and consists of a 550-metre-long mural between Ponte Mazzini and Ponte Sisto in Rome, showing eighty huge figures created by removing the *patina* of dirt from the walls running along the embankment of river Tiber. The figures, or scenes, are major events in the history of the city, ranging from the mythical she-wolf feeding the twins, to iconic city landmarks, sensual

---

35 Ibid., p. 49.
36 L. Larcan, 'La mia Roma cupa e geniale, William Kentridge racconta il suo capolavoro da street artist tra Ponte Mazzini e Ponte Sisto', *Il Messaggero*, 6 April 2016.

Anita Ekberg splashing in Trevi fountain, bombs during World War II, Pasolini's death, and refugees landing in Lampedusa. It is a work of art characterized by site-specificity and transitoriness. The former is given by the presence of the river:

> 'La storia di Roma viaggia sul Tevere, dalle acque riemerge per essere restituita a Roma', riflette l'artista. E confessa Kentridge che 'l'idea della location è legata anche alla vicenda di Giorgiana Masi ricordata da una lapide a ponte Garibaldi, la studentessa di 18 anni uccisa nel 1977 durante una manifestazione.'[37]

Kentridge's statements confirm that *Triumphs and Laments* creates a new mental and spatial landscape by merging the personal, sentimental values attributed to the scenes depicted and the universal value of the city's history. As often in Kentridge's art, 'Rather than representation [...] figuration and narrative become a way of relating the inner landscape (personal memory) with the outer landscape of social and political events at large'.[38]

However, his artwork is made transitory by the action of urban pollution on the drawings: it is estimated that in three or four years the designs will disappear because of the smog depositing on it. The idea of *pentimento* and the defacing of walls, which also emerged in Vladislavić's short stories, gain a new meaning: using Rosalinde Krauss's definition, Kentridge's art is often a 'palimpsest', carrying the idea of writing and erasure:

> Yet, erasure is also a metaphor for the healthy questioning of the certainties and preconceptions lying behind human relations in what might only appear to be an increasingly interactive and democratic world of the digital era. It questions the notion that any definite statement is ever possible; it denies the value of complete or binary theories of politics and social relations (or of any finished artwork, for that matter).[39]

---

37   Ibid.
38   C. Christov-Bakargiev, *On Defectibility as a Resource: William Kentridge's Art of Imperfection, Lack and Falling Short*, ed. by Carolyn Christov-Bakargiev, *William Kentridge*, (Milan: Skira, 2004), p. 33.
39   Ibid.

Therefore, a wall can also be a democratic challenge as well as an act of tolerance, underlining the relativity of ideological positions. Kentridge drew on his earlier experiences as actor and director to design on the wall in Rome a series of scenes or *tableaux* which constitute not only a narrative continuum but also a procession. Viewers can find there the sense of theatricality that characterizes his art:

> The theatricality of his imagery, which is sometimes vaudeville act of intention and feeling and sometimes a cruel choreography of power relations. [...] The kinetic expressivity of these 'performance pieces'arrests their form and line, and creates in the viewer a desire for the next moment, the about-to-come, the anticipation, the final realization of the gesture, so the story, the parable can be told.[40]

The theatricality has also been enhanced by the inauguration ceremony held on 21st April 2016, planned by Kentridge, which presented a double parade (the 'triumphs' and the 'laments') of forty musicians and singers, who danced with the stencils used to design the scenes on the wall, accompanied by music. Both the drawings on the wall and the show are just another version of the 'shadow procession', one of Kentridge's great favourites:

> Understanding that the blankness of the shadow, the lack of psychological depth, may be an asset — that understanding the world not only through individual psychology is often appropriate and stronger. [...] What shadows as objects, silhouettes or puppets do, is make the mediation conscious. The world of shadows tells us things about seeing that are invisible by the light of sun.[41]

---

40 Ari Sitas, *Processions and Public Rituals*, ed. by N. Benezra, S. Boris, D. Cameron, *William Kentridge*, Chicago Museum of Contemporary Art and New York Museum of Contemporary Art (New York: Harry Abrams, 2001), p. 59.

41 William Kentridge, *In Praise of Shadows*, ed. by C. Christov-Bakargiev, *William Kentridge*, p. 159.

Hence, shadows are evocative but they cannot be identified with anything too subjective on the part of the viewers, who feel psychologically detached as much as physically distinct from the wall of shadows. Although they cannot identify with the shadows, the viewers can identify with the artist because walking along the wall is 'a vicarious experience of the physical component of the artist's creative process'.[42] As Kentridge explains:

> Walking, thinking, stalking the image. Many of the hours spent in the studio are hours of walking, pacing back and forth across the space gathering the energy, the clarity to make the first mark. It is not so much a period of planning as a time of allowing the ideas surrounding the project to percolate.[43]

Movement and artistic production; movement and ideas; movement and journey, displacement, migration: these are conceptual fields that Kentridge has investigated in his career and that made him particularly sensitive to places where different kinds of movement are involved. This is the case with another decorated wall he presented in 2012 for one of Naples's underground stations, the most beautiful metro station in Europe according to the *Daily Telegraph*. It consists of two mosaics showing a procession of figures taken from the city's past and present (e.g. Vesuvius, San Gennaro, Capodimonte's porcelain statuette, musicians, etc.) but also some of Kentridge's recurrent figures such as the Compass Man, the Man with a Megaphone and Kentridge's *doppelganger*. In his work the artist also included pieces of the city map as well as decorations similar to those found in the archaeological sites of Pompei and Ercolano. Both the mosaics in Naples and the stencils in Rome clearly reveal common ideas and procedures, and they show how Kentridge has manipulated the wall to let it bear the sentimental values of a community as well as an artistic message that mixes historical

42   Shinji. Kohmoto, in W. Kentridge, *What we see & what we know: thinking about history while walking, and thus the drawings began to move* (Kyoto: The National Museum of Modern Art, 2009), p. 150.
43   Kentridge, *What we see & what we know: thinking about history while walking, and thus the drawings began to move*, p. 120.

awareness, beauty, mystery and lightness in urban environments or areas that are not normally associated to those values.

Ivan Vladislavić and William Kentridge do not only know each other very well but they have been engaged in a long-lasting dialogue about art, narration and the city. For instance, Vladislavić quoted Kentridge in *Portrait with Keys*, and Kentridge's book, *William Kentridge: Tapestries* (2008), hosts Vladislavić's short story *A Farm in Eloff Street*. The works that have been considered here are a good viewpoint over their art and South Africa, and the image and the idea of the wall, as well as its concrete 'living' presence, have the power of coagulating a number of central themes in their art. Vladislavić and Kentridge use the wall to show how an inevitable and fundamental architectural element has often been charged with ideas of prevarication and exclusion on the one hand, but it has also been transformed into a manifesto of freedom and creativity on the other. In the texts analysed here, the wall is a metaphor of a place — South Africa, Italy, the world — of frustrated potentialities, and hopes of social harmony; it is also a spokesman of a series of messages, periodically or accidentally erased and rewritten, that make it a palimpsest of memories which, though hidden, are preserved; finally, it is a mosaic of universal sentimental values linked to the human condition. Although walls have different roles in Vladislavić's and Kentridge's works, they never lose their building ability to segment space. In history, space has frequently been enclosed, banned or limited to free movement by the building of walls, but when these limitations have proved themselves arbitrary, people have found ways of penetrating, re-inventing and transforming them. Rephrasing De Certeau, in strategies, the spaces are produced, tabulated and imposed; in tactics, spaces are manipulated and diverted.[44] The walls pictured by Ivan Vladislavić and William Kentridge represent various tactics to keep memory while refusing time; to inhabit space without occupying it.

---

44 "[…] strategies are able to produce, tabulate and impose these spaces, […], whereas tactics can only use, manipulate and divert these spaces", M. de Certeau, *The practice of everyday life*, p. 30.

Bibliography

Barnard, Rita, *Apartheid and Beyond: South African Writers and the Politics of Place* (Oxford–New York: University Press, 2007).

Bonito Oliva, Achille, 'William Kentridge: Between Utopia and Dystopia', in *Streets of the City (and Other Tapestries): William Kentridge* (Milan: Electa, 2009), pp. 24–27.

Christov-Bakargiev, Carolyn, 'On Defectibility as a Resource: William Kentridge's Art of Imperfection, Lack and Falling Short', in *William Kentridge*, ed. by Christov-Bakargiev (Milan: Skira, 2004), pp. 29–39.

Concilio, Carmen, 'The Wall as Signifier in Ivan Vladislavić', in *Postcolonial Gateways and Walls*, ed. by Daria Tunca & Janet Wilson (Leiden–Boston: Brill Rodopi, 2017), pp. 205–217.

_____, "Il muro nella mente: Nadine Gordimer tra nuova e vecchia censura", in *Antropologia*, n. 2 (Rome: Meltemi, 2002), pp. 115-137.

_____, *Ivan Vladislavić. Johannesburg. Street Addresses / Johannesburg. Uno stradario* (Turin: Tirrenia Stampatori, 2007).

_____, "Villa Toscana a Johannesburg, di Ivan Vladislavić", in *L'Italia nelle scritture degli altri*, ed. by Piero de Gennaro (Turin: Trauben, 2011), pp. 119-132.

_____, "The Wall as Signifier in Ivan Vladislavić", in *Postcolonial Gateways and Walls*, ed. by Daria Tunca & Janet Wilson, (Leiden-Boston: Brill Rodopi, 2017), pp. 205-217.

De Certeau, Michel, *The Practice of Everyday Life* (Berkeley: University of California Press, 1985).

Deleuze Jacques, and Guattari Felix, *Anti-Oedipus* (London: Continuum, 2004).

Garb, Tamar, 'A Land of Signs', *Journal of Contemporary African Art*, 26, (Spring 2010), Nka Publications, 6–29.

Guercio, Gabriele, 'Becoming Aware in a World of People on the Move', in *William Kentridge: Tapestries*, ed. by Carlos Basualdo (New Haven: Philadelphia Museum of Art, Yale University Press, 2008), pp. 43–59.

Guarracino, Serena, 'The Dance of the Dead Rhino: William Kentridge's Magical Flute', *Altre Modernità*, 4, (10:2010), 268–278.

Guidotti, Valeria, "Magical Realism Beyond the Wall of Apartheid? Missing Persons by Ivan Vladislavić", *Coterminous Worlds. Magical Realism and Contemporary Post-colonial Literature in English*, ed. by E. Linguanti, F. Casotti, C. Concilio (Amsterdam: Rodopi, 1994), pp. 227-244.

Holland, Heidi, and Adam Roberts (eds.), *From Joburg to Jozi. Stories about Africa's Infamous City* (Johannesburg: Penguin, 2010).

Larcan, Laura, 'La mia Roma cupa e geniale. William Kentridge racconta il suo capolavoro da street artist tra Ponte Mazzini e Ponte Sisto', *Il Messaggero*, 6 aprile 2016.

Kentridge, William, 'In Praise of Shadows', in *William Kentridge*, ed. by Christov-Bakargiev (Milan: Skira, 2004), pp. 156–161.

Kentridge, William, *What We See & What We Know. Thinking about History while Walking, and thus the Drawings Began to Move* (Kyoto: The National Museum of Modern Art, 2009).

Krauss, Rosalind, 'The Rock: William Kentridge's Drawings for Projection', *October*, 92 (Spring 2000), 3–35.

Mbembe, Achille, and Nuttal Sarah (eds.), *Johannesburg. The Elusive Metropolis* (Durham–London: Duke University Press, 2008).

Sitas, Ari, 'Processions and Public Rituals', in *William Kentridge*, ed. by Neal Benezra, Stacy Boris, Dan Cameron (New York: Chicago Museum of Contemporary Art and New York Museum of Contemporary Art, Harry Abrams, 2001), pp. 59–65.

Vladislavić, Ivan, *The Exploded View* (Johannesburg: Random House South Africa, 2004).

_____, *Missing Persons* (Claremont: David Philip Publishers, 1989).

_____, *Propaganda by Monuments and Other Stories* (Cape Town: David Philip Publishers, 1996).

_____, and Hilton Judin, *blank___ Architecture, Apartheid and After* (Rotterdam: NAi Publishers, 1998).

_____, *The Exploded View* (Johannesburg: Random House South Africa, 2004).

_____, *Portrait with Keys: Joburg & What-What* (Cape Town: Umuzi, 2006).

_____, 'A Farm in Eloff Street', in *William Kentridge: Tapestries*, ed. by Carlos Basualdo (New Haven: Museum of Art, Yale University Press, 2008), pp. 97–107.

_____, and Goldblatt David, *TJ Johannesburg Photographs 1948–2010: Double Negative* (Rome: Contrasto, 2010).

_____, *The Exploded View* (Johannesburg: Random House South Africa, 2004).

MAKING THE I APPEAL TO THE EYE: VISUAL SUBJECTIVITY IN *JANE EYRE* 2006 BBC MINISERIES ADAPTATION

Daniela Salusso
(University of Turin)

Charlotte Brontë's *Jane Eyre* has been rewritten, translated, analysed and adapted so many times that it may seem virtually impossible to say something new. However, BBC 2006 miniseries directed by Susanna White manages to do something unique, in that it is at the same time the most faithful and the most innovative cinematic rendition of the novel. Its greatest merit is twofold: it finds a subtle but effective way to visualise the book's first-person narration and at the same time, it transfers into visual form what Barthes called the 'distributional' and 'integrational functions'[1] of the text.

White's adaptation features an exquisite performance from Toby Stephens, whose Rochester is simultaneously stern and vulnerable, and also from Ruth Wilson as a strong, balanced, yet passionate Jane. It is divided in four episodes, each one-hour long, all ending in a cliffhanger, the typical plot device of serialised fiction. The first part tells the story of Jane from her childhood until she first arrives at Thornfield and ends when she discovers Rochester lying in bed surrounded by flames. The second episode deals mainly with the development of Jane and Rochester's relationship, and ends when Jane is sent back to Lowood to attend to her dying aunt. Here we are left with another cliffhanger: while Rochester and Miss Ingram disappear riding in the woods, we catch a glimpse of an unknown black-haired figure looking from the window of the North Tower. The third part sees Jane returning and the marriage proposal, and ends right where the existence

---

1   Roland Barthes and Lionel Duisit, 'An Introduction to the Structural Analysis of Narrative', *New Literary History,* 6:2, (1975), 237–272.

of the mad woman in the attic is revealed. The fourth episode, finally, follows Jane during her time at Marsh End and ends with a flashforward of the two protagonists' future life.

The first episode opens with a sequence where a young girl seen from behind is wandering among the dunes in a deserted landscape, wearing a red sari-like dress. We cannot see her face, but our eyes follow her footsteps on the sand. A panning shot of the surroundings follows, and when the camera is again on the little girl, this time she is facing the viewer, sitting down and playing with the sand. What does all this have to do with Jane Eyre — one might wonder — but then the camera shows us a close-up of the girl's face, and her fierce, elfin look overcast only with a line of sadness reveals that she is, indeed, our beloved heroine. Slowly the camera zooms in on Jane's eyes, until the sand dunes fade and we are taken back to late 19th century England, where the protagonist is sitting on a chair, wearing a skirted outfit with puffed sleeves in the typical Victorian fashion and reading a book, *Voyages and Travels*. This cinematic technique allows the director to reproduce the first person narrative effect without using either Jane's voiceover or the first person perspective, which would be characterised by point-of-view shots or subjective camera. It is what Bruce Kawin called 'mindscreen' or 'the field of the mind's eye'.[2] Mindscreen, differently from visual or auditory modes, refers to an image which the viewer perceives as belonging to a specific consciousness in so far as it 'records mental events and indicates mentation'.[3]

Also the passing of time is treated as a recording of mental events from Jane's point of view: after her friend Helen Burns and many others have died at Lowood, Jane is sitting in the garden drawing. Death is shown as a rite of passage, after which Jane becomes a teenager. Then the camera zooms in on Jane's charcoal drawing, which soon turns into a painting. Her hand has changed, it is more expert, holding a brush instead of a pencil,

---

2   Bruce Kawin, *Mindscreen: Bergman, Godard, and First-Person Film* (Princeton, N.J.: Princeton University Press, 1978), p. 10.

3   Kawin, p. 170.

and when the camera shows us Jane's face, we already know that she is an adult, different and yet the same. We are with Jane from the very beginning, well aware that the story unfolding before our eyes is her story. The voice that captures, compels and mesmerises us in the book is Jane's voice, therefore adapting the book and grasping the so-called spirit of the author is finding Jane's voice and perspective. As Sara Lodge puts it: 'You cannot get past Jane Eyre, if you want to read Jane Eyre. Her voice, her "I", is the controlling medium through which the story is conjured.'[4] Despite this being the starting point, Lodge questions whether the controlling voice of the protagonist engages 'our sympathy, submerging us in her consciousness' or whether it 'alienates us from a narrator so self-involved', and further on wonders whether Brontë 'speaks through Jane, endorsing her point of view' or whether 'the novel [...] is designed to let us see the difference between Jane's biased, subjective vision and that of others'.[5] White's interpretation resists all Postcolonial bees in the bonnet, from the unreliability of the narrator to the precariousness of the protagonist, always threatened and shadowed by the hidden, untold stories of minor characters whose forgotten points of view are essential to reconstruct a puzzle-like reality. The story, instead, is told straight.

First we need to establish what the story is. As already mentioned before, it is useful to recall Roland Barthes' theory of narrative as it was adapted to film plots by McFarlane.[6] Barthes divided narrative functions into two groups: the distributional and the integrative.[7] The distributional functions are made up by the linear sequence of events, and they are easily transferred to another medium. Integrative functions, on the other hand, such as character traits or atmospheres, are only adaptable.[8] Functions, then, are further

4   Sara Lodge, *Charlotte Brontë – Jane Eyre* (London: Palgrave MacMillan, 2009), p. 31.
5   Lodge, p. 33.
6   Brian McFarlane, *Novel to Film: An Introduction to the Theory of Adaptation* (Wotton-under-Edge Gloucestershire: Clarendon Press, 1996).
7   Barthes, p. 246.
8   McFarlane, p. 13.

divided into cardinal and catalysers, the former being turning points in the plot and the latter being the triggers. Identifying and thus transposing distributional and integrative forms is quite a straightforward task: we could agree, for instance, that Jane being sent to Lowood and her arrival at Thornfield are examples of distributive functions, while the Gothic element or the bleakness of Jane's childhood can be regarded as integrative. However, when cardinal and catalysers are to be found, things become more complicated and edges blur. In fact, most of the pivotal moments are such either because of the effect they have on Jane (so the catalyser is the moment itself and the effect becomes the cardinal point, an example of which may be Jane and Rochester's first meeting) or because they are triggered by Jane's feelings or reasoning (hence, the catalyser is internal rather than external, like in the case of Jane's leaving and her subsequent decision to return).

The problem any director as to face is how to show, visualise Jane's thoughts and inner motives. A number of strategies are adopted by Susanna White: the first is the all-connecting symbolism of red and grey. While in the novel symbols have an evoking function (fire and ice are objective-correlatives of the contrast between passion and oppression; the memory of the red room comes back every time the protagonist feels a threat to her emotional or intellectual freedom), a cinematic rendition cannot afford generalisations and universalisations, in that characters, places and situations have to be rooted in the here and now:

> Telling is not the same as showing. Both stage and screen adaptations must use what Charles Sanders Peirce called indexical and iconic signs — that is, precise people, places, and things — whereas literature uses symbolic and conventional signs.[9]

The symbolic use of red and grey in the 2006 miniseries is an example of this; all symbolism revolves around Jane, it is her map for understanding the world, the connections she makes between

---

9   Robert Giddings, Keith Selby, Chris Wensley, *Screening the Novel: The Theory and Practice of Literary Dramatization – Insights* (London: Palgrave Macmillan, 1990), p. 6.

things. Let us take the very beginning of the first episode, where Jane is reading the book *Voyages and Travels*, and her imagination travels to a desert.

In the novel, Jane is reading a different book, Bewick's *History of British Birds,* and interestingly enough, the landscapes evoked are cold, icy ones, which Lodge believes are 'equivalent to the harsh emotional climate in which she lives at the Reeds' house.'[10]

> They were those which treat of the haunts of sea-fowl; of 'the solitary rocks and promontories' by them only inhabited; of the coast of Norway, studded with isles from its southern extremity, the Lindeness, or Naze, to the North Cape — 'Where the Northern Ocean, in vast whirls, Boils round the naked, melancholy isles Of farthest Thule; and the Atlantic surge Pours in among the stormy Hebrides.' Nor could I pass unnoticed the suggestion of the bleak shores of Lapland, Siberia, Spitzbergen, Nova Zembla, Iceland, Greenland [...] Each picture told a story; mysterious often to my undeveloped understanding and imperfect feelings, yet ever profoundly interesting.[11]

Then why does White decide to depict Jane's imagination as travelling to a warm place rather than a cold one? The answer lies in the intrinsic difference between the novel and the film: in the novel we have insight into Jane's mind, we know her fears and wishes because the first person narration makes us acquainted with those intimately, yet at the same time the harsh, bleak environment of the Reeds's house is not told directly but simply evoked. Therefore, Jane's ambivalent fascination with the solitary icy landscapes helps the viewer create a mental and physical image of her tribulations. On the contrary, in the film viewers are shown the house and all the characters that live in it; what we lack, instead, is direct insight into Jane's mind, her desire that she will later express 'to escape somewhere warm'. Furthermore, we are given another visual clue of the coldness and harshness of the house: the predominant colour is grey, the sun depicted in the illustration being the only red spot in the entire room.

---

10   Lodge, p. 45.
11   Brontë, p. 12.

The symbolism of red and grey permeates the series, grey being an objective correlative not only for the bleakness of Jane's childhood, but especially for her plainness. In the novel, she is always wearing a 'black stuff dress', whereas in the four episodes she seems to be always choosing greyish outfits for herself. This leitmotif is the perfect visual rendition of the well-known self-description of Jane Eyre as 'plain, obscure and little'.

Red, instead, associated with fire, is the symbol of passion; the director cleverly steers away from the temptation of interpreting passion in *Jane Eyre* as being only the romance, and depicts it rather as Brontë had intended, a physical and spiritual force that lives inside Jane, which must be explored but also kept at bay. Red is the colour of her wild imagination (the red sari) but it is also the colour of the haunted room she is sent to when she is supposed not to have behaved well. Several times throughout the story, we see Jane having to fight the memories of the red room. It still haunts her, even after she has grown into womanhood. Whenever she feels like her independence or her self-worth is in jeopardy, Jane recalls the horrors she felt inside it. Instead of resorting to flashbacks, White makes a very interesting choice: she disseminates the series with red details that become, quite literally, a *fil rouge* that helps us perceive and decode events from Jane's point of view. A very clear example of this is the presence of a thin red scarf that Jane sees from time to time wafting in the wind from the North Tower. The red scarf is the visual equivalent of 'the laughter of Grace Poole' which is mentioned throughout the book, the foreboding of a hidden mystery, already symbolically linked with fire, and a subtle way to suggest that someone is being imprisoned and throwing tantrums there, much as Jane was kept inside the red room against her will. As Sally Shuttleworth reminds us, 'there are parallels between the angry child shut in the red room, and the mad wife confined to the attic'.[12] Nevertheless, as I said before, this seems to be a case of

---

12   Sally Shuttleworth, *Jane Eyre and the 19th century woman*, Discovering Literature: Romantics and Victorians, British Library Website Archive.

Jungian synchronicity[13] rather than an implicit reference to the Postmodern reading of Bertha as Jane's double.[14]

This connection is further exemplified by the presence in the film of another red scarf, however smaller and more faded in colour: it is the one Jane wears the morning after she saves Rochester from the fire; she will remove it the moment she finds out Rochester has gone to Miss Ingram's house, and then she will wear it again when the master returns. Jane's scarf seems to be the visual counterpart of the moments in the text where she admits her feelings for Rochester, as to say that she gave herself permission to show them. Emblematic is the scene where Jane takes off the scarf in front of the mirror after she learns that her master is courting another woman: while untying it she says aloud 'You were mistaken, Jane Eyre'. The removal of the scarf, thus, in one gesture, manages to show us Jane's feelings, which in the book are described in a lengthy inner monologue that begins with self-deprecation:

> I pronounced judgment to this effect: That a greater fool than Jane Eyre had never breathed the breath of life; that a more fantastic idiot had never surfeited herself on sweet lies, and swallowed poison as if it were nectar. 'You,' I said, 'a favourite with Mr. Rochester? You gifted with the power of pleasing him? You of importance to him in any way? Go! your folly sickens me. And you have derived pleasure from occasional tokens of preference — equivocal tokens shown by a gentleman of family and a man of the world to a dependent and a novice. How dared you? Poor stupid dupe! (303)

It then continues with the realisation that she must hide her feelings, however strong:

---

13   In his book *Synchronicity: An – Acausal – Connecting Principle* (Princeton: Princeton University press, 1960), Carl Gustav Jung coined the word "synchronicity" to describe "temporally coincident occurrences of acausal events."

14   For further investigation on this matter, see: Sandra M. Gilbert and Susan Gubar, *The Madwoman in the Attic – The Woman Writer and the Nineteenth-Century Literary Imagination* (New Haven and London: Yale University Press, 2nd edition, 2000).

Every good, true, vigorous feeling I have gathers impulsively round him. I know I must conceal my sentiments: I must smother hope; I must remember that he cannot care much for me. For when I say that I am of his kind, I do not mean that I have his force to influence, and his spell to attract; I mean only that I have certain tastes and feelings in common with him. I must, then, repeat continually that we are for ever sundered: and yet, while I breathe and think, I must love him. (332)

By encapsulating Jane's thoughts in a single gesture, White manages to maintain the protagonist's inner motives, which is the highest form of fidelity. Words can be sacrificed, whereas motives cannot, in that they are the catalyst underlying all action.

The second device is making the inner catalysts manifest by means of an opposite strategy, consisting in changing or adding words that are not in the original work. An example of this can be found at the very beginning of the first episode. With the exception of her screaming once she is locked up in the red room, Jane does not speak for the first ten minutes. She is being pulled away from her secluded safe space behind the 'red moreen curtain', mocked, ridiculed, trampled on physically and psychologically by her cousins but still she does not utter a single word. The first time she opens her mouth is when her aunt mentions her plan to send her to Lowood because, despite trying, she does not know how to deal with Jane, to which the young girl replies 'You have not tried very hard. My uncle's wish is that you treat me like one of your children' already expressing that desire for equality that will drive most of Jane's actions. The girl's remark, although this precise exchange never happened in the novel, aptly summarises Jane's feelings and adds the immediacy of a dialogue:

This reproach of my dependence had become a vague sing-song in my ear: very painful and crushing, but only half intelligible. Miss Abbot joined in — 'And you ought not to think yourself on an equality with the Misses Reed and Master Reed, because Missis kindly allows you to be brought up with them. They will have a great deal of money, and you will have none: it is your place to be humble, and to try to make yourself agreeable to them.'[15]

15   Brontë, p. 18.

It is generally accepted that a cinematic rendition has to show what the book says, but sometimes also the reverse is true. Jane's feelings, which she voices throughout the novel, must be expressed in the film by creating a dialogue that is not in the text, because some things are too important to be simply hinted at. We are in the presence of another catalyst here, one that explains Jane's repulsion for any kind of injustice. Throughout the text Jane is called wicked, beast, deceitful, strange, a roving, solitary, queer, frightened, shy little thing, and plain. Despite this, she speaks her own mind and treats everybody as equal, regardless of age or social status. Jane's awareness begins in her childhood and fully develops in her adulthood, when she will stand up to Mrs. Ingram and her speech about God giving us good blood or bad blood, and finally, in her relationship with Rochester.

Similarly, after the fortune-teller incident in which Jane is tricked by Rochester into admitting her feelings, the woman notices something about her master that gives her hope things may be changing for the best after all:

> One thing specially surprised me, and that was, there were no journeyings backward and forward, no visits to Ingram Park: to be sure it was twenty miles off, on the borders of another county; but what was that distance to an ardent lover?[16]

In the book it is Jane's thought, but in the miniseries the remark is uttered by Mrs. Fairfax, thus allowing the viewer to share Jane's hope.

The reverse happens when in the novel it is Mrs. Fairfax who introduces Rochester's character to Jane before they even met, by saying: 'He is rather peculiar, perhaps: he has travelled a great deal, and seen a great deal of the world, I should think. I dare say he is clever, but I never had much conversation with him.'[17] In the film this dialogue never happens; we are shown, instead, when Jane enters his study and sees the maps lying on the desk and his collection of butterfly and insects, conveying the idea that he is a

---

16   Brontë, p. 469.
17   Brontë, p. 198.

traveller, certainly erudite, and probably a loner. Susanna White seems to always find a balance between showing and telling, and is never afraid to apply minor variations to dialogues and situations in order to say what needs to be said and show what needs to be shown.

The third visualising device is the most complex of all, because it consists in showing what is not said but only implied, in other words, recreating pivotal scenes in all their complexity, distributional and integrative functions included. Adaptations have always been criticised for impoverishing the book's content due to necessary omissions in the plot, and at the same time visualisation has been regarded as destroying many of the subtleties with which the printed word could shape the internal world of a literary work. As I have said before, this is not always the case, since visualisation can open up other kinds of questions. Perhaps in the book we are wondering about the characters' appearance to the extent of which it has not been described by the writer, but in a film we are wondering about characters' motives: in one case, we read between the lines, in the other case, we read between glances and smiles. However, actions speak louder than words only if they are chosen very carefully.

This technique is employed especially in the depiction of Jane and Rochester's relationship. During their first meeting, the change that Rochester brings to Jane's monotonous life is introduced by shifting back and forth between Jane's lonely, silent and dreamy-like scenery and the racing horse accompanied by dramatic music. The role of music is fundamental, as Hutcheon reminds us:

> Visual and gestural representations are rich in complex associations; music offers aural 'equivalents' for characters' emotions and, in turn, provokes affective responses in the audience; sound, in general, can enhance, reinforce, or even contradict the visual and verbal aspects.[18]

The juxtaposition of silence and music reproduces the effect Brontë created, namely showing the importance of Rochester's

---

18   Hutcheon quoting Abbott in Linda Hutcheon with Siobhan O' Flynn, *A Theory of Adaptation* (London: Routledge, 2013), p. 108.

arrival to the audience, but not to Jane. The power hierarchy that is established in this scene subtly captures the atmosphere of the novel. Jane persistently offers help while Rochester, after apparently scorning her, immediately assumes a charming, teasing air, showing gratefulness in the end. Jane, noticing this change in attitude, assures him she is an independent young woman by pointing out that she will 'post her letter first' before hurrying back as he suggests. Hence, the very hard to capture power dynamic, which is the integrative function, has successfully been translated from novel to film. Some of the protagonists' further exchanges are slightly modernised in language, for instance when Jane is caught taking a book from the library, she apologises for not asking permission, to which Rochester replies 'You're an intelligent woman, what do you need permission for?' This stylistic choice certainly happens in order for the dialogues to better appeal to the public, but above all to keep the delicate balance of the power game realistic and fluent. In addition, almost every time the two protagonists speak there is a close-up on their expressions, and every time Rochester finishes talking, the camera goes back to Jane, as to indicate that what really matters is her reaction to his words, once again bringing the first-person narration to life.

Another extremely interesting choice regards White's decision to depict Jane and Rochester's deep connection by inserting an original speech that mimics Brontë's style, and the addition of a set of twins. Rochester's speech is delivered in the first episode, while he and Jane are sitting on the grass with Adele, looking at the wildlife around. It powerfully shows the insight and deep understanding Rochester has in Jane's soul and brings together all the leitmotivs of Jane's life: the grey-red symbolism and the reference to fire, the image of the caged bird afraid of being beaten as an objective-correlative for Jane's childhood, the willingness to escape paired with the desire to grow:

> There is a bird. It's a nondescript grey colour. It is accustomed to in not moving too quickly, not to draw attention to itself for fear of being beaten. It wishes it could be in a cage. But sooner or later, slowly, day by day its wings grow very strong. And if you were to look very closely, you would see brilliant, scarlet feathers hidden under its drab

wings. Until one day, it has grown so confident, it flaps its red wings
and flies straight upwards into the sky and those lucky enough to catch
it in flight, think they have caught a glimpse of a firebird. Then it flies
away somewhere warm and never comes back. It's true, there's one
here in Thornfield in the gardens if you look very hard.

The function of these lines in the first episode is to foretell
Jane's future decision to leave which formally will be triggered
by the discovery of Bertha, but psychologically will have to do
with the desire of becoming a fully independent woman. Much in
the same way, two identical twins are introduced at Rochester's
house party, whose function is to prepare us for the almost
telepathic connection between the two protagonists, exactly like
one of the aristocrats at the party wonders: 'Don't you believe
that two minds could be so attuned as to communicate across
countries?'

Finally, probably the most problematic integrative function to
transpose into film is the flirtatious quality of Jane and Rochester's
dialogues. Visualising, and therefore disambiguating, an
exchange whose very essence is ambiguity itself is no easy task.
Brontë's writing alludes to flirtation without giving us precise
stage directions on what the characters do with their bodies while
talking, but we do perceive a certain atmosphere:

> Mr. Rochester, as he sat in his damask-covered chair, looked different
> to what I had seen him look before; not quite so stern – much less
> gloomy. There was a smile on his lips, and his eyes sparkled, whether
> with wine or not, I am not sure; but I think it very probable. He was,
> in short, in his after-dinner mood; more expanded and genial, and also
> more self-indulgent than the frigid and rigid temper of the morning;
> still he looked preciously grim, cushioning his massive head against
> the swelling back of his chair, and receiving the light of the fire on his
> granite-hewn features, and in his great, dark eyes; for he had great, dark
> eyes, and very fine eyes, too – not without a certain change in their
> depths sometimes, which, if it was not softness, reminded you, at least,
> of that feeling.[19]

---

19   Brontë, p. 247.

With these premises, it is not surprising that the following conversation in which Rochester asks Jane whether she thinks he is handsome and she replies, briskly, 'No, Sir' is accompanied by the typical mannerisms of flirtation in the TV series: after Jane answers, she looks away and half smiles, blushing. The director is showing us what happens the moment Jane starts noticing that Rochester has 'great, dark eyes, and very fine eyes, too' and he notices he is being noticed.

Similarly, deep sensuality pervades the fire scene: we can see only two silhouettes in the dark, their voices are hushed, their bodies very close, visually reproducing Jane's account 'He paused; gazed at me: words almost visible trembled on his lips, but his voice was checked', 'Strange energy was in his voice, strange fire in his look'.[20]

In addition, when Jane returns to the room she repeatedly kisses the hand Rochester had shaken before saying goodnight. This detail is not in the text, nevertheless it perfectly captures Jane's excitement:

> I regained my couch, but never thought of sleep. Till morning dawned I was tossed on a buoyant but unquiet sea, where billows of trouble rolled under surges of joy. I thought sometimes I saw beyond its wild waters a shore, sweet as the hills of Beulah; and now and then a freshening gale, wakened by hope, bore my spirit triumphantly towards the bourne: but I could not reach it, even in fancy – a counteracting breeze blew off land, and continually drove me back. Sense would resist delirium: judgment would warn passion. Too feverish to rest, I rose as soon as day dawned.[21]

These two scenes explicate a sexual tension that is already present in their novel counterpart, however mitigated. There is one scene, however, that White decides to alter radically. The scene in question happens at the end of the third episode, after the unfinished wedding, when Jane makes her decision to go away. Unlike in the novel, where it happens in chronological order, the

---

20   Brontë, p. 268–269.
21   Brontë, p. 288.

event in the series is divided into two flashbacks that are presented when Jane lives with the Rivers family. In addition, the scene is sexually charged. Jane and Rochester are lying on the bed, while he is caressing and kissing her, a drastic change from the novel where Jane turns her head away from any attempts Rochester makes to get closer. The oversexualisation of the scene may seem gratuitous, but in fact it is not, since it visually explains the real reason behind Jane's departure: the sexual tone of the scene is a way to state once again that Rochester may have power over Jane's body, but he does not have any over her soul. 'Conscience held Passion by the throat' says Jane in the novel, and so does Wilson's Jane experience an inner conflict. The powerful sexual attraction is the very reason why Jane has to leave:

> He released me from his clutch, and only looked at me. The look was far worse to resist than the frantic strain: only an idiot, however, would have succumbed now. I had dared and baffled his fury; I must elude his sorrow: I retired to the door.[22]

In the novel, the moon speaks to Jane in a dream 'My daughter, flee temptation' To which she replies 'Mother, I will.' Showing the temptation, though, enables the reader to understand Jane's choice.

My critique of White's 2006 miniseries purposefully avoids comparisons with the other cinematic renditions of *Jane Eyre,* since the analysis has been carried out not on the basis of a presumed fidelity or infidelity to the novel, but rather starting from the opposite view, according to which all adaptations are interpretations, works of artistic creativity. Following Hutcheon:

> When an adaptation is compared with the literary work it is based on, the stress is on the ways the film creators move within the field of intertextual connections and how they employ the means of expression offered by the filmic art to convey meanings.[23]

---

22   Brontë, p. 688.
23   Hutcheon, p. 35.

Susanna White's series succeeds in conveying not only the deepest meanings of the text, but also its style, its spirit, and above all the voice of Jane Eyre, which still resonates today and makes the character appealing over and over again. When the fourth and last episode end and we see a flashforward of Jane and Rochester's family gathering, it feels almost as if we could hear Jane's voice whispering 'Viewer, I married him.'

Bibliography

Barthes, Roland and Lionel Duisit, 'An Introduction to the Structural Analysis of Narrative', *New Literary History*, 6:2 (1975).

Brontë, Charlotte, *Jane Eyre* (London: Penguin Books Limited, 2013).

Giddings, Robert, Keith Selby, Chris Wensley, *Screening the Novel: The Theory and Practice of Literary Dramatization: Insights* (London: Palgrave Macmillan, 1990), p. 6.

Hutcheon, Linda, Siobhan O'Flynn, *A Theory of Adaptation* (London: Routledge, 2013), p. 108.

Kawin, Bruce, *Mindscreen: Bergman, Godard, and First-Person Film* (Princeton, N.J.: Princeton University Press, 1978).

Lodge, Sara, *Charlotte Brontë – Jane Eyre* (London: Palgrave Macmillan, 2008).

Lowe, Dunstan, and Shahabudin, Kim, *Classics For All: Reworking Antiquity in Mass Culture* (Cambridge: Cambridge Scholars Publishing, 2009).

McFarlane, Brian, *Novel to Film: An Introduction to the Theory of Adaptation* (Wotton-under-Edge, Gloucestershire: Clarendon Press, 1996).

Shuttleworth, Sally, *Jane Eyre and the 19th Century Woman*, Discovering Literature: Romantics and Victorians, British Library Website Archive.

ACKNOWLEDGEMENTS

We would like to thank Paola Brusasco, Michela Borzaga, Valerio Fissore, Lucia Folena, Mariangela Mosca for their precious readings at various stages of the manuscript production.